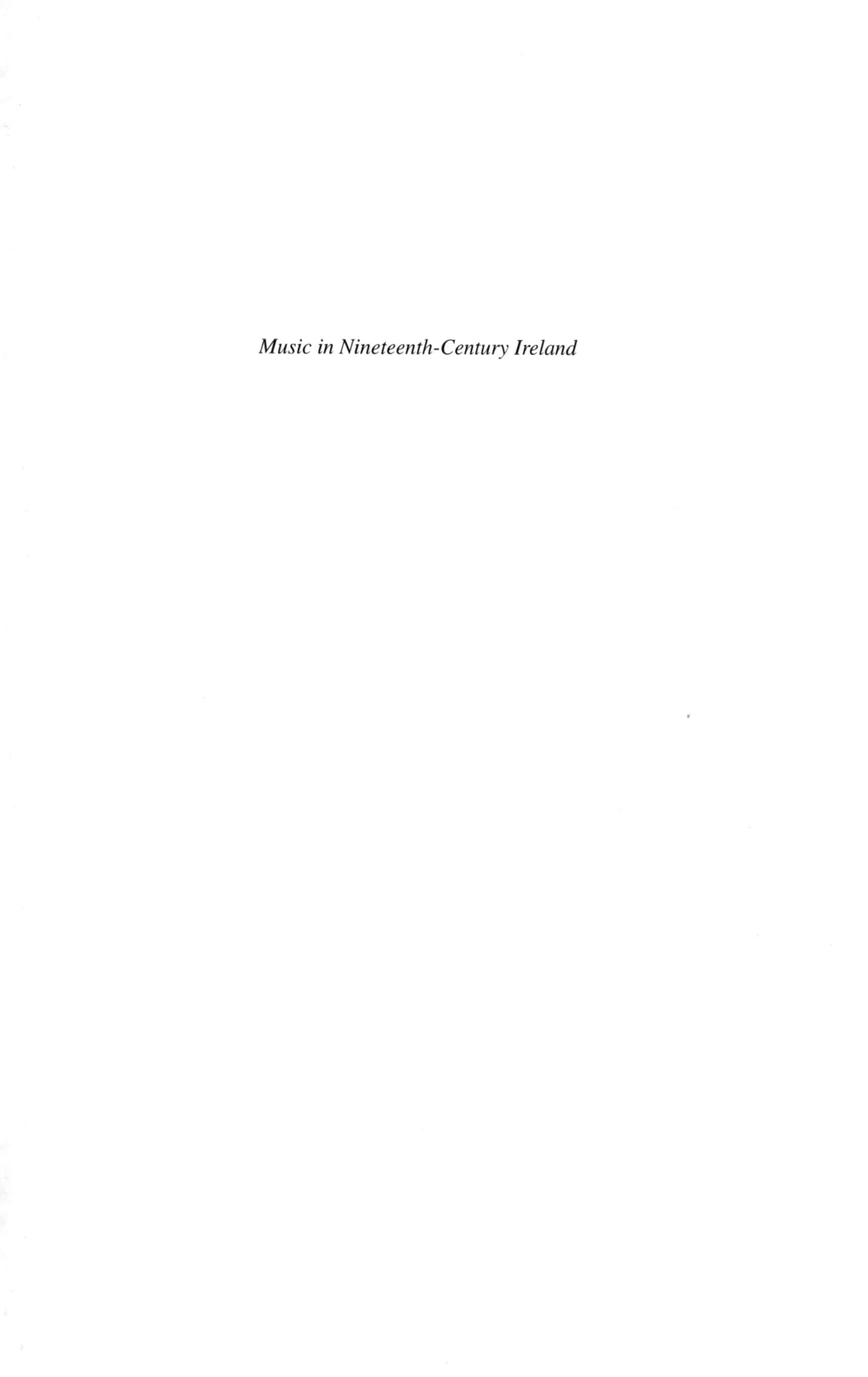

Music in Nineteenth-Century Ireland

IRISH MUSICAL STUDIES
General editors: Gerard Gillen and Harry White

1 *Musicology in Ireland* (1990)
2 *Music and the Church* (1993)
3 *Music and Irish Cultural History* (1995)
4 *The Maynooth International Musicological Conference 1995 Selected Proceedings: Part One* (1996)
5 *The Maynooth International Musicological Conference 1995 Selected Proceedings: Part Two* (1996)
6 *A Historical Anthology of Irish Church Music* (2001)
7 *Irish Music in the Twentieth Century* (2003)
8 *Bach Studies from Dublin* (2004)
9 *Music in Nineteenth-Century Ireland* (2007)

Irish Musical Studies

9: MUSIC IN NINETEENTH-CENTURY IRELAND

Edited by
Michael Murphy & Jan Smaczny

FOUR COURTS PRESS

Published by
FOUR COURTS PRESS LTD
7 Malpas Street, Dublin 8, Ireland
email: info@four courts press.ie
http://www.four courts press.ie
and in North America by
FOUR COURTS PRESS
c/o ISBS, 920 N.E. 58th Avenue, Suite 300, Portland, OR 97213.

© Four Courts Press and
the several authors 2007

ISBN 978–1–84682–024–3

A catalogue record for this title
is available from the British Library. All rights reserved. No part of this publication
may be reproduced, stored in or introduced into a retrieval system, or transmitted,
in any form or by any means (electronic, mechanical, photocopying, recording
or otherwise), without the prior written permission of both the copyright
owner and publisher of this book.

Published in association with
The Society for Musicology in Ireland
Aontas Ceoleolaíochta na hÉireann

Typeset by Carrigboy Typesetting Services.
Printed by Athenaeum Press, Gateshead, England.

Contents

CONTRIBUTORS	7
PREFACE	11
ACKNOWLEDGMENTS	13
ABBREVIATIONS	14

I NATIONALITY

1 Cultural theory, nostalgia and the historical record: opera in Ireland and the Irishness of opera during the nineteenth century 15
Harry White

2 From national sentiment to nationalist movement, 1850–1900 36
Ita Beausang

3 Constructs of nationality: the literary and visual politics of Irish music in the nineteenth century 52
Barra Boydell

II THE FOLK TRADITION IN TRANSMISSION

4 ''Twas one of those Dreams that by Music are Brought': the development of the piano and the preservation of Irish traditional music 74
David Cooper

5 Irish folk music collectors of the early nineteenth century: pioneer musicologists 94
Jimmy O'Brien Moran

III CHURCH MUSIC AND MUSICIANS

6 Strange voices in the 'Land of Song': Belgian and German organist appointments to Catholic cathedrals and churches in Ireland, 1859–1916 114
Paul Collins

7	The Armagh Cathedral Collection in the fabric of Ireland's musical history *Anne Dempsey*	130

IV EDUCATION AND SOCIETY

8	The transmission of song in national schools of mid nineteenth-century Ireland: social, religious and political values in canon *Marie McCarthy*	149
9	Singing and sobriety: music and the Temperance Movement in Ireland, 1838–43 *Maria McHale*	166
10	For the purpose of public music education: the lectures of Robert Prescott Stewart *Lisa Parker*	187

V MUSICAL INSTITUTIONS

11	The Society of Antient Concerts, Dublin, 1834–64 *Paul Rodmell*	211
12	Concert auditoria in nineteenth-century Belfast *Roy Johnston*	234
13	The musical press in nineteenth-century Ireland *Michael Murphy*	252

VI EUROPEAN PERSPECTIVES

14	Musical national traditions in Ireland and the Czech lands in the nineteenth century: similar roots, creative divergences *Jan Smaczny*	278
15	Wagner, Bayreuth, and the Irish image of Germany *Joachim Fischer*	293

CHRONOLOGY *Axel Klein*	305
SELECT BIBLIOGRAPHY	312
INDEX	317

Contributors

ITA BEAUSANG studied piano at the Cork School of Music and at the Read School of Music, Dublin. A music graduate from UCC, she retired on marriage from a teaching post in the Cork School of Music and subsequently worked as lecturer and administrator in DIT Conservatory of Music and Drama. Her book *Anglo-Irish Music, 1780–1830* (Cork UP, 1966) is the standard work on the period and she was research assistant to Professor Aloys Fleischmann for his contribution to *A New History of Ireland*. She is currently acting as an advisory editor for the forthcoming *Encyclopaedia of Music in Ireland* (UCD Press [hereafter *EMIR*]) and is writing a biography of the composer, Ina Boyle.

BARRA BOYDELL is Senior Lecturer in music at NUI Maynooth, and has published widely on the history of music in Ireland: his books include *Music and Paintings at the National Gallery of Ireland* (National Gallery of Ireland, 1985), *Music at Christ Church before 1800: Documents and Selected Anthems* (Four Courts Press, 1998), and *A History of Music at Christ Church Cathedral* (Boydell & Brewer, 2004). He is general editor of *EMIR* for which he was awarded a Government of Ireland Senior Research Fellowship by the Irish Council for the Humanities and Social Sciences in 2005–6. He serves on the council of the Society for Musicology in Ireland of which he was a founding member and served as Honorary Secretary from 2003 to 2006.

PAUL COLLINS is Lecturer in Music at Mary Immaculate College, University of Limerick. His research interests embrace music theory during the Baroque, seventeenth- and eighteenth-century keyboard music, and nineteenth- and early twentieth-century Catholic church music. His first book, *The Stylus Phantasticus and Free Keyboard Music of the North German Baroque*, was published by Ashgate in 2005. He is assistant style editor and an advisory editor for *EMIR*.

DAVID COOPER is Professor of Music and Technology in the School of Music, and Dean of the Faculty of Performance, Visual Arts and Communications, at the University of Leeds. He is the editor of a new edition of George Petrie's *The Petrie Collection of the Ancient Music of Ireland* (Cork UP, 2002) and the author of monographs on *Bartók's Concerto for Orchestra* (Cambridge UP, 1996) and Bernard Herrmann's scores for the films *Vertigo* (Greenwood Press, 2001) and *The Ghost and Mrs Muir* (Scarecrow Press, 2005). He is co-editor, with Kevin Dawe, of the volume *The Mediterranean in Music: Critical Perspectives, Common Concerns, Cultural Differences* (Scarecrow Press, 2005). His recent publications on Irish music include a study of Seán Ó Riada's score for *Mise Éire* in Miguel Mera and David Burnand's *European Film Music* (Ashgate, 2006).

ANNE DEMPSEY graduated from Queen's University, Belfast, with a BMus hons. in 2003. She completed a Master's degree at Queen's in the following year which included an extensive catalogue of the Armagh Cathedral music collection which has formed the basis of her contribution to this volume. She is an independent scholar and self-employed musician working as a piano tutor, piano accompanist and performer, and teaching most recently at the Sperrin Integrated College in Magherafelt.

JOACHIM FISCHER is Senior Lecturer in German, Joint Director of the Centre for Irish-German Studies and Deputy Director of the Ralahine Centre of Utopian Studies at the University of Limerick. He was joint organiser of the conference 'Wagner and Wagnerism: Contexts – Connections – Controversies' at the University of Limerick, 2002. His current major research area is Irish-German connections. Among his recent book-length publications are *Das Deutschlandbild der Iren 1890–1939* [The Irish image of Germany 1890–1939] (Carl Winter Verlag, 2000) and, co-edited with Grace Neville, *As Others Saw Us: Cork through European Eyes* (Collins Press, 2005).

ROY JOHNSTON is an independent scholar. In retirement he completed in 1996 a doctoral dissertation entitled *Concerts in the Musical Life of Belfast to 1874*. Material from the dissertation has appeared as conference papers, chapters in books and the monograph, *Bunting's 'Messiah'* (Belfast Natural History and Philosophical Society, 2003.) He contributed a chapter on 'Music in Northern Ireland since 1921' to vol. 7 of *The New History of Ireland* and has written entries on a number of Ulster musicians for the forthcoming *Dictionary of Irish Biography*.

AXEL KLEIN studied at Hildesheim, Germany, and Trinity College, Dublin and graduated in 1990. His 1995 PhD thesis on twentieth-century Irish art music was the first major work in this area (published in German in 1996). Further publications include *Irish Classical Recordings – A Discography of Irish Art Music* (Greenwood Press, 2001) and many articles in books and journals. He also co-edited *Irish Music in the Twentieth Century* (*IMS* vii) and *The Life and Music of Brian Boydell* (Irish Academic Press, 2003). As an independent scholar he has lectured in Ireland, the UK, and Germany, and in 2004 he went on a lecture tour to the United States which included Harvard, Princeton and Boston College.

MICHAEL MURPHY is Lecturer in Music at Mary Immaculate College, University of Limerick. With Harry White he co-edited *Musical Constructions of Nationalism* (Cork UP, 2001). His research interests include the music of Mieczysław Karłowicz, and various aspects of Irish music history in the nineteenth and twentieth centuries which will be published in *EMIR* and the *Dictionary of Irish Biography*. He was elected Honorary Secretary of the Society for Musicology in Ireland for 2006–9. Forthcoming projects include a monograph on the music of Karłowicz (Mellen Press) and an anthology of documents of Irish music history.

JIMMY O'BRIEN MORAN is perhaps best known as a performer on the uilleann pipes. He has lectured part-time at the Waterford Institute of Technology and at the University of Limerick. He was awarded his PhD from the University of Limerick in 2006 for his dissertation on the nineteenth-century piper, Paddy Conneely. He is a frequent contributor to *An Píobaire*, the bulletin of Na Píobairí Uilleann, and he has had articles published in *The Companion to Irish Traditional Music* (ed. Fintan Vallely, Cork UP, 1999) and *The Encyclopaedia of Ireland* (Gill & Macmillan, 2003). He is Fulbright-Culture Ireland visiting Professor in Irish Studies (Irish Traditional Music) at Boston College, 2007–8.

MARIE MCCARTHY is Professor and Chair of Music Education at the University of Michigan. Her research focuses on the social, cultural and historical foundations of music education, and the transmission of music process across cultures. She is author of two books, *Passing It On: The Transmission of Music in Irish Culture* (Cork UP, 1999), and *Toward a Global Community: The International Society for Music Education, 1953–2003* (ISME, 2004), and has edited several books and authored numerous book chapters and journal articles.

MARIA MCHALE is a graduate of University College Cork, with an MA from City University, London, and a PhD from Royal Holloway, University of London. Her doctoral dissertation, 'A Singing People: English Vocal Music and Nationalist Debate, 1880–1920', is an interdisciplinary study of the issues surrounding cultural nationalism during the English musical renaissance. Her other research interests include historiography, music and gender, music and religion and most recently, aspects of cultural nationalism in nineteenth-century Ireland. She has taught at the University of London and the University of Sydney, and currently holds a Government of Ireland Post-Doctoral Fellowship at UCD. She will be contributing a number of articles to *EMIR*.

LISA PARKER is a graduate of NUI Maynooth, where she is currently pursuing a doctorate on Robert Prescott Stewart. She has contributed the article on Stewart to *Die Musik in Geschichte und Gegenwart* and is preparing articles on John Echlin, John and William Neale, Richard Pockrich, John Andrew Stevenson and Stewart for *EMIR*.

PAUL RODMELL is Senior Lecturer in Music at the University of Birmingham. He is the author of *Charles Villiers Stanford* (Ashgate, 2002) and has also written on Italian opera in nineteenth-century Dublin, and Verdi reception in Great Britain and Ireland. He is currently engaged on a long-term research project on British opera and operatic culture between 1875 and 1918. Other research interests include art music and its culture in Britain throughout the Victorian and Edwardian periods.

JAN SMACZNY is Hamilton Harty Professor of Music, and former Head of School, at Queen's University, Belfast. He has published extensively on the music of the Czech lands, in particular opera, and the life and works of Dvořák and Martinu; he has also, in recent years, produced studies of Mozart and the twentieth century, Mozart and Prague, and Goethe and the Czechs. In 2006 he was elected President of the Society for Musicology in Ireland.

HARRY WHITE is Professor of Music at University College, Dublin and General Editor of *Irish Musical Studies* and *EMIR*. He was inaugural President of the Society for Musicology in Ireland (2003–6), and in March 2006 was elected to membership of the Royal Irish Academy. In 2005–6 he was Government of Ireland Senior Research Fellow in the Humanities, and he is currently writing a study of music and the Irish literary imagination. His most recent book is *The Progress of Music in Ireland* (Four Courts Press, 2005).

Preface

Reading history as a series of convenient chronological divisions is a compromised if pragmatic and understandable activity. The century, for some reason, has come to the rescue of commentators as a convenient way of parcelling out a continuum shot through with divisions which rarely fall with considerate tact on the bookends of each hundred years since the year nought. The over-arching categories often adopted by histories of music: ancient, medieval, renaissance, baroque, classical, romantic, and, most problematically, modern teach us that well-meaning attempts at being helpful in fact often create new unhelpful distinctions particularly where music is concerned. Matching up the musical baroque with the architectural or religious baroque is problematic, and attempting to align musical romanticism with literary romanticism is an activity almost doomed to failure. Better to put our editorial hands up and admit that music with its natural tendency to relate to religion, philosophy, literature, social history and politics will never happily be shoe-horned into a portion as bite-sized as a century.

The year 1800 with the Act of Union might seem a seductive starting point, but then what about 1792, the year of the Belfast Harp Festival? Certainly, this summative event can be seen as a means of commemorating the end of a tradition. But of even greater moment is its role in determining the trajectory of the development of the 'folk', 'traditional', even 'popular' voice in Ireland during the next century and, along with the impact of Moore, in America and Europe. Looking for an end to what inevitably must be considered another 'long century' 1900 has little to commend itself as a terminus; 1914 might seem a plausible end point were it not for the Easter Rising of 1916 and the establishment of the Irish Free State in 1922. So even before attempting to factor in 1789 or 1918, the nineteenth century addressed in this volume is untidy, bloated at either end and shot through with evident links with the past and present. As it happens, the Chronology presented at the back of this volume begins with the birth of Thomas Moore (1779) and ends with the birth of Brian Boydell (1917): the former sets an important seal on music and, more broadly, culture in nineteenth-century Ireland, and the latter, along with Aloys Fleischmann and Frederick May, represents the generation that made a decisive break with it. Those dates, then, are symbolic rather than definitive. Thus a volume presented as *Music in Nineteenth-Century Ireland* should perhaps be better, though far less neatly entitled, 'Music in Ireland in the long, untidy, but identifiably nineteenth century'. In common cause with historian colleagues, our aim is to map a continuum in the hope that the guide provided creates its own definitions.

Were this volume to have been assembled thirty years ago, its content would likely have been both slighter in extent and rather different in terms of theme.

Studies of composers and strands of influence in the classical canon as it developed in Ireland might well have loomed large. The present volume, reflecting the interests of musicology today, leans more toward aspects of nationalism in nineteenth-century Ireland, how the folk tradition was propagated, musical institutions both sacred and secular, and education. Building on a thriving interest among musicologists in archival work, social history and performance, the volume endeavours to create a broad picture not just of what music was like, but how it was delivered and received in a number of diverse centres. As such, the volume is intended to be of broad use not just to the musical scholar, but to the historian and anyone interested in the patterning of music in the development of Ireland in the nineteenth century. In attempting to maximise the usability of the volume, a Select Bibliography of important publications contemporary to the period is appended to the Chronology; neither bibliography nor chronology is intended to be comprehensive but they identify most of the seminal figures and publications, and the nature of their contribution to musical life.

The thematic categorization of this volume should not be an obstacle to comparisons between chapters in other sections. Just as the reader will find ready comparisons between institutions and societies in Dublin (Paul Rodmell, Ita Beausang), Belfast (Roy Johnston) and Armagh (Anne Dempsey), so too one can identify aspects of musical life in the Czech lands (Jan Smaczny) that both mirror and diverge from that in Ireland. The European dimension is also common to Paul Collins' and Joachim Fischer's chapters, the former dealing with the influx of continental church musicians to Ireland, the latter with Wagnerism, a theme also found in Michael Murphy's chapter. Barra Boydell, David Cooper and Jimmy O'Brien Moran examine aspects of the folk music tradition using a variety of methodologies: Boydell's iconographic approach addresses broader social issues pertaining to the study of folk music in the nineteenth century, a theme that resonates with O'Brien Moran's chapter on various collectors, while Cooper explores the role of the piano in preserving the repertoire. The role of music in the mobilization of social groups is explored in three different contexts by Marie McCarthy, Maria McHale, and Lisa Parker: the formal education of children, the links between the temperance movement and international trends in social amelioration, and the single-handed efforts of one of Dublin's domineering personalities respectively. Harry White pursues the experience and influence of opera in Ireland to its literary afterlife in the works of Joyce and Shaw in a chapter that signally addresses the role of musicology in Irish studies.

Michael Murphy & Jan Smaczny

Acknowledgments

In preparing such a wide-ranging volume, the editors owe a debt of thanks, first of all, to their contributors all of whom were not only punctual but forbearing in their acceptance of suggested alteration. In addition, the editors would like to thank Michael Adams and his staff at Four Courts Press, and the General Editors of *Irish Musical Studies*, Harry White and Gerard Gillen.

The editors wish to thank the following institutions for their assistance and permission to reproduce copyright material: the Ulster Folk and Transport Museum, Bristol Museums and Art Gallery, the National Gallery of Ireland, the University of Limerick and an anonymous private owner for the illustrations in Chapter 3; the Trustees of Boston Public Library, the National Library of Ireland and the Royal Irish Academy for the musical examples in Chapter 5; Charles Nono for the hitherto unpublished image in Chapter 6; the Governors and Guardians of Armagh Public Library for the material in Chapter 7; the Board of Trinity College for the image in Chapter 10; the Linenhall Library, the Ulster Museum, Clanmill Housing Belfast, the Lawrence Collection at the National Library of Ireland, and the Ulster Museum for the images in Chapter 12; the Royal Irish Academy for the image in Chapter 13.

Special thanks are due to Ita Beausang who undertook 'extra-mural' archival research in response to the editors' queries regarding the bibliography and chronology. We also wish to thank Gareth Cox, Mary Immaculate College, University of Limerick, for reading the manuscript; Yo Tomita, Queen's University, Belfast, for his help in preparing the digital manuscript, and Aisling Kelly, Mary Immaculate College for her technical support.

Funding was provided by Queen's University, Belfast, for which the editors are very grateful.

The editors also wish to acknowledge the support of the Society for Musicology in Ireland.

Abbreviations

CE	*Cork Examiner*
DDE	*Dublin Daily Express*
DE	*Daily Express*
FJ	*Freeman's Journal*
GMO	*Grove Music Online* <www.grovemusic.com>
IMS v	*Irish Musical Studies*, v: *The Maynooth International Musicological Conference 1995 Selected Proceedings: Part II*, ed. Patrick F. Devine and Harry White (Dublin: Four Courts Press, 1996)
IMS vi	*Irish Musical Studies*, vi: *A Historical Anthology of Irish Church Music*, ed. Gerard Gillen and Andrew Johnstone (Dublin: Four Courts Press, 2001)
IMS vii	*Irish Musical Studies*, vii: *Irish Music in the Twentieth Century*, ed. Gareth Cox and Axel Klein (Dublin: Four Courts Press, 2003)
IT	*Irish Times*
The Keeper's Recital	Harry White, *The Keeper's Recital: Music and Cultural History in Ireland, 1770–1970* (Cork: Cork University Press, 1998)
MT	*Musical Times*
SN	*Saunders' News-letter*
NG	*The New Grove Dictionary of Music and Musicians,* ed. Stanley Sadie (London: Macmillan, 1980)
NG II	*The New Grove Dictionary of Music and Musicians. Second edition*, ed. Stanley Sadie and John Tyrrell (London: Macmillan, 2001)
NLI	The National Library of Ireland
NUI	The National University of Ireland
QUL	The Library at Queen's University, Belfast
RIA	The Royal Irish Academy
RIAM	The Royal Irish Academy of Music
TCD	Trinity College, Dublin
UCC	University College, Cork

Cultural theory, nostalgia and the historical record: opera in Ireland and the Irishness of opera during the nineteenth century

HARRY WHITE

LISTENING TO THE PAST

Derek Mahon's poem 'Ghosts' is an acknowledgment of the difference between an imagined past and a real present: 'We live the life our parents never knew/ When they sang "Come back to Sorrento".'[1] But the poem also affirms that the past remains a foreign country, even when imagination is made good by experience. The ghosts in an Italian hotel room in the 1990s may appear more real than the nostalgia of a popular song heard in Ireland during the 1940s, but they are ghosts nevertheless. We cannot recover them except through poetry and song. They, too, lead a life we cannot properly know.

The ghosts of opera in Ireland during the nineteenth century are likewise difficult to summon, although they have been memorialized to dramatic effect by Irish literature and by the fiction of James Joyce in particular. They are the ghosts of a tradition which, were it not for Joyce's attachment to it, might seem irrelevant to that reception history of the Irish mind which fastens upon musical constructions (and deconstructions) of nationalism at every turn. However strenuously we seek to distinguish between these constructions and the historical record, the ghosts themselves betray, as they do in Joyce, the function of music in Ireland as a definitive and compelling code of memory, whether this code is explicitly nationalist or not. The operas which stand behind these solitary spirits of remembrance can seem unrelated to the afterlife of Irish cultural history, so that when we survey them, the mere record of the operatic past can seem even more illusory than the imagined one which literature so strikingly provides.

This historical record has been, until recently, a largely undiscovered country. That this is no longer the case is due to scholars such as Joseph Ryan, Christopher Morash and Axel Klein, but the achievement of this record has brought its own bewilderments, and chiefly the bewilderment occasioned by the act of recovery itself. As Joseph Ryan remarks, '[T]he study of Irish opera offers a good example of the gap between what one might reasonably expect and what actually occurred.'[2] But reasonable expectations are not often satisfied by the record of Irish musical history. One reason for this is that musical history itself,

---

[1] Derek Mahon, 'Ghosts', from *Selected Poems* (Allen Lane: Penguin, 2001), p. 113. [2] Joseph Ryan, 'Opera in Ireland before 1925', *IMS* vii, 39.

when it behaves as a model of generic survey does not work well in a country where European genres are peripheral expressions of musical experience. Ghosts of another kind can seem to surface once this has been observed (and chiefly the ghosts of nationalist culture), but in any case the eurocentricism of a musical record dependent on the valence of genre can and does produce more problems than it resolves. When Klein poignantly observes that 'virtually every other Western country can listen to its own musical past, [whereas] Ireland – apart from its ethnic traditions – cannot', the temptation to explore this observation by examining afresh the concept of an 'Irish musical past' becomes paramount.[3] 'Listening to the past' in Ireland may require a mode of perception that transcends the dismal record of musical genres. The very impoverishment of that record, especially by contrast with its abiding and potent afterlife in Irish literature, is sufficient reason to ask 'why' questions in addition to 'what' questions of musical life in Ireland during the nineteenth century.

If, for example, we seek the extent to which nineteenth-century Ireland affords an operatic past for contemporary European and North American musical history, the short answer will be none whatever. Richard Taruskin's *The Oxford History of Western Music* (2005) furnishes a convenient and recent example of Ireland's complete absence from the history of opera, not because Ireland is musically unimportant, but because historians of musical culture as diverse as Carl Dahlhaus, John Caldwell and Taruskin tacitly are in agreement about how the European musical past is to be reconstructed.[4] The fundamental requirement by which Ireland might belong to such a past is simply not there. The reasons for this absence are self-evidently available from almost any reading of Irish history, but in any case there is not much to recommend a contrast between 'European opera' and 'Irish culture', unless we concede that the former is a fabric of local variants across time and place. Other than remarking that nineteenth-century opera assumes the central condition of music as an intelligencer of romantic drama, revolutionary politics and (proto-) nationalist perspective, we cannot really simplify its material complexity in favour of its existence or absence in Ireland.

It is just such a reductionism, however, which tends to obtain when the recovery of Ireland's musical record is in question. When Klein estimates the production of some 280 operas by Irish composers in the period 1780–1925, of which about 30 are devoted to Irish subjects or represent the ethnic repertory (or both), we are not much nearer to an explanation for the peripheral status of opera

---

3 See Axel Klein, 'Stage-Irish, or the National in Irish opera, 1780–1925', *Opera Quarterly*, 20:1 (2005), 27–67, here 27.   4 Although the German romantic address on Celticism is acknowledged by Carl Dahlhaus in *Nineteenth-century music* (English trans. J. Bradford Robinson, Berkeley: University of California Press, 1989), it is an unmistakable convention (one might say a law) of musical history which demands that musical works (and their currency in contemporary reception history) remain pivotal in the narrative, so that in each of the three cases mentioned here, Ireland's lack of such works axiomatically entails the absence of any corresponding account of music in Ireland. For Caldwell's reading of Irish composers in Britain (in *The Oxford history of English music* (Oxford: Oxford University Press, 1999)), see below. See also Klein's critique of Nicholas Temperley (Klein, 'Stage Irish', 28ff), which addresses a similar problem.

in Ireland by comparison with its organic presence in Europe, even if our grasp of the historical record is substantially improved.[5] Klein is right to observe that the history of English opera in the nineteenth century is dominated by Irish (or Irish-related) composers, but it is likewise fair comment to note that Ireland was especially receptive to the English operas of Balfe, Wallace, Benedict, and Sullivan. The sporadic existence of 'Irish' opera must therefore be distinguished from the sustained reception of Italian and English variants, especially in Dublin theatres from the 1840s onwards. Christopher Morash has observed that 'Italian opera … for most of the 1840s had *almost completely overwhelmed the sound of the spoken word on Irish stages*',[6] a striking claim which is premonitory of the conditions which would have allowed original Irish opera to exist as a central, rather than a peripheral mode of dramatic engagement. But those conditions did not arise, nor could they in a country so dramatically denuded of the infra-structural provisions which opera requires. 'Young Ireland' and Italian opera did not consort with each other in the formative years of cultural nationalism, however popular *The Bohemian Girl* may have proved in Dublin. One almost seemed to entail a rejection of the other. Nevertheless, before the story of Irish opera became the story of English opera, Balfe's early ascendancy on the London stage provoked in the Dublin press not only a competent defence against those charges of plagiarism which his early operas excited, but also an aspiration which Balfe was not to fulfil:

> The great secret – that to which Italian dramatic compositions are greatly indebted for their success and from want of attention to which all dramatic attempts in music, upon our stage, greatly owe their failure – is this: *the action of the piece must be carried on in the music*. Why is the writing of the words entrusted to the dolts and dunces hitherto employed? Why are not such poets as our countrymen, Moore and Anster, enlisted in the dramatic cause? Why are not the libretti of the best of the standard Italian operas submitted to them, and the necessary plan of the composition developed? Surely, our history would furnish many an attractive theme for the drama, and let us remind the two eminent composers, to whom we have chiefly adverted in this article [Balfe and Rooke], that they have a country – that country has a music, breathing with every passion, every affection, that moves and swells in the human heart … It lies upon the surface of the history of music – that the more composers have consulted national music – the music of the people – the more have the beauties and attractions of their style been enhanced. The Venetian, Neapolitan, and other native airs of Italy are clearly the foundations upon which have been built the loveliest structures of the Italian muse. It was Weber's attention to the music of Switzerland and the Tyrol, which imbued his writings with all that depth of feeling and affection which pervades them … The accusations against Balfe

---

5 Klein, 'Stage Irish', 34.   **6** Christopher Morash, *A history of Irish theatre, 1601–2000* (Cambridge: Cambridge University Press, 2000), p. 107. My emphasis.

have been grounded on the extent of his imitative powers. Why then, should not these men resort to our native mines, the riches of which are yet unexplored? Their powers stand unquestioned.[7]

As it transpired, Balfe's powers were to remain otherwise engaged. The author of this extract not only harbours and represents a theme which would sound throughout the nineteenth century – the prospect of cross-fertilising indigenous and European modes of musical discourse – but misconstrues Italian and German opera to this end. In this respect, the allusion to Moore is characteristic of a desire to unite Irish poetry and European music which (in Ireland) was destined to remain largely unsatisfied. The volition itself would founder on the illusory (and fallacious) reading of romantic opera as a conjunction of 'native airs' (whether Italian or otherwise) and compositional technique. Even from Balfe's own point of view, the exhortation here to 'resort to our native mines' impracticably eclipses the essence of his achievement, which was virtually to have invented a species of English opera that would dominate the London stage for decades. (To be fair, it is only very recently that this achievement has received anything like its due consideration, insofar as British music historians have, almost as a matter of convention, subscribed to the general view of widespread failure with regard to English opera between the death of Handel and the advent of Benjamin Britten.)[8] From an Irish perspective, however, the impact of Balfe's English operas and the regular institution of seasons of Italian opera, notably at the Theatre Royal (Dublin) throughout the period 1830–80, must have reinforced the conviction that something more than the popularity of individual arias (to say nothing of the cult which attached to individual singers) might be had from an art form that 'completely overwhelmed the sound of the spoken word on Irish stages'. The desire for a masterwork would naturally arise from such a conviction.

THE NATIONAL LONGING FOR FORM

This desire is more difficult to identify in music than in literature, where its presence has been more or less a *donnée* in postcolonial critical discourse. Citing a famous passage from *Ulysses*, in which this desire is explicitly addressed, David Lloyd observes that 'Joyce alludes here, in compressed fashion, to the principal concerns that continue to play through Irish cultural nationalism: the desire for the masterwork; the opposition between the spirit of peasant song,

---

[7] From an unsigned article entitled 'National music and musicians' published in *The Citizen*, 1 (Dublin: 1839), transcribed by Ite O'Donovan. The author is possibly George Petrie. [8] For an instructive commentary on this convention, see Nicholas Temperley, 'Great Britain' in *The New Grove Dictionary of Opera*, ed. Stanley Sadie (London: Macmillan, 1992), ii, 523: 'Opera does not have deep roots in Britain. Only in the last hundred years, at most, has a flourishing tradition of English-language opera, in the fullest, continental, sense, existed. Most writers have been tempted to treat the earlier history in a teleological fashion: as a series of faltering steps towards the presumed goal reached perhaps with *Peter Grimes* in 1945.'

"racy of the soil", and the hybrid "flowers of corruption"'.[9] This opposition will seem familiar to anyone conversant with the cultural history of music in Ireland, but it is salutary to acknowledge that the literary *topos* of longing, what Declan Kiberd terms 'the national longing for form' remains current in Irish critical discourse long after the nineteenth century.[10] Kiberd's concession to the idea of 'total poetic silence' (formulated by the poet Thomas Kinsella) allows him to situate the Irish literary renaissance against 'the virtual absence of good writers in both languages [i.e. Irish and English] through the whole nineteenth century'.[11] Although this seems an extreme perspective to take on Thomas Moore, Maria Edgeworth, James Clarence Mangan and Samuel Ferguson (among others), the binding force of this estimation, which is widely shared, is strongly reminiscent of the 'Land without Music' version of English musical history during the same period. It is precisely this sense of longing, the desire for a masterwork once again, which likewise animates the perception of English music between the death of Purcell and the advent of Elgar. The tension between English opera and the German musical imagination aggravated this longing, especially because the former was so explicitly dependent on the structural precedents of Italian models (Bellini and Donizetti) whereas the latter, because of its abstract condition of expression (put plainly, the ascendancy of instrumental genres), remained difficult of access. The Victorian longing for musical form was not confined to opera, but it had little success elsewhere, except in the closely-related genre of oratorio.

If the English musical renaissance can be fairly characterized as an attempt to satisfy this longing (and in the process emancipate domestic music from the imaginative constraints of number opera) we cannot afford to overlook this attempt, if only to distinguish it from the context of opera in Ireland. To find a voice for English music which might escape the anxiety of Italian influence and the burden, in Bernard Shaw's favourite diagnosis, of German sententiousness required an infrastructural commitment which would never be realized in Ireland except as a projection of colonial musical discourse. Dublin satisfied itself with repeated runs of Italian opera and the 'English' (or 'Irish') *Ring*, notwithstanding occasional (and painful) attempts to domesticate the idiom of English opera by representing the icons of 'native music' on the stage. It is not simply that the national longing for form would attain literary rather than musical expression, but that musical experience, and specifically the experience of opera (Balfe, Benedict, and the Italians), would become a prelude to fiction and drama in Ireland rather than to musical composition. The achievement of opera as a

---

9 David Lloyd, 'Adulteration and the nation', in *Anomalous states: Irish writing and the post-colonial moment* (Dublin: Lilliput Press, 1993), pp 88–124; here p. 101. **10** Kiberd uses this phrase (which originates as a general usage in Salman Rushdie's *Midnight's children*) as a chapter heading in his *Inventing Ireland* (Harvard: Harvard University Press, 1996). As Kiberd and Lloyd (among many others) demonstrate, it is a longing which is both contemplated and fulfilled by *Ulysses* (1922). **11** See Declan Kiberd, 'Writers in quarantine? The case for Irish studies', *The Irish writer and the world* (Cambridge: Cambridge University Press, 2005), pp 52–69; here p. 55. Kiberd refers to an essay by Kinsella entitled 'The divided mind', first published in 1972.

domestic genre, as Klein decisively demonstrates, was so sporadic and naively conceived that it could scarcely rival literature on its own terms, even if, as I wish to argue here, the staging of opera in Dublin had a formative influence on literature.[12]

THE ADULTERATION OF CULTURE

To propose that the terminus of opera in Ireland was literary rather than musical is an argument that depends on a reading of Irish cultural history which affirms the hegemony of literary revival over every other consideration or mode of expression at the close of the nineteenth century. The ascendancy of verbal culture, specifically with regard to opera, may well be expressive of that tension between the loss of one language and the mastery of another which gives the Irish Literary Revival its impetus, but the faltering narrative of opera in Ireland gains considerably if it is read as something other than a chronicle of failure. To understand the genre in Ireland as a poorly represented local variant is clearly legitimate, but it is no less viable to think about opera in Ireland, and hence the 'musical past' in Ireland, as a construct which is determined by its reception history, and above all by the reception history afforded to it by writers such as Shaw and Joyce. More particularly, we can show that Shaw strategically defines himself as a writer in relation to European opera (pre-eminently Wagner) and in this process rejects the currency of British and Irish opera in preference to his own species of 'opera without music'. Likewise, Joyce's structural reliance on Wagner speaks at first to a reception of opera in Dublin (principally as a code of memory) which allows the static condition of repeated runs (interminable seasons of Balfe and Wallace) to attain a vital afterlife in fiction. In the aftermath of fiction and drama, we seem to be presented with verbal operas of the Irish mind, as it were, rather than with any substantial body of opera during or after the nineteenth century. What is striking in Joyce and Shaw, for example, is that an intimate engagement with the genre of opera itself, whether nostalgic or formative, produces a literature self-consciously regulated by musical considerations. It is a literature, one might suggest, which is adulterated by music.[13]

---

12 Those operas from the late eighteenth and early nineteenth centuries by John O'Keeffe, J.B. Logier, and John Stevenson which Klein discusses establish a clear convention of musical identity which would hold firm throughout the nineteenth century: for an opera to be 'Irish', it had to represent prominently a folk melody. The excerpts from O'Keefe's *The Wicklow Mountains* (1796) and Logier's *Brian Boroimhe* (1810) published by Klein (Klein, 'Stage Irish', 30ff) affirm this convention, which would endure as late as 1896 and Stanford's opera *Shamus O'Brien*. Klein's identification of a 'gap of nearly forty years' between one Irish opera (Samuel Lover's *Il Paddy Whack in Italia*, 1841) and the next (John William Glover's *The Deserted Village*, 1880) is sufficient to demonstrate how slender the Irish operatic repertory would remain throughout the nineteenth century, even if Klein's rather stringent definition of 'Irish opera' (which excludes Balfe and Benedict) partly accounts for this reduced presence.   13 Although the influence of music on Joyce and Shaw has long been recognized, it is only very recently that critics have engaged with opera as the true domain of imaginative precedent in their work. Shaw's extensive experience as a

This suggestion stems from a theory of hybridization which David Lloyd has adapted to Irish cultural nationalism and which he develops in order to distinguish between Joyce's dismantling of cultural autonomy, and the formative phases of this autonomy which accumulated such force in the late nineteenth century. Lloyd nominates several instances of 'cultural purification' which are incorporated in national institutions including the Gaelic League, the Gaelic Athletic Association, the Irish Literary Revival, the National Theatre and so on, but of particular relevance here is his reading of Douglas Hyde's essay 'Gaelic Folk Songs' (1890). This essay, along with Hyde's more prescriptive 'The Necessity for De-Anglicising Ireland' (1892), offers a diagnosis of 'the Gaelic genius' which is, as Lloyd argues, radically expressive of Irish cultural autonomy in opposition to received notions of narrative intelligibility. Amongst much else, it determines the transmission of Gaelic culture in which the static condition of music and the 'unsequacious' nature of the Gaelic verbal imagination are intimately aligned:

> I have found no popular ballads among the peasantry, for to tell a story in verse requires an orderly, progressive and somewhat slow sequence of ideas, and this is the very faculty which the Gael has not got – his mind is too quick and passionate …
>
> But even this characteristic of Gaelic thought is insufficient to account for the perfectly extraordinary inconsequentness and abruptness of the folk-songs … These singers often forgot … the real words of the song, and then they invented others, but more frequently they borrowed verses from any other piece … provided it could be sung to the same tune … What between the 'unsequacious' mind of the original makers, the alterations made by generations of singers who forgot the words, and the extraneous verses borrowed from completely different productions … the most beautiful sentiments will be followed by the most grotesque bathos … [14]

Hyde commends these disjunctions, which are themselves subversive of any claim to an Anglicized notion of 'art' (Lloyd points out that it is the process of oral transmission, rather than any 'tricks of the professional poet', that appeals to Hyde), but of greater relevance here is the simultaneous affirmation of melody as mnemonic formula and the disavowal of narrative order. As Lloyd argues,

---

London music critic and Joyce's pervasive reliance on music in his fiction are obvious justifications for this critical engagement in general terms, but the notion of *Ulysses* (for example) as a *Gesamtkunstwerk* or of *Man and Superman* as a verbal opera presents implications for the corresponding absence of Irish operatic works *per se* in the late nineteenth and early twentieth centuries. For a comprehensive account of Joyce's reception of Wagner see Timothy Martin, *Joyce and Wagner: a study of influence* (Cambridge: Cambridge University Press, 1991). As Martin points out, Wagner's influence on the literature of European modernism was immense. Joyce's adulteration of musical forms can thus be regarded as the extreme manifestation of a pervasive tendency in European poetry, fiction and drama through which Wagner's symbolic apprehension of art is adapted to literary genres. **14** Hyde, 'Gaelic folk-songs', quoted in Lloyd, 'Adulteration and the nation', pp 102–3.

'Hyde's "restoration" of the essential folk-song requires ... the representation of the work of the Gaelic bards as a deviation from the true passion of the people.' When Lloyd adds that 'Irish folk culture is transformed into an ahistorical ground on which the defining difference of "Irishness" can be established over against the homogenizing/hybridizing influence of "Anglicization",'[15] his reading clarifies the vital exclusion of art music from Hyde's agenda.

Although it is obvious that this agenda was eclipsed by the plural tolerance and narrative intelligibility of the Literary Revival (of which it was a part), it is somewhat less apparent that the vigorous adulteration of culture which was brought to bear on the Literary Revival (in essence, the re-imagining of Irish culture in English), continued to affirm the static conception of music which Hyde identifies in this passage; it also affirmed, almost as a matter of convention, the status of music as an intelligencer of verbal meaning.

Both of these affirmations – music as an *a priori* essence, and music as a conduit for verbal expression – were so widespread in Ireland throughout the nineteenth century that they can be used at least partly to explain the static condition and reception of opera, especially when taken in apposition with the monotony and underdevelopment of Irish musical life during the same period. But they can also be advanced to clarify the powerful continuity between folksong and operatic aria which Joyce notably took almost as a matter of course. Joyce's own strong instinct for the adulteration of culture finds a remarkable correlative in the genre of opera itself.[16] The status of opera in his earlier fiction belongs to a wider assimilation of musical set-pieces (arias, ballads, folk songs, the *Melodies* of Thomas Moore) which, in Seamus Deane's phrase, collectively functioned 'like an extended national operetta'[17] in Irish fiction, poetry and drama long before Joyce. Fundamental to this process of assimilation was the iconic projection of opera as a cultural, if notably limited site for Irishness.

THE PATHOS OF PADDY

It speaks to the adulteration of the genre that this site did not belong exclusively to opera. On the contrary, the proximity between opera and spoken drama was so intimate that it is difficult to classify one as a borrowed musical culture without conceding that the other was likewise taken over from English models (even where these were brilliantly exploited by Irish dramatists at work in London). It is no less true that images of the stage Irishman were an invention of the English theatre, however successfully they transferred to Dublin. Klein is worth quoting directly on this point:

---

[15] Lloyd, 'Adulteration and the nation', p. 103.   [16] Which is to say that the 'hybrid' nature of opera, its admixture of music and theatre, is one which might reasonably be expected to appeal to Joyce, given his own (often acute) awareness of linguistic adulteration (Irish and English again), to say nothing of his strong appetite for music as a primary code of expression.   [17] Seamus Deane, 'Poetry and song, 1800–1890', *The Field Day anthology of Irish writing*, ii, ed. Deane (Derry: Field Day Publications, 1991), p. 4.

the trilogy of works that, rather naively, became known as the 'Irish Ring' – Balfe's *The Bohemian Girl* (1843), Wallace's *Maritana* (1845), and Benedict's *The Lily of Killarney* (1862) – were absolutely European operas with English words; the most Irish connotations are to be found in the work of the German-born Benedict ... The Balfe, Wallace and Benedict works featured prominently in the repertory of (mainly) travelling opera companies in Britain and Ireland; Seamus Reilly's overview of operas performed in Dublin between 1888 and 1904 reveals yearly performances of all three, sometimes of up to four runs a year.[18]

This last observation brings us close to Joyce and confirms the prominence of all three operas in his formative years as a writer, but the characterization of these works as 'absolutely European operas with English words' somewhat eclipses the process of cultural absorption by which they later became 'absolutely Irish' through their referential status in Joyce and elsewhere.[19] *The Lily of Killarney*, moreover, provides a special case in which the opera is built on a projection of Irishness that derives from the Boucicault play (to which it is so intimately related) and in turn from the novel by Gerald Griffin (*The Collegians*, 1829). The plot to one side, it is the emphatic concept of 'Irishness' which ties these three versions together, even if the narrative setting of the novel and the operatic medium of *The Lily of Killarney* are self-evidently distinct. Seamus Deane's reading of this difference exactly prefigures the attempt here to understand the opera as an Irish work:

> The most significant alteration in the Boucicault play, and in the opera derived from it ... is not in the roles of the characters so much as in the disappearance from these adaptations of the heavily upholstered prose of Griffin himself. For that is the form of the King's English that is ultimately dominant – self-consciously respectable, wearing its learning on its sleeve, even making its classical quotations, tags, and references a ground bass to the lighter Irish melodies of place names, personal names (Myles-na-Copaleen), and chevilles.[20]

If the currency of transaction for Griffin in 1829 is the King's English, then in 1862 it is the apparel and demeanour of English opera. The metaphor employed by Seamus Deane is actualized to the extent that the respectable 'ground bass' of Griffin's prose finds a correlative in the operatic discourse of Benedict's score. In the vocal libretto, the socially regulative force of dialect has all but disappeared, even if the place names and the chevilles remain.

---

18 Klein, 'Stage Irish', 42–4. **19** The O'Casey trilogy (*The Shadow of a Gunman*, *Juno and the Paycock* and *The Plough and the Stars*), an 'Irish Ring' of a more persuasive kind, frequently (and laconically) relies on the popular resonance of these arias in Irish popular culture at the turn of the century. **20** Seamus Deane, *Strange country: modernity and nationhood in Irish writing since 1790* (Oxford: Clarendon Press, 1998), p. 63.

Of greater significance is Benedict's successful integration of local colour and the claims of English opera: these claims owe much to Balfe, and to Benedict's own experience as a conductor and composer in Germany and Austria, but the succession of fixed forms which he employs (beginning with an overture that proclaims its debt to Weber as unmistakably as it rehearses the prominent themes of the set numbers to follow) confirms the ascendancy of genre over subject matter. Although the melodic line is sometimes inflected to indicate a particularity of Irishness, the opera absorbs such inflections in the fulfilment of well-established generic expectations, as in Hardress' final aria, 'Eily, mavourneen'. Despite the characteristic cheville in the text, the periodic structure, chromatic inflections and melodic structure of the vocal writing realize the demands of an English romantic ballad. Only in the penultimate number of the first act ('Let the farmer praise his grounds') is the melodic writing paradigmatic of Irish folk song, so that the text, with its Irish refrain ('Gramachree ma cruiskeen, slantha gal mavourneen ...') is deftly set to a pre-existent tune.

This discretion with regard to the deployment of ethnic material not only means that the contract between Irish subject matter and English opera is emphatically in favour of the latter, but that a distinct (and new) semantic field of Irishness is created through the confluence of the two. The fixed forms guarantee to the opera its international currency and credibility, so that the Irish subject matter is authenticated by these, rather than the other way around. Those numbers in *The Lily of Killarney* by which James Joyce reliably indicates remembrance and the bourgeois Catholic imagination attain such features in the first instance because of their self-standing popularity as ballads and concert arias.[21] They become detached from the opera, but in that liberation the opera remains a plausible source of Irish sensibility. The arias become songs, and the songs become iconic of urban memory and experience. But it is also fair comment to add that the steady rate of performance which Benedict's opera (together with those by Balfe and Wallace) enjoyed in Dublin (and not only between 1888 and 1904) ensured that the works from which these songs were excerpted would function as a recurring (and significantly static) feature of the Irish cultural matrix, no less than would a small (and likewise static) repertory of Italian works. Opera, in brief, would become Irish by association, and indeed by habituation.

In Colonel Caverly's pattersong from *Patience*, 'the pathos of Paddy as rendered by Boucicault' is among those qualities which are required to make up the essence of a heavy dragoon. Gilbert is almost certainly referring here to Boucicault's own stage plays and to the dramatist's performance in *The Shaughran* (1875) in particular, but the line itself allows us to distinguish between the bathos of stage-Irishry (in a Savoy Opera that incidentally lampoons Oscar Wilde) and the assimilation of Benedict's opera into the fabric of bourgeois Irish culture. Gilbert and Sullivan dominated English opera in the closing decades of the

---

21 *The Lily of Killarney* appears in *Dubliners*, *A Portrait of the Artist as a Young Man*, *Ulysses* and *Finnegans Wake*.

nineteenth century, just as Balfe had done forty years before. By then, and certainly in 1881, the year of *Patience*, the subject of Ireland had drifted from the London operatic stage. In the spoken theatre moreover, the pathos of Paddy seemed a faded trope by comparison with the glittering intelligence of Wilde. Meanwhile in Ireland, as Charles Villiers Stanford would complain, there was 'no opening for a prophet ... who writes operas in his own country'.

Stanford's complaint, in a letter to Robert Prescott Stewart on 2 January 1881, would itself prove to be prophetic: notwithstanding the healthy reception of Balfe, Benedict and Italian grand opera through the closing decades of the nineteenth century, Ireland remained a closed door to new works by composers of any nationality.[22] But the prophecy would also extend to England for the duration of Stanford's operatic career, and with the sovereign exception of one opera, *Shamus O'Brien* (1896), Stanford's persistent difficulties with the genre would remain expressive of a larger indifference ironically contextualized by the enormous popularity of the Savoy Operas during Stanford's formative years as a composer. The story of English opera would remain a chronicle of failure, initiated by a critical press (headed by Bernard Shaw) notably hostile to the viability of such enterprises as Richard D'Oyly Carte's heroic (if impracticable) efforts to create an English National Opera, which culminated in the production of Sullivan's *Ivanhoe* in 1891. This hostility continues to echo in modern commentary. John Caldwell's terse assessment of serious opera in England at the turn of the century in *The Oxford History of English Music* (1999) may stand here as a characteristic indictment: 'Whatever claim Cowen, Thomas, Mackenzie, and Stanford may have to belong to the vanguard of what came to be called the English musical renaissance, it would not be based on their operas.'[23] Although recent studies of Stanford by Jeremy Dibble and Paul Rodmell in particular have somewhat redeemed this bleak judgment, it remains true that the narrative of English musical history, which concedes to Parry and Stanford a pioneering role in the rehabilitation of serious composition, continues to affirm the indictments of Stanford and his contemporaries, and to uphold the censures of Bernard Shaw.

The early reception of Sullivan's *Ivanhoe* by Shaw and J.A. Fuller Maitland, for example, centred upon that work's failure to emancipate itself from what Maitland calls 'the set pieces of old-fashioned opera'[24] and Shaw's more trenchant indictments:

> I maintain that it is disqualified as a serious dramatic work by the composer's failure to reproduce in music the vivid characterisation of Scott, which alone

---

[22] Stanford was writing to Stewart immediately prior to the first performance of his first opera, *The Veiled Prophet*, given in Hanover on 6 February 1881. The letter is folded in with Stewart's copy of the vocal score, now preserved in the library of the RIAM. My thanks to Philip Shields, librarian, for drawing this source to my attention. [23] John Caldwell, *The Oxford history of English music, vol. 2, c.1715 to the present day* (Oxford: Oxford University Press, 1999), p. 253. [24] Fuller Maitland's assessment, originally published in *The Times* is cited by Arthur Jacobs in *Arthur Sullivan: a Victorian musician* (Oxford: Oxford University Press, 1984), pp 326–7.

classes the novel among the masterpieces of fiction ... Take for example Scott's Bois Guilbert, the fierce Templar, the original 'bold, bad man', tanned nearly black, disfigured with sword-cuts, strong, ambitious, going on for fifty, a subject for Verdi or Velasquez. Is it possible to sit patiently and hear the music of the drawing-room, sensuous and passionate without virility or intelligence, put into the mouth of such a figure? Not with all the brass and drum sauce in the world.[25]

Shaw, with his malicious appetite for damning with faint praise, would later allow that 'the Savoy Opera is a genre in itself' and then proceed to nominate Sullivan's one work in this genre without Gilbert (*Haddon Hall*) as 'the highest and most consistent expression it has yet attained'.[26] The underlying tenor of such criticism was that English music was incapable of (and temperamentally unsuited to) a mature achievement in serious opera. The serious genre could not be part of the story, except by way of parody or risible pretension. In such a climate, it is hardly surprising that Stanford failed, other than when he fell back upon the resources of English opera itself and adopted the structural habits of Balfe and Benedict which he had experienced for himself during his teens in Dublin.[27] His experience of *The Lily of Killarney* in particular provided Stanford with a model which illuminates the compositional technique deployed in *Shamus O'Brien*. If *Shamus* is an Irish opera, its claims to that ascription are more securely based than on mere nationality or even subject-matter. It is, rather, the work's narrativity, expressly in terms of an Irishness habituated by the popularity of English (and Italian) opera that makes the case for *Shamus* as an Irish work. This narrativity relates it not only to the history of Irish prototypes on the English stage, but to a more narrowly defined operatic convention by which the English operas of Balfe in particular, which have nothing expressly to do with Ireland, attained secondary meaning as Irish works by means of their faithful and enduring presence in Irish theatres. It is this presence, this conventional degree of reception and assimilation, which accounts in turn for their memorable afterlife in Joyce. The supreme irony in such a reading is that *Shamus*, for all its brilliant success in London, Dublin, Belfast, Limerick, Waterford and Cork, failed to register in any meaningful way in the formation of Irish cultural history.[28]

25 Bernard Shaw, 'A suppressed notice of Ivanhoe' (*The World*, 4 February, 1891), reprinted in *Shaw's music: the complete musical criticism in three volumes*, ed. Dan H. Laurence (London: Bodley Head, 1981), ii, 253–60; here 253–4.   26 Cited in Jacobs, *Arthur Sullivan*, p. 342.   27 For an account of Stanford's experience of opera during his childhood and early youth in Dublin, see Jeremy Dibble, *Charles Villiers Stanford: man and musician* (Oxford: Oxford University Press, 2002), pp 27–32. This account, based in significant measure on the composer's own record, incidentally restores to opera in Dublin a much more positive complexion than might otherwise be the case, insofar as it registers a lively operatic culture (Beethoven, Bellini, Cherubini, Donizetti, Flotow, Gounod, Meyerbeer, Mozart, Rossini, Thomas, Verdi and Weber, in addition to Balfe, Benedict and Wallace), which excluded only Wagner from its purview. Such a record confirms the popularity of English, French, German and Italian grand opera in Dublin, just as it also confirms the general absence of any significant Irish contribution to the genre.   28 For the reactions of the Irish press to *Shamus*, see Dibble, *Stanford*, p. 274. Despite wholehearted endorsement of

Although it satisfied what Jeremy Dibble describes as the 'still insatiable' hunger for comic opera, it could not transcend this function, even when Stanford sought to convert it into a 'grand opera' (by adding sung recitatives) for the continental stage.[29] It would remain trapped within its own generic limitations. Its narrativity of Irishness, both in terms of subject matter and musical structure, would founder and lapse into silence. Only 'the pathos of Paddy' (and the spirit of Boucicault) endured.

TELLING TALES AND DEFERENCE POLITICS

In *The Irish Story: Telling Tales and Making It Up in Ireland*, Roy Foster comments thus on the revival of narrative history in contrast to postcolonial discourses about Ireland in recent years:

> Thinking about the shape of Irish history, or arguing about the accuracy and significance of certain generally accepted themes, one is struck again and again by the importance of the narrative mode: the idea that Irish history *is* a story, and the implications that this carries about a beginning, middle and the sense of an ending. Not to mention heroes, villains, donors, helpers, guests, plots, revelations, and all the other elements of the story form.[30]

Whether history can still function as narrative remains open to question, but Foster's identification of those 'elements of the story form' is in the meantime strongly suggestive of not only history and fiction, but also of opera. Heroes and villains remained the stock-in-trade of the operatic stage in Bayreuth no less than in London at the close of the nineteenth century (and for long after that). These rudimentary prototypes allowed Shaw to cut Wagner sufficiently down to size so as to explain him to the Great British Public, even if his motives for doing so were not to foment a cultivation of English opera, but to clear the path for his own dramatic discourse as 'operas without music'.[31] Nevertheless, for Shaw, as for everyone else who sought to understand the state of music in Britain at the turn of the century, the narrative function of opera remained central: the genre existed to tell a tale. Even the 'ballad opera' (and the ballad itself) did that much.

The tale that Stanford is telling in *Shamus* universalizes Irish history through the agency of romantic prototypes which are musical as well as literary. Stanford knew Le Fanu's ballad well, and although the gestation of the opera dates from about 1891, the composer's already extensive engagement with Irish music (most

---

the work, it failed to form any part of the literary afterlife which attached to Balfe and Benedict: *Shamus* finds no echo in Joyce. **29** See Dibble, *Stanford*, pp 280–1. **30** R.F. Foster, 'The story of Ireland', *The Irish story: telling tales and making it up in Ireland* (London: Penguin Books, 2001), p. 2. **31** See Laurence, *Shaw's music*, i, 12: 'The plays themselves, as Shaw revealed, were conceived on musical principles, being opera without music.' Laurence reports Shaw as commenting that 'Granville Barker was not far out ... when, at a rehearsal of one of my plays he cried out, "Ladies and gentlemen: will you please remember that this is Italian opera".'

notably through his collaboration with the poet and literary historian Alfred Perceval Graves, who wrote the texts for Stanford's *Songs of Old Ireland*, 1882 and *Irish Songs and Ballads*, 1893), and his incorporation of folk melodies into his original compositions, meant that Stanford's assimilation of traditional music was far more extensive than that of any other composer inclined to represent Ireland through the medium of opera. But this intensity of engagement did not alter Stanford's regard for European compositional technique as the fundamental source of operatic narrativity, even if the overture to *Shamus* announces the work's Irishness through the agency of a folksong. Stanford's recourse to Le Fanu's romantic account of an episode from the 1798 rebellion, moreover, did not attenuate in the smallest degree his unionist politics or his stringent disavowal of Home Rule for Ireland. In this regard, Graves's memoir of Le Fanu (1880) contains a salutary observation about the author of *Shamus O'Brien* which might equally apply to Stanford himself:

> We have heard it said (though without having inquired into the truth of the tradition) that 'Shamus O'Brien' was the result of a match at a pseudo-national ballad writing made between Le Fanu and several of the most brilliant of his literary confreres at T.C.D. But however this may be, Le Fanu himself was undoubtedly no Young Irelander; indeed he did the stoutest service as a press writer in the Conservative interest, and was no doubt provoked as well as amused at the unexpected popularity to which his poem attained amongst the Irish nationalists. And here it should be remembered that the ballad was written some eleven years before the outbreak of '48 and at a time when a '98 subject might fairly have been regarded as legitimate literary property amongst the most loyal.[32]

Almost sixty years later, Stanford's empathetic response to the materials of Le Fanu's poem did not embrace the smallest concession to political autonomy. On the contrary: he would later withdraw his opera from circulation for fear it should promote Home Rule in the second decade of the twentieth century. It was a move, as Jeremy Dibble indicates, which was adumbrated by his resignation in 1900 from the Irish Literary Society, specifically in protest at Yeats' condemnation of British colonial rule (in South Africa, no less than in Ireland).[33]

In his letter to Stewart of 1881, Stanford had described his first opera, based on 'The Veiled Prophet of Khorassan' from Thomas Moore's *Lalla Rookh* (1817),

---

[32] Alfred Perceval Graves, 'Memoir of Joseph Sheridan Le Fanu' (1880) as retrieved from <www.encyclopediaindex.com/b/pclp110.htm> (accessed 2 August 2006). See also Alfred Perceval Graves, 'Joseph Sheridan Le Fanu', *Irish literary and musical studies* [1914] (repr. New York: Books for Libraries Press, 1970), pp 51–70. Dibble, *Stanford*, pp 13–18 attributes decisive importance to Le Fanu's influence on the 'Tory Patriot' formation of Stanford's father and on the composer himself.   [33] Dibble, *Stanford*, p. 368. It is worth adding that despite this withdrawal, Stanford continued to be much involved in the promotion of Irish folk music, as in his vice-presidency of the Irish Folk Song Society (London, 1904) or his publication of his edition of the Petrie Collection between 1902 and 1905.

as 'an Irishman's work on an Irish poet's story', a formula that might reasonably be applied also to *Shamus*. But the 'Irishman's work', as with Benedict's setting of Boucicault, is in this case a romanticising of Ireland in terms of English opera, and by 1896, decidedly old-fashioned English opera at that. In this connection, Arthur Sullivan's correspondence with Boucicault himself during the composition of *Ivanhoe* proves to be extremely germane: Sullivan had repudiated the older dramatist's offer of assistance with the libretto (following his break with Gilbert) on the grounds that 'the whole tendency of stage music now is to get rid as much as possible of songs, duets and other *set pieces* and to become as *dramatic* as possible.'[34] But it was 'songs, duets and set pieces' which continued to preoccupy Sullivan, and, following him, Stanford. Stanford's note at the head of the vocal score of *Shamus* advertises that 'the composer has only used two traditional folk-songs in this opera' ('Father O'Flynn' and 'The Glory of the West'), but this revealing disavowal of musical stage-Irishry (and stage-Englishry, for that matter, given that the second of them is a march associated with Cromwell) does not supervene Stanford's reliance on 'Father O'Flynn' (who is also a character in the opera) not only to head the overture but to provide a set piece in the finale of the first act.

Of even greater significance, however, is the fluency with which Stanford adopts the theatrical technique of his youth, to such an extent that it is difficult to hear in *Shamus* anything other than an adroit reprise of the operatic discourse which Balfe and Benedict had so skilfully exploited decades earlier. *Shamus* is the rhetoric of ballad opera brought to bear on a libretto which is already the stuff of romantic comedy. The violence, betrayal and reprisals of 1798 are eclipsed by comic melodrama in the text before Stanford has set a line. Le Fanu's poem (and the additions by Stanford's librettist, George Jessop) is a mythology of racial stereotypes which was not only acceptable to Stanford's patriotic unionism but which itself demanded the validation of currency on the English stage. Libretto and score collude in this understanding, by which the exotic projection of time, place and character occludes any danger of contemporary resonance other than to celebrate, as always, the quick-witted Celt and his honest, if lugubrious, Saxon masters. Shamus himself is not the stage-Irishman of Tory propaganda (the simian buffoon with his absurd – and often violent – pretensions to liberty) but the proud provincial whose courage and independence are preferable to the treachery and opportunism of the collaborator (Mike Murphy). This mutual recognition of moral integrity (as between Shamus and his captor, Captain Trevor) touches upon a characteristic trope of mid-Victorian fiction: the benevolent relations which can exist between the centre and the periphery, especially when deference politics remain not only tenable, but (at least to the centre) ethically justifiable.

Such relations had long disappeared from Irish politics by the time Stanford came to write *Shamus O'Brien*, but this does not mean that they were void of meaning for the composer himself. To judge from Stanford's biography, indeed,

---

34 Sullivan in a letter to Boucicault dated 6 June 1890 and cited in Jacobs, *Arthur Sullivan*, p. 317.

the reverse was the case, insofar as the explicitly unionist admixture of loyalty to Empire and to Ireland, both of which Stanford inherited from his father, continued to inform his political sensibilities throughout his life.[35] His disillusion with the Ireland of Land Reform and agitation for Home Rule calls to mind Roy Foster's compelling diagnosis of Anthony Trollope's disenchantment with Ireland in his late fiction:

> Trollope had written Ireland into his panoramic vision of Victorian English life, but in his last year, and his last novel, he saw Irish nationalism beginning to write Ireland out of the Union. This would prove such a successful operation that the Irish dimension of Trollope's English identity has tended to recede: forgotten along with the British identity of the Victorian Irish middle class, Catholic as well as Protestant, who produced generations of Phineas Finns.[36]

Trollope would make his disillusion explicit in his last novel, *The Landleaguers* (unfinished at the time of his death in 1882), but Stanford behaved otherwise: the score of *Shamus O'Brien* attests from beginning to end a striking nostalgia for the kind of operatic projection of Irishness which made Benedict famous in 1862. The creation of set pieces, discrete ballads, patter songs, choral numbers and folk tune arrangements: it is all there in *Shamus*, just as it had been in *The Lily of Killarney* a generation earlier. As in the earlier work, Stanford's skilful recourse to mainstream opera assimilates (and domesticates) in turn the Irishness of the text, and makes it acceptable to late Victorian taste. In place of 'heavily upholstered prose', once again, there is the panache and virtuosity of Stanford's compositional technique.

It is the nature of this technique – its committed recovery of an older operatic tradition, its emphatic preference for *buffo* variants of musical drama, its integration of musical Irish identity cards and the apparatus of conventional opera, and its discrete moments of memorable lyricism – which confirms Stanford's bad faith as a writer of Irish music. This is all the more evident when *Shamus* is contrasted with two other Stanford works that closely neighbour it: his arrangement of *The Irish Melodies of Thomas Moore: the Original Airs Restored* (1895) and the *Requiem* (1897).[37] In the present context, the Moore arrangements are much less significant than the *Requiem*, except to note that they affirm, at close proximity to the opera, Stanford's abiding interest in preserving (or restoring) Irish music according to a powerful, if underdeveloped notion of authenticity. The equation of these melodies (and many others) with an identifiable and stable projection of Irishness was not unique to Stanford, but he, more than any other

---

[35] See, for example, the correspondence between Stanford and Erskine Childers cited and discussed in Dibble, *Stanford*, pp 404–6. [36] Foster, *The Irish story*, 'Trollope and the memory of Ireland', p. 146. [37] Stanford also set another Le Fanu ballad, *Phaudrig Crohoore* in 1895. Stanford's extensive Irish settings, arrangements and original compositions based on Irish folk song deserve a self-standing assessment which they have yet to receive.

composer (before or since), engaged with the materials of Irish music to such an extent that sooner or later (and usually sooner, as in the case of *Shamus*) the quotation in full of an Irish melody became the only reliable indicator of a work's authentic Irishness. Even where Stanford could defeat this convention, as he did in setting the *echt*-Irish *Shamus* as a romantic opera, the dutiful presence of the traditional air was never far away.

It is the *Requiem*, however, which throws the deliberately stylized (and retrospective) compositional technique of *Shamus* into sharp relief. Whatever its stylistic derivations, it is hard to escape the impression that here Stanford is writing as himself, without any sense of cultural obligation to those English expectations of Irishness which he felt impelled to satisfy in *Shamus*. Written in 1896 in memory of Lord Leighton and first given under Stanford's direction in Birmingham in November of the following year, the *Requiem* travelled quickly and consolidated the composer's reputation not only in England but in Germany.[38] Dibble's perceptive judgment on the work's closing movements speaks to its dramatic flair, its structural intelligence and operatic conception:

> The Agnus Dei is one of Stanford's most visionary choral movements with a dramatic tension he rarely equalled in other choral works. Its theatrical demeanour and rhetoric are thoroughly suggestive of an operatic finale in which the Lux Aeterna has the same aura as a final act of redemption. Indeed, it might be argued that in this movement, Stanford came closest to writing his finest operatic conclusion.[39]

In this reading (which elsewhere acknowledges the fundamentally symphonic cast of Stanford's thought, especially in terms of motivic variation), the *Requiem* is redeemed from its own reception history, which originated in genuine acclaim but which rapidly progressed into obscurity. Klein pithily remarks that Stanford was 'too Irish for the English, too English for the Irish, and too German for both',[40] a judgment which brilliantly summarizes the predicament in which the composer found himself, whatever path he might pursue. The chameleon-like condition of his immense facility as a composer (which allowed him to inhabit too many musical worlds at once), meant that he was easy prey to Shaw's merciless accusations of artistic posturing. He would soon come to represent that dominant reading of Victorian music as a mode of respectable aspiration (rather than enduring achievement), to which so many of his compositions have been consigned by posterity. Stanford and Parry: a pair of sirens blest only by their professional peers, but otherwise eclipsed by the passage of time, and by the music of Edward Elgar.

Shamus O'Brien went the same way, although it did not disappear as quickly from circulation as the *Requiem*. Its eventual obscurity was, in any case, hastened by Stanford's own withdrawal of the work against the tide of Home Rule. It now

---

[38] See Dibble, *Stanford*, p. 299. [39] Ibid., p. 298. [40] Axel Klein, *Irish classical recordings: a discography of Irish art music* (London: Greenwood Press, 2001), p. 145.

exists in the mausoleum of musical neglect, strikingly symbolized by the old Royal Edition in which the vocal score first appeared, and to which so many forgotten monuments of Victorian music glumly belong.

THE ARRAIGNMENT OF ART

Perhaps we ought to be grateful that Shaw did not comment publicly on *Shamus* or the *Requiem*, given his otherwise tireless denunciation of Stanford's music, but it is not difficult to conjecture that he would have been somewhat more sympathetic to *Shamus* than to anything which smacked of 'oratorio mongering' or the influence of Johannes Brahms.[41] Shaw's notorious incapacity in this latter regard did not prevent him from championing Elgar, whose mastery of two genres Shaw had hitherto dismissed (the oratorio and the symphony) changed Shaw's mind about the future of English music.[42] But Elgar's ascendancy confirmed Stanford's demise, a process which was well underway by the time Shaw had taken on the English theatrical establishment and embarked on a career as a dramatist that stemmed directly from his experience as an indefatigable thinker about music, and about the role of European music in England in particular. Reception history would favour Shaw and Elgar, and not Shaw and Stanford.

This latter pairing is worth a moment's further consideration, especially given Stanford's persistent attempt to find his voice as a composer of opera and Shaw's ebullient recognition of his own plays as opera without music. Shaw and Stanford dominated English music as critic and composer respectively, if to obviously different ends. Shaw's reaction against the musical establishment is self-evidently in striking contrast to Stanford's success within its folds, but the two shared common ground nevertheless. They were close Dublin contemporaries (Stanford was four years' Shaw's senior), both were from the same Tory Protestant milieu, and both sought a better musical life in London. Although neither one disparaged his Irishness (even if Stanford seems to have assumed it and discarded it at will), neither hesitated to adapt himself to the canons of English taste. Shaw's motives for doing so were vitally different from Stanford's: he arraigned music in England (the strident jeer of the autodidact extended to almost every British composer) just as he would arraign the theatre, in order to clear a path for his own

---

[41] The fact that Lucy Shaw (sister of GBS) took part in the first production of *Shamus* may or may not account for Shaw's silence; in the same vein, it is not entirely fanciful to conjecture that Shaw's antipathy towards Stanford may have originated in a degree of personal resentment: Michael Holroyd reports that Robert Prescott Stewart claimed responsibility for having driven Vandaleur Lee (the 'damaged Svengali' of the Shaw household) from Dublin. Given that Stewart was Stanford's teacher, Holroyd's suggestion that Shaw's 'particular disdain' for Stanford may have originated in Vandaleur Lee's expulsion may have good grounds. See Michael Holroyd, *Bernard Shaw, volume 1, 1856–1898: the search for love* (London: Chatto & Windus, 1988), pp 48–9.   [42] For a characteristic comment on Brahms, see 'Circenses', *The World*, 24 December 1890, repr. in Laurence, *Shaw's music*, ii, 233–9; here 235: 'I really cannot stand Brahms as a serious composer. It is nothing short of a European misfortune that such prodigious musical powers should have nothing better in the way of ideas than incoherent commonplace.'

engagement with spoken drama. Shaw's experience (and assimilation) of Wagner in particular formed an essential prelude to a whole body of work that would begin in earnest with *Widowers' Houses* (1892) (originally and significantly entitled *Rhinegold*). One significant by-product of this engagement was to realize that 'Irishness' was an English invention. This recognition lies at the heart of *John Bull's Other Island*.

Stanford, by comparison, did not see this, and struggled as a consequence to represent Irishness as a separate entity, even when his solution to this problem, as in *Shamus*, lay in writing an English opera. One especially shrewd observation from Shaw on this problem, as it manifested itself in Stanford's symphonic writing, deserves prominence in this regard:

> It is only in the second subject of this movement [the last movement of the *Irish* Symphony], an original theme of the composer's own minting, that the form and the material really combine chemically with sonata. And this satisfactory result is presently upset by the digression to the utterly incompatible aim of the composer to display the charms of his native music. In the first movement, the sonata writer keeps to his point better: there are no national airs lifted bodily into it. Nevertheless, the first movement does not convince me that Professor Stanford's is a symphonic talent any more than Meyerbeer's was. In mentioning Meyerbeer I know I run the risk of having the implied comparison interpreted in the light of the Wagnerian criticism – that is, as a deliberate disparagement. I do not mean it so.[43]

Although this passage comes from one of Shaw's better-known indictments of Stanford, it seems fair to take Shaw at this word when he affects not to disparage Stanford by likening him to Meyerbeer. The implicit comparison with another composer of opera is a shrewd insight, and so also is the effort to disabuse British music (as it then was) of its obligations to the 'native charm' of folk music. But Shaw's scepticism in regard to Stanford never abated. His music would always be arraigned by his compatriot's critical intelligence.

Other arraignments would follow, not least in Ireland. In Dublin, the dreary disavowal of 'Saxon music', together with the likewise jaded affirmation of a 'wealth of [Irish] melody' simply reinforced the polarization of two cultures when a controversy arose from Stanford's short-lived Presidency of the Feis Ceoil:

> we therefore welcome and applaud the decision of the Feis Executive, and we rejoice that it is destined to be made clear that we possess amongst the treasures of our nation a wealth of melody, both rare and beautiful, and within limits of our shores musicians and vocalists cultured and dowered with all the gifts which make the glory of the art they love … if, in too many cases, we have to allow the Saxon to make our boots, he shall never make our music.[44]

---

[43] Shaw, 'Going Fantee', *The World*, 19 May 1893, repr. in Laurence, *Shaw's music*, ii, 876–83; here 881.
[44] From an article entitled 'The Irish feis', published in *The Nation*, 20 June 1896, and cited in Dibble,

In the event, Stanford's Irish Symphony would nevertheless serve as a model for Irish art music, notably inspiring a composition prize which others secured by emulating precisely that wholesale 'lifting' of folk tunes into the symphonic structure which Shaw had repudiated.[45] But the passage cited above apostrophizes Douglas Hyde's concept of 'De-Anglicisation' (in essence, the 'Irish Ireland' project) just as its celebration of melody affirms Hyde's reading of the 'unsequacious' Irish imagination, propped up, as it were, by the unchanging mnemonics of a folk tune.

By the end of the nineteenth century, Stanford was out, but the cultural nationalism which his own collections of Irish melodies had helped to foster was in, as never before. In this climate, Irish opera seemed a more remote prospect than ever.

PORTALS OF IRISHNESS

More than a century after Stanford and *Shamus*, it would be easy to suggest that opera was to remain (for the most part) remote from the Irish cultural matrix.[46] The historical record is there to support this reading, as Klein has so recently and conclusively demonstrated. If I am persuaded to argue otherwise, it is only because opera in Ireland found its terminus in fiction and drama (as in Joyce and Shaw), where the innately adulterated condition of the genre itself found expression in work which explicitly represents an alternative to musical composition. To show how this happens is clearly work for another day, but in the meantime it is useful to conclude by referring again to the difference between the empirical poverty of Irish opera and the richer afterlife which cultural history can provide. This is not to deny the sovereign importance of seeing things as they are, but simply to suggest that constructs of the 'musical past' and the 'operatic past' may not be confined to the domain of actual composition. Joyce's fiction and Shaw's plays can fairly be construed as literature which is radically informed by the paradigms of art music in general and opera in particular, if only because both writers were so explicit about their intentions in this regard. Joyce's remembrance of things musically past in *Dubliners* and *Ulysses*, and Shaw's reliance on *Don Giovanni* in *Man and Superman* exemplify the creation of literary texts in which music is formative rather than incidental or metaphorical. Within the folds of

---

Stanford, p. 284.   **45** For details of the competition and the choice of Stanford's *Irish* Symphony as a model, see Dibble, *Stanford*, pp 343–5.   **46** Norman Lebrecht begins his controversial account of Covent Garden by remarking that 'In the middle of most great cities there stands an opera house: part monument, part amenity.', Norman Lebrecht, *Covent Garden: the untold story: despatches from the English culture war, 1945–2000* (London: Simon & Schuster, 2000), p. 1. Most great cities, but not all, and not Dublin. Even if we were to limit our comprehension of opera in Dublin to the performance of works written and first given elsewhere, the nineteenth century would show itself to be incomparably more hospitable to the genre than the twentieth. This is an observation which gains ground particularly at mid-century and the disappearance of visiting companies from the Dublin operatic scene after 1945.

these texts, opera enjoys a structural and expressive significance which it otherwise would not attain in an Irish context. In turn, such texts allow us to reconstruct an operatic past which the historical record of composition does not as easily disclose. 'Listening to the past' in a verbally dominated culture may not mean listening to a handful of works which prove the general rule of silence or indifference. The operatic and the dramatic are often closely allied in modern Irish literature, even if this alliance is evidently in favour of the spoken theatre.[47]

Vincent Cheng's remark some years ago that a more plural conception of Irish cultural history has meant that the 'portals of Irishness' are beginning to open up is one that might profitably be applied to studies of music in Ireland and especially to the reception of music in Ireland, whether that music is 'Irish' or not.[48] In this respect, the challenge with regard to opera is to follow the trace of music as it disappears from view and then re-emerges as something other than itself. Stanislaus Joyce provides an exemplary indication of how this challenge might be met in his critical speculations about the reception of 'The Dead':

> The comedy of the supper table is excellent and so is the end. I wonder will any scruffy old professor recognize Jim's ability to write general noise on paper, a kind of comic chorus, and to balance it against solo and silence.[49]

In that unmistakably operatic reading of his brother's fiction, Stanislaus Joyce points towards the missing history of Irish opera. We might profitably follow his lead.

---

[47] The prominence of music as a formative (and thematic) model in the work of Irish dramatists (including Shaw, Synge, O'Casey, Friel and Murphy) centres upon operatic prototypes to the extent that a substantial body of work for the theatre can legitimately be construed as a substitute for opera. [48] Vincent J. Cheng, 'Authenticity and identity: catching the Irish spirit', in *Semicolonial Joyce*, eds Derek Attridge and Marjorie Howes (Cambridge: Cambridge University Press, 2000), pp 240–61; here p. 259. [49] From Stanislaus Joyce's *Triestine Book of Days* (1907), cited in John McCourt, *The years of Bloom: James Joyce in Trieste 1904–1920* (Dublin: Lilliput Press, 2000), p. 127.

From national sentiment to nationalist movement, 1850–1900

ITA BEAUSANG

A nation is the same people living in the same place ... Or also living in different places.[1]

THE DUBLIN MUSICAL LANDSCAPE

The musicians who peopled Irish musical life during the second half of the nineteenth century certainly lived in the same place. However, as decreed by professional, religious and class distinctions they also lived in different places, sometimes overlapping but more often sealed into separate domains. As Ireland recovered from the effects of the devastating famine which had reduced the population by half, musical life continued as usual in Dublin in the churches, theatres and concert halls. The dominant musical figures such as John Smith, professor of music at Trinity College Dublin, his successor Robert Prescott Stewart, and the numerous members of the Robinson family, belonged to the Protestant ascendancy. The founders and professors of the Irish Academy of Music were connected to the Protestant cathedrals, and were active as members and conductors of the principal musical societies.

With the growth of the Catholic middle class a new constituency was beginning to emerge, exemplified by John William Glover,[2] organist of St Mary's Cathedral, Marlborough St, Dublin, who was professor of vocal music to the Normal Training College of the National Board of Education. In 1851 Glover founded the Royal Choral Institute, aimed at training choristers from the working classes to perform works which were 'at present exclusively confined to the private musical societies'.[3] He launched the Institute with a performance of *Messiah* by 150 performers, and announced an ambitious series of oratorios for which the choristers would be exempt for the first time from subscription fees.[4]

'LAND OF SONG' SAID THE WARRIOR BARD

However, the death of Thomas Moore on 25 February 1852 turned Glover in a new direction. Less than a month later he was music director for a 'Grand

---

1 James Joyce, *Ulysses* (Paris: Shakespeare & Company, 1922), p. 317. 2 John William Glover (1815–99), composer, organist, teacher. 3 *FJ*, 1 November 1851. 4 Ibid. The Institute, which lasted until 1855, gave performances of *Messiah, Samson, The Creation, Alexander's Feast, Elijah, Judas*

National Commemoration of our Gifted Countryman, Thomas Moore Esq.', held on two consecutive nights in the Antient Concert Rooms, at which 'The Irish Melodies will conclude each evening and will comprise the most esteemed of those imperishable lyrics'.[5] The performers were drawn from different sides of the social spectrum: David Richard Bell Esq. recited Milton's monody on the death of Lycidas, and Moore's 'Melologue on National Music'; the soloists included Gustavus Geary and Richard Smith (son of John Smith), stipendiaries at Christ Church cathedral; while the 'Powerful Chorus' came from the Royal Choral Institute.[6]

The Moore bandwagon had taken off. Writing from London, Lady Morgan was the first to propose a monument to Moore in St Patrick's Cathedral where he would be close to Swift.[7] A meeting of the friends and admirers of Moore was called 'for the purpose of providing a Public Testimonial in his native city to the National Poet of Ireland'.[8] With the earl of Charlemont as President the General Committee was named, consisting of fifty-eight members from the highest echelons of Irish society.[9] Two further meetings were held in quick succession and lists of subscriptions from all over the country were published.[10]

Meanwhile public support continued for two 'Grand National Concerts' organized by Glover, for which an advertisement stated 'The musical selections will consist altogether of the most esteemed compositions of our late illustrious countrymen'. In fact according to the review of the first concert:

> The programme comprised selections from the choicest melodies of the bard of Ireland together with some *morceaux* of choral music from the compositions of the great masters. Both theatres were fairly crowded on last evening, other places of amusement of considerable attraction were open, and we believe well-attended, and still our city afforded to the national concerts a numerous and highly respectable attendance of the lovers of Irish and classical music.[11]

Gustavus Geary lost no time in announcing a 'Grand Full-Dress Subscription Concert, to gratify the desire so universally expressed by the citizens of Dublin, since the death of our lamented Bard, for a concert of music exclusively Irish, in which the *Melodies* should form a principal feature.'[12] It was noted in the review that:

Maccabeus, Mozart's *Requiem*, Rossini's *Stabat Mater* and Schumann's *Paradise and the Peri*. **5** Ibid., 22 March 1852. **6** Ibid. **7** Ibid., 23 March 1852. **8** Ibid., 30 March 1852. **9** In addition to members of the aristocracy and officers of the crown the committee included the antiquarians Henry Hudson, George Petrie and William Wilde; the nationalist historian, Madden; the poets, Samuel Ferguson and John Francis Waller; the scientist, Sir William Rowan Hamilton; the physician, William Stokes (biographer of Petrie); and three founding fathers of the Irish Academy of Music, Revd Charles Graves, Walter Sweetman, and William Hudson. **10** Reports of meetings: *FJ*, 30 March and 10, 17 April 1852. **11** Ibid., 8, 10, 13 April. On 12 April (Easter Monday) two productions of Boucicault's play *The Corsican Brothers* were running concurrently in the Theatre Royal and the Queen's Theatre; the Tyrolese Vocalists were in the Music Hall; and the conjurer, Robert Houdin, was presenting *Soirées Fantastiques* and Magic Wonders at the Rotunda. **12** Ibid., 8 April 1852.

the most interesting section of the evening was the selection from Horncastle's collection of Irish songs. Mr Geary with some trouble succeeded in obtaining possession of the poetry and music of some half-forgotten Irish melodies – not to be found in Moore's collection – but all breathing the very soul of native harmony, and racy of the wild and plaintive sweetness which vindicates the truth of their Irish origins.[13]

Since their publication Moore's *Irish Melodies* had filtered into the national consciousness through various channels. They were sung in drawing-rooms and at concerts, and interpolated into opera performances. They were played by regimental bands on state occasions, by bands at meetings of Father Theobald Mathew's temperance movement, and at Daniel O'Connell's 'monster meetings' at historic sites. The dichotomy between Moore's life, spent mostly in England as a pet of the aristocracy, and his role as Ireland's national bard did not reduce the popularity of 'one whose songs have thrilled in melody through every Irish heart, quickening the pulse and flushing the cheek of "patriot, soldier, and lover" and inspiring all with a deeper love of Ireland'.[14]

Glover's promotion of Moore continued in 1853 with a series of three 'Grand Irish National Concerts' in the Royal Irish Institution, 5 College Street, where Glover held vocal and pianoforte classes. An unusually political note was sounded in a review of the first concert:

> The busts of Moore, Grattan and Curran, which adorned the walls of the room, carried the minds of the audience back to the time when the aspiring genius of the poet sung the wrongs and sorrows of his country, and when his two brilliant contemporaries proclaimed in burning eloquence the injustice done to Ireland.[15]

The concert began with 'Let Erin remember the days of old', arranged for vocal quartet, which was performed

> with much spirit and with all the animation which this fine martial lyric so richly merits ... A novel instrument, of great capability and compass, was introduced for the first time in this country on the occasion; it is called the euphonium, and produced a very harmonious effect, under the skilful management and brilliant instrumentation of Professor Glover, in several pieces from Bunting's collection of Irish melodies. The splendid violin performance of Mr Levey in selections from Irish music constituted a very pleasing feature of the evening's entertainment.[16]

On 28 May Glover conducted the first concert in honour of Moore's birthnight, which was to become an annual event in the Dublin musical calendar.[17]

[13] Ibid., 23 April 1852. [14] Ibid., 23 March 1852. [15] Ibid., 18 May 1853. [16] Ibid. Richard Michael Levey [O'Shaughnessy] (1811–99), professor of violin at the Academy of Music, leader of Theatre Royal orchestra, published *The dance music of Ireland*, 2 parts (London: 1858, 1873). [17] Ibid., 20, 30 May

Later in the year Queen Victoria and Prince Albert came to Dublin to attend the Great Industrial Exhibition, held at Leinster Lawn, under the auspices of the Royal Dublin Society. Moore's popularity in royal circles was confirmed by the report that Prince Albert asked for a copy of 'Though the last glimpse of Erin', which was sung at a concert in the vice-regal lodge.[18]

By 1855 the appetite for undiluted Moore at concerts had begun to pall. According to an account of the annual Moore birthnight concert it

> confirmed us more than ever in our opinion that the lyrics of Moore are unsuited to form an entire programme for a musical entertainment ... Besides Moore, with all his genius, was not a musician. He had a finely attuned ear for melody, but harmony or grand choral effects he knew little or nothing of, and hence were all his adaptations intended for the drawing room, and to take them into the Concert hall, save in detached pieces, is putting them out of their place, and calculated to destroy those refined impressions they are certain to make in the quiet of home.[19]

The inauguration of the Moore statue in College Street on 14 October 1857 brought a renewed outpouring of public homage for the national bard.[20] When the speeches by the various dignitaries were over 'the vast concourse of people ... remained for a time listening to the performance by the military band of selections from the *Irish Melodies*'. Gustavus Geary had arranged a Moore Commemoration concert for the same evening, but as it clashed with an important operatic event – the first performance in Dublin of *La Traviata*, with Marietta Piccolomini[21] as Violetta – the concert was postponed until the following evening. Perhaps in deference to public demand in a year when there were no less than five Italian opera seasons in Dublin, only the first half was devoted to Moore, the second half consisted of selections from popular operas:

> The idea of a musical celebration on an occasion when the country was engaged in paying an enduring tribute to the fame of the greatest of lyric poets, was a happy one, and its appropriateness was the more striking when the programme for the evening showed that the chief portion of the entertainment would consist of a judicious selection of some of the most beautiful and popular of the poet's glorious lyrics ... The most lasting, and at the same time the highest, tribute to poetic genius is to make his songs familiar as household words to the people for whom they are written, and let them oft be sung not merely in the homes of the rich and poor alike, but also in the halls dedicated to musical enjoyment.[22]

1853. **18** Ibid., 1 September 1853. **19** Ibid., 29 May 1855. **20** It was described as 'a grotesque effigy' in Walter Strickland's *Dictionary of Irish artists* (Dublin and London: 1913), ii, 122. It was commissioned from Christopher Moore (1790–1863), following a competition in which John Hogan, the leading Irish sculptor, was an unsuccessful entrant. **21** Italian soprano (1836–99). Piccolomini had made her debut in 1856 at Her Majesty's Theatre, London, in the first performance there of *La Traviata*. **22** *FJ*, 19 October

As Moore's statue became a Dublin landmark,[23] the term 'national music' became synonymous with the *Irish Melodies* which continued to be performed both in public and in private. There was no sign of a public backlash against Moore's plundering of Bunting's collections. When copyright on the early numbers expired, new editions by Glover and Joseph Robinson were published in Dublin to meet the demand.

CATHOLIC CHURCH ORGANISTS

The growth of the Catholic middle class is evident in the increased number of concerts of national music involving organists of Catholic churches in Dublin city and suburbs, for which the Round Room of the Rotunda was the most popular venue. In 1869 Andrew Keane, organist, St Laurence O'Toole, Seville Place, and James Fanning, organist, Mount Argus, took part in a 'Grand Concert of Irish Music' for which the tickets were advertised for sale at the offices of the nationalist newspapers, *The Nation* and *Irishman*. However, the programme of music by Moore, Balfe, Benedict and Wallace did not appear to have any political connotations.[24] In 1870 the annual concert for Moore's birthnight was conducted by John Glynn, organist, St Saviour's, Dominick Street, who had enlisted a varied cast of performers, including a solo concertina and the band of the 43rd Light Infantry. In addition to the usual Moore's *Melodies* the programme included favourite music by Benedict, Balfe, Wallace, Glover, Samuel Lover and Weber.[25]

'GOD SAVE IRELAND' SAID THE HERO

The first overt use of patriotic music on a concert platform occurred at a 'Grand National Concert' on St Patrick's Day 1871, when the Skinners' Band from the Dublin Liberties played the French national anthem, 'The Marseillaise', and the Fenian anthem, 'God Save Ireland', as a finale to a programme of operatic and national music conducted by Fanning.[26] The Franco-Prussian War had been keenly followed in Ireland where there was considerable sympathy for the French after the fall of Paris on 28 January. The words of 'God Save Ireland', had been written by T.D. Sullivan a few days after the execution of the Manchester Martyrs

---

1857. Part 1: 'Give me the harp of epic song', 'The meeting of the waters', 'The harp that once', Fantasia on Irish airs (Glover), 'Let Erin remember'. **23** Joyce refers to it as 'the droll statue of the national poet of Ireland'. James Joyce, *A portrait of the artist as a young man* (London: Penguin Classics, 1992), p. 194. It was on Leonard Bloom's itinerary: 'He crossed under Tommy Moore's roguish fingers. They did right to put him over a urinal: meeting of the waters.', Joyce, *Ulysses*, p. 155. **24** *FJ*, 6 February 1869. Balfe: 'Lo the early beam of morning', 'The shamrock', 'St Senanus and the lady'; Selections from *The Lily of Killarney*; Wallace: 'Let me like a soldier fall'; Moore: 'Dear harp of my country', 'When he who adores thee', 'O breathe not his name', 'The Coolin', 'I saw from the beach', 'The minstrel boy'. **25** Ibid., 28 May 1870. **26** Ibid., 17 March 1871.

in 1867.[27] Sung to the air of a popular marching song of the Confederate Army, the ballad subsequently became the unofficial national anthem of successive political movements.

In contrast, the music chosen for the O'Connell Centenary in 1875 did not reflect any blatant political connections. Joseph Robinson conducted two concerts in the Exhibition Palace: *Elijah* in the afternoon, and a concert of music by Irish composers in the evening, which was poorly attended because it clashed with the banquet at the Mansion House. On the following evening 3,000 people attended a Grand Popular Concert for which the Leinster Hall was opened to hold the overflow from the Concert Hall. Glover conducted 500 instrumentalists and singers in a performance of his oratorio, *St Patrick at Tara*, extracts from the O'Connell Centenary cantata, *Tara*, and Irish melodies, including 'The harp that once' translated into Irish by Cardinal McHale.[28]

The release from prison in England of Michael Davitt and other Fenian prisoners in January 1878 marked a watershed in the use of national music as a political tool. In 1878 a 'Grand Irish Ballad Concert', conducted by Peter Goodman, organist, St Peter's, Phibsborough, was held in the Rotunda under the management of the Incorporated Brick and Stonelayers of Dublin, in aid of the Released Political Prisoners' Fund. The Brass Band of Trade played a selection of Irish music, including the signature tune of the Young Ireland movement, 'A nation once again'.[29] Later in the year Davitt and Chambers gave accounts of prison life at a meeting of the Fund in Belfast, while the Belfast Band 'discoursed music appropriate to the occasion'.[30]

The celebration of the Moore Centenary in May 1879 was preceded by a three-day Irish Harp Revival Festival in the Rotunda. The performers included a Swedish harpist, Adolf Sjoden, as well as a choir of pedal harps, a trio of ancient Irish wire-strung harps, a Welsh harper, 'one of the last surviving of the Celebrated Blind Irish harpers' and celebrated Irish pipers.[31] Ten years earlier Glover's daughters, Emilie and Madeline, had organized a series of vocal and harp concerts 'in an effort to bring our national instrument prominently forward hereafter, so that it may no longer be said that "The harp is silent in its native clime"'.[32] There were some reservations about the present revival: 'If it should seem strange that a foreigner is an organizer of the scheme it is comfortable to find that the best names in our country have rallied round him to lend their gifts to his work.'[33] These included Glover, Robert Prescott Stewart, R.M. Levey and three other professors from the Royal Irish Academy of Music, Wilhelm Elsner, Carl Lauer and Luigi Carracciolo.

---

27 Timothy Daniel Sullivan (1827–1914), editor of *The Nation,* lord mayor of Dublin 1886–7. He gave lectures on 'The Songs of Ireland' in Kingstown in 1884 and in Dublin in 1887; see *FJ*, 2 February 1884 and 6 June 1887.   **28** Ibid., 6, 7, 9 August 1875.   **29** Ibid., 11, 12 March 1878.   **30** Ibid., 25 May 1878.   **31** Ibid., 5 May 1879.   **32** Ibid., 6 December 1869.   **33** Ibid., 5 May 1879: 'The Irish Music will be comparatively illustrated by Scottish, Welsh, English, Norwegian, Danish, Swedish and other National Airs'. The first half of the programme included music by Mozart, Oberthür, Knight, and Gounod's *Meditation on Seb. Bach's Prelude* (sic) which was played on the violin, harmonium and harp by Levey,

On the actual day of the centenary a 'Great Musical Festival and Literary Celebration' was held, at which Moore's *Melodies* reigned supreme. Subscription tickets ranged from half a guinea to half a crown for the afternoon concert, conducted by Joseph Robinson, which was attended by the largest crowd ever seen in the Exhibition Palace. The programme which opened with 'When through life unblest we rove', sung by a chorus of 200 voices, also included an oration by Lord O'Hagan and a *Centenary Ode* by Denis Florence McCarthy, read by Chancellor Tisdall of Christ Church.[34] In the evening a chorus of 250 voices, and a band of harps including Sjoden, took part in a Grand Popular Concert, conducted by Glover, with ticket prices from one to three shillings. A choral fantasia, *One hundred years ago*, specially composed for the occasion by Glover, was performed, and afterwards a 'Grand Promenade Concert of Irish Music' by combined bands, numbering 100 performers, rounded off the celebrations.[35]

The imprisonment of Davitt in Portland Jail and Parnell in Kilmainham Jail gave renewed impetus to the organizers of concerts in aid of political prisoners. In January 1882 a fund-raising 'Grand National Concert' was held in the Rotunda under the auspices of the St James' Branch of the Ladies Land League and the Political Prisoners' Aid Society. It was conducted by John Glynn, and consisted mostly of popular vocal music by Balfe, Wallace and Moore.[36] Glynn's concert on St Patrick's Day was noticeably more political, with the inclusion of 'My land' and 'Those penal days' by Davis, and recitations by John Kells Ingram and Charles Gavan Duffy, founders of the Young Ireland movement.[37]

Eighteen eighty-two was also the year of the unveiling of the O'Connell Monument and of the Exhibition of Irish Arts and Manufactures in the Rotunda. Joseph Robinson, veteran of the 1853 exhibition, was in charge of the music for the opening ceremony of the Exhibition. It was reported that the historic Round Room had undergone a transformation 'the full extent of which can scarcely be recognised; the magnificent ceiling chandeliers and wall decorations on which time has wrought sad havoc have been renovated completely'. The first part of the concert consisted of choral music by Handel, Mendelssohn and Haydn. The second half started with a march that Robinson had written especially for the occasion based on 'Silent O Moyle', followed by favourite Moore's *Melodies*. The closing item, the overture to *William Tell*, was described in the preview as 'one of the finest Rossini has written, and having regard to the subject of the opera an extremely appropriate *morceau* on an occasion when Irish nationality will in two forms be notably celebrated'.[38]

The links between music and politics came strongly to the fore in 1883 at a concert held in the Rotunda on the evening after the Parnell banquet, during

---

Stewart and Sjoden. **34** Thomas O'Hagan (1812–85), first Catholic to hold the office of lord chancellor. The Revd Chancellor Charles Edward Tisdall DD also recited at Moore's birthnight concert in 1880; see *FJ*, 28 May 1880. **35** Ibid., 28, 29 May 1879. **36** Ibid., 9 January 1882. **37** Ibid., 17 March 1882. **38** Ibid., 14 August 1882. Part I: Selections from *The Hymn of Praise*, *The Creation*, the 'Hallelujah' Chorus. Part II: March, Robinson, 'Kathleen mavourneen', 'O where's the slave', 'The harp that once', 'Avenging and bright', 'Let Erin remember', Overture *William Tell*; see *FJ*, 16 August 1882.

which Parnell had been presented with a National Tribute of £37,000. The concert, under the auspices of the Parnell committee, was organized by John O'Donnell, a prominent band musician. The patrons included the lord mayor and deputy mayor of Dublin, the Catholic archbishop of Cashel, Dr Croke, and civic dignatories from Cork, Clonmel, Waterford and Nenagh. The flags, patriotic banners and decorations from the banquet remained for the concert, and it was reported that it was confidently expected that the majority of the Irish Parliamentary Party, including Parnell himself, would attend.

The programme opened with 'A nation once again' and included two other ballads by Davis, 'The Volunteers of 1782', and 'Annie dear'. John O'Donnell played his composition, 'Irish-American Polka', on the cornet, introducing the airs 'Hail Columbia' and 'O'Donnell Abu'. Other notable items were 'The wearing of the green', one of the popular songs from the '98 rebellion, and 'The Irishman,' composed specially for the concert by Joseph Robinson. Moore's *Irish Melodies* were given a new significance; 'The harp that once' was sung in Irish, and 'Let Erin remember', performed by the entire concert party, provided the rousing finale.[39]

The connection between Irish music and the Irish language movement was formalized in a series of concerts held in the Rotunda by the Gaelic Union, a precursor of the Gaelic League.[40] In 1884 a complimentary benefit was held there for John O'Donnell, 'for his recent spirited effort by means of Irish concerts to popularise our native language and music'. The concert, which was under the patronage of the lord mayor, William Meagher MP, was conducted by Brendan Rogers, a musician who was also an Irish language scholar.[41] In the interval between the first and second half of the programme short addresses on the Irish language and Irish music were delivered by the Revd Dr Samuel Haughton FTCD, and Thomas Sexton MP.[42] The two speakers came from very different backgrounds: Thomas Sexton MP for Sligo, had been in prison in Kilmainham Jail with Parnell and was active in the Land League; Samuel Haughton MD, professor of geology at Trinity College, Dublin, was the father of biomechanics in Ireland and a strong critic of Darwin's theories. However, both were united in extolling the value of Irish music and the language.

The distinguished audience represented various sectors of Irish society, including Michael Cusack, who later in the year would be one of the founders of the Gaelic Athletic Association (GAA), the Revd Maxwell H. Close MRIA, Vice-President of the Gaelic Union, two MPs, and the chief magistrate. On the following day a newspaper review reported the speeches in full. The music included John O'Donnell's cornet solo, 'O'Donnell Abu' and 'Eileen aroon', sung in Irish with harp accompaniment.[43]

---

39 Ibid., 11 December 1883. **40** The Gaelic Union was founded in 1878 by Douglas Hyde and others, following the break with the Society for the Preservation of the Irish Language. It was superseded in 1893 by the Gaelic League. **41** Brendan Rogers (1849–1932), composer, lecturer, organist. **42** *FJ*, 2 February 1884. **43** Ibid.

The Gaelic Union's next venture was 'a Grand Literary and Musical Entertainment to be held in the interests of the Irish language'.[44] The concert was a mixture of popular music by Lover, Wallace and Moore, with recitations by the Revd Chancellor Tisdall. His delivery of Denis Florence McCarthy's poem, 'The Centenary of Moore', originally performed by him at the Moore Centenary in 1879, 'The Death of Marmion' by Scott and some humorous recitations were the main attractions of the evening.[45] The only concession to the Irish language was the song 'Eibhlin a rún'.

In 1885 the newly-founded GAA held a concert to celebrate the anniversary of another national poet, Robert Burns. The Revd Maxwell Close took the chair for a programme of Scottish music and Highland dancing, and Michael Cusack of the GAA gave a short address, in which he drew a comparison between the superstitions revealed in Burns' 'Hallowe'en' and Bryan Merriman's 'Midnight Court':

> They were contemporaneous, and it was hardly possible that there could have been any communication between them, yet the Gaelic inspiration revealed its workings in both poems in exactly identical forms.[46]

The names of Archbishop Croke and Parnell appear together as patrons of the first annual St Patrick's Day concert held in 1885 by the Dublin district of the Irish National Foresters, a Friendly Society with nationalist leanings founded in 1877, which had branches all over the country. The concert was organized by John O'Donnell, and the programme included the mandatory 'The wearing of the green' and an Irish-American March composed by O'Donnell, dedicated by permission to Parnell.[47] In 1886 T.D. Sullivan attended the concert in the Rotunda:

> The platform was tastefully arranged with the banners of the Irish National Foresters and on it were also displayed portraits of Parnell and Davitt. Around the balcony were hung green bannerettes and national mottos such as 'God Save Ireland', 'The Land for the People', 'Ireland a Nation' and 'Peace and Plenty'. The first part of the programme concluded with the singing in solo and chorus of the National Anthem, 'God Save Ireland'. The solo part was entrusted to Mr B. Leslie, but he discharged his task rather indifferently and spoiled the effectiveness of the anthem which the audience was not slow to demonstrate ... The proceedings closed with the singing of the National Anthem by the audience.[48]

Michael Davitt's name was added as patron for the 1887 concert.[49] He had just returned to Ireland with his American bride, Mary Yore, from Oakland, California.

---

[44] Ibid., 18 April 1884. [45] Tisdall reappeared in 1888 when he and Maud Gonne performed readings at a 'Grand Concert of Irish Music' in aid of the Dublin City Hospital. *FJ*, 5 November 1888. [46] Ibid., 28 January 1885. [47] Ibid., 17, 18 March 1885. [48] Ibid., 18 March 1886. [49] Ibid., 16 March 1887.

The patrons for the fifth concert in 1889 were named as Archbishop Croke, Davitt, Parnell and William O'Brien MP.[50] By the end of the year Parnell had been cited as co-respondent in the O'Shea divorce case, which ended his association with concerts of national music. Soon after her arrival in Ireland the name of Mrs Michael Davitt appeared in large capital letters in an advertisement for a charity concert in the Rotunda, under the patronage of Dr Edward Walsh, archbishop of Dublin, in aid of the church and schools, North William Street. The concert attracted huge public interest:

> Before the doors of the Round Room were opened a throng of vast dimensions had gathered outside the building. Further out long lines of carriages took up positions, the occupants patiently waiting for ingress. At length the doors opened and the rush of people came with such overwhelming force that the stewards were powerless, and before anyone well knew what had happened every seat was occupied, while the passages were filled to overflowing. The doors were then closed in the face of fully as large a number of persons as were inside the hall; but in spite of all efforts to provide accommodation several hundred people who had tickets were unable to gain admission.

After a summary description of the first items on the programme the reviewer continued:

> The appearance of Mrs Davitt was the signal for an outburst of the most unbounded enthusiasm, the greeting being one of the heartiest and most fervent it is possible to imagine. After the cheering had ceased Dr Cruise began the accompaniment to Gounod's very trying song, 'Ave Maria', amid a stillness that betokened the rapt attention of the audience. Mrs Davitt has a pure soprano voice of great clearness and considerable power.[51]

As an encore she sang 'O'Donnell Abu' and later in the programme 'The wearing of the green.' Her final encore was 'The star-spangled banner'. Despite her success on this occasion there is no further trace of Mrs Davitt singing in public.

Following the competition for amateur bands which was held at the Irish Artisans' Exhibition in 1885 John O'Donnell suggested that an annual band contest should take place under the auspices of the Irish National League. In 1887 seven bands took part in the contest which was staged over six nights in the Leinster Hall. It was announced that William O'Brien MP would present the United Ireland Challenge Cup, and that the finale would consist of a performance of 'God Save Ireland' by fourteen massed bands, directed by R.M. Levey.[52]

The baritone, William Ludwig,[53] was the first Irish singer to exploit the potential of America for concert tours of Irish music. America had provided a

---

[50] Ibid., 16 March 1889. [51] Ibid., 10, 11 May 1887. [52] Ibid., 26 September 1887. See Timothy Dawson, 'The City Music and City Bands', *Dublin Historical Record*, 25:102 (June, 1972). [53] William

home since the Great Famine for thousands of Irish exiles, who had welcomed and given financial support to Parnell, Mitchell and many other political leaders.[54] Ludwig had toured there extensively with the American Opera Company since 1886:

> Mr Ludwig has undertaken an enterprise of national importance by the production of Irish national songs and music in America. This is being done for the first time and undoubtedly his courage and enterprise merit the amplest encouragement. Everything that brings Ireland her cause her music and her history before the millions of the 'Ireland across the ocean' must help to deepen and intensify the feeling for the Old Land at home.[55]

In 1888 Davitt and John Dillon attended Ludwig's 'Grand Popular Concert of Irish National Music' at the Leinster Hall, in advance of his American tour. The highly-charged programme of rebel songs traced the course of nationalist history: 'The memory of the dead', 'The boys of Wexford', 'The death of Owen Roe O'Neill', 'The Irish rapparee' and 'The wearing of the green'.[56] Ludwig returned to the Leinster Hall in 1890 for two concerts of 'Irish National Music'. The programme opened with 'Lament for Patrick Sarsfield', and included 'selections from the old bards down to Villiers Stanford and Sir Robert Prescott Stewart'.[57]

A NATION ONCE AGAIN

In the last decade of the nineteenth century the groundswell of cultural nationalism led poets, musicians and politicians to become involved in the activities of the National Literary Society (1892) and the Gaelic League (1893). This in turn led to the foundation of the Feis Ceoil and the Oireachtas, which were both held for the first time during the same week in May 1897:

> The project of the Feis was conceived over two years ago by some members of the National Literary Society, and in this connection it is worth recalling that the Gaelic League and the Oireachtas had their origins in this excellent society. At the beginning it was merely to be a festival of old Irish music and its purpose was to be confined solely to educate the public ear to the beauty and value of the old Irish airs.[58]

Ludwig [Ledwidge] (1847–1923), baritone, succeeded Charles Santley in 1877 as chief baritone of the Carl Rosa Opera Company, excelled in Wagnerian roles, and sang at the O'Connell Commemoration concerts in 1882.   **54** The Irish National League of America was founded in 1883 by Parnell, Davitt, and John Dillon.   **55** *FJ*, 20 October 1888.   **56** Ibid., 22 October 1888.   **57** Ibid., 17 February 1890.   **58** Ibid., 18 May 1897.

As the names of Glover, Robinson and Stewart faded others entered the musical spectrum. Annie Patterson,[59] Signor Michele Esposito,[60] and Vincent O'Brien,[61] three very different personalities, would exert considerable influence on Irish musical life in the future. Patterson, a pupil of Stewart, was the first music graduate of the new Royal University and a passionate advocate of Irish music. She was a member of the National Literary Society and the Gaelic League, and a founder member of the Feis Ceoil and the Oireachtas. In 1897 she and the folk music collector, Patrick Weston Joyce, acted as advisors on Irish music for both events.

At the opening ceremony of the Oireachtas in the Rotunda in 1897 Douglas Hyde recited an ode in Irish, and Annie Patterson conducted a performance of a prize Rallying Song that she had set to music. Harpers and Irish pipers played for an audience that included George Sigerson,[62] and Eoin MacNeill.[63] In 1899 the adjudicators included Annie Patterson and Vincent O'Brien, Douglas Hyde was master of ceremonies and the conductor [steward] of the competitions was Patrick H. Pearse.[64]

Encouragement for the Irish language extended to the Feis Ceoil when the Society for the Preservation of the Irish Language presented a prize for the best singing of a song in Irish.[65] In 1899 it was reported that the entries for singing in Irish at the Feis Ceoil had risen to a total of 29 (17 solo, 12 choirs):

> One outcome of the competitions will be that singing in Irish will be more frequent on the platform than it has been hitherto. If this prove so and if capable singers at public performances showed the melodic and singable quality of the language, the Feis Ceoil will have given the Gaelic movement perhaps the most important stimulus it has yet received in the way of popularizing it amongst the Irish-speaking public.[66]

A special newspaper article, 'Appreciation and criticism', published after the first Feis Ceoil called for a more national flavour in the compositions, 'without prejudice' to Esposito's work.[67] There were no entries for ancient Irish harp, which prompted the Gaelic League to intervene:

> Recently the Gaelic League in Dublin got a consignment of Irish harps which were purchased by members, but of course it is too early to look for any successful results yet, though it leaves us not without hope that the Feis may witness the playing of a band of Irish harpers on the Irish harp.[68]

---

59 Annie Patterson (1868–1934), composer, conductor, lecturer, journalist, organist. **60** Michele Esposito (1855–1929), pianist, teacher, composer, came to Dublin as professor of pianoforte at the RIAM in 1882. **61** Vincent O'Brien (1871–1948), choir master, conductor, singing teacher, organist Rathmines, Dominick Street, Clarendon Street churches; director Palestrina Choir at St Mary's Pro-Cathedral 1903–48. **62** George Sigerson (1836–1925), physician, scholar, professor of zoology and biology, catholic university; founder member Feis Ceoil. **63** *Evening Telegraph* [hereafter *ET*], 14 April 1897; 10, 17, 18 May 1897. **64** Ibid., 8 June 1899. Pearse, the future revolutionary leader of 1916, was then aged nineteen and teaching Irish in Dublin schools. **65** Ibid., 5 March 1897. **66** Ibid., 18 May 1899. **67** Ibid., 5 March, 29 May 1897. The adjudicator was Ebenezer Prout. The winning compositions were Esposito's cantata *Deirdre*, and *Greenoge*, an orchestral overture by James C. Culwick, composer, teacher at the RIAM, conductor St Ann's Choral Union, Orpheus Choral Society. **68** Ibid., 5 May 1898.

In 1899 a leading article on the Feis Ceoil reflected the aims of the Feis:

> All that is best in musical, literary and national life has rallied to the Feis Ceoil. Its promoters have demonstrated that the ancient musical art of Ireland was of a high order, that those who sneered at it were merely steeped in modern vulgarities themselves; and the conception of a modern Irish musical school is not, as some musicians told us, a sort of heresy; or as others said, an idea doomed to failure for want of capacity; but that both are realities which bid fair to give Ireland a great and distinctive place of her own, such as she once held as a home for creative art. Every entertainment will be Irish of the Irish, and all will show the versatility and diversity and the great beauty of Irish work in music and poetry, both archaic and modern.[69]

The National Literary Society continued to promote Irish music as an essential part of the Gaelic revival. In January 1899 the President, Sigerson, and Council of the Society gave an 'At Home' at the Leinster Hall, Molesworth Street:

> It was a social function of considerable interest for it was highly indicative of the better spirit which is now pervading the times, a spirit of wider sympathy and loftier aims, a desire among all classes and creeds to combine and commune together for the furtherance of those objects and ideals which can alone make a nation great and respected. There was a very large and fashionable gathering, music, art and literature being brilliantly and numerously represented.[70]

Many of the songs were in Irish and included arrangements by Culwick, Esposito and Patterson. During one of the intervals W.B. Yeats 'made a brief but highly interesting statement' with reference to the Irish Literary Theatre, which included the following remarks:

> And now let me add a word on the sense in which I see the word 'national'. There is undoubtedly a most interesting awakening of national life in Ireland (applause). It consists of a drawing together of men of all creeds and parties in the service of the idea of Ireland. This gathering, the most exceptional ever held by the National Literary Society, is evidence of it. But this movement needs not merely enthusiasm but definite intellectual ideas, universal ideas, and perhaps the creation or introduction of new forms of expression. I noticed recently an article in a Dublin newspaper contending that great art is not national. This I absolutely disbelieve. All imaginative art is national; it may be merely in its expression of the sentiment and thoughts of a certain people or more often in the choice of its actual themes.[71]

Later in 1899 the society assumed the mantle of the Moore Anniversary at its closing *conversazione* of the season, with a lecture on Moore by the President,

69 Ibid., 15 May 1899. **70** *ET*, 11 January 1899. **71** Ibid.

George Sigerson, in which he claimed that 'millions of our race only know Irish history through the songs of Moore'.[72]

The awakening of national life in Ireland was also reflected in the increasing number of patriotic commemorations. John O'Leary, the veteran Fenian leader, presided at the Thomas Davis anniversary concert in 1895 and at the annual Emmet anniversary commemorations in the Rotunda.[73] The celebration of the centenary of the '98 rebellion surpassed all previous events. Preparations began in 1897, bringing a welcome respite to nationalists from Queen Victoria's Jubilee, which was officially celebrated in Dublin during the year. In September John O'Leary presided at a meeting of the '98 Centenary Committee in City Hall, which was attended by delegates from America, England, Scotland and all parts of Ireland.[74] Ludwig, who was touring with the Carl Rosa Opera Company, returned to Dublin for a well-timed series of concerts, conducted by Vincent O'Brien, featuring the songs of the United Irishmen and the ballads of '98. A second series of four concerts was held in January with singers, pipers, harpists and step dancers:

> Last evening in the Round Room, Rotunda, the first of the series of Mr William Ludwig's '98 concerts of Irish music was given to a crowded house. The concert was under the patronage of the Right Hon. The Lord Mayor who attended with a party, and the representative character of the audience was a very noticeable feature. Almost every class, from the professional to the artisan was represented. The programme was most comprehensive embracing as it did songs of humour, love and war, lamentations, songs of the United Irishmen and street ballads ... The entry of Mr Ludwig was the signal for a burst of enthusiasm. The audience cheered and applauded him to the echo.[75]

Ludwig's familiar repertoire of rebel songs charmed the audience. When he sang the 'The rising of the moon', the audience insisted then on 'The wearing of the green' to the same tune. The concert ended with 'The French are on the sea'. As the date of the centenary approached Ludwig gave a further series of six concerts in March, under the patronage of the '98 Centenary Committee.[76]

On 23 May, the anniversary of the rebellion, torchlight processions took place all over the country, accompanied by bands playing martial music. In South Dublin nine bands took part in the commemoration at Rathfarnham.[77] In September an impressive demonstration was organized by the '98 Centenary Committee for the unveiling by the IRB leader, James Stephens, of a memorial tablet at 9 Bridge Street, where Oliver Bond, the United Irishman, was arrested

---

[72] Ibid., 31 May 1899. [73] Ibid., 4 March, 4 November 1895, 5 March 1896. [74] Ibid., 7 September 1897. [75] Ibid., 11 January 1898. 'Lament for Owen Roe O'Neill', 'Molly Bawn', 'The boys of Wexford', 'The memory of the dead', 'Billy Byrne of Ballymanus', 'The croppy boy'. [76] Ibid., 17, 19 September 1897; 10, 11, 12, 15 January 22, 23, 28 March 1898. Additional songs included 'Fineen the rover', 'The green above the red', 'The priests of '98', 'Twenty men from Dublin town', 'Orange and green', and 'Up with the green flag'. [77] Ibid., 23, 24 May 1898.

in 1798. The commemoration also celebrated the anniversaries of patriots Robert Emmet, Bartholomew Teeling, Matthew Tone and John McIntosh. The procession marched with nine bands from Christchurch Place and wreaths were placed en route on graves at St Michan's, Arbour Hill military prison and St Catherine's Church. The music included funeral dirges, 'The Marseillaise', 'Let Erin remember', 'The boys of Wexford' and 'The memory of the dead'.[78] On the morning of the demonstration full instructions were published on the protocol for the occasion:

> It is specially requested that during the playing of funeral dirges, as arranged for by the programme, at the several scenes of patriot martyrdom on the line of route all heads should be covered and remain so while such music is being played by each band heading contingents. The commemoration is of a serious character, and the bands attending should pay strict attention to the programme of marching music arranged for, and no levity should exist during the playing of funeral dirges; punctuality of the assembly is also earnestly desirable.[79]

In October several fife and drum bands played national music at a demonstration in the Rotunda, organized by the Amnesty Association, to welcome back recently released political prisoners.[80] The quasi-military aspect of these events is reflected in an account of a procession to Glasnevin Cemetery on the anniversary of the Manchester Martyrs, which reported that 'the contingents marched quickly to the stirring music of popular national airs'.[81] In 1899 brass bands, and fife and drum bands from Dublin, Bray, Kingstown and Dundalk led the procession from St Stephen's Green to Glasnevin Cemetery for the Wolfe Tone and Manchester Martyrs Commemoration.[82]

Since the eighteenth century the dance tune, 'St Patrick's Day', had been played as an anthem with 'God save the Queen' by regimental bands on ceremonial occasions and in the theatre. It was traditionally played at the annual trooping of the colours on St Patrick's Day in Dublin Castle Yard, in the presence of the lord lieutenant. However, a newspaper report of the ceremony at the Castle in 1899 was subtitled 'A Curious Incident', with the caption '"St Patrick's Day" not played':

> The trooping of the colours has been always associated with the National Festival in Dublin, but as if apparently to further accentuate the disfavour with which the military authorities regard anything connected with the distinct nationality of Ireland, the Irish national anthem which has annually formed part of the musical programme of the occasion was omitted today.[83]

---

78 Ibid., 21, 26 September 1898.   **79** Ibid., 24 September 1898.   **80** Ibid., 20 October 1898.   **81** Ibid., 21 November 1898.   **82** Ibid., 20 November 1899. Fife and Drum Bands: St Kevin's (Dublin), Lord Edward (Kingstown). Brass Bands: St James', Gas Company Employees', Incorporated Brick and Stonelayers' (Dublin), Bray Brass Band, Emmet (Dundalk).   **83** Ibid.

The account also noted that the shamrock was not worn by the soldiers of the 1st battalion of the Argyle and Sutherland Highlanders who performed the trooping of the colours, nor by their commander-in-chief, Lord Roberts of Kandahar.[84]

THE BIRTH OF A NATION

In *National Music of Ireland* (1846) Michael Conran had written:

> Selections from our national music should form part of our own concerts, for we find that whenever an original melody of Erin is heard in such instances, it at once finds its way to the heart, not less effectively than the elegant melodies of other climes.[85]

Since the death of Moore national music had been a constant at many levels in the growth of cultural nationalism. In the oft-quoted words of Davis: 'Music is the first faculty of the Irish and scarcely anything has such power over them.'[86] During the second half of the nineteenth century the power of national music was manifested to varying degrees at Moore birthnight concerts, at Ludwig's concerts, at St Patrick's Day concerts, at meetings of the National Literary Society, at processions to gravesides and political commemorations. The transition from national sentiment to nationalist movement was inexorable, as the echoes reached even Dublin Castle.

In 1900 an account of a concert given by the Central Branch of the Gaelic League in the Rotunda, at which the eighteen-year old James Joyce sang Hyde's 'Is aobhinn dhuit' to the air of 'The croppy boy', viewed national music from another perspective:

> The work that is done by the Central Branch – an organisation whose objects are really literary and not musical, and whose advocacy of Irish music is but a means to an end – in bringing these charming airs before the public is deserving of much praise.[87]

Perhaps it was as a means to an end that national music had forged connections between the same people living in the same place – or also living in different places – to found a nation.

---

84 Ibid., 17 March 1899.   **85** Michael Conran, *The national music of Ireland* (Dublin: Duffy, 1846), p. 283.   **86** Charles Gavan Duffy, *Memoirs of a patriot* (Dublin: Duffy, 1890), p. 109.   **87** *FJ*, 7 December 1900. The concert also featured two singers who were later characterized by Joyce in *Ulysses*: Mr J.C. Doyle, who sang 'An cailín deas' and 'Slán le Máig' and Mr [Blazes] Boylan, who 'gave the "Cruiskeen Laun" in a very pure tenor voice'. Ibid.

Constructs of nationality: the literary and visual politics of Irish music in the nineteenth century

BARRA BOYDELL

The historical study of the music of aural traditions necessarily draws on documentary and iconographical sources to supplement what can be learned from examples of the music appearing in written arrangements or in published collections which become increasingly common during the nineteenth century. It is, however, widely recognized that the transcription into notation of music of an aural tradition, carried out by musicians from a literate and thus distinct musical background, involves translation: the music is necessarily reshaped according to the concepts and parameters of notation systems developed by and for what is effectively a 'foreign', literate musical world, as well as by the person making the transcription.[1] The language and musical culture of the educated Anglo-Irish society who constituted the public for which in 1724 John and William Neal produced the first published collection of Irish traditional music were very different from that of the musical tradition represented in print.[2] Through their arrangements for 'violin, German flute or hautboy' the Neals were translating these tunes of harpers and other musicians into the musical notation of the world of the contemporary art music tradition. The music was inevitably altered and filtered through notation, through the often meaningless transliteration of Irish titles (not to mention the Italianizing of Carolan's name to 'Signor Carrollini') and even through the provision in one case of a bass and variations 'in the Italian manner'.[3] An important historical document though it is for our understanding of traditional music at the time, the Neals' *Collection* ends up telling us as much if not more about the Neals and their public as it does about the practice of Irish traditional music. So too the later collections of Edward Bunting and George Petrie with their tunes adapted for piano, to cite the better-known publications of Irish music of the late-eighteenth to mid-nineteenth centuries, reveal much about the collectors such as Bunting and Petrie, the public for whom they published, and their attitudes towards the country's indigenous musical traditions, but perhaps less than one might wish for about the actual details of the music and its performance.[4]

I gratefully acknowledge the permission by the various owners to reproduce the pictures illustrated in this article. My thanks are also due to Nicholas Carolan and the Irish Traditional Music Archive, to Sotheby's, to the Viscountess Dillon, and to Dr Adrian Scahill.   **1** See for example the case cited below of George Petrie collecting music in the Aran Islands in the mid-nineteenth century (note 43).   **2** The term 'traditional music' is used here in a generic sense to refer to Irish music of the aural tradition, notwithstanding the distinct social and cultural origins of harp music.   **3** John and William Neal, *A collection of the most celebrated Irish tunes proper for the violin, German flute or hautboy* (Dublin: 1724), facs. ed. Nicholas Carolan (Dublin: Folk Music Society of Ireland, 1986).   **4** Edward Bunting, *A general collection of the ancient Irish music* (London: Preston, 1796); *A general collection of the ancient music of*

These reservations concerning transcriptions of aural musical traditions apply equally to literary references to Irish music and dance in novels, diaries and other writings, and to the iconography of musicians and dance. The author describing a musical performance or dance, the artist portraying musicians and dancers, each selects according to their particular literary or visual perspectives and requirements, and those of their readership or public. The identity both of the author or artist and of their public has a major bearing not just on what is represented, but on what meaning lies behind the representation, whether literary or visual. These questions, which have been termed 'visual politics' within the context of iconography,[5] are of particular interest for the nineteenth-century portrayal of Ireland and of Irish music.

Sydney Owenson's seminal novel of romantic nationalism, *The Wild Irish Girl* (1806), was written at a time when much of the defining imagery of Irish nationalism was being established. Also known by her subsequent married title of Lady Morgan, Sydney Owenson (1776?–1859) was the daughter of an Irish Catholic actor renowned for his stage portrayal of Irish characters, and an English Protestant mother, Jane Hill. She enjoyed a prolific and successful career as a writer, both in Ireland and in England, as well as being a minor composer and arranger of songs (including a set of Twelve *Original Hibernian Melodies* dating from around the same time as *The Wild Irish Girl*).[6] Subtitled 'A National Tale', *The Wild Irish Girl* enjoyed enormous success and contributed significantly to the creation of Irish romantic nationalism. In this novel Owenson set out to define the myths of Irish identity and origins through the medium of fiction, drawing both on her own experience[7] and by reference to the acknowledged antiquarian authorities of her time.

Horatio, the son of an English nobleman, has been banished to his father's Irish estate as a punishment for his dissolute life. On the wild Atlantic coast he finds a remote and exotic, partially-ruined castle perched on a promontory, in which dwell a deposed Gaelic king (the Prince of Inismore), their retainer a wise Catholic priest Father John, and the king's beautiful daughter Glorvina; the former wealth and influence of their kingdom has now been reduced to this literally ruinous condition. Horatio is welcomed into this remote remnant of the ancient Gaelic world and soon falls passionately in love with Glorvina: he learns about the history, culture and language of Ireland, a country he has always

---

Ireland (Dublin: W. Power, and London: Clementi, 1809); *The ancient music of Ireland arranged for the pianoforte* (Dublin: Hodges & Smith, 1840); George Petrie, *The Petrie collection of the ancient music of Ireland* (Dublin: The University Press, 1855). **5** See Fintan Cullen, *Visual politics: the representation of Ireland, 1750–1930* (Cork: Cork University Press, 1997). **6** *Twelve original Hibernian melodies, with English words, imitated and translated from the works of the ancient Irish bards* ... (London: Preston, c.1805). **7** For example, Owenson's footnoted commentary on a description of a May festival: 'In the summer of 1802 the author was present at a rural festival at the seat of an highly respected friend in Tipperary, from which this scene is partly copied', *The Wild Irish Girl*, ii: 187 (144) (page references are given here to the original edition (in three volumes, London: Richard Philips, 1806) [hereafter *The Wild Irish Girl*] followed, in parentheses, to a modern edition ed. Kathryn Kirkpatrick (Oxford: Oxford University Press, 1999)).

scorned. But he must hide his true identity, for it was his own ancestor who was directly responsible, some centuries earlier, for the ruin of this Gaelic family whom he has come to love and respect.

The narrative of *The Wild Irish Girl*, which is cast in the form of a letter-novel, regularly sets up opportunities for one of the characters, usually Father John or Glorvina, to expound to Horatio and to the reader on aspects of Irish culture, history and traditions. At one stage Horatio's questions about the harp ('And is this, Madam, ... the original ancient Irish harp?')[8] lead to a discussion of Ireland's 'national music'. As an Englishman Horatio comments that:

> we [English] thought as little of the music of her country, as of every thing else that related to it; and that all we know of the style of its melodies, reached us through the false medium of comic airs, sung by some popular actor, who, in coincidence with his author, caricatures those national traits he attempts to delineate.[9]

Glorvina responds with a commentary on Irish music which combines antiquarian claims for the antiquity and former pre-eminence of Irish music with subjective musings on how

> Our national music ... like our national character, admits of no medium in sentiment: it either sinks our spirit to despondency, by its heart-breaking pathos, or elevates it to wildness by its exhilarating animation'.[10]

Owenson's exposition of clichés about Irish music without providing any concrete information reflects the novel's wider concern to promote Ireland's cultural identity. Owenson was reflecting an idealized, even sentimentalized perception of Irish music prevalent at a time of growing nationalist feeling in the years following the Act of Union, a perception soon to find widespread popular expression in Thomas Moore's *Irish Melodies* which began to appear the year after the publication of *The Wild Irish Girl* and the musical settings of which bear as little relationship to the realities of Irish traditional music as does the Ireland represented by Glorvina and her father to contemporary reality. This perception of Irish music was founded not on the observation of contemporary musical practices so much as on a yearning for an imagined past nurtured by antiquarianism and Romantic nationalism. In this regard it is no surprise that Ireland's music is represented most strongly in *The Wild Irish Girl* through the imagery and symbolism of the harp.

Irish harpers, notably Turlough Carolan (represented in Neal's *Collection* and later collections of his music published during the eighteenth century), had enjoyed some popularity within Anglo-Irish society,[11] and by the later eighteenth-

---

8 *The Wild Irish Girl*, i, 219 (71).   **9** Ibid., i, 223–4 (72).   **10** Ibid., i, 226–7 (73).   **11** Collections of Carolan's music were published in Dublin by Denis Connor in 1748, and by John Lee in 1778. Richard

century antiquarians were focussing attention on the Irish harp and its music as *the* music of Ireland's identity.[12] But the harping tradition was by then in sharp decline: when Edward Bunting was commissioned to record the music played at the Belfast Harpers' Festival in 1792 the aim was specifically to '*reviv*[*e*] the antient music of this country' (my italics). The gathering of harpers in Belfast was as much an expression of the harp as a symbol of Ireland's identity and culture, a symbol prominently used by the United Irishmen during the final decade of the century, as it was an attempt actually to engage with and understand its music. Despite the Belfast festival, by the end of the century the harp's currency as an abstract symbol, in forms often far-removed from that of the real instrument, far outweighed its familiarity as an actual instrument of music.[13] The harp *was* Ireland, but *what* exactly was the harp and how did it relate to the reality of contemporary traditional music? Herder's ideas of 'folk music' as embodying the soul of a nation contributed to a growing interest during the early nineteenth century in native musical traditions. In Ireland, at least initially, any more inclusive interest in the songs, the dances or the music of pipers which might better have reflected the broader realities of 'folk' or traditional music was however largely eclipsed by this obsessive focus on the harp as the iconic representative of 'ancient' Irish music and culture.

This emphasis on the Irish harp is clearly seen in *The Wild Irish Girl*. From the first time Horatio encounters Glorvina, she is closely associated with the Irish harp, which becomes a central symbol of the novel. *The Wild Irish Girl* appeared a year before the first volume of Thomas Moore's *Irish Melodies* which would popularize the harp as *the* symbol of Irish national identity through songs like 'The Harp that Once thro' Tara's Halls', 'The Origin of the Harp', 'The Minstrel Boy' and many others. But, as Joep Leerssen comments:

> in the years between the United Irishmen and Moore, it was surely the string-tugging Glorvina who co-opted the harp icon most powerfully. [Sydney Owenson] herself was an enthusiastic strummer ...[14]

Noting that her poem *The Lay of the Irish Harp* published in 1807 foreshadows Moore, Leerssen even speculates that there may have been a degree of rivalry between Moore and Owenson as to which of them could claim to be the principal

---

Edgeworth (father of the novelist Maria Edgeworth) employed a harper over a period of about twenty-five years between the 1730s and 1767 (see Nora Grealis, 'Aspects of musical activity in Anglo-Irish homes outside Dublin during the eighteenth and early nineteenth century', MA diss. (NUI Maynooth, 1995), pp 119–122. Mrs Delaney refers a number of times to an Irish harper playing at her houses in Co. Down in the 1740s and 1750s (*Autobiography and correspondence of Mary Granville, Mrs Delaney*, ed. Lady Llanover (5 vols.) (London: Richard Bentley, 1861–2): ii, 368, 580–2; iii, 508–9). **12** See in particular Joseph Walker, *Historical memoirs of the Irish bards* (Dublin: for the author, 1786; London: T. Payne & Son, 1786). **13** Barra Boydell, 'The iconography of the Irish harp as a national symbol', *IMS*, v, 131–45; 'The United Irishmen: music, harps and national identity', *Eighteenth-Century Ireland*, 13 (1998), 44–51. **14** Joep Leerssen, *Remembrance and imagination: patterns in the historical and literary representation of Ireland in the nineteenth century* (Cork: Cork University Press, 1996), p. 59.

player, and indeed champion, of the national harp. When first drawn to the castle Horatio clambers, unseen, up to a window through which he sees Glorvina playing her harp to her father and the priest:

> the Prince ... listened to those strains which spoke once to the heart of the father, the patriot, and the man – breathed from the chords of his country's emblem – breathed in the pathos of his country's music – breathed from the lips of his apparently inspired daughter![15]

The harp plays a central role as the relationship develops between Horatio and Glorvina, a relationship which it even comes to symbolize. The first, as yet unspoken exchange of their feelings for each other takes place in the presence of the harp: following the sounds of 'a harp tuning in an underneath apartment', Horatio finds Glorvina:

> She was alone, and bending over her harp; one arm was gracefully thrown over the instrument, which she was tuning; with the other she was lightly modulating on its chords ...

They sit down and:

> For a moment she raised her glance to mine, and we both coloured, as if she read there – I know not what!
> 'I beg your pardon,' said I, recovering from the spell of this magic glance – 'you made some observation, Madam?'
> 'Not that I recollect,' she replied, with a slight confusion of manner, and running her finger carelessly over the chords of the harp, till it came in contact with my own, which hung over it. The touch circulated like electricity through every vein. I impulsively rose, and walked to the window.

Then:

> abruptly drawing in my dizzy head [from the open window], I perceived her's ... leaning against her harp, and her eye directed towards me ... [16]

In the concluding section of the novel, in the darkness before the dawn of its emotional climax (it ends happily with Horatio and Glorvina's marriage, representing Owenson's hopes for the mutually-loving unity of Irish and English ideals), Horatio returns after an absence to the castle, which he finds silent and deserted. He wanders through the deserted rooms lit only by moonlight, not knowing what has become of his beloved Glorvina and her family:

---

15 *The Wild Irish Girl*, i, 160–1 (52).   **16** Ibid., i, 209–13 (68–9).

> While he stood rapt in horror and amazement he heard the sound of Glorvina's harp, borne on the blast which sighed at intervals along the passage ... he flew to that room where the harp of Glorvina always stood ... [it] was still breathing its wild melody when he entered, but he perceived the melancholy vibration was produced by the sea breeze (admitted by the open casement which swept at intervals along its strings) ... [17]

Here the harp, the very soul of the absent Glorvina, finds its identity in nature, sounding of its own accord, like an Aeolian harp, in the absence of its owner.

The close association of the harp with Glorvina suggests her identification as occupying a position somewhere between the fair maiden of the earlier, Irish-language *aisling* poems, found wandering in poverty and distress and representing Ireland itself, oppressed under English rule, and that of the later nineteenth- and early twentieth-century personification of 'Erin', who stands or sits with her hand resting on a harp.[18] Glorvina is only 'wild' in the sense of her association with the 'wild' Irish setting of the novel and in her not being a member of 'fashionable' society: throughout the novel Owenson emphasizes her cultural accomplishments, underlining the intellectual equality, or even suggested superiority, of native Irish culture compared with that of England. Glorvina is repeatedly portrayed as a veritable scholar of both Classical and contemporary European literature and thought. In addition to her accomplishments as an embodiment of all that is seen as best in Gaelic Irish culture, including her dancing 'her national dance' the Irish jig with unequalled grace and elegance, Glorvina speaks Italian; she reads Rousseau, Goethe and Chateaubriand in their original languages; she studies Classical texts in Greek and Latin; she engages with ease in philosophical discourse.[19]

In his study of nineteenth-century cultural nationalism in Ireland Joep Leerssen describes *The Wild Irish Girl* as being sometimes uncomfortably balanced between being a novel and

> a sort of tourist's guide to Ireland, the charms of the Irish landscape, the pleasant and pathetic character of the poor but honest Irish peasant, the impressive and fascinating history and antiquity – and not in the last place, the great cultural accomplishments of Ireland.[20]

If the harp primarily reflects the 'great cultural accomplishments of Ireland' which underpinned its symbolism with both antiquarian and Romantic nationalist echoes, Leerssen's description of the novel as being in part a 'tourist's guide to Ireland' might suggest the presence of information of a more factual, informative

---

17 Ibid., iii, 209–10 (234).   **18** For selected examples of the portrayal of Erin with a harp, see Jeanne Sheehy, *The rediscovery of Ireland's past: the Celtic Revival 1830–1930* (London: Thames & Hudson, 1980), pp 76, 88, 176, 183, Plate 1.   **19** *The Wild Irish Girl*, i, 126, 247; ii, 148, 185, 193, 225 (41, 80, 132, 144, 146, 157) etc.   **20** Leerssen, *Remembrance*, p. 55.

nature about Irish musical practices. Owenson does in fact provide extensive, quasi-scholarly information on the Irish harp and its supposed origins in lengthy footnotes drawn from antiquarian sources including Joseph Cooper Walker's *Historical Memoirs* and others. A visit to Ulster undertaken in the latter part of the novel by Horatio and Father John, who has become both a tutor in matters Irish (both, it must be said, to Horatio and to the reader) and something of a father-figure to him, provides an opportunity for Owenson to describe a meeting with the historical figure of Denis Hempson, the oldest of the surviving Irish harpers, who died aged over 110 in 1807. Owenson draws both on her own visit to Hempson in Magilligan, Co. Derry in 1805 and on an account by a local Protestant clergyman, the Revd Sampson, who described finding him in bed, fully dressed and with his harp kept under the bed clothes, a detail repeated in the novel. This episode provides not only a climax to Horatio's odyssey through the 'exotic' world of Gaelic Ireland, but also the occasion for what is Owenson's most extended footnote (nearly three full pages of small print in the modern edition) in which she cites Revd Sampson's account in full.[21]

Aside from the dominance of the harp in the musical allusions in the novel there are also brief references to musicians and dancing. These however do not contribute significantly to an understanding of contemporary traditional musical practices. A description of a May Day celebration (*bealtaine*) mentions 'two blind fiddlers, and an excellent piper' and when music is provided for dancing the reader is merely told that 'the piper ... struck up one of those lilts, whose mirth-inspiring influence it is almost impossible to resist'. Brief observations such as these are however again amplified by detailed footnotes on bagpipes and on dancing drawing primarily on antiquarian authorities. Owenson's comment that 'the Irish jig, above every other dance, leaves most to the genius of the dancer' introduces a narrative focussed on Glorvina's excellence as a dancer and Horatio's admiration of her dancing.[22] Later in the novel, during their travels together, Horatio and Father John encounter 'a very indifferent fiddler and a tolerable piper' and there is further dancing,[23] while subsequently, following their visit to Denis Hempson the harper, the priest engages in a commentary on how the former bardic tradition 'has finally sunk into the casual retention of an harper, piper, or fiddler, which are generally, but not universally, to be found in the houses of the Irish country gentlemen'.[24] Although her novel is set in the present, Owenson's concern was not to portray the Ireland of her day but rather to emphasize the antiquity of Irish culture based on a romanticized vision of the past, an imagined lost 'golden age' of which the harp was one of the foremost symbols. Contemporary musical practices had but a passing relevance within this context.

---

21 *The Wild Irish Girl*, iii, 96–108 (199–203), of which the footnote occupies parts of 97 and 107 and almost the entire of 98–106 (199, 202, and the entire of 200–1). Edward Bunting cites Owenson's account in the extensive 'Dissertation of the Irish harp and harpers' in his third published collection *The ancient music of Ireland* (Dublin, 1840), pp 73–6. **22** *The Wild Irish Girl*, ii, 187, 191–8 (144–8). **23** Ibid., iii, 81, 86 (194, 196). **24** Ibid., iii, 118 (206).

Barra Boydell

Illustration 3.1: 'Portrait of a Lady as Hibernia' by Robert Fagan (1761–1816), Private Collection

A comparable view is found in contemporary Irish iconography where visual references to music are dominated by the harp as a symbol of national identity, most often in highly stylized, symbolic forms.[25] By contrast, the representation of musical performance through the depiction of actual music making by the rural or urban-poor population among whom traditional music thrived is relatively rare. A close parallel with Owenson's literary representation of the harp can be seen in the contemporary 'Portrait of a Lady as Hibernia' by Robert Fagan (1761–1816), an artist of Irish descent who considered himself to be Irish[26] (see illustration 3.1). As Hibernia, the female personification of Ireland, the lady is shown leaning on a highly stylized harp whose strings are broken, symbolising the country's spirit broken by the Act of Union of 1800 which brought Ireland under the direct political and economic control of England. The relative dating of the painting and the novel is not known, but it is tempting to trace the influence of *The Wild Irish Girl* on the artist: Glorvina was cited above as being described at one stage with 'her [head] ... leaning against her harp, and her eye directed towards me ...',[27] a pose closely matching that of the lady in Fagan's painting.[28] Note too the wild

25 See note 13. **26** See catalogue of Sotheby's London sale 'British paintings', 15 November 1989, p. 92 (lot 61). **27** *The Wild Irish Girl*, i, 213 (69). **28** This painting could perhaps be an imaginary portrait of Glorvina, but by tradition in the family who owned it up until recently it is a portrait of a Mrs Scott, the

scenery behind, as in the setting of the novel, and how the lady holds in her left hand the music of the patriotic melody *Erin go bragh* (Ireland for ever!), a tune specifically referred to in the novel some pages later on, when Glorvina's fingers

> seemed impulsively to thrill on the chords of the harp – her eyes, her tear-swollen beautiful eyes, were thrown up to heaven, and her voice, 'low and mournful as the song of the tomb', sighed over the chords of her national lyre, as she faintly murmured Campbell's beautiful poem to the ancient Irish air of Erin go Brack [*sic*]![29]

Leerssen identifies a profound change in attitudes towards Irish culture on the part of Anglo-Irish writers and commentators from about the 1820s. The core of this change was a shift from the emphasis on Ireland's past which had animated Owenson's *The Wild Irish Girl* to a focus on popular tradition as expressed though the peasantry. Herder's belief that the genius and soul of a people could be found in their folk poetry and music was now being applied in Ireland. As Leerssen comments:

> The Irish peasantry, until then seen as the pauperized, brutish and sullen dregs of a dead old culture, full of disaffection and hatred for their new ruler, gain cultural interest. They come to be seen, in Romantic, Grimm-like fashion, as the repository of quaint superstition and primordial folk and fairy tales.[30]

The result was an idyllic view of Ireland as 'a mere province or backwater where timeless characters go about their humble and picturesque ways', a conservative and unionist view of Ireland in marked opposition to the continued glorification of ancient culture which would characterize the nationalist Young Ireland movement of the 1840s.[31] Leerssen is referring in particular to the process of collecting folk tales and legends which was initiated in Ireland by Crofton Crocker, whose *Fairy Legends and Traditions in the South of Ireland* was published in 1825. This movement is also reflected in the developing interest in collecting Irish music. From Bunting through Petrie to Joyce and others later in the nineteenth century, folk song collectors visited the remotest parts of the country to collect 'folk music' directly from the people who played and sang it. It is no coincidence that a change can be observed at this period in the manner in which traditional musicians come to be viewed, for which the visual arts provide clear if infrequent examples.

---

wife of a glass maker in Wandsworth, London, and mistress of one of the family (private communication, 17 October 2005). This might explain the lady's décolleté pose and air of sexual invitation, not attributes normally associated with Hibernia unless to suggest Ireland here as 'submissive', even 'emasculated' by the Act of Union.   **29** *The Wild Irish Girl*, i, 228–9 (74). 'Campbell's beautiful poem' is not identified, but the Scottish poet Thomas Campbell (1777–1844) is represented in Bunting's 1809 collection (see note 4 above), in which his poem 'There came to the beach a poor exile of Erin' repeats the popular motto 'Erin go bragh' but is set to the air *Blaith na Seud* ('Thou blooming treasure') (Bunting, *A general collection*, pp 64–5).   **30** Leerssen, *Remembrance*, p. 162.   **31** Ibid., p. 170.

With rare exceptions the portrayal of Irish traditional musicians in art (as distinct from evocations of ancient, 'bardic' harpers) had to wait until ideals of the nobility of the simple rural life began to attract artists in the 1820s. The market for these artists was the wealthier urban classes, not only in Ireland but also in England and further afield. This was the very same market for whom Irish music was effectively defined by Thomas Moore's *Irish Melodies* which appeared between 1807 and 1834. The vast gulf between Moore's *Irish Melodies*, with their tunes regularized with piano accompaniments and set to English texts little related to their origins, and the actuality of Irish traditional music mirrors the distance between the music as practised and its portrayal in the art of the period. Musicians are portrayed in paintings as objects of interest, but often too as an exotic 'Other' for the well-to-do Irish or English art public, different or strange, a 'simple' rural people, perhaps to be pitied and deserving of charity and sympathy, but observed at a safe distance from the comforts of the Victorian drawing room. For the English art market, Ireland was geographically close but in other ways as different as a distant colony, tantalizingly attractive to observe from a safe distance. As Leerssen observes, 'Ireland as experienced and imagined in the nineteenth century was not so much a real country as a chronotope, bent in political space and warped in historical time'.[32]

This new interest in Irish musicians is manifested in the visual arts in two distinct categories: portraits of individual musicians (usually pipers); and rustic genre paintings in which the musician is placed within a wider context of rural life. The first of these categories can be further divided between paintings and drawings produced for public view, and the more spontaneous context of life sketches. In contrast to a finished painting in which the subject matter may be adapted to suit public expectations, life sketches may generally be assumed more accurately to reflect reality. Such sketches will, however, reflect the interests of the artist and cannot necessarily be accepted without question as impartial iconographic evidence. A number of drawings and watercolours of pipers from life exist from the nineteenth century, a relatively early example of which is a sketch from a volume of watercolours executed in the Waterford area *c*.1820.[33] (See illustration 3.2.) Here a seated piper accompanies a couple dancing in what is apparently an accurate portrayal, or accurate in so far as the artist's technique permitted. The rural poor were becoming a subject of sufficient interest to attract the attention of artists, in this case the Waterford-born Sampson Towgood Roch (1757–1847). However, the piper and dancers here are not of greater interest to the artist than any of the others (market vendors, cobblers, women drawing water, etc) included in the volume.[34]

---

[32] Ibid., p. 7. [33] One of the earliest known examples of a sketch from life of an Irish piper is dated 1760; see *The cries of Dublin &c: drawn from the life by Hugh Douglas Hamilton, 1760*, ed. William Laffan (Dublin: Irish Georgian Society, 2003), p. 135. [34] For a discussion of this volume of sketches see W.H. Crawford, 'Provincial town life in the early nineteenth century: an artist's impressions', *Ireland: art into history*, ed. Brian P. Kennedy and Raymond Gillespie (Dublin: Town House, 1994), pp 43–59; also Rosemary Ffolliott, 'Provincial town life in Munster', *Irish Ancestor*, 5:1 (1973), 34–41.

Illustration 3.2: Piper and Dancers, Co. Waterford c.1820, by Sampson Towgood Roch (1757–1847), Ulster Folk and Transport Museum

A number of early- to mid-nineteenth-century drawings and sketches of musicians can be linked specifically to the growing interest in folklore. A pencil sketch of 'An Irish Piper' (see illustration 3.3), for example, is by the novelist, artist and song composer Samuel Lover (1797–1868), one of a number of people who published versions of folk and fairy stories in the aftermath of Crofton Croker's *Fairy Legends and Traditions*. These folk and fairy tales 'occupied a niche in the interstice between fact and fiction, amusing a middle-class readership with something that was both entertaining and instructive, a window on the exotic folk-life of the Irish peasantry',[35] a description equally applying to these images of pipers. A second example is provided by Frederick William Burton's portrait of the Galway piper Paddy Coneely (see illustration 3.4). Burton, who was born in Co. Clare in 1816, would go on to become director of the National Gallery in London in 1874, for which position he was knighted. He was a close friend of Samuel Lover and became friendly with and was actively encouraged by George Petrie, the most significant of the collectors of Irish music during the first half of the nineteenth century. Indeed, Burton painted this portrait while accompanying Petrie through Connemara in 1839.[36] Becoming a popular print when it was

---

[35] Leerssen, *Remembrance*, p. 163. Lover's *Legends and stories of Ireland* first appeared in 1831.
[36] George Petrie, a gifted violinist who had been actively collecting Irish music since his late teens, first published the fruits of his important work as a folk song collector in 1855 (see note 4). Coneely was the source of a number of the songs and tunes in Petrie's collection (*The Petrie collection of the ancient music of Ireland*, ed. David Cooper, Cork: Cork University Press, 2002, passim). For Petrie's account of Coneely see note 38 below. See also Jimmy O'Brien Moran's chapter in this volume for extensive discussion of Coneely.

Illustration 3.3: 'An Irish Piper' by Samuel Lover (1797–1868), National Gallery of Ireland

engraved for the *Irish Penny Journal* in October 1840 and exhibited at the Royal Hibernian Academy in 1841, 'The Galway Piper' is one of a number of Burton's Connemara paintings (including 'The Aran Fisherman's Drowned Child', one of his best known paintings) which, to cite Marie Bourke

> reflect the mood of the period: they are part of a search for 'national identity'. They reflect an interest in antiquity and the past, and treat contemporary Irish subjects in a sensitive and objective manner.[37]

Images such as these are among the most detailed iconographic records we have of traditional musicians from the nineteenth century, and yet they tell us little about the context of their music-making: for whom did the pipers play? Where did they play? Did they accompany dancing or were they performing instrumental solos? In the case of Burton's 'Galway Piper', the public who would have seen it

---

[37] Marie Bourke, 'Rural life in pre-famine connacht: a visual document', in *Ireland: art into history*, ed. Kennedy and Gillespie, p. 63. Despite details including the omission of the coat hanging on the chairback and the more raised but less realistic way in which the pipes are held, the engraving in the *Irish Penny Journal* is directly based on Burton's watercolour sketch; see Jimmy O'Brien Moran's chapter in this volume (illustration 5.1) for this image.

Illustration 3.4: 'Paddy Coneely, a Galway Piper' by Frederick William Burton (1816–1900), National Gallery of Ireland

exhibited at the Royal Hibernian Academy or engraved in the *Irish Penny Journal* was not concerned with musicological accuracy: its interest was in an image which reflected an idealized and patronizing representation of 'folk' life as reflected in Petrie's essay on Coneely which it accompanies in the *Irish Penny Journal*.[38] Samuel Lover's piper, an informal sketch rather than a worked image for exhibition, is casually dressed and was sketched as he played, seated apparently on a simple bench. In contrast, Burton's piper, clearly a more finished work executed with a public in mind, wears smart clothing and is seated on a chair: we know from Petrie's account that he and Burton met Coneely on the road outside Galway, that they subsequently 'kept [him] with us for a fortnight', and that he 'will only play for the gentry or the comfortable farmers. He will not lower the dignity of his professional character by playing in a tap-room or for the commonalty'.[39] Burton's portrait, however, presents the piper in a formalized style, dressed in a manner which perhaps suggests playing 'for the gentry or the comfortable farmers' but which provides little actual evidence of the context of his music-making. Whether or not he played for the Galway gentry, this was a world apart from that of Burton's and Petrie's publics.

38 [George] P[etrie], 'Paddy Coneely, the Galway Piper', *Irish Penny Journal*, 1:14 (3 October 1840), 105–8.   **39** Ibid., 106, 108.

When a piper *was* depicted in context, that context might have little to do with reality, but everything to do with creating a setting to appeal to the ideals of the picture's intended public. The clothing of the exotic in an acceptable form is shown most clearly by Joseph Haverty's painting of 'The Blind Piper' dating from *c.*1844 and certainly the most famous nineteenth-century image of an Irish musician (see illustration 3.5). The piper in question, Patrick O'Brien, was a well-known piper who frequented the streets of Limerick. The detail of his pipes suggests an accurate, almost photographic attention to realism, but the setting has been fundamentally altered. In tune with the interests of his public, again that of the Royal Hibernian Academy exhibitions for whom it might have been inappropriate to portray the piper playing in the squalor of a city street, Haverty transfers him to this sylvan setting and shows him accompanied by his daughter who sits to his left, hinting at a reference to the 'maid of Erin', the nineteenth-century female personification of Ireland. Shorn of the harsh realities of the present, this painting allows its public to engage with the folk traditions of the peasantry presented in a suitably Romanticized, even 'sanitized' manner that does not offend the politeness of the drawing room.

Interestingly, Haverty painted a second version of the same painting, which is clearly intended for a different context (see illustration 3.6). Here the same piper is placed in a setting which grants him entry to the world of the gentry. Instead of the bare-footed peasant girl clad in traditional red skirt we have a rosy-cheeked, elegantly-dressed young girl, clearly from a wealthy family. Clutching a bouquet of flowers and accompanied by her pet dog, she stretches her hand out towards the piper almost with a gesture of ownership. From being a piper who scraped a living in the streets of Limerick, Patrick O'Brien has entered the service of the 'big house'. With these two very different interpretations of the same subject, Haverty portrays folk culture, in this case a piper, in ways designed to appeal, it would appear, to different patrons: he offers them not the reality but what they want to see. The world of traditional music, and with it an aspect of Irish identity, is imagined or reinvented to suit the viewer.

In addition to his significance as a folk music collector, George Petrie was one of the foremost Irish topographical artists of his day and an early pioneer of Irish archaeology. Interestingly, however, he does not include musicians in his numerous and often well-peopled watercolours and drawings of the Irish landscape. Here Petrie reflects established artistic norms in presenting an idealized rather than a realistic landscape: where his views include figures, as often they do, these serve merely to give exaggerated emphasis to the scale and grandeur of the landscape or to bring life to an urban setting or featured building.[40] Only rarely do people form a more prominent feature in his paintings, but in such cases the attention is not on an individual but on a group of people acting collectively and anonymously, usually in the context of some religious or other custom hallowed by time.[41]

---

[40] For examples and discussion of Petrie's topographical paintings see Peter Murray, *George Petrie (1790–1866): the rediscovery of Ireland's past* (Cork: Crawford Municipal Art Gallery, 2004). [41] Paintings

Illustration 3.5: 'The Blind Piper' by Joseph Haverty (1794–1864), National Gallery of Ireland

It can seem difficult to reconcile these images by Petrie the artist, so devoid of musical representation, with Petrie the avid collector of Irish music as described thus by his friend and biographer William Stokes, referring to a visit to the Aran Islands:

> Inquiries having been made as to the names of persons 'who had music' ... an appointment was made ... to meet ... at some cottage near to the little village of Kilronan ... To this cottage, when evening fell, Petrie, with his manuscript music-book and violin ... used to proceed. Nothing could exceed the strange picturesqueness of the scenes which night after night were thus presented ... It would have required a Rembrandt to paint the scene. The minstrel – sometimes an old woman – sometimes a beautiful girl or a young man – was seated on a low stool in the chimney corner, while chairs for Petrie and O'Curry[42] were placed opposite: the rest of the crowded audience remained standing. The song having been given, O'Curry wrote the Irish words, when

including more prominent groups of figures include 'The last circuit of the pilgrims at Clonmacnoise' (*c*.1828) and 'St Brigid's Well' (*c*.1829); repr. Murray, *George Petrie*, pp 20, 23. **42** Eugene O'Curry, a native Irish-speaker and colleague in the Ordnance Survey, accompanied and assisted Petrie on many of his folk song collecting trips.

Illustration 3.6: 'The Blind Piper' ('Limerick Piper') by Joseph Haverty, University of Limerick

Petrie's work began. The singer recommenced, stopping at a signal from him at every two or three bars of the melody to permit the writing of the notes, and often repeating the passage until it was correctly taken down, and then going on with the melody, exactly from the point where the singing was interrupted ... [43]

And so the process continues until Petrie plays the melody back to the islanders on his violin, the translation of the music from its original context into that of the educated, classically-trained musician already accomplished before the very ears of those whose music it was. This process would reach its conclusion in Petrie's published versions of the tunes to which, in accordance with contemporary practice, he added piano accompaniments. This description of a musical event provides a very apposite illustration of the similar act of 'translation' that was being effected in the visual arts when the Irish peasantry, including musicians, were being depicted for the urban Irish and English audiences. Stokes' expression of the painterly quality of the above scene was in fact an accurate reflection, if not perhaps of the work literally of a Rembrandt, at least of that of the rustic genre painters of the mid-nineteenth century.

[43] Cited after *The Petrie collection*, ed. David Cooper, pp 13–14.

Illustration 3.7: 'Children Dancing' by Trevor Thomas Fowler (1800–81), National Gallery of Ireland

The poet Wordsworth had expressed the belief that human passions could be seen at their purest in 'low and rustic life', in contrast to the polite conventions and concealed feelings of sophisticated society,[44] while Fintan Cullen notes:

> In the first half of the nineteenth century, in both literature and the visual arts, Ireland was frequently represented through its peasant class. National character, it was thought, exhibited itself most strongly and visibly in the rural poor.[45]

This sense of discovering true, unalloyed feelings and emotions in the lives of the simple peasantry lay behind the emergence of rustic genre painting, a style of painting made fashionable in the 1830s in particular by the Scottish-born artist David Wilkie. Although Wilkie visited Ireland in 1835 with 'a picture or two of a national kind in his head' and subsequently exhibited two Irish paintings at the Royal Academy in London, musicians do not feature in either of these.[46] The new-found interest in Irish rustic life on the part of British artists influenced by Wilkie did however result in a number of other artists turning to subjects which include musicians and music-making.

[44] Christiana Payne, *Rustic simplicity: scenes of cottage life in nineteenth-century British art* (Nottingham: Djanogly Art Gallery/Lund Humphries, 1998), p. 6.   [45] Cullen, *Visual politics*, p. 116.   [46] 'The Peep-O-Day Boy's Cabin' and 'The Irish Whiskey Still'; see Cullen, *Visual politics*, p. 116.

Barra Boydell 69

Illustration 3.8: 'The Irish Piper' by Alfred D. Fripp (1822–95), Bristol Museums and Art Gallery (K266)

An Irish-born artist who contributed to this genre was Trevor Fowler, born in Dublin in 1800 but who emigrated to America in 1837. His painting 'Children Dancing at a Crossroads', dating from one of his return visits to Ireland, evokes this idealized view of 'simple peasantry' with its cheerful, rosy-cheeked, barefoot children (see illustration 3.7). This painting gives us a view of a freer form of Irish dancing prior to the invention by the Gaelic League in the late nineteenth and early twentieth centuries of what came to be regarded as 'traditional' Irish dancing: upper body straight and rigid, arms held straight down, with all the movement in the legs.[47] This glimpse of earlier dance styles is however largely incidental to the painting's major concern, the portrayal of a sentimental scene clothed in some of the clichés of Irish peasant life, which Cullen lists as including:

> rustic interiors of the shebeen or cottage … quaint customs and modes of dress, criminality, striking beauty in the women, fine features in the men and a colourful mischievousness in the near-naked children …[48]

Here, apart from the cheerful, barefooted children, the clichés include the 'drunken Irishman' suggested by the liquor-swilling man at the right of the

---

[47] For a summary of the modern invention of 'traditional' dance, see Vincent Comerford, *Ireland* (London: Arnold, 2003), pp 193–7.   [48] Cullen, *Visual politics*, p. 121.

painting, and a pig rooting at a broken bottle in the left foreground. The more or less accurate portrayal of music and dance is clearly subordinated to the broader narrative of the painting.

The paintings discussed above are by Irish artists (or, like Fagan, artists who regarded themselves as Irish) who provided varying constructs of the imagined identity of their country. They all, however, came from urban or well-to-do backgrounds that were set sharply apart from the poor, rural world that they were portraying and which they were viewing essentially as outsiders. An English artist who contributed to this genre and who provides an outsider's view of Ireland and the Irish was the Bristol-born artist Alfred Fripp (1822–95). In 1843 Fripp made the first of three visits to Ireland in search of subject matter. Like Wilkie, he exhibited his paintings in England at the Society of Painters in Watercolours. His numerous watercolours of the later 1840s include Irish peasant subjects with titles such as 'The Rosary', 'The Holy Well', 'Interior of a Galway Cabin', 'The Bog Cabin', 'A Pilgrim at Clonmacnoise' and, in 1850, 'The Irish Piper' (see illustration 3.8).[49] Fripp's 'The Irish Piper', a classic example of the rustic genre painting, must count among the most striking images of Irish music from the mid-nineteenth century, but it tells us as much or more about the attitudes towards Ireland of an English artist and of the public for whom he was painting as it does about traditional music-making.

An elderly piper, almost certainly blind (perhaps a cliché, but often true with pipers, as with harpers) sits outside a row of rough cottages in a wild landscape, with mountains behind and a river and bridge in the distance. He is surrounded by children and women who clearly reflect Cullen's cliché category of 'striking beauty'. The women, wearing shawls and other distinctively Irish dress, are smiling, absorbed in the music while interrupted in their daily chores, with pails of milk or water. An older woman to the right holds a young child in her arms, who points towards the piper. One young girl leans on the piper's shoulder, another crouches on all fours at his feet, looking up at him as he plays. In the middle distance another woman, her attention as if suddenly attracted by the music as she emerges from her cottage, turns around to listen to the piper.

Adjectives such as 'Romanticized' and 'sentimentalized' may be overused, but surely here they are no exaggeration. Fripp does not ignore the poverty – the bare feet, the simple, very basic cottages (with the incongruous exception of the diamond-pained window in the right foreground, an English style of window quite out of keeping for a small and remote Irish cottage) – but effectively he idealizes this reality, echoing an earlier aesthetic in which, as Brian Kennedy observes 'in portraying a happy peasantry in their pictures, the artists ignored the hardship of life in a thatched cottage, and, instead, convey a moral message. Patrons were to be spared reminders of poverty, famine, and poor housing and sanitary conditions'.[50] But rural Ireland in 1850 was certainly no romantic idyll

---

49 See H. Stuart Thompson, 'George A. Fripp and Alfred D. Fripp', *Walker's Quarterly*, 25–6 (1928), 84–95. **50** Brian P. Kennedy, 'The traditional Irish thatched house: image and reality, 1793–1993',

as Fripp might have us believe, with the smiling faces, the children playing, the sense that the poor, rural peasantry lives a charmed, carefree existence. This is a rural Ireland which had barely emerged from the worst famine experienced in Europe for centuries in which millions, predominantly from just such marginal rural communities as depicted in this scene, had died or been forced to emigrate. A further aspect which reflects the extent to which this painting presents an imagined rather than a necessarily accurate portrayal of traditional music-making is that the piper's audience is entirely one of women and children: what has happened to the men? In fact there are two men in the far distance, one on the bridge looking down at another with a cart below. The men are not just incidental to the painting: they are specifically excluded from the music, from the feminine world of art and emotions. Fripp presents music as feminine, a world in which the piper, being old and frail, presents no threat – he is not the handsome, manly young piper of Burton's painting of the Galway piper, dressed up in his smart frock coat.

Individual details of the piper and his instrument in Fripp's painting may be realistic in themselves but the setting – a *tableau vivant* depicting that oldest of conceits, the happy peasant – certainly is not. An image such as this, exhibited in London in 1850, serves a political as well as an artistic purpose, reassuring the English public that, despite the harrowing images and accounts of the Great Famine published just a few years before in the *Illustrated London News*, the public conscience could be set at rest. Rural Ireland could again be viewed comfortably as an exotic Other, a world remote from, and yet so geographically close to the civilized world of the London drawing room. Fripp's 'Irish Piper' tells us little of substance about the practice of Irish music in the mid-nineteenth century. It does however tell us considerably more about Victorian England's perceptions of Irish identity in particular and of attitudes to rural poverty in general. As such, it is a classic example of visual politics in which music plays an essentially incidental, if not unimportant role.

The examples of the literary and visual portrayal of Irish traditional music cited here are associated with the fine arts of literature and painting or otherwise with the upper classes of society; but the information they provide (or fail to provide) on contemporary musical practices, and the aspects of literary and visual politics which they may represent, are not limited by class or context. In conclusion, two undated picture postcards from the late nineteenth century demonstrate many of the points raised above but expressed within the field of popular art (see illustrations 3.9 and 3.10). Both do indeed provide detailed pictures of *uilleann* pipers and their instruments (note in one instance the piper's foot support, a feature recurring in nineteenth-century portrayals of standing pipers but no longer used), but these are subsumed within a veritable catalogue of clichés which, through the medium of the picture postcard, were very probably aimed at the émigré Irish-American market: in both cases the jovial Irishman; in

Visualizing Ireland: national identity and the pictorial tradition, ed. Adele M. Dalsimer (Boston and London: Faber & Faber, 1993), p. 168.

Illustration 3.9: 'The Irish Piper' (picture postcard, *c.*1900), unsigned. Irish Traditional Music Archive

one, the innocent audience of children, the girl either carrying her baby sibling or perhaps playing at being 'mother', the thatched cottages, and even a round tower in the background; in the other, a country lane with, in the background, a two-storied cottage of distinctly un-Irish style. Once again, and not so very far removed from the scene portrayed by Fripp, an idealized world is presented which presents largely imaginary views of Ireland, but views in which the piper plays a central role.

Nineteenth-century nationalism encouraged the identification of selected aspects of a country's culture and history as iconic symbols of nationality. Irish nationalism inherited a direct role for music within this imagery due to the harp's existence as the country's symbol since early-modern times, an imagery central to Sydney Owenson's retrospective construction of nationality in *The Wild Irish Girl*. As interest developed in native 'folk' traditions during the nineteenth century attention increasingly turned to the country's indigenous musical traditions. It is significant that the major nineteenth-century collectors of Irish folk music, Bunting, Petrie and Joyce, most often used the adjective 'ancient' to describe this music: they were collecting what was valued not so much as the living musical tradition of their own day but as the remnants of an ancient Irish

Illustration 3.10: 'Irish Piper'
(picture postcard, *c.*1900),
by John Carey (1861–1943).
Irish Traditional Music Archive

culture.[51] While some nineteenth-century artists did feature harps in contexts of Irish antiquity,[52] those interested in contemporary Irish rural life portrayed a world from which the harp had now disappeared. In the absence of this iconic symbol, contemporary musical practices were of incidental, if essentially exotic interest within the iconography of Irish rural life.[53] The literary and iconographical representation of Irish music in the nineteenth century, whether viewed from within the country or by outsiders, was little concerned with the recording of actual musical practice or that of related activities such as dance. It would not be until later in the twentieth century that Irish traditional music, valued as a living tradition rather than primarily as a remnant of the past, would begin to assume the defining role it does today in popular perceptions of Irish identity.

51 For Bunting and Petrie see note 4 above; Patrick Joyce, *Ancient Irish music* (Dublin: McGlashan & Gill, 1873), with later collections titled *Irish music and song* (Dublin: Gill, 1888) and *Old Irish folk music and songs* (Dublin: Hodges, Figgis, 1909). **52** Notably Daniel Maclise, e.g. his 'Marriage of Aoife and Strongbow' (National Gallery of Ireland) with its detailed portrayal of an Irish harp modelled closely on the Trinity College ('Brian Boru') harp. **53** For further examples see Samuel McCloy's 'The Arrival of Phadrig na pib' (1873), Erskine Nicol's 'Cover the Buckle' (1854) and Howard Helmick's 'The Country Dancing Master, West of Ireland' (1874) illustrated and described in *A time and a place: two centuries of Irish social life*, ed. Brendan Rooney (Dublin: National Gallery of Ireland, 2006), pp 29–35.

"'Twas one of those Dreams that by Music are Brought': the development of the piano and the preservation of Irish traditional music[1]

DAVID COOPER

> She looked up at him for a moment, coloured deeply, and played something else. He took some music from a chair near the pianoforte, and turning to Emma, said, 'Here is something quite new to me. Do you know it? – Cramer. – And here are a new set of Irish melodies ...'
>
> Jane Austen, *Emma*

Aloys Fleischmann's monumental index, *Sources of Irish Traditional Music c.1600–1855*, amply evidences the currency of Irish and Scottish folk material in print during the latter part of the eighteenth century.[2] From around 1780 the number of collections of songs and pieces seems to have increased exponentially, and Fleischmann lists more than twelve hundred individual items published between 1790 and 1799. That this proliferation should come so close on the heels of Johann Gottfried von Herder's *Stimmen der Völker in Liedern* (1778–79) is surely not coincidental, for it reflects a burgeoning interest in, and enthusiasm for, 'the music of the people' that fuelled, and was itself fuelled by, the development of literary Romanticism. Herder's fascination with folk music was, of course, influenced by the Ossianic poetry largely fabricated by Macpherson, and in Ireland, Charlotte Brooke would defer to the spirit of Macpherson's Ossian in her translations of Irish poetry in the *Reliques of Irish Poetry*, first published in 1789.[3] For Brooke, 'the beauties of the music of this country are, at present, almost as little known as those of its poetry. And yet there is no other music in the world so calculated to make its way directly to the heart: it is the voice of Nature, and Sentiment, and every fibre of the feeling breast is in unison with it.'[4]

If the founding of the Royal Irish Academy in Dublin in 1785 (three years after the achievement of partial legislative independence for 'Grattan's Parliament') reveals an increasing interest in the Gaelic literary heritage of Ireland at least for

---

1 The title of one of Thomas Moore's *Irish Melodies*. **2** Editor, Aloys Fleischmann; assistant editor, Mícheál Ó Súilleabháin; associate editor, Paul McGettrick, *Sources of Irish traditional music, c.1600–1855* (New York: Garland, 1998). **3** Charlotte Brooke, *Reliques of Irish poetry: consisting of heroic poems, odes, elegies, and songs, translated into English verse: with notes explanatory and historical; and the originals in the Irish character. To which is subjoined an Irish tale* (Dublin: George Bonham, 1789).
4 Quoted in Brendan Clifford and Pat Muldowney, *Bolg an tsolair, or, Gaelic magazine: containing Laoi na sealga, or, the famous fenian poem called THE CHASE, with a collection of choice IRISH SONGS translated by MISS BROOKE, to which is prefixed an abridgement of Irish grammar, with a vocabulary and familiar dialogues, Patrick Lynch and Charlotte Brooke* (Belfast: Athol Books, 1999), 133.

some members of the Anglo-Irish Protestant ascendancy, the scholarly consideration of Irish music was not so apparent. Joseph Cooper Walker's *Historical Memoirs of the Irish Bards* (1786),[5] and an article by William Beauford in the fourth volume of *Transactions of the Royal Irish Academy*,[6] do include transcriptions of several caoines, but the vast majority of publications consisted of 'favourite country dance' tunes or hits from popular stage shows.

The prolix title of Edward Bunting's 1796 publication, *A General Collection of the Ancient Irish Music Containing a Variety of Admired Airs Never Before Published, and also the Compositions of Conolan and Carolan; Collected from the Harpers &c. in the different Provinces of Ireland and Adapted for the Piano Forte with a Prefatory Introduction*, indicates the scope and seriousness of his intent.[7] Although John Parry and Evan Williams had published a collection of *Antient British Music* in 1742, and Daniel Dow *A Collection of Ancient Scots Music* around 1778, this is the first use of the term 'ancient' with reference to Irish music in the title of a work in Fleischmann's survey. The impetus for the collection, the first of three volumes of Irish music published by Bunting in 1796, 1809 and 1840 respectively, was the Belfast Harp Festival of July 1792, organized by a committee involving members of the radical, and largely Presbyterian, Belfast Society for Promoting Knowledge. The festival was premised upon the preservation of what was seen as a largely moribund Gaelic musical culture, and in his preface to the 1796 collection (published by the Belfast Society for Promoting Knowledge) Bunting made it clear that he believed that much of the repertory sprang from remote antiquity. I would suggest that his usage here does not simply indicate the much more constrained employment of the word in the Academy of Ancient Music, established in 1726 as the Academy of Vocal Music, or the Concert of Ancient Music, founded in London in 1776 to play art music of earlier generations. In the concluding paragraph of his preface, Bunting remarks that:

> It is a debt which every man owes to his country, to search for and perpetuate the records of other days, to oppose, as far as he can, the destructive ravages of time, and to render permanent the fleeting productions of every species of genius; productions of an era so remote in the present case, as to baffle our attempts to ascertain their exact station on the scale of events ... In paying them all due attention, we do not merely gratify the natural feeling of national pride; we are tracing the progress of the human mind, and endeavouring to restore a page in the history of man.

---

5 *Historical memoirs of the Irish bards: an historical essay on the dress of the ancient and modern Irish: and a memoir on the armour and weapons of the Irish* (Dublin: Printed for the author, by Luke White, 1786).   **6** William Beauford, 'Caoinan: or some account of the antient Irish lamentation', *Transactions of the Royal Irish Academy*, 4, read 17 December 1791, 41–54.   **7** Although the date of 1797 has been suggested for the first volume (for example by Brian Audley in 'The provenance of the *Londonderry Air*', *Journal of the Royal Musical Association*, 125/2 (2000), 206), there is strong evidence that it was published in 1796. See Colette Moloney, *The Irish music manuscripts of Edward Bunting (1773–1843): an introduction and catalogue* (Dublin: Irish Traditional Music Archive, 2000), pp 161–2, note 18.

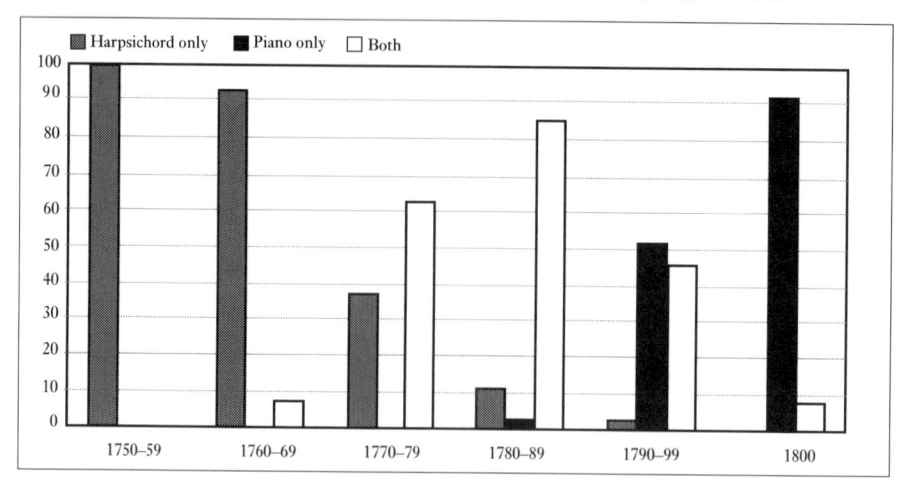

Figure 4.1: An analysis of Hess' data on harpsichord and piano designation in solo keyboard music published in England between 1750 and 1800. The dependent (y) axis indicates the percentages of each category of work in each decade.

Given this imperative to preserve, and the 'utmost reverence' with which the harpists apparently treated the music, it is significant that Bunting should have chosen the piano as the medium for its performance. There are a few collections of Irish music utilising the piano identified by Fleischmann that predate this volume, for example, *John Lee's Collection of Country Dances for the Present Year 1791* has 'proper basses for the Harpsichord or Piano-Forte'[8] and *Cooke's Selection of Twenty One Favourite Original Irish Airs* published in Dublin around 1795 are 'arranged for the Piano-Forte, Violin or Flute',[9] but otherwise there are hardly any that specify uniquely the instrument. In Albert Hess's examination of the transition between harpsichord and piano as principal keyboard instrument in an article published in the *Galpin Society Journal* in 1953, he considered the trend in instrumental designation provided on the title pages of keyboard music in English publications between 1750 and 1800.[10]

Figure 4.1 presents an analysis of the data presented by Hess of solo keyboard music published between 1750 and 1800: publications which according to the title were composed for the harpsichord alone; works written either for the harpsichord or the piano; and works which were published specifically for the piano. Although Hess's sample is not particularly comprehensive (a total of 289 individual works), it is assumed here that it is reasonably representative of the population. The trend is certainly unambiguous, with a massive decline in the proportion of publications written uniquely for solo harpsichord between 1770 and 1800. The turning point appears to lie in the period between 1780 and 1789,

---

8 Fleischmann, *Sources*, p. 556.   **9** Ibid., p. 577.   **10** Albert G. Hess, 'The transition from harpsichord to piano', *Galpin Society Journal*, 6 (1953), 75–94.

with the piano beginning to be asserted as the primary instrument in the final decade. A similar tendency can be discerned in the solo keyboard works of Clementi, many of which were published for piano or harpsichord until the late 1780s, with a gradual shift to the solo piano, though some of his publications from the first decade of the nineteenth century still indicate either instrument. As Nicholas Temperley notes:

> Well before 1800, the piano's victory over the harpsichord had become an accepted fact in London. For instance Cramer, from his op. 1 (1788) onwards, firmly used 'piano forte' alone on the title-pages of his published works.[11]

It is generally considered that Henry Walsh gave the first concert performance on a 'forte piano' (described in an advertisement in *The Dublin Journal* as 'that much admired Instrument') in Dublin in May 1768,[12] and according to the *Reminiscences* of the singer Michael Kelly, the piano was in widespread use in Dublin during the 1770s.[13] Research by Teahan on instrument makers in Ireland demonstrates a general increase in piano manufacture in Dublin over the final two decades of the eighteenth century, with at least a dozen factories being active during the period,[14] and although inevitably these would have been low-volume enterprises, they would certainly have been established in response to a fashion for the new instrument among the aristocracy and gentry.

Edward Bunting came to prominence in Belfast in the seventeen eighties as a child prodigy, having taken on the job of assistant to a certain Mr Weir (or Ware), the organist of St Anne's Church (which stood on the site on which St Anne's Cathedral would later be built), at the age of eleven.[15] According to George Petrie, writing in 1847, Bunting also deputized for Weir as a piano teacher, and apparently:

> After a few years spent in this manner, he became a professor on his own account; and as his abilities as a performer had become developed his company was courted by the higher class of the Belfast citizens, as well as by the gentry of its neighbourhood, and, in short, the boy prodigy became an idol among them.[16]

His 1796 volume is indisputably written for a hammered rather than a plucked keyboard, since it makes the most of the dynamic and articulatory potential of the instrument.[17] The facsimile of Preston and Son's original edition engraved by Thomas Straight of 7 Lambeth Walk, Surrey, which was published by the Linen Hall Library, Belfast, in 1996 reveals much more clearly than the corrupt pirate editions that followed the progressive nature of Bunting's approach to the

---

11 Nicholas Temperley, 'London and the piano: 1760–1860', *Musical Times*, 129 (June, 1988), 289–93; here 290.   **12** Virginia Pleasants, 'The early piano in Britain (*c*.1760–1800)', *Early Music*, 13:1 (1985), 39–44; here 40.   **13** Ibid., 40.   **14** John Teahan, 'A list of Irish instrument makers', *Galpin Society Journal*, 16 (1963), 28–32.   **15** George Petrie, 'Our Portrait Gallery – No. XLI. Edward Bunting', *Dublin University Magazine*, 29 (1847), 64–73; here 67.   **16** Ibid., 67.   **17** It is ironic, perhaps, that Seán Ó

instrument. This can be seen to follow the example of a number of contemporary composers, and particularly the group of composer pianists now described as the 'London Pianoforte School', in its detailed application of expressive markings.[18] Bunting employs a relatively wide variety of dynamics for the period: *ff*, *f* (and *for.*), *Fz*, *rf*, *sfor*, *p* (and *pia.*) and *pp*; as well as '*dim:*' and hairpin *diminuendo*, and '*cres:*' and hairpin *crescendo*. Articulation marks found in the arrangements include the staccato dot and stroke, and the portato marking, as well as an assortment of shorter and longer slurs.

It could be argued that although Bunting was writing for the piano, he was drawing on the characteristics of the harping tradition in his arrangements. The pieces in the 1796 collection were either collected at the 1792 Harp Festival, or on subsequent trips to counties Tyrone and Londonderry in Ulster and to Connaught, and, as Colette Moloney points out, this volume 'is perhaps the most authentic of the three in that it has the least amount of editorial intervention.'[19] Although Bunting arranged a number of the tunes from the harping tradition, there are relatively few 'basses' to be found in his manuscripts or edited collections that are explicitly transcribed from harpers' performances. A small number of the transcriptions in Bunting Manuscript 29 held by the library of Queen's University, Belfast – a volume begun by Bunting in 1792 and finished in 1805 according to an inscription on its front end-paper – do contain indications of what appear to be basses. For example, 'The Banks of Claudy' on page 3, 'Burn's March' on pages 30–1, 'Callena Vacca Sheo Shurse' on page 46, 'Callena Vacca' on page 48, 'Lady of the Desert' on page 52, 'Veaaghan Gleash' on pages 54–5, 'First Part of a Veaaghan Gleash' on pages 56–7, and 'John Scotts [*sic*] Lamentation' on page 158 all feature such indications.[20] However, the vast majority of the transcriptions give little impression that Bunting was concerned to record details of accompaniment or other aspects of performance practice from musicians. Those which do exist (in the later volumes and the manuscript sources) are of two main types, heterophonic ones in which the bass part runs parallel to, or incorporates, the melody, and 'tonic-drones' based around inversions of the tonic chord.[21] According to Moloney, Bunting's main changes to his manuscript sources fall into three types: the adaptation of modal tunes to conform to the major-minor tonal system; the alteration of melodies for harmonic reasons; and the omission of ornaments noted in his draft notations.[22]

Riada should choose to return to the harpsichord in the 1960s as a replacement for the harp in his arrangements for Ceoltóirí Chualann.   **18** A pirated edition which was published by W. Power & Co. of Dublin forms the first part of an edition containing all three Bunting volumes, titled *The ancient music of Ireland*, published by Waltons Publishing in 1969 and reprinted in 2002. This appears to have originally been printed between 1807 and 1826 (see Moloney, *The Irish music manuscripts*, p. 162). It contains many inaccuracies, transposes the order of two of the pieces, and omits a large number of markings of dynamics and articulations.   **19** Moloney, *The Irish music manuscripts*, p. 58.   **20** Page numbers refer to the markings which appear on the manuscript and not to the numbers given in Moloney's index. See the Bunting Collection in the Digital Image Library of the Special Collections at QUL. Bunting's spelling is given here.   **21** See Moloney, *The Irish music manuscripts*, pp 75–83.   **22** Ibid., p. 59.

Example 4.1: 'A cha[i]linigh a bhfaca sibh Seorsa', the sixth tune from Bunting's 1796 volume in the Preston & Son edition.

Example 4.1 presents the sixth tune from the 1796 collection, 'A Cha[i]linigh a bhFaca Sibh Seorsa[?]' or 'Girls Have You Seen George?', which clearly exhibits both of these practices. In fact, the lower stave of the first two bars simultaneously involves a melodic doubling and an implied tonic chord drone in E minor whose archaic quality is to a degree undermined by the fairly conventional harmonisation and cadential structure of bars 4–8 (IV–I–V–I–V–I in G major). Heterophony is re-established in bars 13–18 and 21–4, and Bunting avoids the temptation to end with a facile perfect cadence. An even simpler application of the tonic drone technique is seen in number 50, 'Is Iombo Éru [Is Im Bó agus Eiriu] &cc' ('An Irish Lullaby'), in which a hexatonic melody is accompanied throughout by repeated octave Gs in dotted minims.

In the main, however, Bunting's harmonisation and accompaniment strategies are consistent with conventional late-eighteenth-century art-music practice, particularly that exemplified by Haydn and Pleyel, both of whose compositions appear in handwritten arrangements by Bunting in MS 20 of the Bunting Irish Music Manuscripts, dated by Colette Moloney between c.1796 and c.1798.[23] A

---

[23] Ibid., p. 29. It is worth remembering that George Thomson employed Pleyel as one of the arrangers of

diatonic framework is generally assumed, with conjunct motion in thirds and sixths, broken-chord accompaniment patterns, and strongly goal-orientated harmony reinforced by the frequent use of secondary dominant chords. By noting these characteristics it is not intended to suggest that such techniques were necessarily antithetical to practices of at least some of the traditional musicians whose performances Bunting recorded. It seems that many of these were influenced by contemporary taste; and as Arthur O'Neill, one of the performers at the 1792 festival, remarks:

> There is a great deal of ancient Irish music lost in consequence of the attachment harpers latterly have for modern tunes, and which is what is now chiefly in vogue: the national tunes and airs being confined only, I may say, to a few gentlemen in the different provinces I have travelled through. And, without the most distant idea of any view or interest, I here declare that if it was not in consequence of the unprecedented and, I may truly say, inspired and spirited conduct of a gentleman of Belfast whose name I will have occasion to mention before I conclude this poor production [Edward Bunting], that I again repeat it – that if it was not for his exertions the compositions of a Dibdin and some other composers of similar productions would in a very few years be a very great means of annihilating our dear Irish music.[24]

O'Neill writes of meeting Bunting in Newry some time after the Harp Festival[25] and of the former playing to him 'Speic Seóigh[e]ach' (or 'Joice's Tune' as it appears in the 1796 collection) on the piano.[26] Although it is very possible that the version played by Bunting to O'Neill on that occasion differed from the one he published in 1796, it is of interest that O'Neill makes no comment on Bunting's style of performance. The first three harmonic events of his setting, a solid $F - G^7 - C$ ($I - V^7$ of V – V) progression supporting the pitches $F_5 - D_5 - C_5$, do not reveal a particular sensitivity to the underlying pentatonicism of the melody, and his approach throughout the rest of the arrangement is unambiguously diatonic. Several chords are arpeggiated (indicated by a vertical curved line), presumably in deference to the harp, but despite this it is idiomatically conceived for the piano.[27]

While allowance must be made for Bunting's relative youth and inexperience (he was only 23 in 1796 when *A General Collection of the Ancient Irish Music*

A Select Collection of Original Scotish [sic] *Airs for the Voice with Introductory & Concluding Symphonies & Accompaniments for the Pianoforte, Violin & Violoncello By Pleyel, Kozeluch & Haydn with Select and Characteristic Verses* (London: Preston, 1793). **24** Donal O'Sullivan, *Carolan: the life, times and music of an Irish harper*, new edition (Cork: Ossian Publications, 2001), Part Four, 'The memoirs of Arthur O'Neill', p. 319. **25** Or 'ball' as he describes it, thinking perhaps of the three 'Granard balls' held in Granard, Co. Longford in 1781, 1782 and 1785. **26** Here and on a number of occasions, Bunting fails to follow the rule of vowel placement in Irish of *caol le caol agus leathan le leathan* (slender with slender and broad with broad). **27** Clive Brown has noted (personal communication) that arpeggiation was widely used in keyboard performance in the period, and thus arpeggio signs may indicate special cases

was published), and for the embryonic state of musical historiography at the time, the ahistoricism of his conception of harmony is noticeable here. In his introduction he remarks that:

> it was discovered that the *most* ancient tunes were, in this respect, the most perfect, admitting of the addition of a Bass with much more facility than such as were less ancient. Hence we may conclude, that their authors must necessarily have been excellent performers, versed in the scientific part of their profession, and that they had originally a view to the addition of *harmony* in the composition of their pieces.[28]

Bunting seems to have regarded 'Thugamar Féin a[n] Samhra[dh] Lin[n]' ('We Brought the Summer with Us') and 'Tá an Samhradh [ag] Teacht' ('The Summer Is Coming') as being particularly 'ancient' tunes, and noted that 'the words of *Coolin* were extant in the reign of Henry VIII [1509–47] a very modern period when compared with that in which the air was composed', suggesting a credibly historical notion of antiquity.[29] For Bunting, the first setting in the collection, 'Ad Ccoigreach [Coigríoch] Má Bin Tú' ('If to a Foreign Clime You Go'), was the 'oldest melody extant', the only evidence for which assertion seems to have been the age of the performer and the unfamiliarity of others in the audience with the air.

Despite the purported antiquity of these three melodies, Bunting's approach remains decidedly contemporary: the harmonisation is goal oriented and diatonic, the tonality is unequivocally major and the harmonic palette is in general restricted to tonic, subdominant and dominant chords. When compared with, for example, the approach taken by Domenico Corri in *A Select Collection of the Most Admired Songs, Duets &c.* (1788), volumes one and two of which seem to have been in Bunting's possession at some time in his life, it will be seen that they reflect a common late-eighteenth-century taste and musical manners.[30] Strangely, for Bunting the 'ancient' Irish music's apparent potential for contemporary harmonization demarcated a subsequent state of decay from 'perfection', the few surviving tunes being 'the wreck of better times, the history of which is either lost, or incorrectly recognised, in a confused series of traditions'.[31]

Petrie's pen portrait of Bunting published in the *Dublin University Magazine* in January 1847 refers to the relative failure of the first volume of *Ancient Irish Music* to appeal to the Anglo-Irish aristocracy, until its mediation by Thomas Moore and John Stevenson:

---

which might not have been arpeggiated as a matter of course. **28** Edward Bunting, *A general collection of the ancient music of Ireland, arranged for the piano forte* (London: Clementi & Company, 1809), p. ii. Bunting's emphasis. **29** Ibid., p. iv. **30** His copies were bequeathed by Charlotte Milligan Fox to QUL in 1916. See Moloney, *The Irish music manuscripts*, p. 159. These sets contain a number of arrangements of songs by Dibdin. **31** Bunting, *A general collection*, p. ii.

Of the popular success of this collection, Bunting himself has spoken but moderately; and, indeed, though it may have had a tolerable sale in his own immediate locality of Belfast, and among the patriotic portion of the middle classes elsewhere in Ireland, we have strong reasons for believing that it never, to any extent, found its way into the houses of the higher orders; and hence the feelings of surprise at the novelty as well as of admiration of the beauty of these melodies experienced by the public generally when they were reproduced by Moore, and forced upon their attention by the fascination of the songs to which he united them.[32]

In the subtitle to his second volume, *A General Collection of the Ancient Music of Ireland: Arranged for the Piano Forte* (1809), a much more expensive volume than the first, retailing at £1 6s., as opposed to 10s. 6d., Bunting indicates that it contains 'some of the most admired melodies are adapted for the voice, to poetry chiefly translated from the original Irish songs by Thomas Campbell, esq., and other eminent poets: to which is prefixed a historical & critical dissertation on the Egyptian, British and Irish harp'.[33] The epigraph to the preface chains together, without acknowledgment and with one slight misreading, quotations from three of Macpherson's Ossianic poems – 'Carric-thura', 'The Night-Song of the Bards' and 'Carthon':

> [O] Bards of other times! Ye, on whose souls the blue host of our fathers rise! strike the harp in my hall; and let me [Fingal] hear the song. Pleasant is the joy of grief; it is like the shower of spring when it softens the branch of the oak, and the young leaf rears its green head. ['Carric-thura', 158]. Raise the song, and strike the harp; send round the shells of joy … Let some grey bard be near me to tell the deeds of other times; of kings renowned in our land, of chiefs we behold no more. ['The Night-Song of the Bards', published in the notes to 'Croma' as an example of what is purported to be much more recent verse than Ossian on similar themes, 192]. Such was the song of Fingal in the day of his joy. His thousand bards leaned forward from their seats, to hear the voice of the king. ['Carthon', 129].[34]

Bunting's quotation stops short at a curiously pregnant juncture, for the following non-cited line reads, rather appropriately given the context, 'it was like the music of the harp on the gale of the spring'.[35] That his second collection should be prefaced by this reference to antiquity through Ossian is perhaps surprising, given that Macpherson had long been discredited as the supposed translator of third-century Gaelic poems. Fiona Stafford has noted the poetry of Ossian is in fact a

---

[32] Petrie, 'Our Portrait Gallery', 69.   [33] Bunting, *A general collection*, p. iii. This is actually marked 'Vol: 1st' on the title page.   [34] Page references are to James Mcpherson, *The poems of Ossian and related works*, edited by Howard Gaskill with an introduction by Fiona Stafford (Edinburgh: Edinburgh University Press, 1996) [hereafter Macpherson/Stafford].   [35] Macpherson/Stafford, *The poems of Ossian*, p. 129.

more complex phenomenon than might be allowed by some critics who would simply see it as forgery, regarding it as 'less the work of an inexpert linguist, or an unscrupulous 'Scotsman on the make' than a sophisticated attempt to mediate between two apparently irreconcilable cultures'.[36] Such a case might equally be made for Bunting, for like Macpherson, he drew his material from an oral tradition, but fashioned the music to be congruent with contemporary taste and prevailing notions of antiquity. The 1809 volume was published one year after the first volume of Thomas Moore's *Irish Melodies* appeared, a volume of twelve songs which included seven tunes taken from Bunting's 1796 collection. In his earlier sets of *Irish Melodies*, Moore employed the Dublin composer Sir John Stevenson as his musical arranger. Stevenson's approach has sometimes been described as stylistically influenced by Haydn, a not unreasonable assertion although Haydn's earliest set of 'Scots' song arrangements, published by William Napier in 1792, seems somewhat old fashioned and foursquare in style when compared with Stevenson's.[37] Haydn's arrangements are scored for voice, violin and continuo, and have a keyboard part that does not appear to be idiomatically conceived for a modern hammered instrument and still employs figured bass.

Bunting rehearsed again his notion that 'the most ancient tunes were, in this respect, the most perfect, admitting of the addition of a bass with more facility than such as were less ancient' in his preface to the second volume. While acknowledging his familiarity with the art music of Italy and Germany, he suggests that 'where public taste is *pure*, the original music of Ireland will be heard with delight'.[38] The 'historical and critical dissertation on the harp' that follows certainly gives the impression that this is to be a work of scholarship rather than a collection of favourite country dances of the type which regularly appeared in the period, but despite this and the verse translations from Irish of Mary Balfour, Dean Swift, Dr William Drennan and others, Bunting's basic approach to the arrangement of the melodies offers even more concessions to bourgeois taste than did the first volume.

In the spirit of the arrangements by Pleyel, Kozeluch and Haydn in George Thomson's *A Select Collection of Original Scotish* [sic] *Airs*, the opening volume of which first appeared in 1793 (see footnote 23), Bunting employs rather elaborate 'introductory and concluding symphonies' – instrumental preludes and postludes – for the songs in the album. Thomson remarks in the preface to his own 1803 edition that 'the symphonies form an introduction and conclusion to the airs, so characteristic, so elegant, and so delightful, and comprise such a rich collection of new and original pieces, that they must be regarded by every musical amateur as an invaluable appendage to the airs'.[39] Thomson goes on to

36 Ibid., p. viii.   **37** For example, in W.H. Carr/W.H. Grattan Flood and Bruce Carr, 'Stevenson, Sir John (Andrew)', *NG II*, xxiv, 378, and in James W. Flannery's *Dear harp of my country: the Irish melodies of Thomas Moore* (Nashville: J.S. Sanders & Company, 1997), where the author remarks that 'Stevenson destroyed the character of many of the airs, especially the older pieces, with stiff piano accompaniments replete with florid introductory "symphonies" that owe more to a watered-down Haydn than to anything in the Irish tradition', p. 101.   **38** Bunting, *A general collection*, p. iii.   **39** George Thomson, *A select*

indicate the musical limitations of his target audience in his note that 'instead of a Thorough-bass denoted by *figures*, which very few can play with any propriety, the harmony is plainly expressed in musical Notes, which every young Lady may execute correctly'.[40]

While tunes had been presented without lyrics or instrumental frames in Bunting's first volume, to be played rather than sung, the 1809 collection looks to a similar market to that of Moore's *Irish Melodies* and Thomson's collections, albeit the songs are interspersed with purely instrumental numbers. Lyrics are presented in English translation throughout, the Irish language being reserved for the titles. Harry White has discussed the circumstances of the exclusion of the Irish texts collected by his collaborator Patrick Lynch from the volume, and suggests that this was probably due to Bunting's antipathy towards Lynch who had turned King's evidence against the United Irishman Thomas Russell (librarian of the Belfast Society for Promoting Knowledge) in 1803.[41]

Example 4.2 illustrates the opening 'symphony' and the first five bars of the vocal melody of the song 'A Phlur na Maighdion' [A Phlúr na Maighdean] ('Thou Flower of Virgins'), whose text by Drennan, is specially 'written for this work, from a literal translation of the original Irish'.[42] The 'symphony' is idiomatically conceived for the piano, and draws on such classical mannerisms as the horn fifths in the right hand in the first bar, the doubling in thirds between bars two and three, the chromatic slide on the last beat of bar 3, and the underlying tonic and dominant harmony; the ornamentation provided by the trills, turn, abrupt arpeggio, melodic fiorituri and accented cadential appoggiaturas in the bass look particularly to the slow movements of Haydn and Clementi piano sonatas. It might even be suggested that the pianistic style is prescient of the nocturnes of John Field.

'A Phlur na Maighdion' is the only song to be offered as an optional vocal duet (a characteristic that underlines its domestic role), and is certainly one of the more elaborate arrangements in the collection, but Bunting demonstrates equally his debt to contemporary art-music practice in many of the other songs. The graceful prelude to 'Eilighe Gheal Chiun' [Eilí Gheal Chiúin] ('The Charming Fair Eily') sports what might be seen as Mozartian broken chord figuration in its melodic balancing of tonic and dominant harmony, and the chromaticism of 'Bhfear Liom na Eire' ('I Would Rather than Ireland'), with its Neapolitan sixth cadential inflections looks to the Mozart of the C minor piano concerto K. 491 and Requiem. While 'Oganaighe Oig' ('The Captivating Youth'), 'An Cota Caol' ('The Slender Coat') and 'Anna na Geraoibh' ('Nancy of the Branching Tresses') undoubtedly exhibit the influence of Haydn and several composers of the London Pianoforte School, Bunting's sensitivity and sophistication should not be underestimated. The traditional performer may regard these arrangements as

---

collection of original Scottish airs for the voice (London: Preston, 1803), p. 1.   **40** Ibid., 1. Thomson's emphasis and upper casing is retained.   **41** White, *The keeper's recital*, p. 42.   **42** Bunting, *A general collection*, p. 22.

Example 4.2: 'A Phlur na Maighdion' from *A General Collection of the Ancient Music of Ireland* (1809)

musically and spiritually antithetical to the tradition from which they sprang, but in his best settings Bunting uses his resources competently and effectively (and often more creatively than Stevenson), and it is unreasonable to regard them as second-rate imitations of Haydn.

Undoubtedly residual traces of harp performance practice do remain in places in this volume. In 'Ím Bó agus Samha Bó' (or 'Burn's March'), for example, which Bunting explains is 'one of the progressive lessons taught young harpers & is the fourth tune generally learnt',[43] he has taken some liberties in terms of figuration and harmony, but these can be regarded as attempts to assimilate the harper's technique into that of the piano. 'Brighid Cruise' ('Bridget Cruise'), while adopting a conventional approach to the cadence over the final three bars, has a relatively simple left-hand part and avoids the broken-chord figures found in the accompaniments of many of the other songs and pieces. 'Maille Dheas Bhan' [Mailí Dheas Bhán] ('The Beauteous Fair Molly') employs a very simple rocking octave pedal motion in the bass, and 'Marcaigheacht in Boinne' ('The Cavalcade of the Boyne') has for the most part a minimal bass line. However, in other pieces, like 'Plangstigh Raighle' ('Planxty Reilly') and 'An tSheann Bheann

---

[43] In item 18 from Manuscript 33 (3) of the Bunting manuscripts, Moloney, *The Irish music manuscripts*, p. 390. See QUL, Special Collections, Manuscript Collections MS 4/29.

Bhocht' [An tSean Bhean Bhocht] ('The [Poor] Old Woman'), especially in the contrapuntal left hand in bars 8–16, Bunting relies more on standard art-music harmonic practices of the period in terms of harmony and texture. In the latter, the written out repeat of the first half of the tune is treated as a two-part invention.

The twenty-eight pages of scholarly introductory material which preface the 1809 collection are dwarfed by the hundred-page 'Dissertation on the Irish Harp and Harping' that opens the 1840 volume of Bunting's *The Ancient Music of Ireland*. This contains essays by Bunting and Samuel Ferguson (the latter including a contribution from George Petrie), and includes a vocabulary of general musical and specific harping terms in Irish, as well as nineteen pages of 'notices of the more remarkable pieces and melodies of the collection'. In his preface, Bunting expounds his curious view (later challenged by Petrie in the introduction to his 1855 collection) of the invariability of traditional melody – that unlike poetry, which is subject to corruption and interpolation, 'a strain of music, once impressed on the popular ear, never varies'.[44] Melodies have, Bunting asserts, been preserved 'in their integrity from the earliest periods' by an intuitive and unconscious assimilation that resists structural modifications. Alterations have been introduced by those who have not heard melodies 'in their original state', such as Moore's collaborator, Stevenson, but 'so long as the musical collector or antiquary confines his search to the native districts of the tunes he seeks for, he may always be certain of the absolute and unimpeachable authenticity of every note he procures'.[45] Bunting summarily dismisses the suggestion made by Moore in the preface to his third volume of *Irish Melodies* of the relative modernity of many the 'finest airs'.

Although Bunting claims that his object 'chiefly is to give the remaining airs of the collection arranged in *true* harp style, for the piano forte', his view of the antiquity and authenticity of the melodies would seem to be at odds with many of his arrangements.[46] In the first chapter of his dissertation ('Of the Characteristics of Irish Melody'), as well as expounding his view of the 'emphatic Major Sixth' as a primary melodic marker of Irishness,[47] he proposes certain structural features 'more observable in the very old class of airs', namely that:

- they are in a major key and in triple time;
- they are in four sections (ABB¹A);
- the second section generally lies in the upper octave relative to the first;
- the cadential structure of the four sections is I – V – IV (or VI) – I.[48]

---

[44] Bunting, *The ancient music of Ireland, arranged for the piano forte* (Dublin: Hodges & Smith, 1840), p. 1. [45] Ibid., p. 2. [46] Ibid., p. 6. [47] The notion is dismissed by Petrie as follows: 'that such tone is indeed a characteristic one, both of Irish and Scottish melodies, I by no means deny; but I cannot concur with Mr Bunting that it is an essential, or even the most characteristic feature of a true Irish melody.' George Petrie, *The Petrie collection of the ancient music of Ireland*, ed. David Cooper (Cork: Cork University Press, 2002). [48] Bunting, *The ancient music of Ireland*, p. 16.

David Cooper 87

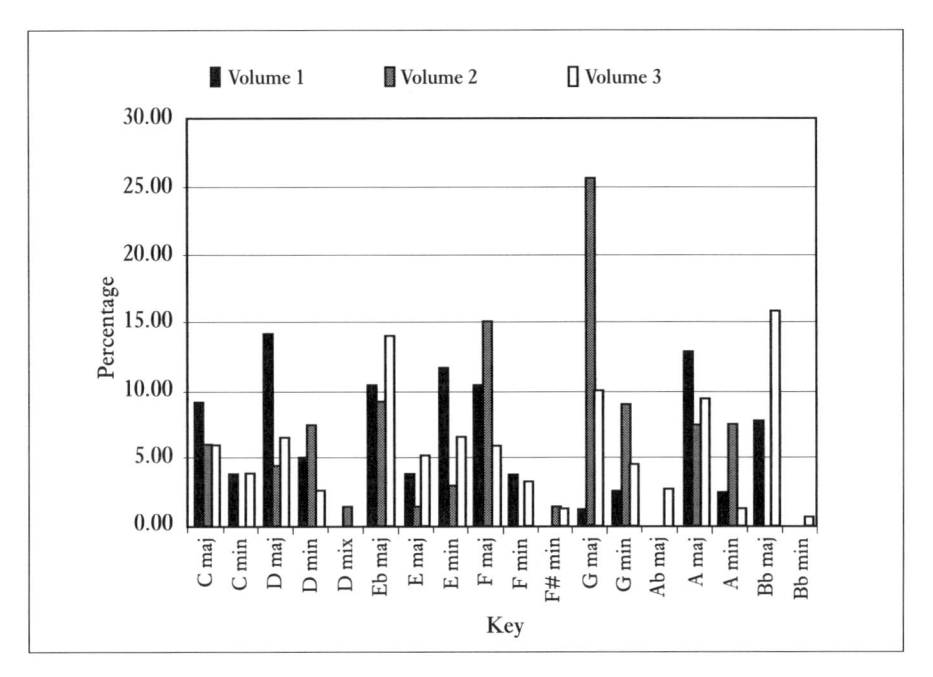

Figure 4.2: Distribution of Pieces by Tonality in the Three Bunting Volumes.

This final point, which clearly presumes a modern, functional approach to the harmonic underpinning of tunes from the distant past, is correlated by Bunting, in a rather wild leap of imagination, to the use of the terms *diapente* (a perfect fifth or 3:2 harmonic ratio) as dominant, and *diatessaron* (a perfect fourth or 4:3 harmonic ratio) as subdominant, by Giraldus Cambrensis (1146–1223) in his *Topographia Hiberniae*.[49] Bunting's comprehension of modulation is certainly at odds with the conception of the term in eleventh- and twelfth-century Britain, where the Latin modulatio indicated a rhythmic measure.

Similarly at variance with post-revival conceptions of traditional practice is the range of keys employed by Bunting, both in this volume and the preceding pair. Figure 4.2 illustrates graphically the percentages of the different tonalities used,[50]

49 Giraldus Cambrensis, translated by Thomas Forester, revised and edited with additional notes by Thomas Wright, *The topography of Ireland* (Cambridge, Ontario: In parentheses publications, 2000). Cambrensis actually notes that 'it is astonishing that in so complex and rapid a movement of the fingers, the musical proportions can be preserved, and that throughout the difficult modulations on their various instruments, the harmony is completed with such a sweet velocity, so unequal an equality, so discordant a concord, as if the chords sounded together fourths or fifths', p. 71. **50** The correlation between Volume One and Volume Two is 0.132, between volume two and volume three 0.545, and between Volume Two and Volume Three 0.284. Although cross tabulation would have provided another appropriate statistical measure, it was felt that the normalization of data sets as percentages indicates more clearly the relative importance afforded to particular keys at the various stages of Bunting's career. However, it is arguable that the absolute numbers as well as relative proportions in any key offers important information, and the

and a characteristic that can be observed in the distribution of flat keys. More than forty percent of the pieces in Bunting's third volume are in the keys of C, F and B♭ minor, and E♭, A♭ and B♭ major. This compares with just thirteen percent in these keys in the 1803 edition of Thomson's *A Select Collection of Original Scottish Airs*. Of course, the range of keys conventionally employed by traditional musicians is driven by exigencies such as string tuning (harp), restrictions of finger position and exploitation of open strings (fiddle), and avoidance of cross fingering (flute), rather than a music-theoretical rationale. Although a collector with absolute pitch might have, for example, notated in E♭ a performance nominally in D major on a violin tuned a semitone sharp, for the non-musically literate musician working within an oral tradition, the key signature would have been an irrelevance.

Perhaps more significant with regard to the range of keys employed by Bunting is the art music practice of the period. A casual perusal of *Sources of Irish Traditional Music c.1600–1855* demonstrates that key signatures of F and B♭ major, and D and G minor, are relatively common in the works referenced by Fleischmann up to 1796. The keys used by Bunting in his 1796 collection, in which E♭ major and F minor in particular become more significant, are strongly correlated to the tonalities of Haydn's sonatas, partitas and divertimentos for solo keyboard written between around 1766 and 1795.[51] Equally, the tonics of the outer movements of Beethoven's thirty-two piano sonatas, composed between 1793 and 1822, lie almost entirely within the range of keys employed by Bunting (only the C# minor op. 27/2 and F# major op. 78 fall outside this range), and there is a moderately strong correlation between the percentages of keys employed across the two repertoires. If the tonics of all the individual movements of the Beethoven sonatas and the tonalities of all the pieces in the three Bunting collections are compared, an even stronger correlation is found.[52] It is probably fair to say that Bunting's tonal mindset was aligned to the art-music models which achieved particular prominence in Britain and Ireland during the period in which he was working.

Of course, the piano of the late 1830s presented a significant advance in terms of tone production from that of 1796, mainly as a result of thicker strings under higher tension and heavier hammers of the later instrument. Capable of a wider range of timbre and dynamics and more resonant than its predecessors, articulation required greater physical effort than the fortepiano and early square piano. Whereas Bunting's use of articulation, ornamentation and dynamic markings in his second volume does not differ dramatically from the first, with relatively widespread use of the accent, staccato dot and stroke, and short slur, the third volume demonstrates a visibly new approach from the opening number (example 4.3).

---

approach of using percentages masks this. For example, in Volume 1, eight tunes (10.39%), in Volume 2, ten tunes (15.15%), and in Volume 3, nine tunes (5.96%) are in F major. **51** The correlation coefficient in this case is 0.746. **52** The correlation coefficient is 0.733.

[Musical score: "Sit Down Under My Protection", By Maclael, ♩=104, or Pendulum 11 Inches. Moderately Quick. Very Ancient, Author and date unknown.]

Example 4.3: 'Sit Down Under My Protection' from *The Ancient Music of Ireland* (1840).

The principle innovations are the widespread use of portato (notated using slurred dots as in the left hand of example 4.3 from bars 2–9), notes with strokes slurred together (as in the right hand of bar 1), and rests to increase the clarity of articulation. It is tempting to assume that the plethora of sometimes contradictory markings is the caprice of an overenthusiastic engraver trying to make most inventive use of his punches, but it seems from evidence in MSS 12 and 13 of the Irish music manuscripts of Edward Bunting held by Queen's University, Belfast as transcribed by Moloney, that these do represent Bunting's intentions. These two manuscripts contain handwritten piano arrangements in Bunting's and an unknown copyist's hand, which are very similar to those that appear in print in 1840, and Moloney suggests that they are likely to have been made in preparation for this publication.[53]

Clive Brown has made a very detailed examination of the notation of articulation and phrasing in his study *Classical and Romantic Performing Practice 1750–1900*, in which he notes that 'there has been little consensus even in the matter of which composers used both dots and strokes to mean different things and which used a single mark with a more variable meaning'.[54] For many

---

[53] Moloney, *The Irish music manuscripts*, p. 36.   [54] Clive Brown, *Classical and romantic performing practice, 1750–1900* (Oxford: Oxford University Press, 1999), p. 201. See also Clive Brown, 'Dots and strokes in Late 18th- and 19th-century music', *Early Music*, 21:4 (1993), 593–597 and 599–610.

Example 4.4a: The opening of Hempson's performance of 'Scott's Lamentation' as transcribed by Bunting.

composers it seems there was scant distinction in meaning between the two forms of the symbol, whether indicating staccato on unslurred notes or portato on slurred ones, though as Brown notes, Haydn did differentiate between slurred strokes and dots in the Trio section of the Minuet of his String Quartet op. 77 no. 1.[55] Even allowing for the fact that Bunting may not have been intending such a refined level of nuance as Haydn was apparently describing, the detail is striking, if at times almost absurd. In the second piece, 'Lady Iveach', 'dotted' portato appears in the right hand against slurred strokes in the left (bars 17, 19, 25 and 27); in 'The Blackbird and the Thrush', slurred strokes are found above stroked quavers separated by quaver rests; and in 'Huish the Cat' quavers have strokes and crotchets, dots. Perhaps most curious of all, in 'Scott's Lamentation for the Baron of Loughmoe' (see example 4.4b), three staccato quavers separated by rests are slurred together.[56] In general, it seems possible that for Bunting the stroke indicated a rather shorter staccato than the dot, in line with the usage advocate by pedagogues such as the French piano teacher Jean Louis Adam.[57]

If Bunting really performed the pieces in the way he appears to be indicating, it suggests an approach to touch and sonority of remarkable variety, though fussiness. It may be he felt that the articulations helped the pianist to emulate the 'true' sound of the harp (though of the vocabulary of the harp on pages 20–8,

---

[55] Brown, *Classical and romantic performing practice*, p. 250. See also the reference to Haydn's Concertante in B♭, H I:105 in Brown, 'Dots and Strokes', 606.   [56] Though such slurred staccato notes separated by rests are used, for example, by Beethoven.   [57] Brown, *Classical and romantic performing practice*, p. 216.

Example 4.4b: The start of Bunting's arrangement of 'Scott's Lamentation for the Baron of Loughmoe'.

only in the ascending and descending glissandi described as Sruith-mor are slurred groups of staccato dotted notes shown), particularly that of harpist Denis Hempson, who in the old Gaelic art-music tradition still played with long curled fingernails and of whom Bunting writes:

> he had an admirable way of playing *Staccato* and *Legato*, in which he could run through rapid divisions in astonishing style ... The intricacy and peculiarity of his playing often amazed the Editor, who could not avoid perceiving in it vestiges of a noble system of practice, that had existed for many centuries; strengthening the opinion, that the Irish were, at a very early period, superior to the other nations of Europe, both in the composition and performance of music.[58]

Bunting presents a piano arrangement of 'Scott's Lamentation' 'as originally performed by Hempson on the Irish harp' between pages 88 and 89 of the dissertation (see example 4.4a), and here almost the full array of articulatory symbols is used in an attempt, it seems, to indicate as authentically as possible Hempson's range of touch. But the detail also seems to suggest an effort to exhibit the pieces in a way that supports the 'scholarly' dissertation that prefaces the work. This associates the music with the apparatus of the 'elevated' art music of the day: the most ancient music of Ireland brought into conjunction with the most 'scientific' music of Europe.

58 Bunting, *The ancient music of Ireland*, p. 73.

Bunting's arrangement (example 4.4b) transforms the lament, which in the 'transcription' of Hempson's performance is largely performed in parallel motion or heterophony, not simply by the modern harmonisation which becomes considerably more dissonant and abrasive as the piece progresses, but by the subtle reworking of the articulation and phrasing. Almost all of the markers of Gaelic antiquity and harp performing practice identified by Bunting have been suppressed in the interests of contemporary musical taste.

Subsequent to Bunting's editions, a number of other collectors and editors offered arrangements of Irish melodies for the piano, including: the artist and antiquarian George Petrie's *The Petrie Collection of the Ancient Music of Ireland* (1855); the philologist and polymath Patrick Joyce's *Ancient Irish Music*, harmonized by Professor J.W. Glover (1872); and Francis Hoffmann's *Ancient Music of Ireland from the Petrie Collection* (1877). Petrie's arrangements, written in the large by his eldest daughter, are generally more musically neutral and passive than those of Bunting, and while clearly being modelled on those in his collections offer a less sophisticated approach to the piano. Petrie remarks in the introduction to his 1855 volume that:

> I might have made this volume one of far higher musical pretensions, and probably, popular interest, by intrusting the harmonization of the airs to professional musicians of known ability, many of whom I am proud to rank amongst the number of my friends. But I knew of none, at least within the latter circle, who had devoted any particular study to the peculiarities of structure and tonalities which so often distinguish our melodies from those of modern times, and I consequently feared that harmonies of a learned and elaborate nature, constructed with a view to the exhibition of scientific knowledge, as well as the gratification of conventional tastes, might often appear to me unsuited to the simple character and peculiar expression of the airs, and require me either to adopt what I might not approve, or, by the exercise of a veto, which would have the appearance of assumption, involve me in collisions which I should desire to avoid.[59]

The use of articulation marks in particular is rationalized, and only dots are used to indicate staccato and portato (the latter more sparingly employed than by Bunting). Accompaniments are, as Petrie suggests, less 'scientific' than utilitarian, with voice leading seldom more complex than might have been found in hymn-tune harmonizations, and this tends to lend them a rather earnest, even pious quality.

Francis Hoffmann's settings of 201 tunes taken from Petrie's collection of more than 2,000 melodies in manuscript show even less interest in demonstrating 'scientific knowledge' and look to a more popular market than Petrie's 1855 collection, with its elaborate scholarly 'notices' on individual tunes. The niceties

---

[59] George Petrie, *The Petrie collection of the ancient music of Ireland* (Dublin: The University Press, 1855), p. xix.

of touch that Petrie retains are largely absent here and harmonizations are, by and large, even simpler. Glover's arrangements in Joyce's *Ancient Irish Music* are sparser still, with neither phrasing nor dynamics, an approach to harmony that at times reduces it to a simple interplay between tonic and dominant chords, and a tendency to employ drones and pedal tones that arguably brings the arrangements closer to the practice of traditional musicians. Glover, in terms that both echo and extend those of Petrie, notes in a letter to Joyce:

> As you have confided to me the task of clothing your Irish tunes in suitable harmonies, I think it necessary to mention that simple as the task may seem, it required some discrimination. Some of the tunes are regular, and subject to the rules of counterpoint; others are wild and desultory, and such as do not readily admit the accompaniment of a bass: while many again are of a mixed kind, partaking of both these characteristics. In giving them suitable harmonies, I have been guided by the obvious principle of not attempting a harmony when doing so would injure the character of the tune, as in case of the Keens and Lullabies. In tunes partaking of the mixed character, I have found it expedient to vary the treatment, so as to be in keeping with the melody; for in many tunes of this class the point and interest lies in a few notes occasionally at the end of each part. In such tunes, by alternating a simple harmony with a bit of vigorous unison – so that the point of the melody will be readily understood – the character of the music is more distinctively preserved. I have avoided all abstruse treatment as out of place; and I have merely endeavoured to give the melodies such natural harmonies as will be in accordance with their character, and at the same time will enable them to be readily caught up by the popular ear, and to be retained there.[60]

With Joyce's and Glover's arrangements, the music begins its return from the sitting rooms of the gentry and middle classes described in Jane Austen's *Emma*, where popular melody sat with the art music of Cramer and Clementi, Pleyel and Kozeluch, Mozart and Haydn, to the vernacular of the peasantry and working classes; from the Gaelic enthusiasms of the Anglo-Irish study to the political activism of Conradh na nGaeilge and eventually Sinn Féin. The piano had developed dramatically in expressive power over the eighty-odd years between Bunting's 1796 and Joyce's 1872 collections of *Ancient Irish Music*, but in Joyce's it recedes into the background, no longer the vehicle of the high-art aspirations of Bunting who saw in his arrangements the synthesis of ancient Gaelic and modern European practices.

---

60 P.W. Joyce, *Ancient Irish music* (Dublin: McGlashan & Gill, 1873), pp iv–v.

Irish folk music collectors of the early nineteenth century: pioneer musicologists

JIMMY O'BRIEN MORAN

The purpose of this essay is to explore some of the attitudes and methodologies of the early nineteenth-century collectors of Irish folk music in order to trace the development of a scholarly and musicological approach.

There are certain parallels between music and archaeology, and collectors and antiquarians often met with some surprise if not resistance when the fruits of their labours confirmed the existence of a sophisticated society in Ireland prior to colonization.

The nineteenth century was one of great change, the middle of which was marked by the catastrophic Great Famine of 1845–9. Shortly afterwards, in 1851, the Society for the Preservation and the Publication of the Melodies of Ireland (SPPMI) was founded. This society was significant in that it epitomized many of the attitudes and interests of these early collectors which differed considerably from those of collectors in the latter part of the century. Its first task was to publish the collection of its president, George Petrie. In a way, the society heralded the end of an era as it folded in 1855 or 1856 with the publication of its first volume, *Ancient Music of Ireland*. Many of the melodies sent to the society by members from around the country had been collected before the Famine and the remainder during or shortly afterwards. This material presents a window through which to view the tradition and its performance practice in that period.

These early nineteenth-century collectors were among Ireland's intellectual and social elite. It is worth noting that two thirds of the council of the SPPMI were members of the Royal Irish Academy. They could not be considered folk musicians although many undoubtedly played arrangements of folk melodies. In general, their musical background and training was in the classical tradition. They were motivated by a love of the music fuelled by patriotic and sometimes nationalist zeal. Unlike the collectors in the latter part of the century they were not, in general, 'of the people'.[1] Nor was their published work intended for the folk from whom it was collected which, again, was in contrast to the later collectors. However, this serves to highlight the great social changes that took place in second half of the nineteenth century.

The term 'great collectors' appears to have been coined by collector, piper and Irish music historian, Breandán Breathnach (1912–85) to describe those who

---

1 Of the later collectors, Francis O'Neill was an accomplished traditional flute player, while James Goodman, although from a family of Anglican ministers, was a native Irish speaker, sang Irish songs and played the pipes. Another distinguishing feature of these later collectors was that they did not indulge in

compiled substantial collections of folk melodies. Beginning with Edward Bunting (1773–1843), Breathnach included George Petrie (1790–1866), the Hudson brothers, William (1796–1853) and Henry (1798–1889), William Forde (c.1795–1850), John Edward Pigot (1822–71) and Patrick Weston Joyce (1827–1914). He also included the later collectors such as James Goodman (1828–96), Francis O'Neill (1848–1936) and Francis Roche (1866–1961) within the group. Although part of Joyce's collection was published by Petrie in some ways he belongs to the latter group in that, socially, he was closer to the music and much of his publishing was done in the late nineteenth and early twentieth century.[2] It is not certain if he played an instrument but his home place in Glenosheen, Co. Limerick, 'was the home of music and song'.[3] Like the earlier collectors he indulged in some analysis of the music but it is largely based on the work of Petrie whose friendship he particularly valued. The market target for his publications appears to have been the ordinary people who had benefited economically and socially from the changes that took place in the latter part of the century.

The lack of interest in collecting texts on the part of the collectors of melody may relate to their limited or inadequate knowledge of the Irish language. However, Bunting considered the texts to have such a value as to personally pay for them to be collected. The 'historian of Galway', James Hardiman (1782–1855) had a collection of song texts, as well as a collection of airs, although this appears to number less than 100.

The criteria for inclusion among this group are varied. Some collectors transcribed hundreds of melodies while others transcribed considerably less but copied extensively from printed and manuscript collections. Some collected to preserve the music while others collected solely with a view to publishing the material. These early collectors concerned themselves with music analysis while at the same time setting the music in piano arrangements, thereby widening the appeal of their publications to include drawing room performers as well as those with a scholarly interest in the music.

The origins of collecting folk music and folklore are often traced to the work of Bishop Thomas Percy whose *Reliques of Ancient English Poetry* (1765) inspired others to become collectors. However, the earliest collection of folk music to be printed in Ireland was *A Collection of the Most Celebrated Irish Tunes*, in 1724,[4] by Dublin music entrepreneurs John and William Neale, which predates the influence of Percy.

Irish folk melodies have been noticed in manuscript collections as early as the sixteenth century, such as in the *Dallis Lute Book* and the *Ballet Lute Book*.[5] Many Irish tunes are to be found in English publications, particularly those of the

---

the same type of analysis as the early collectors.   **2** Joyce published three collections: *Ancient Irish music* (Dublin: McGlashan & Gill, 1873); *Irish music and song* (Dublin: Gill & Son, 1888); *Old Irish folk music and songs* (Dublin: Longmans, Green & Co., 1909).   **3** Joyce, *Old Irish folk music and songs*, p. vii. **4** A facsimile of this volume was republished as *A collection of the most celebrated Irish tunes*, ed. Nicholas Carolan (Dublin: Irish Folk Song Society, 1986).   **5** Trinity College, Dublin, Dallis MS 410/1, Ballet MS D.1.21.

eighteenth century, through which numerous acculturated tunes of Scottish and English origin may also be traced.[6]

The harp tradition was in its death throes when some of the survivors gathered in Belfast for the Harp Festival in 1792. A very young Edward Bunting accepted the daunting challenge of transcribing the music from these performances, thus ensuring his place in the history of Irish folk music as well as sowing the seeds of a lifelong interest in Irish folk-music collecting. Bunting's work was also to have far-reaching consequences in terms of the inspiration it gave to prospective collectors such as George Petrie and William Forde in particular. Bunting published his first selection in 1796 and his second in 1809. In his dissertation on the harp, which appeared in the second volume, Bunting's list of references is impressive and includes Sir Charles Burney (1726–1814) and Sir John Hawkins (1719–89) among many others. A chain of influence can be traced from Bunting through Petrie, Forde and Joyce, to the collectors of the twentieth century.[7]

Petrie was a prominent figure among the early collectors. He approached the study of folk music in a manner parallel to that which he employed in archaeology. Petrie had emancipated Irish archaeology from its amateur antiquarian status through logical, scholarly enquiry and scientific methodology where, according to Herity and Eogan 'his clear-minded approach and ... logic helped to bring Irish antiquarianism from the extremes of the romantic phase into harmony with the more logical and scientific spirit of the nineteenth-century science'.[8] Indeed he viewed the study of folk music as a branch of archaeology, as he remarked in a letter to Lord Dunraven:

> it is my deliberate conviction that we possess nothing of the past so honourable to our national character, or – viewed as a branch of our archaeology – of greater importance to the history of the great Celtic race of mankind to which we chiefly belong.[9]

There is an impression that some of the collectors, and George Petrie in particular, felt they were preserving the culture on behalf of the 'folk' who did not fully appreciate it and were helpless to prevent its demise. In a somewhat longwinded passage he noted:

> In short, I could not but fear that I might be vainly labouring to cultivate mental fruit which, however indigenous to the soil, was yet too refined and delicate a flavour to be relished, or appreciated, by a people who had been, from adversities, long accustomed only to the use of food of a coarser and more exciting nature.[10]

[6] Aloys Fleischmann, *Sources of Irish traditional music* (London: Garland, 1998). [7] Joseph Raftery and David Greene, *Proceedings of the Royal Irish Academy*, 72 (Dublin: 1972). [8] Michael Herity and George Eogan, *Ireland in prehistory* (London: Routledge & Kegan Paul, 1977), p. 8. [9] William Stokes, *The life and labour in art and archaeology of George Petrie* (London: 1868), p. 373. [10] George Petrie, *The Petrie collection of the ancient music of Ireland* (Dublin: The University Press, 1855), p. xi.

In the introduction to his *Ancient Music of Ireland* Petrie admitted that he had some misgivings about how the work might be received by the narrow stratum of society who could afford it.

Elizabeth Crooke suggests that the Anglo-Irish, in the act of owning and preserving some of Ireland's past, justified their position as adopted Irishmen.[11] This can be clearly seen in the biting critique by Samuel Ferguson on James Hardiman's *Irish Minstrelsy* in the *Dublin University Magazine*. Although Ferguson focussed his criticism on the clumsy, unskilful translations chosen by Hardiman which, he felt, sadly misrepresented the beautiful originals, his primary objection was to Hardiman's Catholic and nationalist interpretation of the song texts which denied Protestants legitimacy in Ireland. Wayne E. Hall has outlined Ferguson's motivation thus:

> Ferguson sought to establish that Protestants loved and identified with Ireland as much as anyone did. Through their study, through their recovery of old "Irish" texts and their production of new ones, Protestants would thus also accumulate cultural authority with which to legitimize their political position, eventually to graduate out of their ascendancy role as alien usurpers and to earn a rightful place in Ireland's future.[12]

This concept of cultural authority clearly applied to the collection of folk music also and highlights the fact that there was a certain 'otherness' about the folk who shared the same island but inhabited a different world.

The melodies in the manuscript collections generally carry an attribution to the informant or to another collector as the source of the tune. This practice is to be found in the publications of Bunting and, to a much greater extent, Petrie. It is also commonly found in the collections of Hudson and Forde. The acknowledgment of other collectors as the source of material reveals a widespread interest and a web of collecting activity around the country. Moreover, the acknowledgment of the importance of the informant is noteworthy in a tradition that is generally perceived as anonymous. However, there has always been some recognition of the individual whether as composer or performer. The names of Ó Catháin, Carolan and Jackson immediately come to mind as composers while Hempson (or O'Hampsey) and Gandsey were celebrated as performers.

One musician who attracted the attention of several collectors was the blind Galway piper and singer, Paddy Conneely (*c*.1800–1851).[13] Conneely's rise to national prominence can be traced to an article by Petrie in his *Irish Penny*

---

11 Elizabeth Crooke, *Politics and archaeology ánd the creation of a National Museum of Ireland* (Dublin: Irish Academic Press, 2000), p. 70.   **12** Wayne E. Hall, *Dialogues in the margin* (Washington: Catholic University of America Press, 1999), p. 48.   **13** His surname was variously spelt in different sources and even by the same author on occasion: Henry Hudson and William Forde typically use 'Conneely' in their manuscripts, but Hudson used 'Coneely' in his magazine publications (see below), and Forde once used 'Conneally' in a letter. Petrie used 'Conneely' and 'Coneely' arbitrarily in his manuscripts, but 'Coneely' in his publications (see note 47 below).

Journal on 3 October 1840. Magazines and penny journals were the popular media of the time,[14] and the appearance of an engraving of Conneely (from a painting by F.W. Burton) on the front page of the *Irish Penny Journal* was unprecedented for a folk musician (see illustration 5.1).[15] The three-page article that accompanied it must have made Conneely the best known piper of his time.

Conneely's music was collected by Petrie, the Hudson brothers, Henry Robert Westenra (1792–1860) and William Forde. Westenra, 3rd Baron Rossmore, was a noted performer on the Irish pipes.[16] He met Conneely on several occasions and collected some music from him. Rossmore's music manuscripts appear to have perished. However, ten tunes were sent to Petrie by Rossmore and are copied into the latter's collection, including five which Rossmore attributed to Conneely. William Elliot Hudson's collection does not appear to have survived either but William Forde copied 94 tunes from Hudson's manuscript of which 92 were Conneely's. Altogether some 183 items were collected from Conneely which offer common ground on which to discuss the collectors. While it reflects well of Conneely that he was sought out by many collectors it is also a good indication of the respect in which Petrie was held that he influenced the other collectors to visit Conneely.

Of the five collectors who transcribed music from Conneely two of them published writings on the music they collected and a third left extensive notes among his manuscripts. Evidence can be found in the writings of Petrie, Forde and Henry Hudson to suggest that these collectors were scientific in their approach, with varying degrees of success, in areas of analysis, classification and comparative musicology. George Petrie and Henry Hudson were amateur musicians whose primary careers lay elsewhere. William Forde, however, was a professional musician engaged in performing, teaching, arranging and editing music, and therefore one might expect a deeper analysis from him.

When discussing collectors it is easy to concentrate on the contribution of George Petrie whose activities are perhaps the best documented. However, his collecting achievements and the influence he had on other collectors should not be underestimated. Petrie has been described as a polymath and his interests were certainly varied. His early work as a commercial artist[17] and his years as superintendent of the topographical department of the Ordnance Survey brought him around the Irish countryside where he undoubtedly made many contacts and encountered musical informants. His original purpose in collecting folk melodies was for his own pleasure and, initially, he had no intention to publish. He was a tireless worker in each of his fields of interest and his occasional failure to meet

---

14 See *300 years of Irish periodicals*, eds Barbara Hayley and Enda McKay (Mullingar: Association of Irish Learned Journals, 1987). **15** See Barra Boydell's chapter in this volume for a discussion of the original painting which is also given in illustration 3.4. **16** The first meeting between Conneely and Rossmore is recounted in Frank Thorpe Porter, *Twenty years' recollections of an Irish police magistrate* (Dublin: Hodges, Foster & Figgis, 1880), p. 337. **17** Petrie supplied sketches of topographical scenes for several books such as Thomas K. Cromwell's *Excursions through Ireland* (1821), Wright's *Guides to Wicklow and Killarney* (1821) and James N. Brewer's *Beauties of Ireland* (1825).

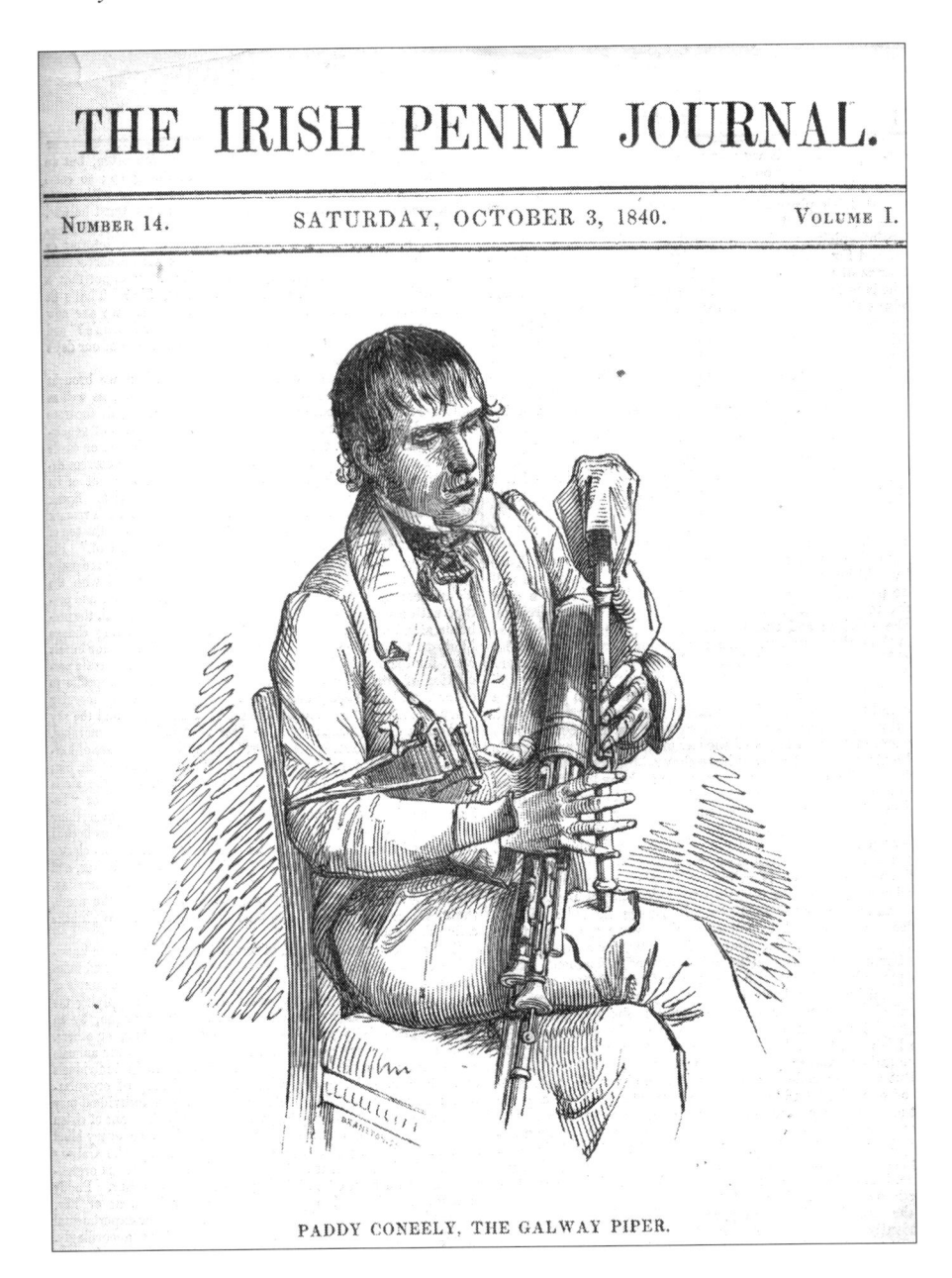

Illustration 5.1: Burton's 'Galway Piper', *Irish Penny Journal*, 3 October 1840

deadlines was due to the volume of projects he endeavoured to complete and the meticulous detail for which he strove. Understandably, the writing up of research caused difficulties, as did publishers' schedules. One instance of this is the catalogue of the antiquities collection held by the Royal Irish Academy which he failed to produce within the given time and which was subsequently completed by William Wilde. His essay on round towers, although submitted in 1833, was not completed in its much-expanded form until 1845. Similar procrastination dogged the preparation of material for his *Ancient Music of Ireland*, the first volume of music for the SPPMI of which he was sole editor. Instead of a volume per year from 1851 to 1855, as was initially intended, only one volume was completed during that period, a contributing factor, no doubt, to the dissolution of the society. However, it is in that volume, as well as the first instalment of the sequel which was set in print but not published until 1884, that we find so much information that Petrie did not otherwise commit to paper. True to form Petrie indulged in great detail, seeking contributions from specialists wherever he felt necessary.

Petrie's delay in producing the first volume of his *Ancient Music of Ireland* caused the society to offer the volume to its members in four fascicles, issued in instalments from 1853 onwards. The introduction which prefaced the complete volume was not included with the first fascicle (1853) which did, however, carry a notice that the society was intending to collect and classify all the melodies in their possession and encouraged members to collect and forward any folk melodies that they might have to the society.

In the introduction of the 1855 volume Petrie stated:

> I have endeavoured to carefully analyse the peculiarities of rhythm and structure found in the airs, as well as in the songs sung to them; I have thus, as I conceive, been enabled to lay a solid foundation for a future general classification of our melodies, which must be free from error, and be of great value in illustrating the origin and progress of our music.

It was Petrie's intention to provide a dissertation on the 'history, antiquity, and characteristic structure of Irish music', in association with Irish scholar Eoghan Ó Comhraigh (Eugene Curry) with whom he had worked in the Ordnance Survey. This dissertation was to be prefixed to the first volume of his *Ancient Music of Ireland*. However, it was never completed. What appears to be a draft copy survives among the Petrie manuscripts in the Irish Traditional Music Archive, Dublin. In it Petrie wrestles with philosophical concepts of taste and the effects of music on the human senses. However, he never quite gets to the analysis of the music as promised in the introduction and main text.

Petrie collaborated with experts on areas with which he himself was not sufficiently familiar. He called on Ó Comhraigh to provide the Irish texts and translations for certain song texts and on Patrick Weston Joyce to explain traditional dances. As in his archaeological studies Petrie had read widely and was familiar with work, similar to his own, on English and Scottish music published by Chappell and Farquahar Graham respectively. In a letter to James Goodman, Petrie wrote:

> I should like to see your set [*sic*] of the boat tune – airs of this class are hard to be got now in Ireland, but they are still common in the Hebrides.

He had a great interest in the history of melodies and to that end he would collect several versions or even fragments. He claimed to have as many as 50 settings of one particular tune although no melody with that number of settings has been traced in his manuscripts. Joyce stated that Petrie never saw Forde's manuscripts.[18] If he did not, it is significant that both collectors were thinking along similar lines of melodic analysis, tune variants and origins. Forde's work was mostly written between 1843 and 1850 while Petrie wrote up his work from 1851 to 1855. Their similar approach supports the notion of a common influence in the work of Edward Bunting.

The notes provided by Petrie to the individual tunes contain a wealth of information. This information was perhaps to form part of the dissertation which Petrie intended to place at the beginning of this volume. Elements of comparative musicology can be found in his approach as he looked to Scottish, Scandinavian, Gothic, Chinese and 'Hindostanee' melodies for similarities. Dance tune types and song structures are discussed. Petrie used the term 'narrative air' to describe a song in 3/4 time frequently having the form aa || ba or some variation of the same. He described the phrases of the 'b' section of this type of song as rising into 'impassioned energy, as if the singer were excited by harrowing recollections, and then returning to their preceding quietness, sink gently down to their final close.'[19] This description agrees with a suggestion of Aloys Fleischmann[20] that the performance style of *sean nós* was more extrovert before the Famine. Petrie also drew attention to unusual song structures which have a phrase length of five bars. The most common song type in Petrie's collection is the love song, followed by ballads. Attention was given to the 'ploughman's whistle' and other songs of occupation such as spinning songs. Also included are drinking songs, 'loobeens' and lullabies. Although he only described modes as major or minor he did identify a hexatonic scale with the absent 4th and other occurrences of the hexatonic scale with an 'emphatic' 4th. He frequently drew attention to the flattened 7th and the unusual use of the melodic minor.

Petrie's surviving music manuscripts are frustrating in their disarray. The majority of the manuscripts were bound into three volumes around 1900 and are now housed in the National Library of Ireland.[21] The original volumes, numbers 1–16, appear to be bound in sequence within the three compilations and may reflect some original chronological order. Other music manuscripts include a

---

18 Joyce, *Old Irish folk music and songs*, p. x.   **19** Petrie, *Ancient music of Ireland*, p. 45.   **20** Fleischmann, *Sources*, p. xxiii.   **21** NLI, MS 9278–80.

handful of tunes in the Irish Traditional Music Archive, and in the library at Trinity College, Dublin, one volume of music and a folder of loose leaves containing tunes were apparently used in the preparation of examples for the 1855 volume.[22] Petrie's habit of rewriting tunes in different keys, and often without reference to the original attribution, adds to the confusion and slightly undermines his reputation as a music scholar. The collection would greatly benefit from palaeographic analysis which might give chronological clarity to the various entries.

Petrie prepared the melodies in piano arrangements for his *Ancient Music of Ireland*, with some help from his eldest daughter Marianne.[23] Aloys Fleischmann exposed Petrie's inability to deal with modal tunes, harmonising them in either major or minor keys. However, he points out that:

> an understanding of the modal system anywhere in Europe at this time would have been confined to a handful of scholars, and the treatment of the tunes by Petrie and his daughter is in accord with the general practice in folk song arrangement throughout the nineteenth century.[24]

This has implications for our next collector, William Forde, but is a criticism that has also been levelled at Bunting. However, this practice may have arisen from the perceived expectations of the potential purchasers of such music publications. Bunting, no doubt, knew better than anyone that the old wire-strung harp, with its fixed tuning, could not deal with accidentals. But such rigid scales might have sounded too alien to the ears of his intended market.

Forde, like Bunting, was a professional musician and author, and arranged and edited over fifty publications on a variety of musical subjects including voice training, flute and piano arrangements. He appears to have approached Irish folk music with the intention of publishing a book entitled *A General Collection of the Music of Ireland* for which he printed a prospectus dated January 1845 and in which he described himself as a scientific musician.[25] Although he promised piano arrangements for the melodies his work never progressed that far.

His manuscripts, which are housed at the Royal Irish Academy, number thirteen volumes and display methodical discipline. One of these is his *General Collection* manuscript in which he brought together many of the tunes contained in the other volumes. Forde had the ability to recognize similarities between melodic variants and some of his work suggests an early approach to the concept of tune families. These melodies, gathered on the same page, frequently have as many as six settings together.

Other manuscript volumes are dedicated to the sources of tunes and carry titles such as *Scotch Airs* or *A Collection of Folk Music Belonging to Various Nationalities* while three are used exclusively to group the collected melodies according to mode, labelling them according to the Tonic Sol-fa method.[26] This

---

[22] TCD, MS 3562–3. [23] TCD, MS 3563. [24] Aloys Fleischmann, 'Petrie's contribution to Irish music', *Proceedings of the Royal Irish Academy*, 72 (Dublin: 1972), p. 212. [25] RIA, MS 24 O 19, 7. [26] RIA,

early use of the term 'folk music' is interesting and may be significant.[27] Unlike Petrie and Hudson, Forde did not publish any commentary about individual pieces and therefore observations on his work and methods must be general. He gave a lecture series in Cork on various aspects of Irish music in 1843–4.[28] From the evidence of his music manuscripts and the surviving lecture notes it is Forde who displays the most scholarly approach to the music.

Forde's prospectus suggests the following themes to be discussed in the book:

Music known to the ancient Irish as a regulated system different from the musical system of modern Europe:– Principles of the Irish music:–
The structure of Irish melody proves it was the offspring of cultivated art:–
Music, as a cultivated art, not created or practised by any people in a state of barbarism:–
Common origin of the Irish and Scotch music:– The Welsh music from a different source:–
The music of the continental nations of Europe has no affinity with the Irish:–
The probable source of the Irish system of music traced to the great civilized nations of ancient Asia, Egypt and Greece:–
The accounts remaining of the ancient Greek music describe certain remarkable melodic features:– The same are found in the living music of Ireland, China and Java:– – To a great extent they exist also in the music of India, and in the Gregorian music of the Roman Catholic Church:– They are not practised in the modern European system of music:– Greece owed the first knowledge of art and science to the pre-civilized nations occupying Asia-Minor, Syria and Egypt:– Irish history, tradition, language, monuments (and music) point to the same regions
The state of the art at various periods in the island:–
The musical instruments of the Irish:– The bards and musicians:–
The Irish style of music merits preservation as a source of variety and novelty in musical composition, as well as for its beauty and originality[29]

Forde's list of headings for his book was comprehensive. Bunting had previously touched on some of these themes although not in as much detail.

Like Bunting and Petrie, Forde was familiar with the writings of Burney, with his particular focus on 'ancient Greek music', and appears to have been up to date with the musicology of art music. He was obviously a pioneer when it came to applying it to Irish folk music. In a transcription of one of his lectures he claimed:

MSS 24 O 27, 24 O 33 and 24 O 34. **27** Frank Llewelyn Harrison claims that the term 'folk music' was not coined until several decades after 1846 but this collection carried the title by 1844. Frank Llewelyn Harrison, 'Irish traditional music: fossil or resource?' *Ó Riada Memorial Lecture 3* (Cork: UCC Irish Traditional Music Society, 1988), p. 18. **28** The *Southern Reporter* of 6 January 1844 carries one of many advertisements for Forde's lecture series: see Ita Hogan, *Anglo-Irish music, 1780–1830* (Cork: Cork University Press, 1966), p. 210. **29** RIA, MS 24 O 19, 7.

I have since discovered that a point escaped the observation of Burney, the great musical historian, which lies directly in the path of the searches for affinity between the Greek and Irish music.[30]

Forde relied heavily on published material and the collections of others and his collection amounts to almost 1,900 melodies. The number of these he personally transcribed is relatively small, perhaps not exceeding 350 items. Although his transcriptions do not show any particular advantage over those of the other collectors, it is to be regretted that Forde never published his book. His surviving lecture notes suggest that his failure to secure sufficient subscription denied Irish music of a most important work.[31]

Henry Philerin Hudson, a dentist, was an amateur musician who, with his brother William Elliot Hudson, organized the 'Dublin Festival of Music' in 1831. He was a member of several Dublin musical societies and published an English translation of Beethoven's *Mount of Olives* with a piano arrangement by Vincent Novello, a copy of which is housed in the Boston Public Library. When his brother took over *The Citizen or Dublin Monthly Magazine* in 1841 Henry edited the music section entitled 'The Native Music of Ireland'. In it he published piano arrangements of Irish music from his own collection as well as some compositions which he modelled on folk melodies.

It would appear that his main purpose in publishing the music was to disprove a statement, privately expressed by Edward Bunting, to the effect that no modern composition had the characteristics of traditional melody. Bunting declared that the last composer of traditional-sounding melody was the Limerick piper Walker Jackson who died in 1798. To prove him wrong Hudson set about composing melodies based on traditional ones. To this end he analysed tunes and identified scale patterns and structures on which he based his own compositions. He published his music as genuine folk melodies giving false sources and suggesting similarities to, for example, Carolan tunes.

These fabricated sources appear to have been couched in partial truths. One frequently quoted source for his compositions is the 'Farmer and O'Reilly' collection. Hudson had begun his collection by copying 78 tunes from the manuscripts of lexicographer and Irish teacher Edward O'Reilly in 1812. O'Reilly and Edward Farmer, another teacher of Irish, appear to have formed a teaching partnership about the year 1817. There is no mention of Farmer in Hudson's manuscripts:

> This is drawn from a MSS book compiled years ago, which we shall call the "Farmer and O'Reilly collection". Edward Farmer was a country schoolmaster

---

[30] RIA, MS 24 O 22, Forde likens what he calls the Greek chromatic scale to the pentatonic and hexatonic scales (which he describes as 'broken scales') often found in Irish folk music.   [31] Caitlín Uí Éigeartaigh, 'The Irish Music collection of William Forde: an essay in comparative musicology' (unpublished paper at Irish Traditional Music Archive). Forde's MSS are currently being prepared for publication by Uí Éigeartaigh.

who had settled in Dublin ... and taught, (amongst other things) the Irish language ... (Edward) O'Reilly was found in a small house at Harold's Cross: he, in addition to the copy of his dictionary, communicated a collection of native airs. From this, and from others handed by Farmer, the collection in question was made up, and with the addition of several airs noted down at the time, as sung by the people in the country.[32]

George Petrie, in a letter to James Goodman, states that he had seen the O'Reilly collection in about 1842, around the time Hudson was writing, yet he does not allude to Farmer as contributor to the collection. Referring to the melody 'The Old Coulin' he stated:

> I first set it from the singing of Paddy Conealy [sic], the Galway piper, about five-and-twenty years ago, and shortly afterwards got a set of it very slightly differing from a folio manuscript volume of Irish songs and tunes written by Edward O'Reilly, the Irish lexicographer.[33]

Significantly, he never publicly admitted his deception although his manuscripts contain an admission and explanation.[34] However, one of his comments in *The Citizen* put forward his argument, almost named Bunting (as an antiquarian) and tried to refute Bunting's theory:

> Some more learned antiquarian may say that there is no proof that this is an old air, and that some of the triplets are not of the antique character. Suppose it to be modern, what it the result? ... then, if you will, we have here an unstudied effusion in modern times, conceived in all the essential attributes of the ancient music ...[35]

With the genuine traditional melodies he also provided accompanying commentary, some of it relevant to the music but much of it politically charged and highly amusing in style:

> It is a happy thing with us, that, whilst the labours of other and abler men are recovering the historic truths respecting the lives and fortunes of our Irish heroes of former days, which the jealousy, bigotry, and villainy of the maintainers of the "British interest" had too long falsified and obscured, – we in our humble way, are rescuing from oblivion many of those heart-stirring tunes with which our people welcomed those same heroes, in the days of their power and glory. 'Sarsfield's Quick-step' here it is, 'A Sarsfield to the rescue, ho!'[36]

---

[32] Henry Hudson, 'The native music of Ireland', *The Citizen, or Dublin Monthly Magazine*, January 1841.
[33] Stokes, *Life*, p. 351.   [34] Five of Hudson's manuscript books are in the Boston Public Library (M 374 a.3–7) and a photostat copy of the Hudson manuscripts is housed in the National Library of Ireland. Hudson's explanation is written on the end-page of NLI MS 7258.   [35] *The Citizen*, April 1841.   [36] Ibid.,

And again:

> Oh! thick-head! Oh! numbscull [*sic*]! where wert thou born, bred, or reared? – in Doncaster? – in Cockneyshire – or in what other foggy hole in Bullland?[37]

Of the three collectors considered here, Henry Hudson would probably have the least claim to being considered a musicologist but his approach was reasonably analytical. He also included much information about the context in which the music was performed, particularly that of Conneely. Apart from the analysis of tune structure and phrasing, Hudson's writings show an awareness of gapped scales, both hexatonic and pentatonic. He subscribed to the importance of the 'emphatic 6th' in Irish melody as espoused by Bunting, although Petrie remained unconvinced that it was essential. He identified many different song and tune types, including love songs, political songs and ballads and also collected a number of drinking songs.

Unlike Bunting, Petrie and Forde, Hudson occasionally tried to justify his piano arrangements, explaining the reason for his use of certain harmonies. In one instance, confessing that he had included consecutive fifths, he pointed out that Rossini's *Otello* had a series of consecutive fifths and explained that the special effect of them was required by the melody:

> we always think there is a palliation of the crime, when it is committed in conjunction with a contrary motion in some of the other parts, and in the present instance we have that; which, we are inclined to think, was an ingredient in our adoption of the irregularity ... the roughness resulting from the faulty passage had its charm for us, and, with this apology, we must submit our case to the censure of the learned.[38]

It would not be fair, therefore, to dismiss Hudson from the pantheon of early folk musicologists, particularly since it is from him that we get some of the most interesting tunes from Conneely. He collected 143 melodies from Conneely where Forde collected 30 and Petrie about 43. One of the jigs, 'The Munsterman's Frolic', has eleven parts, the usual number for such tunes being two but occasionally stretching to five or six. Another interesting feature is what appears to be the notation of regulators, the closed pipes which sit under the wrist of the piper's lower hand and which play simple chords in occasional accompaniment to the melody. This may be the earliest example of regulator-playing notated from performance.

Another item from Henry Hudson shows the difficulty of transcribing airs (see example 5.1). Traditional performers of songs and slow airs tend to take many liberties or even ignore the metre of a melody while concentrating on the words

December 1842. **37** Ibid., March 1841. **38** *The Citizen*, May 1842.

Example 5.1: Regulators in 'O Connell's Welcome to Clare' (Hudson, NLI MS 7255 No. 389)

or the ornamentation of the tune. Hudson obviously had serious difficulty with the transcription of the melody of 'Máire Ní Thaidhg Óig' and attempted to notate it four different ways. While it is likely that different verses would affect the way the melody is performed, the words used by Conneely were not collected, thus obviating their consideration. These notations are obviously from repeated performances but they highlight the difficulty of field transcription. It is interesting that William Elliot Hudson's collection contains only one setting of this melody.

The methodology of these pioneer collectors is interesting and varied (see example 5.2). Bunting transcribed many airs but also paid collectors to do the work for him. None of the others are known to have employed professionals but, although their collections contain their own fieldwork, they all copied from published collections and from the manuscript collections of others, including each other. George Petrie offered music from his collection to Thomas Moore, Francis Holden and Bunting.

William Stokes, in his biography of Petrie, gave a description of the collector's method of transcription, notating the melody first and playing it back on his violin for approval of the informant:

Example 5.2 a, b, c and d: Four attempts to transcribe 'Máire Ní Thaidhg Óig' (Hudson, NLI MS 7255 No. 402)

The song having been given, O'Curry wrote the Irish words, when Petrie's work began. The singer recommenced, stopping at a signal from him at every two or three bars of the melody to permit the writing of the notes, and often repeating the passage until it was correctly taken down, and then going on with the melody, exactly from the point were the singing was interrupted. The entire air being at last obtained, the singer – a second time – was called to give the song continuously, and when all corrections had been made, the violin – an instrument of great sweetness and power – was produced, and the air played as Petrie alone could play it, and often repeated.[39]

Henry Hudson must have used a similar approach since he described, in *The Citizen*, how Conneely had a very clear idea of the correct setting of the tune. There is little evidence as to what instrument Hudson played other than piano (some family members played the flute) but he must have been able to play back what he had transcribed to get the piper's opinion of the setting:

whilst he possesses the power of varying to a remarkable degree, he is one of the most faithful preservers of the original text of our airs; and, indeed, he is a stickler for every note and point of an air which he has once thoroughly fixed to his satisfaction, far beyond anybody we have yet had the fortune to meet with.[40]

The idea of the informant being a 'stickler for every note' and correcting the collector's transcription is both surprising and amusing. His role as musician allowed him to transcend social barriers, placing him on an equal footing with his collectors with whom he could discuss his music. Petrie describes Conneely as having 'a high opinion of his music talents, and a strong feeling of decent pride'.[41]

Forde, who collected during the famine, described how 'a mutton chop twice a day' was keeping his informant, piper Hugh O'Beirne, alive.[42] The collector ultimately transcribed over 180 melodies from him. Forde played the flute and could have conveniently played back the notations on that instrument. However, this is not specifically stated.

The relationship between the collector and the informant is an interesting one. Forde appears to have worked very well with O'Beirne, collecting a huge number of items from him. Unfortunately he left no commentary on his work with Conneely. However, despite having copied 92 tunes of Conneely's from the manuscripts of William Elliot Hudson, Forde still sought him out in 1847 for a further 30 melodies. Henry Hudson's affection and respect for Conneely is very obvious from his commentary. In the *Dublin Monthly Magazine* (a new series of *The Citizen* since 1842) of January 1843, Hudson asked:

---

39 Stokes, *Life*, p. 317.   **40** *The Citizen*, April 1842.   **41** [George] P[etrie], 'Paddy Coneely, the Galway piper', *Irish Penny Journal*, 1:14 (3 October 1840), 105–8, here 108.   **42** Pádraig de Brún, 'Hugh O'Beirne, piper', *Ceol*, 5:1 (Dublin: 1981), 25.

Example 5.3(a): 'The Virtue of a Kiss' (Petrie, NLI MS 9280 No. 1961)

Example 5.3(b): 'The Virtue of a Kiss' (Hudson, NLI MS 7255 No. 376)

When you hear the air of Máire Inis Toirc, will you refrain? We received it from our own dear, blind, sad, cheerful friend, Paddy Coneely [*sic*].

Petrie, too, enjoyed a good working relationship with Conneely although he indicated a disapproval of certain traits of his character such as Conneely's enjoyment of horse racing and hunting. His description of Conneely in the *Irish Penny Journal* article contained a warmth that is absent from his references in the *Ancient Music of Ireland*.

Many of the transcriptions of Conneely are surprisingly consistent, even down to a similarity in the notation of ornaments. In the following examples a setting collected by Petrie is remarkably close to Henry Hudson's transcription of the same tune.

The differences between the two settings are very slight given that more than two years had elapsed between the two performances (see example 5.3). The uniformity is even more remarkable considering that traditional musicians usually try to vary the setting every time the tune is played. Petrie wrote straight semiquavers to Hudson's semiquaver triplets. Hudson's attempts to capture the detail of ornamentation are also interesting especially the improvisatory flourish in bar 12. Hudson transcribed several of these in other tunes.

Example 5.4(a): Hudson's interpretation of the rhythm in 'Johnny Gibbon's March in '98' (Hudson, NLI MS 7256 No. 471)

Example 5.4(b): Forde's interpretation of the rhythm in 'Johnny Gibbon's March' (Forde, RIA MS 24 O 19 p. 100, No. 7)

Discrepancies in rhythmic interpretation occasionally occur in the collections. Because Irish music is played with a rhythmic swing where the usual emphasis prolongs the accented beats there is an understood swing to the rhythm when reading notation of Irish music. Hudson writes out a march in 6/8 which is not unusual for a march. However, in this instance it does not sound correct. Forde interprets the rhythm in 2/4 presumably with a heavy swing or *inégal* interpretation (see example 5.4).

The formation of the SPPMI in 1851 began with a nationwide request for melodies to be collected and sent to them. These appear to comprise a large part of the collection of John Edward Pigot, secretary for the society. Many of these melodies were added to Petrie's collection. Henry Hudson, who was also a member, had sent out a similar request in *The Citizen* ten years earlier and the results can be seen in his manuscripts:

> Since we commenced the publication of our 'National Melodies,' we have received several contributions to our stock of unpublished Irish Airs from various individuals, anxious, like ourselves, to assist in preserving the relics of the 'days of our glory.' We have also received *promises* of valuable contributions from several others, and feeling assured that there is still an immense harvest to be reaped, which may wither away on the land and be for ever lost, if not speedily 'stored,' we think we have shown sufficient freedom from *selfishness* in our undertaking, to warrant us *now* in calling on all the readers of the *Citizen* – on every one at least whose heart glows with the love of his native country, to assist us, by contributions of any unpublished Irish Airs or Songs which he may possess, in preserving the memory of the glories and misfortunes of our forefathers.[43]

Although Forde died before the formation of the SPPMI, he had transcribed from musicians, had copied extensively from published collections and gladly accepted tunes sent to him by friends, thereby anticipating the work of the society.

43 *The Citizen*, April 1841.

The attention to detail and the search for accuracy reflects Petrie's obsession with purity of versions. He believed that, despite the variation in the song settings he collected, the words required the singer to adhere to the original melody. This was in direct contrast with Bunting's less plausible theory that the harpers preserved the best versions. But why, therefore, did Petrie avoid collecting texts while Bunting paid to have them collected? With regard to collecting texts, Petrie was no different to Forde and Hudson. Part of his difficulty lay in his limited knowledge of the Irish language, but he abhorred what he perceived as licentiousness and vulgarity in the songs many of which he felt were later adaptations to old airs. However, if the preservation of the original melody depended on the song words it would surely be affected by new texts. This contradicts his theory that the melody was best preserved by singers. In fact, traditional melodies vary from singer to singer while variation within the verses of a song is also a trait valued within the tradition. Petrie, in a letter to James Goodman some three years before his death, wrote:

> I feel almost glad that you have exhausted the stock of tunes of your 'old friend, ex-piper Kennedy' [Goodman's informant], so that you may have time to collect from the peasant singers, by whom, as I have always found, our melodies are most purely found.[44]

These concerns do not appear to have troubled some of the other collectors as much. Both Hudson and Forde were content to notate Conneely's music whether he sang or played it.

P.W. Joyce, although he did not collect music from Conneely, freely altered and edited music he collected or even copied,[45] much as a traditional player might alter a setting to make it more suitable to their style or their instrument.

Some collectors display a strong bias in the material they chose to collect. A comparison with the repertoire in collections made slightly later in the nineteenth century by folk musicians for their own use[46] suggests prejudice and selectivity on the part of some well-known collectors. Petrie, in the article he wrote about Conneely in the *Irish Penny Journal*, stated:

> Paddy can play not three tunes, but three thousand: in fact we have often wished his skill to be more circumscribed, or his memory less retentive, particularly when, instead of firing away with some lively reel, or still more animated Irish jig, he has pestered us, in spite of our nationality, with a set of quadrilles or a galloppe, such as he is called on to play by the ladies and the gentlemen at the balls in Galway.[47]

44 Stokes, *Life*, p. 351.   **45** Caitlín Uí Éigeartaigh, 'The collector as editor', *Éigse Cheol Tíre*, 2 (Dublin: 1976), 7.   **46** John 'the Boss' Murphy (1875–1955), who learnt much of his fiddle repertoire from his father William (1831–1911), left music manuscripts which contain a wider variety of traditional genres, including quadrilles and galops, than appears in the manuscripts of collectors such as Petrie. This collection has been privately published as *The Boss Murphy musical legacy*, ed. Colette Moloney (Churchtown: 2003).   **47** Petrie, 'Paddy Coneely', 106.

It is perhaps unsurprising not to find a quadrille among the Conneely tunes in Petrie's collection. Hudson, on the other hand, wrote in *The Dublin Monthly Magazine*, January 1843: 'The first tune he desired us to take down from his playing was "Moll Rooney's Pig"' suggesting that he allowed Conneely dictate the choice of music. While Hudson collected a considerably greater number of melodies than the others it is interesting to see the variety of material in his collection. There is a conspicuous number of dance tunes, particularly reels. Other dance types such as polka and slide rhythms, more typically found later in the century, are also represented. 'Toper's Songs' (drinking songs) which might have scandalized Petrie, also appear frequently.

That Conneely was an important carrier of tradition is without question. The fact that four prominent collectors and an aristocratic piper should seek him out is significant and affirms his importance.

The legacy of the Irish folk music collectors of the early nineteenth century is manifold. From Bunting we have the only record of the failing harp tradition before its ultimate demise. Not only did he collect the melodies but he also made a study of the terminology which, although imperfect and perhaps incomplete, is effectively all that we know about that tradition. The other collectors have left an interesting musical map, albeit generally without song texts, of Ireland prior to the social and cultural upheaval caused by the Great Famine. Breandán Breathnach once remarked that the efforts of these collectors could rest on shelves without any detrimental effect on the tradition.[48] However, they remain an important resource for scholars of Irish folk music, offering an insight into the performance style and repertoire before the Famine. They also present a valuable supplement to the traditional repertoire. In an age when so many new 'compositions' are being forced on the public ear through recordings, the time seems opportune to open these stores harvested in years of musical plenty and invigorate the tradition with them once again.

---

[48] Breandán Breathnach, 'The use of notation in the transmission of Irish folk music', *Ó Riada Memorial Lecture 1* (Cork: UCC Irish Traditional Music Society 1985), p. 2.

Strange voices in the 'Land of Song': Belgian and German organist appointments to Catholic cathedrals and churches in Ireland, 1859–1916

PAUL COLLINS

In Belgium it is believed that the best musicians migrate to Ireland on account of the wonderfully melodious old organs and because Irish audiences are very appreciative of their efforts.[1]

Is the 'Land of Song', with its great traditions and rich inheritance of national music, not capable of teaching aspiring musicians to play the organ, or to train a choir competent to render the music for the ceremonies in our churches? Has not the Feis Ceoil for many years been bringing promising young organists to light? What has become of these? [...] It is sad to think that, in view of the limited number of [church organist] positions, and in face of the amount of unemployment at present in the musical profession, foreigners are brought over when a vacancy occurs.[2]

Concluding his handbook entitled *The Reform of Church Music*, the Belfast-based organist and choirmaster Arthur de Meulemeester (1876–1942) comments:

What the Catholic University of Louvain has done for the upholding, for the restoration of Irish academic learning and for Irish culture, is but a grateful reversal of history, – an example which is being emulated in the matter of ecclesiastical musical art, by the great and famous Lemmens Institute of Malines, which is now represented in this country by so many of its erudite disciples.[3]

Six graduates of the Lemmens Institute are known to have been working at Irish cathedrals and churches by 1916, all but one being employed by the Congregation of the Most Holy Redeemer (the Redemptorists). Formerly known as the École de Musique Religieuse, which was founded by the Belgian organist Jaak Nikolaas Lemmens (1823–81) in 1878, the institute at Malines (Mechelen) opened its doors in 1879. In March of the same year, *Lyra Ecclesiastica*, the bulletin of the newly formed Irish Society of St Cecilia, brought news of the establishment of the institute to its readers. An English version of Lemmens' prospectus, published '*in extenso*' by the bulletin, was introduced as follows:

---

[1] 'Ireland, land of Belgian organists—remarkable facts', *Irish Independent*, 22 August 1930, 8. [2] Letter from 'Marcato' to the Editor, *Limerick Leader* [hereafter *LL*], 6 September 1930, 10. [3] Arthur de Meulemeester, *The reform of church music* (Dublin: Catholic Truth Society of Ireland, 1936), p. 110.

Illustration 6.1: Charles Louis Nono (1834–95), organist-choirmaster at Sts Peter and Paul's Pro-Cathedral, Ennis, from 1859, courtesy of Charles Nono, grandson of the organist depicted.

Academy of Sacred Music at Malines, Belgium

Under the august protection of His Eminence the Cardinal Archbishop of Malines; of their Lordships the Bishops of Belgium; and under the direction of M.J. Lemmens. This Academy is established for the purpose of training and advancing to the highest degree of proficiency, organists, choirmasters, and vocalists, for the service of the Holy Catholic Church.[4]

The English version of Lemmens' prospectus was provided by Francis Prosper De Prins (1829–84), the Belgian organist of Limerick's Redemptorist church (Mount St Alphonsus) from 1862 to 1884.[5] Francis and his brother, Léopold, who was organist at St Mary's Cathedral in Cork and a composer, were among the few Belgian organists working in Ireland before 1900. The first of the Belgian arrivals, more likely, was Charles Louis Nono (1834–95), who studied at the

---

4 *Lyra Ecclesiastica* [hereafter *LE*], March 1879, 51.   **5** Ibid., 51–2.

Academie van Schone Kunsten in Roeselare, graduating there in 1856 or 1857 (see illustration 6.1).[6] He arrived in Ennis in 1859 to take up the dual appointment of organist-choirmaster at the Pro-Cathedral of St Peter and St Paul and music teacher at St Flannan's College.[7] In 1860 the *Clare Almanack* informed its readers that at the unfinished 'Parish Roman Catholic Chapel' in Ennis

> There has lately been erected a magnificent organ, built by Mr. White of Dublin, which cost the large sum of £600. Monsieur Nono, the organist, has formed a choir for sacred music.[8]

Like other Belgian and German musicians that secured appointments as organists in Ireland, Monsieur ('Mons') Nono made a significant contribution to cultural life in his town of adoption. In addition to teaching harmonium, piano and singing, he directed the Ennis Amateur Band during the 1860s, imported musical instruments, and tuned and repaired pianos.[9] His 'grand concerts', held at such venues as Ennis town hall and Tulla courthouse, were greatly appreciated and frequently featured Madame Nono (Wexford-born Ellen O'Byrne) and 'the Mesdemoiselles Nono' as vocalists.[10] One of his sons, 'Donat' (Donatus, *b*.1872), who according to the 1901 census was an 'organist' and 'professor of music', taught at St Flannan's College from 1901 to 1916 and succeeded Charles Louis as organist at the cathedral.[11]

As the hub of Catholic church music reform during the late nineteenth century was Germany, it was to the Kirchenmusikschule at Ratisbon (Regensburg), founded by Franz Xaver Haberl (1840–1910) in 1874, that Irish ecclesiastics had looked in order to supply the Irish Church with badly needed musical expertise. Six years before the founding of the Ratisbon school, German efforts at reform had peaked with the establishment by Franz Xaver Witt (1834–88) of the Allgemeiner Deutscher Cäcilien-Verein and the journal *Musica Sacra*, the latter propagating the new society's reformist principles. Francis and Léopold De Prins, like other Belgian and German organists working in Ireland during the period covered by this chapter, were devoted advocates of Cecilian reform.[12] Francis, 'possessing great musical taste, with the power to impart it successfully to others', had previously held the 'eminent' position of organist to the Dominican church in

---

6 See Herman Kerstens, *Vlaamse Organisten sinds 1900 in het Buitenland* (Norbertijnenabdij van Tongerlo: Kempense Cultuurkring, 2002), p. 7.   **7** See John Chartres Molony, *The riddle of the Irish* (London: Methuen, 1927), p. 33. Nono, as one might expect, became a member of the nascent Irish Society of St Cecilia, being listed in the supplement to the April 1879 issue of *LE*.   **8** *Clare Almanack*, 1860, 46. **9** As a 'Professor of Music and Singing', Nono's local rivals were W.H. Algair and Herr Holts; see Tim Kelly, 'Ennis in the nineteenth century'. MA diss. (University College, Galway, 1971), pp 272–3.   **10** See, for example, the notice advertising 'Monsieur Nono's Grand Evening Concert' in the *Clare Journal*, 14 February 1867.   **11** Donat is undoubtedly the 'Dominic' referred to in the 'Register of cathedral organists' given in *Music in Ireland: a symposium*, ed. Aloys Fleischmann (Cork: Cork University Press, 1952), p. 161.   **12** There were, of course, notable indigenous musicians who were staunch Cecilians, like Joseph Seymour (organist at St Andrew's Church, Westland Row, Dublin), Brendan Rogers (organist at Dublin's Pro-Cathedral), and John Murray (organist at the Cathedral of the Assumption in Thurles).

Louvain,[13] and was probably recruited by Belgian-Province Redemptorists, who had established their Congregation's first community in Ireland at Limerick in 1853.[14] Reporting on the formal dedication of Mount St Alphonsus, which took place on 7 December 1862, the *Munster News* noted that the 'musical portion of the proceedings', under the direction of De Prins, was rendered by 'the first exclusively male choir formed in Limerick, in a Catholic Church', the choir numbering 'close on seventy.'[15] It was further remarked that when the Belgian organist first assembled his 'choral corps of one sex', its members

> were with few exceptions ignorant of music. They began no further back than two months ago, and yet on Sunday last, they rendered the service in a manner that reflected infinite credit on their talented instructor, and the judgment of the Fathers in having secured his valuable services.[16]

Even before the appearance of the first issue of *Lyra Ecclesiastica* in 1878, Francis and Léopold De Prins had edited a quarterly journal entitled *St Cecilia* (from 1876),[17] and the brothers were ardent members of the Irish Society and committed supporters of its bulletin.[18] Of *St Cecilia* and its editors, *Lyra* gave the following assessment:

> This ably-conducted and beautifully edited publication has now been before the public for two years, and was the first practical effort made in this country to bring Cecilian music within the reach of our choirs and choristers. The Messrs. De Prins have been favourably known for many years past (one in Limerick and one in Cork), as almost the only organists who persistently applied themselves to upholding and practically applying the principles of the Cecilian Society in their respective choirs, and the selections they have already published in their quarterly journal prove the soundness of their judgment in Church musical matters, as well as their artistic discernment.[19]

---

13 See 'The Redemptorist Fathers.—Dedication of Mount St. Alphonsus Church—Sermon by the Most Rev. Dr. Moriarty', *Munster News and Limerick and Clare Advocate* [hereafter *MN*], 10 December 1862, 3. **14** Other Redemptorist foundations were to follow at Dundalk (St Joseph's, 1876) and Belfast (Clonard, 1896), both of these communities employing Belgian organists. Redemptorists in Baltimore, the first episcopal see of the Roman Catholic Church in the United States, were also supportive of liturgical music reform during this period: see Ann Louise Silverberg, 'Cecilian Reform in Baltimore, 1868–1903', PhD diss. (University of Illinois at Urbana-Champaign, 1992), pp 287–9.   **15** *MN*, 10 December 1862, 3.   **16** Ibid.   **17** *St. Cecilia. Quarterly Journal of Catholic Church Music by the best ancient and modern composers*, ed. MM De Prins (London: Burns & Oates. Dublin: M.H. Gill & Son)   **18** Francis and Léopold were listed as members of the Irish Society of St Cecilia in the supplements to the March and April 1879 issues of *LE*. The June 1879 issue requested subscribers in the Limerick region to forward their annual subscriptions to Francis De Prins, while earlier in the same year, Francis and Léopold were among the first to report to *LE* on liturgical music outside of Dublin (see Kieran Anthony Daly, *Catholic church music in Ireland, 1878–1903: the Cecilian reform movement* (Dublin: Four Courts Press, 1995), p. 51).   **19** *LE*, January 1879, 40.

Further evidence of the De Prins brothers' commitment to Cecilian ideals may be gleaned from the accounts they forwarded to *Lyra* in 1879 of their St Patrick's Day and Holy Week liturgies. Léopold ('the talented organist and choirmaster of Cork Cathedral') wrote:

> On St Patrick's Day, we had a grand solemnity at the cathedral, the Mayor and the Corporation present, the bishop and chapter also present at High Mass. The music of the Mass was Zangl's of the Cecilian catalogue, for four voices, organ and wind instruments. I had seventy voices in the chorus, and every chorister sang his part right well. The effect was very fine, and I received not only the congratulations of his Lordship but also those of the Corporation. They all said they never heard anything more effective and religious at the same time.[20]

The following month, Francis reported on the Holy Week ceremonies at Mount St Alphonsus:

> The music sung on Palm Sunday at the blessing of the palms and the procession which followed, was that prescribed in the *Processionale Romanum*. The Ordinary of the Mass sung on that day was Haller's *Missa Quarta*; the Proper of the Mass was sung in Gregorian ... The Mass on Easter day was Haller's celebrated *Missa Assumpta est*, for four equal voices; this Mass is, perhaps, one of that grand composer's finest specimens of Church Music we know of.[21]

After the establishment of the church music institute at Malines in the same year, the brothers, it would seem, took an added interest in developments in sacred music in their native country. On Christmas Day 1882 Francis introduced a *Messe en re* by Lemmens to Mount St Alphonsus,[22] while *Lyra's* music supplements of 1883 included 'two little motets for three voices' by Palestrina, which had been forwarded to the bulletin by the Limerick-based Belgian. The motets, the bulletin noted, 'were first published ... by direction of the Cardinal Archbishop of Malines, a great lover of real Church Music'.[23] Following the death of Francis in July 1884, the July/August issue of *Lyra* lauded the influential Cecilian's efforts at promoting 'the standard of true liturgical music':

> The Irish Society of St Cecilia can badly afford the loss which it has sustained in the death of one of its most sincere and zealous working members, Mons F.P. de Prins of Limerick ... Years before our Society was established, the standard of true liturgical music, in opposition to the frivolous style which then prevailed, was raised in the Redemptorist Fathers' Church in Limerick by the

---

20 *LE*, April 1879, 62. **21** *LE*, May 1879, 72. **22** See *LE*, February 1883, 15. **23** *LE*, September/October 1883, 64.

Messrs de Prins, with the joyful approbation of the Fathers and there, under the cross of the mission the true music of the Church has flourished and waxed strong in a congenial atmosphere ... Setting himself steadily against the 'solo' system and thus depriving himself at first of the countenance and help of most of the educated musicians, who were strongly devoted to this system, Mons de Prins, out of untrained material, educated, trained and brought to efficiency, a choir of forty men and boys, now for the most part readers of music and capable of singing, in a style which leaves nothing to be desired, the most difficult works of the ancient and modern church writers.[24]

In mid 1898 the Belgian composer Jozef Bellens (1876–1939), a Lemmens laureate (1897), was appointed organist to Mount St Alphonsus.[25] A composer of sacred music and works for organ, Bellens's output included a motet, *Salva nos, Domine*, for SATB and organ, and a *Missa prima* and *Ave Maria*, both for two equal voices and organ.[26] Like his fellow countryman and organist Joseph Sireaux, who was based in Dundalk, Bellens became involved in the relief of Belgian refugees at the start of the Great War, being a member of the reception committee that welcomed 40 such refugees to Limerick in December 1914.[27] He remained in Limerick until 1919, when he returned to Belgium to teach music at a seminary in Hoogstraten.[28] On behalf of Bishop Robert Browne of Cloyne, who had enlisted his help in sourcing a qualified organist-choirmaster for St Colman's Cathedral in Cobh, Bellens contacted the institute at Mechelen and secured German-born Alphonsus Graff, who remained at St Colman's from 1902 to 1908. In a letter to Browne dated 19 October 1901, Bellens assured the bishop of Graff's suitability for the position:

It gives me very much pleasure to let you know, I have succeeded in getting a really good musician for your cathedral, Mr Alphonsus Graff, a German by birth, but now a naturalized Belgian. He studied at the School for Churchmusic, the well known Lemmens Institute, established in Mechlin [*sic*] by the bishops of Belgium, over which the great catholic composer Edgar Tinel is director, and where I studied myself. His diploma from this school qualifies him to hold the position of organist and choirmaster in any church or cathedral ... I knew him always to be a most respectable young man, a good catholic and a thorough musician. The director, Edgar Tinel, wrote me also to recommend him highly to your Lordship. He is now about 36 years of age. I must say, that your Lordship will be fortunate in securing him.[29]

---

24 *LE*, July/August 1884, 54.　**25** See Bellens's advertisement in *MN*, 31 August 1898, 2.　**26** These three works appeared in supplements to the Belgian journal *Musica Sacra* in 1897/98 (17:12), 1911/1912 (31:3–7), and 1912/1913 (32:5) respectively.　**27** See 'Belgian Refugees', *LL*, 23 December 1914, 3.　**28** See 'Departure of Mr J P Bellens', *MN*, 26 April 1919.　**29** From the Bishop Robert Browne Papers held at Cloyne Diocesan Centre, Cobh.

At St Joseph's Church in Dundalk, the Redemptorists engaged Belgian musicians from 1903. In that year Jan Juliaan Stuyck (1880–1957), who graduated from the Lemmens Institute in 1901, succeeded Thomas Vincent Parks as organist.[30] Like his own successor, Joseph Sireaux, who was employed from 1905 to 1910, and who subsequently became organist at St Patrick's Church, Dundalk (1910–19), Stuyck returned to Belgium after the Great War.[31] Following Sireaux's move to St Patrick's, Firmin Van de Velde (1888–?) was appointed organist at St Joseph's (1910–12), being succeeded by Jan Baptist Van Craen (1864–?) in 1916.[32] In late 1912, having 'sollicited [sic] the vacant place of Organist in the Pro Cathedral of Galway and Professor of music in the College', Van de Velde, on foot of a request made by Bishop Thomas O'Dea, forwarded details of his qualifications to Father Heinrich Bewerunge at Maynooth.[33] In the second of three letters written by the Belgian organist to Bewerunge concerning the Galway post, Van de Velde gives a comprehensive account of the requirements for the music component of his diploma from the Lemmens Institute:

> I send you here enclosed a copy of my diploma. I dare say, you would like to know the different subjects which were the matter of my examination. Besides the examination on latin, religion and liturgy, the examination on music embraced the following points:
>
> *In private —*
> To compose a counterpoint for four voices on a chant or cantus firmus there and then assigned, and to pass over successfully to the soprano, bass, alto and tenor.
>
> *With closed doors* — Practice on the organ —
> Prelude for a Gregorian chant, there and then designated. Accompaniment to Gregorian melodies, there and then designated.
> To execute in counterpoint and with pedal, a choral of J.S. Bach, the melody of which was fixed there and then.
> To answer questions on the history of religious music.

---

30 Stuyck was also a composer, his works including an *Ave Maria* for SATB and organ, op.10, and a Toccata for organ, op.21.   **31** With the opening of a Belgian Relief Fund in Dundalk in 1914 and the arrival of Belgian refugees, Sireaux ('J. Siraux'), in a letter to the *Democrat and People's Journal* (14 November 1914, 5), expressed his thanks to the people of Dundalk for their support of a fund-raising concert (see also *Democrat and People's Journal*, 7 November 1914, 5).   **32** Kerstens claims that Van Craen, who graduated from the Lemmens Institute in 1890, spent a period as organist of Carlow's Cathedral of the Assumption (see Kerstens, *Vlaamsa Organisten*, p. 24). The 'Register of cathedral organists' in Fleischmann's *Music in Ireland* (p. 161) concurs with this, noting that Van Craen was at Carlow in 1892. A year later, in 1893, Van Craen was appointed organist to St Peter's in Phibsborough, Dublin (see *LE*, November 1893; also Daly, *Catholic church music*, p. 147).   **33** Letter from Van de Velde to Bewerunge, dated 12 October 1912 (Father Cornelius Mulcahy Papers, Limerick Diocesan Archive).

In public —
To execute an organ-piece, marked out eight days before the examination.
To read at first sight an organ-piece with pedal, marked out there and then.
To improvise in ecclesiastical style of music on a theme marked out there and then.
To execute an organ-piece, selected from the works of the musical masters, found in the repertory of the applicant and pointed out there and then.
To execute a piano-piece, selected from the works of the musical masters, found in the repertory of the applicant and pointed out there and then.[34]

The most significant of the early Belgian appointments was undoubtedly that of Arthur de Meulemeester (1876–1942) by the Redemptorists in Belfast in October 1898. Described as 'the ideal church organist—a man who combined brilliant musical genius with deep and fervent piety',[35] de Meulemeester was a prolific composer of sacred music and 'a tireless campaigner and leading voice in the area of church music reform, not only in the north of Ireland, but throughout the country.'[36] The touchstone for all such reform, according to the Belgian, was Pius X's *Motu Proprio* ('Tra le sollecitudini' [Among the cares]) on the renewal and regulation of sacred music. Commenting that 'the Law on Church Music' had been 'completely and clearly laid down' in the 1903 papal document,[37] the Clonard organist echoes R.R. Terry's earlier observation that

The Holy Father has spoken, and matters which were regarded as subjects for discussion have been removed from the region of controversy to the region of obedience ... The day for individual comment and for individual expression of opinion has happily gone for ever ... [38]

De Meulemeester, who entered the Lemmens Institute in 1894, was a student of Edgar Tinel, and graduated at Mechelen in 1898. At Clonard, he established himself as an energetic 'apostle of the liturgy and champion of good church music', and the Clonard Domestic Archives remark upon the accomplishment of the Belfast church choir under his direction.[39] Clonard's Domestic Chronicle records, for example, that at the laying of the foundation stone of the Redemptorist church by Bishop John Tohill on 4 October 1908, the music

---

34 Letter from Van de Velde to Bewerunge, dated 16 October 1912 (Father Cornelius Mulcahy Papers, Limerick Diocesan Archive). Convinced that he had 'all the necessary qualifications to carry out the duties' of his 'profession' to Bewerunge's 'greatest satisfaction', Van de Velde, in his final letter regarding the Galway post (dated 29 October 1912), suggested that the Maynooth-based German priest, 'before taking a final decision', should 'have a "concursus" between the different applicants'.   **35** E.H. Jones, C.Ss.R., 'Chevalier de Meulemeester, K.O.L., K.O.C.B.', *Redemptorist Record*, 6:5 (September/October 1942), 151.   **36** Mary Regina Deacy, 'Continental organists and Catholic Church music in Ireland, 1860–1960', MLitt diss. (National University of Ireland, Maynooth, 2005), p. 86.   **37** De Meulemeester, *The reform of church music*, p. 14.   **38** R.R. Terry, *Catholic church music* (London: Greening, 1907), pp 39–40.   **39** See James Delaney, 'Church music reform', *Irish Ecclesiastical Record*, 68 (July–December, 1946), 242. For a fascinating insight into de Meulemeester's interaction with Redemptorists at Clonard, see James Grant,

was rendered in a faultless style by the meticulously trained choir of Clonard under the conductorship of Monsieur de Meulemeester, the well known organist and composer. All pieces were sung with rare beauty and taste, the solemnity and impressiveness of the sacred music being fully expressed.[40]

De Meulemeester's sacred music was regularly sung by Clonard choir, his motets, in particular, being included on all major feasts.[41] One notable occasion that featured a work by the Belgian was the 'opening' of the new organ on 26 May 1912:

At the twelve o'clock Mass the following, among other pieces, were beautifully sung by an augmented choir:– 'Singenberger,' 'Jesu Dulcis Memoria,' 'Ave Maria Arcadelt,' Lemman's [sic] 'Easter Sonata,' and Meulemeester's 'Hymn to St Cecilia.' M. Meulemeester presided at the organ, and the effect produced by the superb instrument, played by a master hand, was indeed memorable.[42]

Keenly aware of the competent, loyal service given by Lemmens graduates to the Irish Church, de Meulemeester, writing in 1935, stressed the need for 'more judicious' organist appointments. Failure to make appointments 'with the necessary discrimination' had led to a situation where good organs were 'in the hands of "executioners" instead of "executants," – in the hands of so-called organists'.[43] Poor organists and choirmasters were directly responsible for 'the unworthy condition' of sacred music in Ireland, 'the scarcity of efficient organists' being 'at the root of most existing defects in the art of Sacred Music.'[44] In 1905, thirty years before he wrote his handbook on church music reform for 'all who are concerned in the progress of ecclesiastical art', de Meulemeester had attempted to fulfil the 'crying necessity' for training for Irish organists when he 'submitted a scheme for an inter-diocesan School of Church music' to Bishop Henry Henry of Down and Connor.[45] Due to the bishop's sudden death, however, the proposal progressed no further.

The Westphalian-born priest, musician, and scholar, Heinrich Bewerunge (1862–1923), like de Meulemeester, knew that the training of organists and choirmasters would have to become 'the pivot of reform.'[46] In an article published in the *New Ireland Review* in 1900, Bewerunge, who had been appointed to a new chair of 'Church Chant and Organ' at St Patrick's College, Maynooth, in 1888, outlined the qualities required of one who would 'judge on the suitability of any music for Church services.' His description accurately profiles the musicians from mainland Europe who secured positions at Catholic cathedrals and churches in Ireland at the end of the nineteenth century:

One hundred years with the Clonard Redemptorists (Dublin: Columba Press, 2003), pp 189–94.
40 *Clonard Domestic Chronicle*, i, 124.   **41** See Jones, 'Chevalier de Meulemeester', 151.   **42** *Irish News and Belfast Morning News*, 27 May 1912, 6.   **43** De Meulemeester, *The reform of church music*, p. 77.
44 Ibid.   **45** Ibid., p. 74.   **46** Ibid., p. 68.

> First of all he should be a pious Catholic, and, more particularly, be thoroughly familiar and sympathetic with the Liturgy of the Catholic Church. Secondly, he should be a good musician with a good historical training. He should have a fair knowledge of all the principal classes of music, and be particularly familiar with Gregorian Chant and the Palestrina style, the two classes of music that admittedly form the culminating points in the history of Church music. Of these two kinds of music he should thoroughly understand both the technical construction and the spirit that pervades them, and he should be able to perform them in a satisfactory manner.[47]

The reason for the paucity of such 'men' among Ireland's church musicians is as clear to the German scholar as it would be to de Meulemeester over thirty years later:

> we are severely handicapped by the almost complete impossibility for our young musicians to get a proper training in Church music. One of the results of this impossibility is that a considerable number of the more important positions of organists have to be filled with musicians imported from England or the Continent. This is not as it ought to be. But even apart from this, the general condition of Church music in this country is sadly affected by the want of opportunities for the training of organists and choirmasters.[48]

Bewerunge's appointment to the influential academic position at Maynooth confirmed the 'foreign musician' as 'an authoritative figure' in Irish Catholic church music.[49] Before Bewerunge's arrival, however, the Irish Church had already benefited from the expertise and musical leadership offered by at least eight German musicians, and a further eight known Germans would secure employment at Irish cathedrals and churches between 1888 and 1916. From the 1860s, German organists and choirmasters were working in Dublin (Alois Volkmer), Bray (Herr Stein), Dundalk (Alphonse [?] Heurmann), Limerick (Caspar Anton Wötzel,[50] Carl Arnold[51]), Cork (Herr Thinnes, Hans Conrad Swertz, Aloys G. Fleischmann), Cobh (Hans Merx, Rudolf Niermann), Kilkenny (Herr Moomaier,[52] Herr Weickert,

---

47 Heinrich Bewerunge, 'Cecilian Music', *New Ireland Review*, 13:2 (1900), 82. In his prospectus for the institute at Malines, Lemmens had already remarked that 'in order to direct Church Music, or to play in the house of God the noble instrument that alone becomes it, the fervent Christian and the skilful professional must be united in the same person' (see *LE*, March 1879, 51). **48** Bewerunge, 'Cecilian Music', 84. **49** Deacy, 'Continental organists', p. 32. **50** Originally from Mainz, Caspar Anton Wötzel (1828–73) was appointed organist-choirmaster to St John's Cathedral in early 1862. A 'highly distinguished professor of music' and composer, he had previously served in the administration of the Governor-General of India as 'conductor of the musical service in the department', 'Catholic Church', *MN*, 1 February 1862, 3. **51** Arnold became organist-choirmaster at St John's Cathedral in 1876. He had previously lived 'for many years' in Belgium and England, and came to Limerick 'recommended by … Cardinal Manning … and other Catholic dignitaries in England.' A 'distinguished student' of the School of Music in Aix-la-Chapelle (Aachen), he also studied at Roulers in Belgium; see 'The musical profession', *MN*, 14 October 1876, 3. **52** Listed as Herr 'Moomaier' in the supplement to the April 1879

Rudolf Niermann, Joseph A. Koss), Longford (Alphonse Haan, George Oberhoffer, Rudolf Niermann), Thurles (Maximillian Scherrer), Carlow (Gustav Haan), Ardee (Carl William Rothe), Tuam (Hans Merx[53]), and Loughrea (Joseph A. Koss).[54] Bewerunge, no doubt, was highly influential in the appointment of German organists to churches in Ireland and elsewhere, as the career of Rudolf Niermann attests.[55] On 7 February 1908, the parish priest of St Oswald's in Ashton-in-Makerfield (Liverpool archdiocese), Ardfinnan-born former Maynooth student Father James O'Meara, wrote to Bishop Browne of Cloyne, recommending Niermann as a successor to Alphonsus Graff:

> Herr Niermann has asked me to write you a testimonial letter on his behalf. Through Father Bewerunge I secured his services to help my organist and teach my choir while he is disengaged. I have no hesitation in recommending him. He is a thoroughly trained musician and understands Church music and choir training perfectly. He has done excellent work here even in a few weeks and I feel sure he will prove a valuable acquisition to any church that secures his services permanently.[56]

Despite the bleak picture painted by Bewerunge in 1900 regarding the training of Irish Catholic organists, some efforts had been made to ameliorate the situation. In addition to Irish-based continental organists taking on students, some Irish organists, like C.J. Hanrahan from Limerick, had travelled to Mechelen and elsewhere to undertake further study. The 'Cecilian Intelligence' section of the January 1880 issue of *Lyra* proudly announced that

> at a *concours* given by the organ class in the recently established church music school of Malines, under the direction of M. Lemmens, an Irishman and a member of our society (Mr Hanrahan of Limerick) distinguished himself, and was warmly commended by the critical jury present.[57]

Alois Volkmer, a stalwart Cecilian first mentioned in *Lyra Ecclesiastica* in 1879, was Joseph Seymour's predecessor at St Andrew's Church in Westland Row, Dublin, and taught organ at St Patrick's College, Maynooth (prior to Bewerunge's arrival there) and at the Royal Irish Academy of Music.[58] In 1880, *Lyra* included a notice advertising organ lessons at the RIAM, Catholics being urged to consider the particular merit of studying under Volkmer:

issue of *LE*, the organist of St Mary's Cathedral in Kilkenny is referred to as 'Moosmair' in the 'Register of cathedral organists', *Music in Ireland*, Fleischmann, p. 161.　**53** Merx appears as 'Hans Marx' in the 'Register of cathedral organists', *Music in Ireland*, Fleischmann, p. 161.　**54** See *Music in Ireland*, Fleischmann, pp 160–2.　**55** We know also that Joseph A. Koss was appointed organist-choirmaster to Loughrea Cathedral by Bishop O'Dea in 1905 'on the recommendation of Father Bewerunge', 'Kilkenny Singer's achievement', *Kilkenny People*, 21 May 1949. Born in Westphalia, Koss studied church music in Aachen and subsequently spent five and a half years as organist at a church in Weseke, Münsterland.　**56** From the Bishop Robert Browne Papers held at Cloyne Diocesan Centre, Cobh.　**57** *LE*, January 1880, 8.　**58** Volkmer is listed as a member of the central council of the Irish Society of St Cecilia in *LE*, January

> The class has been organized under the direction of Sir Robert Stewart ... The Professors acting under him are Dr Jozè, Mr Marchand, and Herr Volkmer, organist to St Andrew's, Westland Row [*sic*]. Catholic pupils will have a special advantage in studying under Herr Volkmer, as besides his acknowledged ability as an organist and contrapuntist his acquaintance with the Catholic Liturgy, acquired during his residence in the church music school at Ratisbon, will enable him to prepare them in all that they should know to fit them for the position of organists in our churches.[59]

The previous year, pleased to announce that 'a fair beginning' had been made regarding the introduction of Cecilian works to some of Dublin's major churches, *Lyra* noted that

> In St Andrew's, Westland-row, it [Cecilian music] is no longer a novelty, as for some time past under Mr Scott, as choir-director, assisted by Herr Volkmer as organist, and a select choir, some of the most beautiful *morceaux* of the Cecilian catalogue and many of its masses have been rendered with true devotional effect.[60]

Hans Conrad Swertz (1858–1927), born in Geldern in Rhine-Prussia, also studied at the Ratisbon Kirchenmusikschule, and was appointed assistant organist to Herr Thinnes at St Vincent's Church in Sunday's Well, Cork, in 1879.[61] Influenced by continental sacred music practice, Vincentian Father Edward Gaynor (1850–1936) had formed St Vincent's Palestrina Choir at the Cork church in the 1870s, and may well have been responsible for recruiting Swertz and his predecessor. Thinnes, who returned to Germany after Swertz's arrival in Cork, had introduced works by German Cecilian composers to St Vincent's, and was described as 'a *real church Musician*, a man who knows as if by instinct what is suitable and what is not for the House of God, and who will admit of nothing else.'[62] In 1890 Swertz was appointed organist and choirmaster at the Cathedral of St Mary and St Anne in Cork, and he also taught organ, singing, composition and advanced harmony at the city's newly established School of Music. When he immigrated to Philadelphia in 1906, his son-in-law, Aloys Fleischmann senior ('der Ältere', 1880–1964), succeeded him at the cathedral.[63]

1879, 33; see also Daly, *Catholic church music*, pp 47, 116. Joseph Seymour, Volkmer's successor, was a former pupil of Léopold De Prins.   **59** *LE*, January 1880, 8.   **60** *LE*, January 1879, 36. The same report on Cecilian music in Dublin further remarked that at High Mass on St Andrew's Day in 1878, 'the organ accompaniments, preludes, and interludes were all of a character with the vocal portions of the Mass and played with Herr Volkmer's accustomed ability'.   **61** Only the previous year, Swertz had become organist at the Church of St Jakob in Dachau. See Joseph P. Cunningham and Ruth Fleischmann, 'Aloys Georg Fleischmann, 1880–1964: the contribution of a German musician to Irish choral music sacred and secular', *Irish-German biographies*, ed. Joachim Fischer and Gisela Holfter (Galway: Arlen Press, forthcoming).   **62** Letter from Father J. Hanley (St Vincent's) to *LE* dated 2 January 1879 (published in *LE*, February 1879, 46).   **63** Swertz lost a lot of money through stock market speculation, and it appears that he decided to move to the United States to recoup his losses; see Cunningham and Fleischmann, 'Aloys Georg

Fleischmann, the most significant German church musician to arrive in Ireland after Bewerunge, studied at the Royal Academy of Music (Königliche Akademie der Tonkünste) in Munich, and had been a student of Joseph Gabriel Rheinberger (1839–1901). After taking up the post of organist-choirmaster at the cathedral (where he remained until the end of 1960), he endeavoured to implement the principles of the 1903 *Motu Proprio*, which had famously called for the exclusion of women from choirs.[64] In addition to substituting boys' voices for those of women, Fleischmann abandoned the masses of Haydn, Mozart, and Gounod, and in obedience to the decrees of the *Motu Proprio*, privileged plainchant and sixteenth-century polyphony. This transition, involving both personnel and repertory, proved a difficult one for the cathedral's congregation, and provoked 'considerable opposition' at first.[65] Fleischmann's reconstituted choir consisted of approximately 50 boys and 40 men, and as well as singing plainchant and works by a variety of sixteenth-century composers, they also performed works by Rheinberger and music by Fleischmann himself and his contemporaries, including Vinzenz Goller (1873–1953). Within five years of arriving at the cathedral, Fleischmann had won the plaudits of clergy and laity alike. In 1908 the cathedral administrator hailed the German as a 'master' in the training of boys' voices,[66] while a later administrator affirmed that the organist had earned the 'golden opinions' of people throughout Cork city.[67] Also worthy of note is Fleischmann's contribution to musical life outside of the organ gallery, which, like that of other Belgian and German organists domiciled in Ireland after c1860, was considerable. He directed the Cork Choral Union and the School of Music Choral Society, and in 1912 founded the Filedha Ladies' Choir.[68] He also taught singing

Fleischmann'. A second reason for Swertz's departure from Cork is likely to have been his despondency at the implications of Pius X's 1903 *Motu Proprio* for his mixed choir at the city's cathedral. After his arrival in America, Swertz became organist of Philadelphia's Visitation Church, a position he held until his death in 1927. In his letter of application (dated 29 June 1906) for the position at Cork's cathedral, Fleischmann remarks that if appointed, he would be in position to 'save the [Swertz] family from pending ruin and to help the children to finish their education', Fleischmann Papers, UCC archives, quoted in Cunningham and Fleischmann, 'Aloys Georg Fleischmann'. **64** See *Music in Ireland*, Fleischmann, p. 272. De Meulemeester, zealously supportive of Pius X's desire for the reform of church choirs, would later remark that 'female voices are naturally sentimental ... rather than inspiringly devotional: they please the ear,—but disturb the heart and mind; they are unsuited for truly religious music, however impeccable and artistic their renderings may be', *The reform of church music*, p. 23. **65** *Music in Ireland*, Fleischmann, p. 272. The exclusion of women from choirs in the wake of the *Motu Proprio* undoubtedly caused considerable disenchantment among singers, organist-choirmasters, and clergy. After establishing fine mixed choirs at St Vincent's and at the cathedral in Cork city respectively, Father Gaynor and Hans Conrad Swertz were among those completely disillusioned by the ban on women imposed by Pius X; see Deacy, 'Continental organists', p. 41. Such disappointment must have been further sustained by what one writer described as the 'more or less general view ... that the Holy Father sent his message to the whole world when he really desired merely to correct some musical abuses in Italy', H.T. Henry, 'Music reform in the Catholic Church', *Music Quarterly*, 1:1 (1915), 102. **66** Testimonial letter (10 February 1908) written by Canon Richard McCarthy for Fleischmann's application for a post in Germany (Fleischmann Papers, UCC archives; see Cunningham and Fleischmann, 'Aloys Georg Fleischmann'). **67** Testimonial letter (29 May 1911) written by Canon Martin Murphy for Fleischmann's application for a post in Augsburg (Fleischmann Papers, UCC archives; see Cunningham and Fleischmann, 'Aloys Georg Fleischmann'). **68** See *Music in Ireland*, Fleischmann, pp 270–1.

and piano at the seminary in Farrenferris. In 1916 however, he was sent to Oldcastle in Co. Meath with about 450 other German civilian internees, and was transferred to the Isle of Man two years later.[69] During his absence from Cork, which lasted until September 1920, Fleischmann's wife, Tilly, fulfilled his duties at the cathedral.

Alphonse and Gustav Haan also held posts at Irish cathedrals during the late nineteenth century, Alphonse at St Mel's Cathedral, Longford, and Gustav at the Cathedral of the Assumption in Carlow. In 1888 Alphonse, a faithful Cecilian, responded to *Lyra's* request for reports on church choirs:

> Dear Sir, – As invited by *Lyra Ecclesiastica*, I beg to communicate a brief statement about St Mel's Cathedral Choir, Longford, which is conducted by the organist, Mr Alph. Haan, and *is entirely voluntary*. It consists of thirteen singers at present, who meet twice a week for practices, each practice lasting three quarters of an hour. As this country, and this town particularly, is very damp, colds are frequent, and consequently attendance at practices at certain seasons rather irregular.[70]

Depite the 'difficult circumstances' at Longford, where the choir received 'no encouragement whatsoever, either moral or material',[71] Haan's commitment was unflagging, as evidenced by the following account of the Holy Week ceremonies of 1889:

> The very extensive programme of Holy Week music, as contained in the "Officium Hebdomadæ Sanctæ," Ratisbon edition, was rendered, as usual, with elevating solemnity, appropriate to the sacred functions, by the rev. clergy, as well as by the [cathedral] choir, and with strict observance of the liturgical laws, from the "Hosana Filio David," at the blessing of the Palms, to the "Deo Gratias Alleluja" on Easter. His Lordship Most Rev. Dr Woodlock, who was celebrant at all functions, was highly pleased with the performances, especially of the "Tenebræ" Good Friday morning, and High Mass on Easter Sunday. The music was taken mostly from the "Officium Hebdomadæ Sanctæ," from four Masses, by Witt; two by Schweitzer, and one by Singenberger. The motets were by Palestrina, Lotti, Witt, Zange, and Haan.[72]

Gustav Haan (*d*1922), who succeeded Jan Baptist Van Craen as organist of Carlow Cathedral in 1894, also taught music to the seminarians at St Patrick's College, Carlow. Given this latter duty, which involved the establishment of a college choir, his appointment was almost certainly inspired by Bewerunge's arrival at Maynooth six years earlier. Haan's dedication is best captured, yet

---

69 See Cunningham and Fleischmann, 'Aloys Georg Fleischmann'. **70** *LE*, August 1888, 84. See also Daly, *Catholic church music*, p. 100. **71** Bewerunge, reporting on music at St Mel's Cathedral in *LE*, June 1893, 43. **72** *Irish Catholic*, 4 May 1889, 6.

again, in press reports of the important cathedral ceremonies of the liturgical year, in which the cathedral and college choirs participated. Such reports also complement *Lyra* in offering a window on the repertories (largely Cecilian) of church choirs during the late nineteenth century, the works of Witt, Haller, Mitterer, Kaim, Singenberger and other Cecilians constituting the staple diet of many choirs during this period:

> On Easter Sunday ... The music was exquisitely rendered by the combined Cathedral and College choirs, Mr Haan presiding at the organ, and the music was as follows:– Proper of Mass and Credo (Gregorian), Kyrie, Gloria, Sanctus, and Benedictus from Mass in honour of St Ignatius, by Jos. Gruber; Agnus Dei from Mass in honore Spiritus Sancti, by Singenberger; Offertory piece, 'Regina coeli jubila.'[73]
>
> The celebration of the great feast of Pentecost commenced on Saturday morning ... The music was excellently rendered by the College choir. Mr G. Hann presided at organ ... On Whit Sunday was Solemn High Mass at 11 o'clock ... The music was beautifully rendered by the combined Cathedral and College choirs and was as follows:– Proper of Mass and Credo were Gregorian, Kyrie (new) was by Hohnerlein, Gloria, Sanctus (new) and Benedictus were by Gruber; Agnus Dei by Singenberger. Offerory piece was the Offertory of the day, 'Confirma hoc Deus,' by Canon Haller. Mr G. Haan conducted.[74]

Hans Merx, who moved from Youghal in early 1904 to become organist at Tuam Cathedral, was also responsible for establishing a college choir, that at St Jarlath's College, where he had been appointed Professor of Music.[75] The choir first sang at Mass in the cathedral in February 1905, the *Tuam Herald* noting that 'they had three beautiful Masses in unison, by German composers.'[76] In May 1905 Merx returned to Youghal and subsequently held posts at the cathedral in Cobh and in Canada.

The period 1859–1916 saw the appointment of approximately 10 Belgian and 17 German organists to Catholic cathedrals and churches in 15 of Ireland's 26

---

[73] 'Conclusion of Holy Week at Carlow Cathedral', *Nationalist and Leinster Times*, 2 April 1910, 4.
[74] 'Whit Sunday at Carlow Cathedral', *Nationalist and Leinster Times*, 21 May 1910, 4. [75] Merx studied in Aix-la-Chapelle (Aachen), with Professor Steinhaur in Düsseldorf, and at the conservatoire in Cologne. At the age of 17 in Aix-la-Chapelle, Merx 'had already passed ... all those difficult examinations which are required in Germany for the conferring of those Diplomas as Organist and Choir-master which are at least equal in academic value to the degree of a B.Mus. in the United Kingdom. The examinations, which lasted eleven hours a day for three days, included the following subjects:—Organ and piano-playing, choir-conducting, Gregorian Chant and Liturgy, Harmony and Counterpoint, and a thorough knowledge of the old masters of Church Music, especially of the sixteenth century composers, such as Palestrina and Orlando di Lasso', 'A new organist for Tuam', *Tuam Herald*, 6 February 1904, 2. [76] 'Some memories of the Tuam Cathedral organists', *Tuam Herald*, 19 March 1949, 6. The choir sang publicly under Merx's direction, however, as early as April 1904, when 'the service of "Vespers" was inaugurated in the Cathedral' (see 'The Catholic Church', *Tuam Herald*, 23 April 1904).

dioceses. These musicians provided musical leadership in a Church that had repeatedly failed to afford its native musicians the opportunity to avail of proper training in liturgical music in Ireland. Indeed, despite the efforts of de Meulemeester and the Ennis-based Belgian organist Ernest de Regge (1901–58) to address the issue of training, it was not until 1970, with the establishment of the *Schola Cantorum* at St Finian's College in Mullingar, that an Irish episcopacy began to remedy the situation.[77] Until then, successive generations of continental organists would continue to render their services to the Irish Church.

---

[77] See 'Introduction', *IMS* vi, 29, n.54.

The Armagh Cathedral Collection in the fabric of Ireland's musical history

ANNE DEMPSEY

A study of the Armagh Cathedral Collection of St Patrick's Church of Ireland Cathedral, Armagh, furnishes fascinating evidence of a vibrant musical city in Ireland from the middle of the eighteenth century to the early twentieth century. A contextual investigation of the collection, not previously undertaken, throws light on an aspect of music in the north of Ireland that has until now been relatively hidden and certainly undervalued. The collection highlights the inherent contrasts between music in the world of the cathedral and town society while still showing how these two apparently 'separate' worlds were inextricably linked; it also provides a glimpse of a world, far removed from today's, when church and community interests are not so closely intertwined.

The Armagh Cathedral Collection consists of 429 volumes, containing a total of some 4,000 pieces of music and comprising a variety of sacred and secular vocal and instrumental items in printed and manuscript sources. This repertory was performed over a period of almost 200 years from the 1770s[1] through to the 1950s.[2] The focus of this chapter is the nineteenth-century repertoire; it is interesting to note that the vast majority of the music appears to have been performed during the nineteenth century and just over a third of the collection features composers who were writing during this time. Research has revealed a fascinating dual-purpose for the collection since the music was performed both in the cathedral and in the city by local musical societies. Links between these areas will be made where appropriate and the circumstances of performances will also be evaluated, but first it is necessary to give a brief outline of the collection's provenance and overall content.

AN INTRODUCTION TO THE COLLECTION

Although the Armagh Robinson Public Library houses the Armagh Cathedral Collection, it is actually owned by St Patrick's, the Church of Ireland Cathedral.[3]

---

[1] The early dates are recorded in the manuscript copies of instrumental works (vols. 424 and 426) suggesting that this music was written by, if not performed in 1774 and 1770 respectively. Vol. 424 (ref. 209) is a manuscript copy of a Requiem in E♭ composed by Niccolo Jomelli (1714–74). Vol. 426 (ref. 1056) is a manuscript copy of Giovanni Gualberto Brunetti's (1706–87) *Gloria in excelsis deo* in D. Both manuscript transcriptions are in full score. [2] The later dates are stamped on the front covers of the choir books. [3] The research which I undertook into the collection, including the creation of the catalogue, was due to the kind permission of the Governors and Guardians of Armagh Public Library.

At present, the provenance of the collection cannot be positively determined; the bulk of it was kept in the cathedral itself, however, other reports state that portions of it were held in the Music Hall, Vicar's Hill.[4] It is believed that a fire in the Music Hall several years ago resulted in the loss of music. Thus, while Handel's *Messiah* was a well established part of the cathedral's repertoire, there is a notable lack of individual vocal or instrumental parts for it in the collection. However, the full score of *Messiah* (ref. 620) located in the collection has an interesting history: the son of Frederick George Carter (former organist of St Patrick's, 1951–66) discovered the score among his father's possessions in Canada; having remembered performing *Messiah* during his time in the choir, he recognized its correct place within the collection and generously returned the score. Carter also observed that a majority of the parts of *Messiah* may possibly be missing. The only remaining part books are a single bass part book (vol. 415) containing a selection of music from *Messiah*[5] and an oboe part book (vol. 182) which includes, along with a number of overtures from Handel's oratorios, that to *Messiah*. It must also be noted that a large portion of the early nineteenth-century cathedral music was mistakenly sold with the possessions of Richard Allott (precentor of Armagh Cathedral) at his death in 1858. According to Rogers, the 'lost' items comprised 'a large and very valuable collection of music, vocal and instrumental, consisting of the entire works of Handel, and nearly all those of the old composers'.[6] The remainder of the collection resided in the cathedral until the recent restoration, when the music was removed to the basement of the Robinson Public Library where it has since resided.

The purpose of the collection was clearly for institutional performance with a significant number of both choral and orchestral anthologies. In addition to the volumes presumably used during cathedral services by the choir, there are a number of mainly instrumental donations and acquisitions whose provenance is indicated by either inscriptions and/or stamps of ownership reading: Armagh Musical Society, Armagh Philharmonic Society, Armagh Amateur Harmonic Society and Orchestral Society. The inscriptions indicate the use of these sources by a variety of musical societies. In addition, there are bound anthologies that were evidently derived from various private collections.[7] Unfortunately it is impossible to establish at this stage with clarity to which organization each volume belonged.

---

4 The Music Hall is located on a road called Vicar's Hill located beside St Patrick's Cathedral. **5** This part book includes *All we like sheep, And the Glory, Break forth into joy, For unto us a child is born, Who is the King of glory?* and *Worthy is the lamb* (ref. 832–837 and 949). **6** Edward Rogers, *Memoir of the Armagh Cathedral with an account of the ancient two copies* (Belfast: 1881). **7** The owners' names were found inscribed on the various volumes. These names include Mrs Cuthbert (ref. 297) who owned a collection of cathedral music, Henry and Elizabeth Goodwyn (ref. 108) who owned Avison's *Eight Concertos*, I. Rouse (vol. 229) and Clarke (vol. 201) who both owned anthologies of secular songs and glees by a variety of composers. Other names mentioned in association with the privately owned anthologies are Revd James, M.B.H Strangways, R.W. Rolston and George R. Lawless, all of whom are referred to later in this chapter.

There are a variety of composers represented within the collection, ranging from the seventeenth century (Michael Ester [East], Orlando Gibbons) through the eighteenth (Corelli and Handel), to the twentieth century including Howells and Ireland. Despite the range of composers found in the collection, Handel emerges as being the most popular in both the instrumental and vocal sections, his works comprising one tenth of the entire collection. A poem, first published by Joseph McKee and later found in the Rennison files, comically highlights the preference for Handel's repertory (see Appendix I). Certain composers of the canon are well represented, with Haydn[8] and Mendelssohn[9] accounting for 2 per cent and 5 per cent respectively; there is, however, a significant lack of music by Bach.[10] The presence of music by John Clarke-Whitfield (1770–1836), Thomas Attwood (1765–1838), William Boyce (1711–79) and Maurice Greene (1696–1755) is an indication of the antiquarian bias apparent in the cathedral repertoire. One third of the composers represented in the collection are English,[11] thus just less than half the music was composed by Englishmen. A striking feature of religious music from this period was the complex and intimate network of composers connected with the cathedral community. Generally, composers studied with each other, dedicated their works to each other, and acted as both composer and editor in many of the collection's printed sources – as many as one fifth of the composers represented here were cathedral organists. Four copies of the Stafford Smith Anthems can be found in the collection (vols. 1310–13). These titles provide prime examples of the strength of the musical tradition in churches at this time where works printed by individual churches (e.g. the choir of Durham Cathedral) were used by choirs throughout Britain. The remaining half of the collection includes a varied range of nationalities including Austrian, Czech, French, German, Irish, Italian, Polish, Scottish, Silesian and Welsh composers. German and Italian composers feature quite strongly, while there are only one or two samples of such traditions as Scottish, Welsh, Czech and Silesian. It is important to note that nationalities such as Polish, Silesian and Czech are featured primarily in the instrumental portion of the collection.

THE VOCAL COLLECTION

Vocal music comprises 70 per cent of the entire collection with the most frequently occurring composers being Thomas Attwood, William Boyce, John Goss (1800–80) and Maurice Greene. A mixture of styles is present within the collection from the *stile antico* of Gregorio Allegri (1582–1652), Albertus Bryan

---

[8] The works by Haydn found within the collection are *The Creation* and a variety of symphonies.
[9] Mendelssohn's works include the *Wedding March* from the incidental music to *A Midsummer Night's Dream*, *Psalm 114*, *St Paul* and *Hymn of Praise*. [10] Within the entire collection, there is a vocal score of Bach's Christmas Oratorio (ref. 113) and Cruxifus (B minor Mass), which is located in *Sacred Minstrelsy* (ref. 1299 and 1300). [11] This statistic includes both Handel, described in *NG II* as English of German birth, and Mazzinghi who was English of Coriscan birth.

(1621–68) and Thomas Causton (c.1520/25–1569) to the more romantic manner of George Job Elvey (1816–93), John Stainer (1840–1901) and James Turle (1802–82). Unsurprisingly, the vocal collection is made up predominantly of sacred music of various kinds: anthems, services (matins, evensong and eucharist), chants, psalms, hymns, requiems, cantatas and oratorios. Approximately 80 per cent of the collection consists of anthems and services while the remainder contains a small number of each of the other genres. Only a small proportion of the vocal collection is secular comprising two anthologies of songs and glees (vols. 201 and 229). Both volumes appear to have been privately owned, by M. Clark and I. Rouse respectively. How they became part of the Armagh Collection has yet to be ascertained.

Joseph McKee's statement that 'There is no doubt that the 19th century was the hey-day of the choir both musically and financially ... the 19th century witnesses the Armagh Choir in full bloom'[12] can certainly be supported. There are many references made in the local papers[13] during this period to the high standards achieved by the choir at St Patrick's: for example 'The anthem ... was performed in that splendid style for which the choir is proverbial.'[14] This level of praise was a regular occurrence in the local papers of the time and on many occasions the choir was rated by the local paper as 'distinguished amongst the cathedral establishments of Great Britain'[15]. Almost fifty years later the choir was still receiving similar commendations: 'the late Bishop Blomfield paid the merited compliment of saying that it was a "model for the world"'.[16] Even allowing for a certain amount of local bias, the consistency of opinion over several decades engenders confidence in sustained standards.

The Rennison files (compiled by the Very Revd Henry Rennison, dean of Armagh 1955–1965), the central source of information detailing when music was performed, span a period of 364 years (from 1600–1964); it was not, however, until 7 October 1845 that the music programme of the cathedral began to be recorded in detail by the local newspaper thus providing a starting point for a study of the repertoire for the second half of the nineteenth century. The files' contents are mainly transcriptions from Diocesan Records, Visitations, the local newspapers and other sources providing information on the cathedral with the focus of each file being its musical life. The newspaper transcriptions provide the most fruitful information about the musical activities in Armagh. This resource provides many insights into the musical activities of a nineteenth-century cathedral as viewed through the pages of a local newspaper. However, a systematic analysis of the music and for what purpose it was written is difficult owing to the inconsistent record keeping typical of the time. Problems were also

---

12 Joseph McKee, 'The choral foundation of Armagh Cathedral (1600–1870)', MA diss. (Queen's University, Belfast: 1982), p. 75.   **13** There are three newspaper sources which feature in the Rennison files: the *Armagh Guardian* [hereafter *AG*], the *Ulster Gazette* [hereafter *UG*] and the *Irish Ecclesiastical Society*. The *AG* was the main local paper recording cathedral events from 1800 to 1879, and from 1879 to 1900 the *UG* became the main source.   **14** *AG*, 12 November 1855.   **15** *AG*, 9 October 1848.   **16** *UG*, 6 January 1894.

encountered in the Rennison files themselves: there are periods in which service lists have not been recorded and it is difficult to assess if they are Rennison's or the newspaper's editorial omissions. But given the detail of Rennison's files and their consistency (it is even noted when the services had not been recorded by the newspapers) it is reasonable to attribute any lacunae to the newspapers.[17] Thus it cannot be assumed that if a work did not feature in the files that it was not performed, rather there is just no written evidence. In addition, information about performance practice, in particular, is somewhat sketchy and incomplete. Nevertheless, the newspapers are the only source of cathedral service lists from this time and in this respect are invaluable.[18]

Inscriptions on various of the works performed have proven to be another valuable source of information offering insights into the ownership of these pieces of music, and often when and where they were performed. Many of the part books have either stamps as follows: 'THE CATHEDRAL/ARMAGH'[19] or handwritten inscriptions reading 'Vicar Choral/St Patrick's Cathedral/Armagh/ January 1916'.[20] In many of the anthologies a stamp is found on a number of pages suggesting the pages were bound together at a later date.

Many of the part books are dated on their front covers which is a reasonable indication of when they were being used by the cathedral, but it cannot be assumed that the music was not used prior to the date provided.[21] On some of the music, dates are written which denote a possible date of performance. The earliest date annotated during the nineteenth century in the vocal music is 20 August 1825 on a piece of manuscript music by R. Cooke and the latest is January 1916 on a number of part books.

The period 1879–88 was rich in information relating to the service lists contained in newspapers. Up until this date the service lists were provided on special occasions such as installations, funerals and the annual visitations of such as bishops and the Lord Primate. The organist during this time was Thomas Osbourne Marks who may well have prompted the vast improvement in the record keeping. There are between one and three entries per year prior to this date in contrast to the eight to sixteen during this time. While the Rennison files highlight Marks' term as organist as being particularly fruitful, McKee notes that Turle's period as organist was probably one of the most rewarding.[22] Nevertheless, this period was one of healthy musical creativity, dynamism and experimentation spanning the Oxford Movement as well as the revival of the choral music of the Anglican Church.[23] During this period service lists were

---

17 Ideally, an examination of newspaper articles is required to confirm this view. **18** The weekly cathedral service lists are to be found in the local paper outlining the specific musical service, the anthems and the hymns. **19** Vols. 208–14, 224, 232, 391, 392, 394, 395, 397, 398, 400 and 403. **20** Inscriptions have been transcribed as quasi-facsimiles, reproducing the exact spelling, capitalisation and punctuation of the sources while also indicating line endings. The sign '/' has been reserved to indicate line endings. Vols. 393–9, 401–2. **21** A comprehensive list of music contained within all of the anthologies can be found in Anne Dempsey, 'The Armagh Cathedral Collection', MA diss. (Queen's University, Belfast, 2003). **22** McKee, 'The choral foundation of Armagh Cathedral', p. 85. **23** Ibid., pp 81, 85.

mainly provided for important religious festivals, for example Epiphany, Lent and Easter, and Advent and Christmas; fewer visitations were recorded and only a small handful of funerals, ordinations and consecrations. In addition, several significant major events such as Queen Victoria's Jubilee celebrations (25 June 1887), a special requiem service for the Armagh railway disaster (22 June 1889) and an annual choral festival held during the summer months, were mentioned.[24]

The service lists provide an indication of the relative popularity of composers at the time. Cooke's service in G and Goss's service in A were both frequently performed in the 1880s but appear to have dropped from favour in the early 1900s. At that time composers such as Steggall, Stainer, Prout, Hopkins and Langdon were heard with reasonable frequency. There is also a group of composers which was evidently popular across the two decades at the end of the century comprising Clarke, Garrett, Nares, Smart, Sullivan and Tours.

To assess the musical activities of the cathedral at this time an analysis of the Rennison files in relation to the number of services that took place (morning, afternoon and/or evening) is instructive. Between 1845 and November 1879 only morning services were recorded, exceptions being two afternoon services that took place on either a consecration or visitation. Then from November 1879 to June 1887 both morning and evening services were recorded marking a rise in the musical activities. Between 1888 and 1890 the services recorded changed to morning and afternoon with only a few evenings. Following this there was a lull until August 1898 with only morning services noted. The period from 1898 to 1900 was richer with regular morning, afternoon and frequent evening services. Again, this expansion of the cathedral's musical activities can be attributed to Marks. During this two-year period there was also a performance of Stainer's *The Crucifixion* and an organ recital. According to McKee, prior to 1840 the choir attended Matins and Evensong on Sunday and sang at Matins on Wednesday and Friday. When the cathedral reopened in 1840 it seems that the number of services increased with Matins sung daily as well as the two choral services on Sunday. The other significant change after 1840 seems to have been the introduction of a more 'choral' approach to the services; in other words, parts of the services which had previously been read were now given over to musical settings for the choir.[25]

Handel's name appears frequently in the Rennison files and music for *Messiah* appeared to be particularly popular on Christmas day in the cathedral. On the twenty three Christmases recorded in the Rennison files between 1849 and 1915 a selection from Handel's *Messiah* appeared. The main anthem was supplied by *There were shepherds abiding in the field*, which was featured on every occasion, with other items including the 'Pastoral' Symphony, *Glory to God*, *For behold darkness*, *For unto us a child is born* and, of course, the 'Hallelujah' chorus. Armagh clearly adopted the custom first introduced by Theodore Aylward for the

---

24 Information collated from Rennison files. **25** McKee, 'The choral foundation of Armagh Cathedral', p. 81.

choir of St George's Chapel, Windsor, of choosing excerpts from Handel's *Messiah*.[26] According to Fellowes this innovation spread through cathedrals very quickly also incorporating music from other oratorios by Handel.[27]

Handel's music also made a significant appearance at Easter Services, most notably on Easter Sunday 1855 when the choir performed *He was cut off, I know my Redeemer, Worthy is the Lamb, Hallelujah* chorus and *Then shall be brought to pass*. This frequent use of Handel's music is in keeping with the proclivities of the organist at the time, Richard Allot. His evident preference was humorously featured in an article in the *Armagh Guardian* (6 January 1851) where the cathedral authorities were urged to give Handel's music more opportunity of being heard, rather than simply at Easter and Christmas.[28] In addition we are reminded of Handel's popularity in the wider community: 'In recognition of both Handel and the choir's popularity, the following article mentions the attendance at cathedral "In expectation of its [the anthem, Handel's *The Ways of Zion Do Mourn*] being repeated, the cathedral was crowded – one of the largest congregations we ever witnessed being present"'.[29]

Funeral services also allow a comparative analysis; these comprised Croft's *Funeral Service* and Croft and Purcell's *Burial Service*. The anthems used were *Blessed are the departed* by Spohr, *I am the Resurrection* by Croft, *Blessed are the dead* and *Brother thou art gone before us* by Sullivan and as processional for the organ, the 'Dead March' from Handel's *Saul*. This conventionally appropriate repertoire mirrored that of St Patrick's Cathedral, Dublin, as a description of Attwood's funeral in March 1838 indicates:[30]

> Greene's *Lord, let me know mine end*
>
> Croft's *Funeral Service*
>
> Attwood's *Evening Service* in F
>
> 'Dead March' in *Saul*.

Towards the end of the nineteenth century excerpts from two larger works were frequently used at special services: Spohr's *The Last Judgment* and *The Crucifixion* by Stainer (premiered in 1887). According to the Rennison files *The Last Judgment* was first performed on 18 December 1897. *The Crucifixion* was performed on 27 July 1894 and 17 April 1897 and Rennison records that it was given for three years running during Lenten services, although each performance is not detailed. The closeness of these performances to the date of the composition's premiere, 1887, is some indication of the cathedral's contemporary taste in repertoire as well as clear evidence of the work's popularity.

---

[26] Edmund H Fellowes, *English cathedral music* (London: Methuen & Co. 1969), p. 219. [27] Ibid., p. 219. [28] McKee, 'The choral foundation of Armagh Cathedral', p. 78. [29] Ibid., p. 100. [30] John S. Bumpus, *English cathedral music, 1549–1889* (London: T. Werner Laurie, 1908), p. 412.

Eight Armagh-based composers who feature in the Rennison files across the period in question had their work performed in the cathedral.[31] Richard Langdon was the cathedral organist from 1782 to 1794.[32] During this time he composed several anthems, psalm chants and an Evensong Service in A, the latter performed once in 1881 and twice in 1884. John Garbett, a counter-tenor and vicar choral from 1799 to 1822[33] composed Responses in A and F, the former reported as being performed as late as 1867. George B. Allen, another counter-tenor and vicar choral, from 1834 to 1863[34] appears to be have been a talented composer with two printed works found in the Armagh Collection: the motet *In the beginning was the word* and a collection of fifteen anthems. In addition to these works there are also manuscripts of Responses in G and another anthem, *The Lord is my shepherd*. Of these works, *By the waters of Babylon* (1879, 1883), *Let my complaint* (1880) and *It is a good thing* (1880, 1882) from the collection of fifteen anthems were performed in the cathedral (dates provided in brackets).

The full identity of a composer called Thackeray is still not known, but he was a tenor and vicar choral between, approximately, 1860 and 1899. He is mentioned as having composed an anthem entitled *Thou O God* and possibly a Service in A which was recorded in the Rennison files as being performed in 1881, 1884 and 1886; he also seems to have been responsible for an anthem, *Open me the gates*. Unfortunately these works are no longer in the collection.

John Clarke was organist of St Patrick's Cathedral from 1794 to 1797 and was probably the most famous musician associated with Armagh Cathedral.[35] In 1814 he changed his name to Clarke-Whitfeld,[36] and it is under this appellation that his works can be found in the collection (totalling 53 pieces of music). His compositions include a variety of anthems and services although within the period in question only *In Jewry is God known* was performed (once each in 1881 and 1885). Bumpus writes that John Clarke 'did much towards raising the character of the musical services in the cathedral of the Irish Primatial'.[37] Clarke-Whitfeld published at various times four volumes of his cathedral music.[38] The Armagh Collection contains one copy of *Twelve Anthems* and three copies of *A Morning and Evening Service with Six Anthems*.

Robert Turle, composer in St Patrick's Cathedral from 1822 to 1872,[39] features in the collection having composed an anthem entitled *Almighty and Everlasting God* and morning chants in E and A, although none of his compositions have been recorded in the Rennison files as having been performed. Thomas Osbourne Marks, the organist from 1872 to 1916[40] has only one composition in the collection, a *Magnificat* and *Nunc Dimittis* in G (ref. 1176–81). This evensong service was performed in 1884, 1888 and 1889 under the direction of the composer.

---

31 This statement is based on my observations of the Armagh Collection of Music and information from McKee's thesis.   **32** Alistair G. McCartney, *The organs and organists of the cathedral church of Saint Patrick, Armagh* (Belfast: Northern Whig, 1999), p. 79.   **33** McKee, 'The choral foundation of Armagh Cathedral', p. 317.   **34** Ibid., p. 309.   **35** McCartney, *The organs and organists*, p. 79.   **36** Ibid.   **37** Bumpus, *English cathedral music*, p. 372.   **38** Ibid., p. 373.   **39** Ibid., p. 82   **40** Ibid., p. 84

The final Armagh composer to feature in the Rennison files is Charles Wood (1866–1926) who was a chorister in the cathedral. Within the collection there is an anthem *I will arise* and a *Magnificat* and *Nunc Dimittis* in E♭. According to the Rennison files the evening service was performed in 1885 and three times in 1899 though obviously given after he had ceased to be a cathedral chorister. A composer who features in the collection but not in the Rennison files is Frederick William Horncastle who was organist from 1816 to 1822. The works found in the collection include a *Te Deum and Jubilate* in E♭ and a *Kyrie* in D both of which are manuscript copies (ref. 1030–1).

Clearly there was a wealth of talent associated with Armagh Cathedral throughout the nineteenth century. Two further facts help consolidate the choir's strong position within the sphere of cathedral music: in June 1859, Mr Turle and four gentlemen of the choir attended the commemoration festival of the centenary of Handel's death in the Crystal Palace, London[41] and a document from 1855 notes the high esteem in which the choir was held nationally:

> The Choir of Armagh ... to use the language of two eminent judges, the Bishop of London and the Dean of Ely and many others also, [is] universally recognised as the model choir of the UK.[42]

There is a significantly larger percentage of manuscript music found in the vocal collection than either engraved or letterpress music. A possible reason for this is one of simple economic expediency for the cathedral musicians who would acquire a vocal score and then copy their own set of parts. Scribes were certainly employed by the cathedral to produce vocal parts for the services. However, throughout the nineteenth century, the existence of the engraved and letterpress printed music reflects the increased popularity of published sheet music. The part books from 1916 to 1950 demonstrate the role played by the *Musical Times* in providing choral music for ecclesiastical establishments. This particular run of part books contains numerous bound copies of Novello Octavo editions of vocal choral music.

One volume found in the collection is of particular interest: Boyce's 'Cathedral Music', published in 1760, was the country's first collection of services and anthems printed in score. Alcock, who originally conceived the idea of such a publication, intended that it should prevent incorrect transcriptions of music.[43] It is the second edition of the work, published by John Ashley in 1788 (vol. 3), that is found in the Armagh collection.[44] Detailed study of the collection reveals that this volume is a likely source for manuscript copies in part books, a practice which accords well with Bumpus' observation that 'it was the custom in many cathedrals to purchase a small number of copies and make manuscript copies of the parts to be used by the choir'.[45]

---

41 See *AG*, 3 June 1859. **42** See McKee's thesis for a discussion of the credibility of this account.
43 Bumpus, *English cathedral music*, p. 256. **44** Ibid., pp 263–4. **45** Ibid., p. 262.

One scribe known to have been employed by the cathedral was J.M.H. Strangways;[46] volumes 204 and 207 both have his initials inscribed on them. As both volumes are vocal scores with a keyboard part they were presumably used as a source for transcribing the vocal parts for the choir.[47] Each volume either contains anthems or services which can be found in manuscript copies in the part books. The evidence for Strangways' ownership is further strengthened by the crest found on each book which reads 'HONOR VIRTUTIS PRAEMIUM/Rev. James M.H. Strangways'. His name is then found along with the list of subscribers on the second folio of the music book.

Volumes 6 (ref. 424)[48] and 8 (ref. 1312)[49] both have the inscription 'Robert Turle Organist' clearly indicating that they were used during his long tenure as organist (1822–72). Both volumes are again in vocal score with keyboard accompaniment, but in this case they were not used for copying parts for the choir as none in manuscript exist.

Pencilled annotations observable in the part books also provide information on when music was performed; for example, from this information we can ascertain that Clarke's *I will lift up my eyes* (vol. 214, ref. 329) was performed on 28 September 1892. While this volume is missing a front page, its music matches that of volumes 23, 208–14 which have the year 1893 marked on the front. The available evidence suggests that music was bound after performance and then continued to be used. Volume 213 (ref. 859),[50] also marked CATHEDRAL/1893, contains a pencilled annotation stating 'Done on the 27th October 1895' a performance not mentioned in the Rennison files thus confirming the fact that these records are not entirely accurate. Conversely, some of these inscriptions also allow us to identify some vocal works which were not given in the cathedral; for example, Mendelssohn's *Hymn of Praise*, of which there are parts for SSATTB (vols. 209–214), has 'Armagh Music Hall' written on the top right corner outlining precisely the venue of the performance.

THE INSTRUMENTAL COLLECTION

The instrumental music[51] comprises approximately one quarter of the entire collection. The instrumental parts appear in both printed and manuscript form. The vast majority of the instrumental section shows a keen antiquarian interest[52] with a clear emphasis on the canon with such composers as Corelli, Haydn,

---

[46] This particular scribe will be discussed in more detail later in the chapter.   [47] The services of vol. 207 can be found in a variety of part books: vols. 375–7, 383–4 and 378–82.   [48] The title of this volumes is 'Sacred Music,/Composed for the Use of/THE CHOIR OF DURHAM/BY/Thomas Ebdon.   [49] The title of this volume is 'Anthems,/Composed for/THE CHOIR-SERVICE/of the/Church of England,/by/JOHN STAFFORD SMITH.   [50] Edward Hopkins, *Let us now go even unto Bethlehem*.   [51] The term 'instrumental' refers to all music which contained instrumental parts, therefore the genre of oratorio has been included in this category.   [52] On this occasion the term 'antiquarian' refers to composers who died before the music appeared to be performed in the Cathedral.

Mozart, Beethoven, Weber, Rossini and Mendelssohn, and ranges from the baroque to early romantic. An article in the *Ulster Gazette* concerning the Armagh Musical Society[53] aids our understanding of the choice of repertoire:

> Societies like this deserve to be encouraged, they give our young people an opportunity of learning the works of our greatest composers, and becoming proficient in an art too much neglected in this country.[54]

The repertory of the instrumental collection illustrates that both the Armagh Musical Society and the Cathedral Orchestral Society shared this view. The only composers that can therefore be viewed as contemporary are the Irish composer Michael William Balfe (1808–70) and the Czech, Johann Wenzel Kalliwoda (Jan Václav Kalivoda, 1801–66). Nor could it be said that performances kept up to date with novelties since Balfe's *Siege of Rochelle*[55] (the overture of which appears in the collection) was premiered 30 years before the overture was performed in Armagh Cathedral. The majority of the instrumental collection features European composers with only 2 per cent by English composers, a situation at extreme variance with the large proportion of music by English composers in the vocal collection.

The instrumental collection also seems somewhat conservative with regard to genre, comprising largely symphonies, overtures, concerti grossi and classical concerti. The dates provided by the copyists indicate that the overtures and symphonies were copied and presumably performed between 1859 and 1868. The only vocal and instrumental parts dated were those for Mendelssohn's oratorio *St Paul* (dated 1865).

The majority of the parts show evidence of performance with clear indications of bowing, dynamics, performance directions and letter cues used for purposes of rehearsal.[56] The instrumental parts in the collection give an indication of what instrumental forces were used. An examination of the orchestral parts of each work reveals that there was a variety of instrumentation though featuring rather reduced forces including: strings, oboe, flute, clarinet, bassoon, horn, trumpets, trombone and piano. The majority of the orchestral works were arranged for a chamber-sized orchestra. On many of the title pages the term Quintetto is used: 2 violins, viola, cello and flute/clarinet or a variant thereof. This type of arrangement was presumably suited to the forces at the Music Society's disposal. There are a variety of instrumental combinations which are not consistent and several indications that there may be parts missing. When considering the sources at hand, the orchestral arrangements were distinctly pragmatic. On some occasions the presence of second violin, oboe and clarinet parts suggests that the first violin,

---

[53] A background history to the Armagh Musical Society will be provided later in the article. [54] *UG*, 22 October 1887. [55] *The Siege of Rochelle* premiered on 27 October 1835 at London's Theatre Royal, Drury Lane. [56] An examination of the markings on the score could provide an interesting insight into what instrumental forces were used and how they were used.

oboe and clarinet parts are missing. While the string section is consistently represented in the parts, the use of wind and brass varied considerably. It could well be that the larger wind and brass forces required for Mendelssohn's *Psalm 114* (flute, oboe, 2 clarinets, 4 horns, 2 trumpets, 3 trombones and timpani) were not actually present. There is no other indication within the collection to suggest the common use of horns, trumpets and trombones. Anthems are only represented by string parts, sometimes for cello only while others may have parts for two violins, viola, cello and basso continuo.

Given the presence of so much large-scale instrumental music in the St Patrick's Cathedral Collection, its role in the cathedral's services needs to be considered. The Rennison files give no indication that instrumental music was performed as part of the cathedral services. Instruments are only mentioned in connection with the Irish Fusiliers who appear to have held an annual service in the cathedral. An article in the *Ulster Gazette* (19 October 1889) reported that the military band played 'Auld Lang Syne' and the 'National Anthem'. It is not clear from the article if this music was actually performed in the cathedral or merely at the entrance. In another article in the *Ulster Gazette* (25 June 1904), there is an explicit reference to the use of an orchestra in the service of the Irish Fusiliers and a brief mention of a 'band of the regiment' in an article dated *Ulster Gazette* (13 October 1906). Presumably the bandsmen brought their music with them since the collection does not appear to contain this sort of repertoire.

The term 'instrumental' occurs frequently in the Rennison files although the context of its use implies that it refers to the organ alone, a usage supported by an address given during the inauguration of a new organ in Ballyshannon church:

> The discourse was eloquent and very appropriate, during which he took occasion to advocate the use of instrumental music in the public worship of God.[57]

The context in which the word 'instrumental' is used in this address tends to support the view that instrumental music was generally not performed in the cathedral.

An alternative explanation for the performance of instrumental music must therefore be sought. Indications provided by the music in the collection suggest possible avenues for the performance of the instrumental music: the Cathedral Orchestral Society at the Music Hall, Vicars Hill, and the Armagh Musical/ Philharmonic Society as evidenced by four different stamps/inscriptions: 'Music Hall, Armagh', 'Cathedral Orchestral Society', 'Armagh Musical Society' and the 'Armagh Philharmonic Society'.

A newspaper article by an unidentified author found in the Armagh Musical Society minute book[58] reveals that from the late 1840s

---

[57] *AG*, 20 August 1858. [58] The primary source for my research was the Armagh Philharmonic Society minute book. I am very grateful to Mr E.W. Lauder who allowed me to access the minute book. The book contains the minutes from all meetings held by the society from its formation in September 1887 to its

weekly practices, commonly called concerts, were held in the Music Hall, Vicar's Hill, by the members of the Cathedral Choir, under the direction of the organist, the late Mr Robert Turle; these concerts, however, were not open to the general public.

According to Grindle,[59] Richard Allott (Junior), nicknamed 'Fiddling Dick', participated in Friday evening rehearsals in the Old Music Hall, Vicar's Hill. He founded the Cathedral Orchestral Society which ran for 80 years (starting c.1846).[60] McKee's thesis[61] also asserts that the musical and orchestral societies gave regular weekly concerts on Vicar's Hill. Therefore it is probable that the music inscribed with 'Music Hall' and 'Cathedral Orchestral Society' was intended for essentially the same organization. This would also explain the presence of instrumental accompaniment in the choral anthems which gave rise to the earlier consideration of the role of instrumental music in the cathedral itself.

The other performing body that requires consideration is the Armagh Philharmonic Society. During a period of twenty-five years several musical societies originated in Armagh under various names. Many of the societies rarely survived more than one or two seasons; however, the Armagh Philharmonic Society, whose music appears to comprise a significant portion of the cathedral collection, enjoyed a lengthier existence. According to the newspaper article in the Armagh Philharmonic minute book, the first musical society of which there is any official record was established in the year 1845 and was called the Armagh Musical Society. This organization had a short-lived existence, surviving only a few years. Over the next 30 years there was evidence of a growing desire by a significant portion of the Armagh community for the revival of such a musical society:

> It is a pity that where there are so many societies we have nothing to encourage the science of music; but leave it to others to applaud and encore the products of the musical geniuses amongst us.[62]

Exactly twenty years after this *cri de coeur* the Armagh Musical Society was re-established in autumn 1878. The following list summarizes the works performed between 1878 and 1887:

---

dissolution in September 1917. Fortunately there are three newspaper articles (which are unidentified) in the minutes which outline the proceedings of each meeting in detail, providing details concerning plans for the society's future while outlining its history. The minute book also contains the programmes and posters for the first three concerts held by the Philharmonic Society in its opening year. In addition the source unexpectedly reveals information on the musical activities at the Music Hall, Armagh. Unfortunately as the year progressed the enthusiasm with which the minute book was kept began to wane: programmes and newspaper articles are no longer included.   **59** W.H. Grindle, *Irish cathedral music* (Antrim: W. & G. Baird, 1989).   **60** T.G.F. Patterson, *Armachiana*, ii, 43–4.   **61** More detail on the musical and orchestral societies to which McKee refers is required in order to establish their connection with the music in the cathedral collection.   **62** *AG*, 16 July 1858.

1878–9	the *May Queen* and **Messiah**
1879–80	*Acis and Galatea* and the **Creation**
1880–1	*The Lay of the Bell* and **Elijah**
1881–2	**Messiah** and a miscellaneous concert
1886–7	*The Holy City* and the **Hymn of Praise**[63]

The majority of works (in bold) outlined in the table can now be found in the Armagh collection.

September 1887 saw a public meeting held with a view to reorganizing the society because of its financial problems. The society found that the expense incurred in procuring vocal soloists was too great. The meeting, reported in the *Ulster Gazette* (17 September 1887), was held in order to gain support from the community. As a result, a committee, responsible for drawing up a new constitution for the society was formed. Essentially, it was hoped that the society would grow in popularity and thus become financially viable.

The first meeting of the new committee of the Armagh Musical Society was held on 1 October 1887 and engendered a number of significant changes.[64] The name of the society changed from the Armagh Musical Society to the Armagh Philharmonic Society, thus explaining the two different inscriptions found in the collection (there is no evidence to suggest that these were two independent organizations which existed simultaneously). At this first meeting of the committee the purpose of the body as 'a society for the practice of instrumental as well as vocal music, embracing all denominations' was declared.[65] Finally, the solution to the society's earlier financial difficulties was solved by the introduction of subscriptions (one guinea and upwards annually, seven shillings and sixpence for performing members and five shillings yearly in advance for non-performing members). A subsequent meeting, held on 22 October 1887, also records the formation of a 'string band.'[66] At some point between the re-establishment of the society in 1887 and its disbandment Thomas Osbourne Marks, then organist of St Patrick's Cathedral, was the conductor of the Philharmonic Society.[67] He could possibly have been the conductor for the entirety of the society's existence a circumstance that would explain why the music has come to be in the Armagh Collection.

The society was again suspended on 24 January 1908, the cause on this occasion being the absence of a suitable concert venue. Up to this point concerts had been held in the Tontine Room which had been demolished to make room for the city hall. Almost two years later, in November 1909, a new Armagh Philharmonic Society was formed when the city hall was procured for concerts.

---

63 More information on these works have yet to be discovered, for example the composers of *The Lay of the Bell*. The list has been copied from the newspaper article. Those works in bold indicate that the music can be found in the collection. **64** The unidentified newspaper source from which this information is taken can be found in the minute book. **65** Ibid. **66** Further information about the string band has yet to come to light. **67** McCartney, *The organs and organists*, p. 84.

Less than 10 years later, on 24 September 1917, the society was again suspended, with no reason given in the minute books.

The small number of programmes which exist in the minute book reveal that instrumental and vocal, secular and sacred music were typically mingled in the same concerts. As can be seen in Appendix II, there was also an eclectic mix of composers and repertory. Although the canon was well represented, there was also a variety of relatively unknown composers such as Kirjule, Pinsuti, Becker, and Randeggar. Each of the three concert programmes included in the minute book contained a selection from an oratorio, songs performed by guest soloists, and concluded with the National Anthem.[68]

Although the Philharmonic Society and the Cathedral were obviously separate organizations, there were clear links between the two bodies thus explaining the presence of music from the Philharmonic Society in the cathedral collection. For example, apart from Marks's dual role as cathedral organist and conductor of the musical society, a Mr Tarleton, vicar choral of Armagh Cathedral in the 1880s, was the soloist at the opening concert of the musical society on 15 December 1887 in the Tontine Room. The committee members and vice presidents were also closely connected to the cathedral; for instance, the Very Revd the dean of Armagh (*c.*1878) was involved in the committee. Thus the cathedral was a major player in the broader cultural activities of the Armagh community.

One of the committee members present at the final meeting in 1917 was one R.W. Rolston. This particular name is significant in connection with Armagh Cathedral because of an inscription found on a number of volumes: 'Presented to Armagh Cathedral Orchestral Society, by R.W. Rolston Esq. March 1919'. One explanation may be that this may have been the music used by Armagh Philharmonic Society, which was presented by Rolston to the cathedral when it was finally decided that the society would not be reformed. Another name found inscribed on the music in the collection is George R. Lawless who acted as chair of the society between 1899 and 1900, thus providing yet another link between the musical society and the St Patrick's Cathedral Collection.

A further connection between the Society and St Patrick's Cathedral is established by the sole identified scribe in the collection, the Revd James Henry Michael Strangways. The minute books reveal that he was paid by the cathedral in 1858 for copying music, and the instrumental overtures, inscribed 'Armagh Musical Society', also contain manuscript music copied by Strangways, thereby confirming his connection with both organizations. The dates provided by Strangways indicate that the overtures and symphonies were copied and presumably performed between 1859 and 1868. Considering that the Philharmonic Society mentioned in the minute book was reformed in 1887, the music must either have been owned by a previous Musical Society or was first used in the Musical Hall by the orchestral society and later owned by the Musical Society.

---

68 See Appendix II for transcriptions of the concert programmes taken from the minute book.

CONCLUSION

The Cathedral Collection of St Patrick's, Armagh, contains significant information about nineteenth-century Irish cathedral music that should prove beneficial to both musicological endeavour and more broadly social history in the north of Ireland in the period. The collection itself is augmented and complemented by a small number of primary sources, found in the Robinson Public Library, Armagh, directly related to Armagh Cathedral.[69] The combined resources of the Cathedral Collection, the Rennison files and the minute book of the Philharmonic Society paint a vivid picture of Armagh as a musical city in the latter decades of the nineteenth and early twentieth centuries. This image is reinforced by another unidentified newspaper article held in the Philharmonic Society's minute book:

> He [Revd S.E. Wilson] said he thought it was very desirable that the society should be thoroughly developed in this musical city of Ireland. They all knew that there was a large amount of local talent. They had excellent teachers of music, and they had a great number of young ladies and gentlemen who were well up in the musical department, and it would be a great pity if there was any interlude in the growth in the society.

The collection and the light it throws on the surrounding community can offer the opportunity for much further study of what was clearly a vibrant musical centre.

APPENDIX I

THE MUSIC HALL GHOST

Near the Cathedral stands a hall
To Music set apart
Where Singin-men and Choir boys small
And fiddlers ply their art.

Their leader late – Precentor Dick –
For many a year and day
There cracked young crowns with fiddlestick
And o'er the choir held sway.

His reign was long – his power was sole –
Nor feared he Lord or Duke
And all did yield to his control
Except one sturdy cook.

---

[69] The primary sources included service lists of the cathedral and a minute book of the Armagh Musical Society.

Dick reverend Music is an art
When cast in classic mould
Loved Handel, Haydn, and Mozart,
With the noble masters old.

But sneered at Mendelssohn and Spohr,
Admired them not the least,
Called Donizetti a "great bore",
Swore Bishop was a "beast".

But all things pass away, and death
O'er took him quick one day
And stopped our stern Precentor's breath,
And turned to dust his clay.

Lo! In the hall the fiddlers scream
Light strains not heard before;
No longer Handel reigns supreme
As in the days of yore.

Now Mendelssohn is all the rage,
And then they pass to worse
And borrow music from the stage,
Not care for Dick a curse.

Der Freitschütz' [*sic*] arias profane the place
One night when storms were loud
When in bursts Dick, with awful face,
All wrapped in funeral shroud.

Then palsied falls each fiddler's hand,
And none know what to do
Til [*recte* Turle] calls out, "Play Handel's 'grand'
Let's give him number two".

Then fiddlers great and fiddlers small
Each plays as best he can
All out of time, and discord all
So scared is every man.

'Twas better thus, for very soon
(Yet of this they cannot boast)
They scraped so sadly out of tune
Away fled Richard's ghost.

APPENDIX II

TWO CONTRASTING PROGRAMMES FROM WINTER 1887

Programme for 12 November 1887

Armagh Philharmonic Society. / A SELECTION / OF / SONGS, TRIOS GLEES, & C., / WILL BE GIVEN IN THE / INFANT SCHOOL ROOM, CHURCH WALK, / ON THURSDAY EVENING, 17TH NOVEMBER, / AT EIGHT O'CLOCK. / CONDUCTOR–T.OSBOURNE MARKS, MUS.D. /

PART–I. / Chorus, "The Gipsy" (Preciosa), WEBER. / Song, "Jack's Yarn," DIEHL. / Rev. W.F. Johnson. / Trio, "Hark! the Curfew," ATTWOOD. / Miss Josephine Bell, Miss Cowan, and Mr. A. Strong. / Song, "The Little Wonder," RODNEY. / Mrs. Coote. / Glee, "Come o'er the Brook," BISHOP. / Song, "There is a Flower," WALLACE. / Mr. Flanagan. / Trio, "A Little Farm," HOOK. / Rev. W.F. Johnson, Dr. Marks, and Mr. Nelson. / Song, "Come Lasses and Lads," _____ / Mrs. W.F. Johnson. / Quartette, "I love my Love," ALLEN. / Mrs. Coote, Miss Marks, Rev. W.F. Johnson, and Mr Nelson. / Part Song, "Madeleine," ROECKEL.

PART–II. / Song, "Once Again." SULLIVAN. / Miss E. McDowell. / Glee, "Come, Dorothy, Come," VOLKSLIED. / Song, "My Fiddle and I," GOODEVE. / Miss Robinson. / Song, "The Death of Nelson," BRAHAM. / Mr. Flanagan. / Quartette, "Call John," AMERICAN. / Mrs. Coote, Miss Marks, Mr. Johnson, and Mr. Nelson. / Glee, "You Stole my Love." MACFARREN. / Song, "The Kissing Gate," COWEN. / Mrs. Coote. / Glee, "The Boatie Rows," WATSON.

DOORS OPEN AT 7.30, / ADMISSION SIXPENCE. / MEMBERS FREE. / W.F. JOHNSON, CLK., / 12TH NOV., 1887. ARTHUR NELSON, HON. SECS.

Programme for 15 December 1887

OPENING CONCERT, / THURSDAY, 15TH DECEMBER, 1887, / AT EIGHT O'CLOCK, P.M. / CONDUCTOR:– T. OSBORNE MARKS, MUS. DOC. / PRINCIPAL ARTISTS. / SOPRANO:– MISS MARY RUSSELL. / CONTRALTO:– MISS KATE WINDSOR, / (LONDON POPULAR CONCERTS.) / TENOR:– MR. T.R. TARLETON, / (ARMAGH CATHEDRAL.) / BASS:– MR. CHARLES KELLY, / (ST. PATRICK'S AND CHRIST CHURCH CATHEDRALS, DUBLIN.) / LEADER OF BAND:– MR. EDGAR HAINES, / (LEADER BELFAST PHILHARMONIC SOCIETY.)

First Violin. / MISS A THACKERAY. / MR EDGAR HAINES. / MR JOHN WALKER. / MR J.H. KERR. / Viola. / MR J.D. PRICE. / MR JOHN BOYD. / MR A NELSON.
Contra Basso. / MR CHARLESWOOD.

Second Violin. / MISS MARKS. / MR J.R. ROLSTON. / MR WALTER WOOD. / MR FRED BOYD. / MR JAMES FARR. / Violincello. / MR EDMUND LEE. / MR ANDREW BOYD.

Flute. / MR HENDREY.

Pianoforte. / MASTER HARRY SMITH.

RESERVED SEATS,– 2/6 UNRESERVED SEATS,– 1/- / TICKETS TO BE HAD AT M'WATTERS'.

PROGRAMME. / PART 1. / CANTATA, – – "RUTH," – – ALFRED R. GAUL. / PART II / OVERTURE,… … … "Tancredi," … … … ROSSINI. / Song, … …… "Last Night," … … … KIRJULF. / (MISS MARY RUSSELL.) / Song, … … "Bedouin Love Song," … … PINSUITI. / (MR CHARLES KELLY.) / Part Song, … … … "All is Still," … … … MACFARREN. / Song, … … "Love smiles but to deceive," … … BALFE. / Song, … … … "Alice," … … … ASCHER. / (MR T.R.TARLETON.) / _____ … … "Reve Après la Danse," … … DOBROWOLSKI. / Song, … … … "Go-od-bye," … … … TOSTI. / (MISS MARY RUSSELL.) / Song, … … … "The Owl," … … … S. ADAMS. / Song, … … "Oh! would I were a Village Girl," … RANDEGGER. / (MISS KATE WINDSOR.) / Song, … … … "The distant Shore," … … SULLIVAN. / (MR T.R. TARLETON.) / Choral March, … "Come merry Comrades all," … … BECKER. / (ARRANGED FOR BAND BY DR MARKS.) / GOD SAVE THE QUEEN, / WITH ORCHESTRAL ACCOMPANIMENT. / M'WATTERS, PRINTER, ARMAGH.

The transmission of song in national schools of mid nineteenth-century Ireland: social, religious and political values in canon

MARIE McCARTHY

The middle decades of the nineteenth century were marked by rapid social and cultural change in Ireland. Some developments such as mass emigration, a decline in the use of the Irish language as the vernacular of the native people, and an increase in nationalist sentiment resulted from circumstances unique to Ireland. Other developments such as the establishment of a national education system and the spread of literacy among the lower social classes were a feature of national development in other countries too. The provision of formal education through the National School System which was established in 1831 played a major role in expanding the consciousness of the native Irish and broadening the range of social and economic opportunities available to them.

In this chapter I will examine one aspect of formal education that provides insight into musical development in mid nineteenth-century Ireland – the transmission of music in national schools. I argue that by examining music transmission in this context, insights can be gained about the manner in which social, religious and political values were reproduced through the institution of schooling. The argument is based on the assumption that schooling reproduces the values of the ruling class in society by establishing and transmitting a canon of knowledge. In this case, I will examine the canon of school knowledge through song repertoire and its transmission in national schools.

As a cultural practice, music functions in highly complex and powerful ways to advance ideologies and to form and transform the identity of the young.[1] In the context of school music education, this is particularly evident. The transmission of music in education can be viewed as a political agent in the formation of national identity, as a social agent in ameliorating the lives of those who belong to lower social classes, as a moral agent to teach goodness, as a religious agent to pass on religious knowledge and values, and as a cultural agent to bring 'good music' to the masses and elevate their tastes. Thus, the process of engaging young people in music learning is not a neutral, apolitical activity but one that can be motivated by the values and ideologies of the larger society in which it occurs. Prior to examining music in national education in the middle decades of the century, it is necessary to describe the larger landscape of musical life and educational development of the period.

---

[1] Christopher Small, *Music, society, and education*, rev. edn. (London: John Calder, 1980), p. 80.

A DIVERSITY OF MUSICAL SUBCULTURES

A survey of musical life in this period attests to the diversity and hegemonic structure of music subcultures, each rooted in different social and cultural ideologies. While clear lines of demarcation existed between different subcultural groups, in this period those lines began to be blurred by changing sociocultural and political values. As English became more widely spoken among the native Irish, the interplay of musical traditions increased and became more complex, evident for example, in the influence of popular English song on the Irish ballad tradition.[2] Some traditional musicians aspired to new social groups and began to assimilate the musical values associated with them. On the other hand, Anglo-Irish groups sought to preserve ancient Gaelic music and appropriate it to their values and musical genres. Such was the complexity of social and musical life in the middle decades of the century. In the context of understanding song transmission in national schools, the most relevant musical subcultures were those that propagated the values of high culture and nationalism.

One powerful subculture that was centred in Dublin and linked to middle-class life in provincial areas, engaged in the performance and dissemination of classical music. This literate and culturally elite group was looking outward to London and to the continent for its models, its repertoire, and its pedagogy. Its social and political status was such that its members were empowered to control the discourse on musical aesthetics and subsequently to influence what was worthy of public performance and of inclusion in a music curriculum for schools and academies.

Within this subculture, interest in the performance of classical music spread rapidly in the middle decades of the century, evident in the massed performance of a thousand musicians at the International Exhibition in Dublin in 1853 and in the first Irish performance of Beethoven's *Choral Symphony* in 1856. At the same time, musical leaders began to show concern for the musical education of performers and audiences and musical societies were founded. The Sons of Handel (1810), later named the Antient Concerts Society, was the embryo Academy of Music; the Dublin University Choral Society was founded in 1837, and in 1851 John William Glover, professor of music at the Normal Training College, established the Royal Choral Institute. According to Joseph Ryan, this Institute represented 'the Catholic response to earlier Protestant initiatives',[3] and a symbol of the rising social status of Catholics.

Music also functioned to promote Irish nationalism in this period. One group who advanced this cause focused on the preservation of Irish musical heritage and founded the Society for the Preservation and Publication of Irish Melodies in 1851. One of the most prominent leaders was George Petrie who collected the

---

[2] Hugh Shields, 'Ballads, ballad singing, and ballad selling,' in *Popular music in eighteenth-century Dublin* (Dublin: Folk Music Society of Ireland and Na Píobairí Uilleann, 1985), p. 31. [3] Joseph J. Ryan, 'Nationalism and music in Ireland,' PhD diss. (National University of Ireland, Maynooth, 1991), p. 197.

music of Gaelic Ireland and made it available in five volumes, beginning with *The Ancient Music of Ireland* published in 1855. The work of Edward Bunting and Thomas Moore also focused on heritage art music. Bunting's work provided musical inspiration and content for Moore's *Irish Melodies*, published between 1808 and 1834. Moore's intention was to provide songs in the English language suited to the drawing rooms of the nineteenth century, using the idioms and sentiments of Irish music. The aim of the melodies was not to appeal to 'the passions of the angry multitude,' but rather to the rich and educated, and those 'who can afford to have their national zeal a little stimulated without exciting much dread of the excesses into which it may hurry them.'[4] Seán O'Boyle summarized Moore's collection as 'nostalgic, pseudo-historical, whimsical, sentimental productions' that were 'in striking contrast to the living Gaelic [songs] ... of the Irish-speaking people'.[5] Throughout the nineteenth century, Moore's collection formed 'the secular hymn-book of Irish nationalism',[6] and his songs found an honoured place in the music curriculum of national schools.

Another genre of song which emerged as part of the nationalist movement was the Irish ballad associated with Thomas Davis and the Young Irelanders. Davis and other Gaelic revivalists believed that music had the potential to unite all people in the name of nationalism. The development of the ballad tradition reflected the changing role of the English language as the vernacular of the native people, and in this instance as the language of this evolving song tradition. Unlike Moore's *Irish Melodies*, which were deemed appropriate for use in national schools, ballads were viewed by those who controlled curriculum content as coarse and politically charged.

A third musical subculture included the various streams of traditional music and dance that flourished in nineteenth-century Ireland. Socially and culturally it developed and functioned in different spaces to that of art music. As already indicated, the clear lines between subcultural groups were becoming blurred, due to the spread of the English language, the growing middle-class Catholic population, and the association of high culture and socioeconomic advancement. The association of traditional music with the native Irish was but one reason why it was unlikely to find a place in the school curriculum. Even more powerful was the argument that orally transmitted music was inferior to that of the classical tradition, a belief that was dominant in all Western countries that developed a music curriculum in public education at this time. Of the various streams of musical life in Ireland, the one which was most likely to be associated with the introduction of music into the national schools was that of the classical music tradition.

---

4 Thomas Moore, in *Irish melodies with miscellaneous poems, with a melologue upon national music* (Dublin: John Cumming, 1833), pp 207–8.   **5** Seán O'Boyle, *The Irish song tradition* (Dublin: Gilbert Dalton, 1976), pp 13–14.   **6** Donal O'Sullivan, *Songs of the Irish* (Dublin: Browne & Nolan, 1960), p. 7.

MUSIC IN THE CULTURE OF THE NATIONAL SCHOOL SYSTEM

As the National School System began to develop in the 1830s, there was considerable discussion about the value of including music in the school curriculum. In the process of deciding the function and form of music in the curriculum, a canon of school music was formed, the principles of which continued to underlie school music in Ireland for the greater part of the nineteenth and twentieth century. Two major sources guided the development of music in the Irish National School System. They were the *Report from the Select Committees on Foundation Schools and Education in Ireland*, 1835–7[7] and Sir Thomas Wyse's *Education Reform*[8] of 1836. Based on discussions in these sources, the primary functions assigned to music in education were social, religious and aesthetic or cultural. Due to the demands of educating all social classes of an increasingly industrialized society, the social influence of music on the lower classes surfaced as dominant. Music would serve to humanize and civilize, to provide a source of innocent recreation, and to elevate life-style and social manners.[9] Music's value in this instance had a strong utilitarian and social bias.

Music was also viewed as an important adjunct to religious education in the schools. This function was in keeping with thinking in Britain and the United States at that time, where a rationale for music in popular education grew out of the need to improve congregational singing in the context of Protestant religious practices. However, in Ireland a sensitive relationship existed between educational agencies and religious denominations. The explicit intent of the Board of National Education was to maintain an educational system which accommodated mixed denominational groups without interfering with the religious beliefs of any pupils. Denominational reactions were negative due to suspicion based on past experience, and this applied not only to the Catholic Church but also to the Church of Ireland and the Presbyterian Church.

A third reason for including music in national education was its cultural or aesthetic value. Sir Thomas Wyse, a Catholic MP who played a central role in planning the National School System[10] emphasized this aspect of music education. During a speech in the House of Commons on 19 May 1835, he said: 'We educate but half the being ... we make him a reading, writing, and counting machine, whom God designed for a thinking, feeling, acting fellow man.'[11] Having evaluated musical practices in contemporary Ireland, he presented a gloomy picture of his findings. With reference to choral music in religious worship he asked: 'But why is such music rare? Why are these voices not heard

---

[7] *Report from the select committees (of the House of Commons) on foundation schools and education in Ireland*, pt.1, Minutes of Evidence taken before the Committee, 1835. [8] Thomas Wyse, *Education reform*, i (London: Longman, 1836). [9] *Report from the Select Committees*, pp 345, 369. [10] John Coolahan, *Irish education: its history and structure* (Dublin: Institute of Public Administration), p. 58; James Johnston Auchmuty, *Sir Thomas Wyse, 1791–1862* (London: P.S. King & Son, 1939), p. 303. [11] Thomas Wyse, *Speech of Thomas Wyse, Esq., M.P., in the House of Commons on Tuesday, May 19, 1835* (London: Ridgway & Son, 1835), p. 8.

in every church and chapel in the land? We are silent, or worse – discordant.'[12] To correct national musical deficiencies, he advocated that music form an integral part of national education.

In addition to identifying the value of music in national education, song repertoire and methodology were also discussed. In the context of music in British schools, the songs of the people, which frequently embodied national legends, were regarded as important means for engendering the national spirit and of forming an industrious, brave, loyal, and religious working class.[13] While this statement was appropriate for Britain, its application to the Irish National School System would be in direct opposition to the British policy of cultural assimilation that dominated the system. The diffusion of national sentiments and the transmission of Irish national legends through singing was not the intended outcome of national education; rather the aim was to instill feelings of nationality with and loyalty to Great Britain, and thereby to bypass and suppress those aspects of culture that might stimulate rebellion against the Crown.

With regard to pedagogical models, British educators imitated the continent and subsequently adopted them for use in Irish education. British music educator, John Hullah, created a method for use in schools that was based on the French Wilhelm method. The Hullah method contained nothing uniquely Irish and was culturally discontinuous with the experience of the majority of the school population. Patrick Keenan, Head Inspector of the National School System, criticized the songs in Hullah's Manual because they 'do not pretend to any national character, … are foreign to all sympathy, … belong to no country, … [and] are sung in no home.'[14] The weakening of identity with native Irish culture was one of the principal aims of the National School System and Hullah's tunes were in accord with this aim.

Already it is evident that the introduction of music into schools was carefully constructed to align with the general goals and values of the National School System. Those values were enshrined in the song literature chosen for transmission and in the methods used to transmit and disseminate those songs in school culture. Viewing this process from the perspective of establishing a canon allows one to access deeper meanings of what occurred as song was transmitted to young people.

THE TRANSMISSION OF SONG AND THE CONSTRUCTION OF CANON

In a general sense, canon means rule, principle, or standard of judgment. In the context of recent literary and poststructuralist theory, a canon represents a centralized source of cultural authority that justifies and reflects the values of the

---

12 Wyse, *Education reform*, p. 187. **13** 'Prefatory minute of the Committee of Council on Education,' in John Hullah, *Wilhelm's method of teaching singing* (1842), reprint. Bernarr Rainbow (Kilkenny: Boethius Press, 1983), p. iv. **14** *Appendix to twenty-second annual report of the commissioners of national education* (1855), p. 74.

dominant culture and imposes those values on the young primarily through educational agencies.[15]

The institution of a cultural or musical canon can be established consciously and explicitly in education. Teachers, artists, and scholars play an important role in instituting a canon, and in helping hegemonic or counter-hegemonic values to be diffused.[16] The most overt manifestation of canon in music transmission contexts is repertoire – national songs, patriotic music, hymns, ballads, traditional airs, instrumental pieces, to name but some categories. Each musical tradition has its own central repertoire; in most instances novices learn a particular set of pieces in sequential order, sometimes related to technical difficulty, other times related to the social or spiritual readiness of the learner. Since song carries verbal messages, participation in communal singing can create a social cohesion and sense of identity in the group,[17] frequently in the name of political loyalty, cultural nationalism, peace, or religious belief.

Music pedagogy, the manner in which music is presented and disseminated, establishes its own canonic structures and procedures. For example, value was placed on music literacy – knowledge of theory and ability to read musical notation, and orally-transmitted folk and popular song were not deemed appropriate for use in school. In reviewing the use of song in national schools, it is clear that songs were chosen from three sources: John Hullah's *Manual*, European art music, and Moore's *Irish Melodies*.

MUSIC IN THE CULTURE OF NATIONAL SCHOOLS

Several school types existed within the National School System, and it is important to identify the differences between them in any study of music education in the nineteenth century: they were model schools, ordinary national schools, and denominational schools.

A model school for teacher training was founded in Marlborough Street, Dublin in 1838. A countrywide network of 26 model schools developed between 1848 and 1867 and they were strictly conducted on the mixed denominational principle. The National Board of Education exercised tight control over these schools, and thus its aims and policies of cultural assimilation were implemented in them. The curriculum included 'extra branches' of instruction such as drawing and vocal music. The pupils were typically from middle-class families and their social background was in accord with the values promoted by school music.[18] Parents and community members recognized in music yet one more of the

---

15 *The canon in the classroom: the pedagogical implications of canon revision in American literature*, ed. John Alberti (New York: Garland, 1995), pp xi, xvii.   **16** Maurice Goldring, *Pleasant the scholar's life: Irish intellectuals and the construction of the nation state* (London: Serif, 1993), Introduction. **17** Barbara Krader, 'Slavic folk music: forms of singing and self-identity,' *Ethnomusicology*, 31 (Winter, 1987), 9.   **18** For example, see *Appendix to seventeenth report* (1850), p. 241.

delights of 'Victorian middle class respectability' which could be developed in the new schools.[19] The Board provided specialists to teach music in these schools. In 1849, James Washington was hired as a peripatetic teacher who spent six months in each school teaching the pupils and teachers. He was the first to bring the Hullah system of music teaching to the district model schools. Other peripetetic music teachers were later employed by the Board: Mr George Washington in Belfast, Mr Quin in Galway, Mr Goodwin in Dublin and Trim, Mr Shiel in Bailieborough, and Mr Wötzel in Limerick.

In contrast, the majority of pupils in ordinary national schools came from rural, economically deprived backgrounds. Parents' attitude towards 'extra branches' of education such as music was not favourable. When vocal music was taught, it was against the wishes of the parents who universally opposed it.[20] The values which surrounded school music, the songs taught, and the manner of performance were disconnected from the traditional, musical life of the majority of rural communities.

A third class of schools, denominational schools, began to develop in late eighteenth- and early nineteenth-century Ireland, when orders of religious sisters were established with the intention of educating Catholic Irish children.[21] Their contribution to Irish education increased in significance as the nineteenth century progressed. In the *Powis Commission Report* (1870), convent schools received high commendation for their music instruction.[22] Board inspectors referred to the 'scientific' manner in which music was taught, how hymns accompanied religious lessons, the singing in harmony of Irish melodies, and the importance the sisters attached to 'the humanizing effects of music.'[23] Since no state funding was forthcoming for denominational schools, many Catholic orders such as the Christian Brothers and some convent schools remained outside the National School System. The Church of Ireland set up its own school system, the Church Education Society, in 1839. Presbyterians changed some regulations to suit the schools that served their members. Gradually, the idealistic principle of mixed denominational education was subsumed under the tenets of various religious denominations.

Given the different social, religious, cultural and political contexts of these school types, the transmission of song in national schools will be explored from three interrelated perspectives – the reproduction of social class, the formation of religious values, and the promotion of political ideologies. In mid nineteenth-century Ireland political agendas were inextricably tied up with religious identity, social aspirations with political affiliation, and musical identity with sociocultural

---

19 *Appendix to nineteenth report* (1852), p. 225.   **20** For example, see *twenty-second report* (1855), p. 45; *twenty-third report* (1856), p. 51.   **21** These orders included the Presentation Sisters (1782), the Irish Sisters of Charity (1813), the Loreto Sisters, (1822), the Mercy Sisters (1831), and the Holy Faith Sisters (1860).   **22** *Royal commission of inquiry, primary education, Ireland (Powis Commission Report)*, iii (1879), p. 284. See also, *twenty-third report* (1856), p. 184; *Twenty-second report* (1855), p. 120; Sr Mary de Lourdes Fahy, *Education in the diocese of Kilmacduagh in the nineteenth century* (Gort, Galway: Convent of Mercy, 1972), p. 95.   **23** *Powis commission report*, iii, 211; Ibid., ii, 139, 467.

values. These intricate tensions of individual and collective identity were constantly in canon and underpinned the practices of music education in national schools.

SONG TRANSMISSION AS A REFLECTION OF SOCIAL CLASS

An examination of song transmission in various school types reveals the social and cultural aspirations of the families whose children attended the schools. In model schools, the aims of vocal instruction were to impart a theoretical knowledge of 'the science of music' and to have pupils perform 'appropriate music.' In the annual inspectors' reports, reference was frequently made to the appropriateness of songs sung on examination occasions, 'care being taken that nothing of an objectionable nature is introduced.'[24]

The aims of school music were consistent with the social and cultural expectations of school communities. Emphasis on music literacy and songs from the classical traditions appealed to a middle class already steeped in literate traditions and high culture. The importance of music in school culture was visible to community members, particularly on public examination days when administrators and significant local figures evaluated the schools. On a typical public examination day when the children performed, audiences of 'respectable and influential'[25] figures were present – clergy, gentry, professional men, mercantile classes, members of the corporation, and the parents of the children.[26]

Music in the culture of each model school had common elements founded on the Hullah method and the use of song that reflected the values and life-style of middle-class families. At the same time, school music varied from region to region. For example, music flourished in centres such as Belfast, Clonmel, and Marlborough Street, Dublin, due primarily to the presence of enthusiastic music teachers and the support of the local community. Music in Dunmanway model school did not develop in the same way. When it was eventually introduced in 1853, an inspector observed that it was viewed in the community as 'something ridiculous,' and not understood as a school subject.[27] Without that base of support, it never thrived there as it did elsewhere. The school's geographical position, rural location, and the values of the school community were likely to have influenced this lack of development.

In the model schools of the south and east, the musical traditions and values identified with the network of 'big houses' were reflected in model schools and served the Anglo-Irish Protestant and rising Catholic middle-class population of rural Ireland. In these contexts music was valued as a social grace, associated with drawing-room pleasures and the English language, and seen to reproduce the values of high culture.

24 *Twenty-first report* (1854), p. 102. **25** *Appendix to twenty-seventh report* (1860), p. 93. **26** *Appendix to sixteenth report* (1849), p. 273. **27** *Appendix to twentieth report* (1853), p. 117.

In ordinary national schools, literacy and numeracy were given high priority both by parents and teachers. Parents considered 'time misspent which is employed on the acquisition of ... subjects not understood by themselves.'[28] There seems to have been little incentive to introduce singing in the curriculum and there is no mention in inspectors' reports that a public concert was part of the examination day's procedures, similar to model schools. Singing was examined like any other subject and evaluated in categorical terms on a 'poor' to 'fair' to 'excellent' continuum. Influential inspectors such as Newell supported the introduction of music into ordinary national schools, believing that school songs would supersede those of 'the humbler classes' which, in his opinion, were for the most part 'vicious trash, hawked about by itinerant ballad-singers; in times of political excitement often seditious, and frequently obscene and demoralizing'.[29] In his view, music education would elevate the tastes of the people and they would refrain from participation in music or musical events that had political overtones.

The social distance between model schools and ordinary national schools was also evident in the language used by inspectors to describe pupils' singing. Singing in model schools was typically described with phrases such as: 'with great ease and correctness,'[30] 'in a finished and artistic style,'[31] 'with taste and feeling,'[32] or 'with a precision, accuracy of taste, and beauty of effect.'[33] In general, singing in ordinary national schools was described in terms such as: 'from first to last painfully discordant,'[34] 'fair proficiency,' 'tolerable,' 'tolerably fair,' 'very little progress,' or 'poor.'

In convent schools, singing was regarded as an indispensable part of female education. Many community members had a middle-class background and based on countrywide evidence describing the fine quality of music education in these schools, it appears that communities typically had trained musicians among their members.[35] Certain religious orders were influenced by continental social and cultural ideals and identified closely with the Jesuit educational aim of 'forming the judgment or developing what the French call "*le gout*" (good taste)'.[36] Music education served the overarching educational goal of blending the aesthetic, the social, and the religious in the total development of the child. This goal permeated the culture of convent schools, evident in Jane McCarthy's study of the contributions of the Sisters of Mercy to West Cork schooling. She wrote: 'Concerts, poetic and dramatic sketches, original playlets and even full musicals, were performed by the children of these schools, in honour of particular occasions, such as the visit of the Bishop, or Reverend Mother's Feast Day, at

---

28 *Appendix to thirtieth report* (1863), p. 189.   **29** *Twentieth report* (1853), p. 113.   **30** *Twenty-second report* (1855), p. 267.   **31** *Twenty-eighth report* (1861), p. 157.   **32** *Twenty-first report* (1854), p. 51.   **33** *Twenty-second report* (1855), p. 100.   **34** Ibid., p. 132.   **35** For example, see Joseph Carroll, 'A history of elementary education in Kerry, 1700–1870,' MEd diss. (University College, Cork, 1984).   **36** Aine V. O'Connor, 'The revolution in girls' secondary education in Ireland, 1860–1910,' in *Girls don't do honours: Irish women in education in the 19th and 20th centuries*, ed. Mary Cullen (Dublin: Women's Education Bureau, 1987), p. 40.

Christmas or on Convent Anniversary days'.[37] If music assumed such a vital role in these convent schools of a geographically remote region of the country, it is likely that it assumed a similar role countrywide. Music was valued within the realm of aesthetic education, providing pupils with musical experiences that were otherwise unavailable to them. Exposure to 'appropriate' music i.e. harmonized, Western art music, would develop musical taste which in turn would refine and enrich the child's social and aesthetic sensibilities. From this perspective, music in convent schools functioned in a manner similar to that of the model schools, with emphasis on songs that reflected and reproduced the values of middle class, Anglo-Irish culture.

The aesthetic, the religious, and the moral dimensions of education came together in singing instruction. Singing immersed pupils in the good, the beautiful, and the divine. In its capacity to integrate religious and cultural ideals into the fabric of everyday school life, singing was perceived not as an 'extra branch,' but rather as an indispensable activity that offered 'self-fulfilment in the highest forms of human expression.'[38]

In Christian Brothers' schools, many students came from a lower socioeconomic class. The brothers provided an education according to the Catholic social ideal. While hymns represented their canon of song, there is evidence that Moore's *Irish Melodies* were also taught. At the North Monastery in Cork, Br. Burke and his colleague, Br. O'Mullane transcribed many of Moore's *Irish Melodies* (and other songs and hymns) to Tonic Sol-fa notation, and had them printed for use in the Christian Brothers' schools.[39] The Cork Christian Brothers schools, according to Blake, were among the first in Ireland to adopt the Tonic Sol-fa method of music teaching. It bridged the divide between the literate traditions associated with social class and a genre of song that the Brothers considered valuable in the education of Irish children. A similar solution in bridging these musical and cultural traditions occurred when Archbishop John McHale translated the lyrics of Moore's *Irish Melodies* into the Irish language and they were published in 1842. He wrote: 'To introduce these *Melodies* to my humbler countrymen, robed in a manner worthy of their high origin, has been my object in the following translation.'[40]

In reviewing the relationship between the teaching of song and the transmission of social values, the inextricable bonds between sociocultural values, and religious and political ideologies come into full view.

---

37 Jane McCarthy, 'The contribution of the Sisters of Mercy to West Cork schooling, 1844–1922, in the context of Irish elementary educational development,' MEd diss. (University College, Cork, 1979), pp 237–8. **38** Ibid., p. 302. **39** Donal S. Blake, 'The Christian Brothers and education in nineteenth-century Ireland,' MEd diss. (University College, Cork, 1977), p. 179. **40** *A selection of Moore's Irish Melodies*, trans. Revd John McHale (Dublin: James Duffy, c.1842, 1871), p. x.

SONG TRANSMISSION AND THE DISSEMINATION OF RELIGIOUS VALUES

As national schools became denominational in practice in the middle decades of the century, there was an increasing desire on the part of patrons (the majority who were clergymen) to make music part of general education, with the goal of improving church music.[41] This development was evident in advertisements for teachers that appeared in *The Irish Teachers Journal* beginning with the journal's publication in 1868. Skills in music were considered favourable if not a prerequisite for teachers:

> The master *must* be able to sing, and instruct the Choir in Vocal Music. (Church Education Society school)[42]
>
> Wanted immediately a Female Teacher who can sing well and play the Harmonium. Along with her school salary, she will have 10 pounds a year for playing and singing in the Chapel every Sunday.[43]
>
> Male and female teachers wanted, for a Mixed National School – must be Church of Ireland. If music is taught, teacher will get 15 pounds.[44]
>
> Wanted immediately, a first-classed R[oman] C[atholic] male teacher. He must have a certificate to teach Vocal Music.[45]
>
> Co. Cork – Bantry Parochial National School – must be member of Church of Ireland, must understand music, have a good voice, and assist in Church choir.[46]

It is evident that not only was the character of the National School System denominational at this time but also that music had a meaningful place in denominational education. In fact, it could be argued that music functioned to advance denominational education by creating a vital link between schools and the religious practices of communities. Clergymen sought to link school and church; a musically skilled teacher could coordinate musical activities in both social institutions.

Music in model schools served as a magnet to attract pupils from all denominations to the new educational system and to impress on the public the goodwill of the Commissioners of National Education. Since Catholic parents were suspicious of religious indoctrination in schools, political strategies were used to alleviate this suspicion. In Clonmel Model School, for example, it was reported that, 'advantage has also been taken of the singing in order to give effect to the devotional exercises of the Roman Catholic pupils at the hour of religious instruction, and they are now able to sing and chant creditably the hymns and

---

[41] Correspondence to the Editor, 'Vocal music,' *Irish Teachers Journal*, 2 (1 May 1869), 112. [42] *Irish Teachers Journal*, 1 (1 February 1868). [43] Ibid., 5 (1 September 1872), 444. [44] Ibid., 5 (15 September 1872), 466. [45] Ibid., 5 (1 October 1872), 478. [46] Ibid., 5 (15 November 1872), 518.

litanies of their Church'.[47] Efforts to attract Catholic children to model schools were halted, however, when the Catholic hierarchy declared a ban on their members attending these schools in 1863.

The schools of the Christian Brothers included singing in the curriculum, based on the *Powis Commission Report* of 1868–70 and sources written from within the Christian Brothers community.[48] Its presence served two ideals, the Catholic social ideal and the national ideal. The manifestation of these two ideals through singing were evident in the work of Br. Dominic Burke of the North Monastery in Cork. He ensured that singing was taught in all classrooms, with an emphasis on Catholic hymns and plain chant in preparation for the feast days of the Liturgical Year.[49]

In Christian Brothers' schools, not only was music regarded as a powerful source for transmitting Catholic doctrine to pupils but also in fulfilling the Catholic social ideal of moral goodness. One Br. Duggan reported to *Her Majesty's Commissioners on Endowed Schools in Ireland* (1857–58):

> The children are taught to sing moral and religious songs; and I myself, in walking out in the neighbourhood, have frequently heard them in their houses singing the songs they had learned in school, and I know as regards what we call 'neglected children,' who have not been taught to read or write until a late period of their lives, that it has been a powerful instrument as regards its moral effects.[50]

Similar to music in other schools, the public relations function of music was important in the Brothers' schools, in this case to affirm Catholic identity. On the annual public examinations in the North Monastery School, Cork, in the 1860s, 'the delightful rendering of difficult music by the large, well-trained choir of boys', was highly appreciated by the large audience.[51] Just as Queen Victoria was greeted appropriately with song on her visit to model schools in 1849, Cardinal Wiseman, first Archbishop of Westminster, was received enthusiastically in the Christian Brothers' schools during his tour in Ireland in 1858. On his entrance to the Richmond Street Schools in Dublin, 'all rose from their seats and knelt down to receive his benediction, after which the school choir sang a very beautiful hymn in praise of the Pope, which was said to have been the composition of His Eminence.'[52] Generally, in Christian Brothers' schools, song was a medium for moral development in accordance with Catholic ideals, and cultural formation in accordance with the prevailing ideal of nationalism. In convent schools, singing

---

47 *Appendix to sixteenth report* (1849), p. 269.   **48** Joseph Hearne and Bernard Duggan, *A manual of school government: being a complete analysis of the system of education pursued in the Christian schools* (Dublin: The Christian Brothers, 1845), pp 33–4; *Powis commission report*, viii, 93; ii, 7, 467.   **49** Blake, 'The Christian Brothers,' p. 178.   **50** Cited in *History of the Institute*, ii (Dublin: Bray Printing Co., 1958–61), p. 248.   **51** Christian Brother, *A century of Catholic education* (Dublin: Browne & Nolan, 1916), p. 139.   **52** *History of the Institute*, p. 279.

served a similar role in advancing Catholic ideals, but cultural formation was planned in accordance with the prevailing values of Victorian society.

Religious music was also in widespread use in nondenominational schools. When Thackeray visited the Dundalk Infant school during his Irish tour which was reported in 1843, he heard the pupils sing a hymn and observed that most of the children were Roman Catholic. 'At this tender age,' he wrote, 'the priests do not care to separate them from their little Protestant brethren.'[53] Later he heard the same children singing their hymns 'in the narrow alleys and humble houses in which they dwell'.[54] Thackeray's description can be interpreted reasonably in two ways. Either he, 'as a friend from England', was attempting to paint a positive picture of nondenominational education in Ireland, or the chanting of hymns was perceived as a common denominator for all religious groups and offensive to none.

Chanting verses and thus committing them to memory, marching, and singing were frequently presented as occurring simultaneously during instruction or school routines. In his visit to an infant school in Wexford in 1842, Kohl observed similar school activities when the children marched into the classroom, chanting a verse to an old British national melody. 'The instruction', Kohl remarked, 'is conveyed in a poetical form, the little pupils learning short verses, which they repeat or sing in chorus, accompanying it sometimes even with pantomimic gesticulation'.[55] Rote-learning of moral and religious verses as part of school ritual was likely to leave deep traces and ensure long-term effects. It is not surprising that the Catholic church viewed education in so-called nondenominational national schools with suspicion and subsequently banned its members from attending them. Singing may have served to transmit hymns common to all Christian denominations in some nondenominational schools, but it functioned in a much more powerful way to advance religious values and practices in ordinary and denominational schools, and ultimately to move national education toward denominational education.

SONG TRANSMISSION AND THE PROMOTION OF POLITICAL IDEOLOGIES

The songs transmitted in national schools were regularly criticized for their lack of reference to and origins in Ireland. Head Inspector of the National School System, Patrick Keenan wrote: 'I don't think that I have heard five different Irish melodies sung in all the schools that I have ever visited.'[56] He continued his criticism of school songs in the *Powis Commission Report* of 1870, arguing that the Hullah *Manual* contained songs that were not suited 'to the ears of Irish children', tunes that were prepared entirely for English schools, with not a single

---

[53] William M. Thackeray, *The Irish sketch-book* (London: Chapman & Hall, 1843), pp 190–1. [54] Ibid., p. 193. [55] Johann Georg Kohl, *Reisen in Ireland* (London: Chapman & Hall, 1843 [trans. from *Reisen in Irland*: Dreden & Leipzig, 1843]), p. 123. [56] *Appendix to twenty-second report* (1855), p. 74.

Irish air in the book. In his opinion, very little attention was paid to 'the cultivation of Irish music, the class of music which the people could best understand and appreciate.'[57] He recommended songs that would allow the 'national strain' to touch pupils' hearts, bind them to their native land and develop within them a great affection for it. Due to his encouragement, J.W. Glover's *School Songs* containing some Irish melodies were published in 1867.[58]

Thomas Davis was also highly critical of the lack of native culture in schools. 'Until the *National Schools* fall under national control,' he warned, 'the people must take *diligent care to procure books on the history, men, language, music, and manners of Ireland for their children*.'[59] Of these aspects of culture, he considered national song to be powerful in shaping identity and it grieved him that it was not being taught in the National Schools. He wrote:

> Our antiquaries may rescue treasures from the depths of time, ... our musicians may revive those strains wherein love, mirth, or glory are sung with angels' voices; but they are never given to the students of our National Schools, though little German airs, and English daubs and the lore of every other land are put within his reach whenever it is possible to do so.[60]

The 'German airs, and English daubs' he referred to here were part of the Hullah *Manual*, a set of songs whose cultural content was generally culturally discontinuous with the communities of national schools. Besides these airs, the most appropriate and indispensable song, and the one which lent solemnity to public singing occasions, was the British National Anthem, 'God Save the Queen'. A description provided by Sir Francis Head of his visit to Marlborough Street Model Schools, Dublin, in 1852, captured the spirit surrounding the performance of this song: 'The whole of the three hundred girls rose, and, as with one voice, commenced with great taste and melody to sing together "God Save the Queen"!! ... Their performance was not only admirable, but deeply affecting.'[61] When Queen Victoria of England visited Ireland in 1849, she went to the Marlborough Street Model Schools where a chorus of 500 to 600 voices sang the national anthem 'with taste and feeling'.[62] If she had visited other model schools of the Board, it is reasonable to assume that her reception would have been similar to that of Marlborough Street.

At one level, the singing of the national anthem was a culminating musical event on the occasion of public examinations; at another level, it was part of a ritual which confirmed for everyone present the cultural goal of the National School system, and its performance was likely to strengthen colonial identity.

---

57 *Powis commission report*, iii, 88. **58** William Noel Kelly, 'Music in Irish primary education,' MA diss. (University College, Cork, 1978), p. 50. **59** *Thomas Davis: the thinker and teacher*, ed. Arthur Griffith (Dublin: M.H. Gill & Son., 1914), p. 35. **60** Thomas Davis, 'Schools and study,' in *Essays and poems with a centenary memoir, 1845–1945* (Dublin: M.H. Gill & Son, 1945), p. 80. **61** Sir F.B. Head, *A fortnight in Ireland* (London: John Murray, 1852), p. 33. **62** 'Her Majesty's visit to the female infant school of the National Board of Education, in Marlborough-Street, Dublin,' *Illustrated London News*, 11 August 1849, 87.

While singing of the national anthem was a common feature of public performances on examination days in model schools, distinctive singing practices developed in different regions. One such region was the Northeast – Ballymena, Coleraine, Belfast, and Newry. Repertoire used in these model schools displayed a certain independence, creating an image of the Northeast as part of the cultural unit of Great Britain. For example, songs performed at the public examinations held at Coleraine in 1852 attest to this wide-ranging repertoire – music of classical composers (Mozart, Morley), glees, Moore's *Irish Melodies*, a German anthem, and Scottish melodies.[63]

In Ballymena's Model Schools, vocal music was divided into hymns and songs.[64] The religious homogeneity of the pupils facilitated the integration of religious and musical instruction. Although bound by the Board's rules and regulations, the development of music in Northeastern model schools demonstrated a certain local initiative and assertiveness. Efforts to integrate community resources and values into the schools seem to have been more prevalent in the Northeast than in other regions. This coincides with Donald Akenson's description of the individuality of this region: 'By 1800 the Northeast had become a coherent regional culture embodying distinct material forms, as well as linguistic and other non-material attributes. This culture was a hybrid, incorporating native Irish and imported English and Scottish components, but dominated by the Scottish elements.'[65]

Since Christian Brothers' schools of this period functioned almost independently of the National Board of Education, the Brothers had the freedom to put their own educational philosophy into practice. In effect, their students were not taught to sing of themselves as 'happy English children'.[66] On the contrary, the national ideal permeated school life and singing served to advance this ideal in school culture. Moore's *Irish Melodies* represented a genre suitable for developing national sentiments. Br. Burke of Cork was active in promoting this new and 'respectable' presentation of Irish airs and since many of the airs were slow and majestic of movement, 'they came to be styled by the schoolboys "Brother Burke's Lamentations."'[67] It seems that other popular Irish music expressing sentiments of nationalism such as political ballads were not used in Christian Brothers' schools in that period.

SINGING IN NATIONAL SCHOOLS: SOCIAL, RELIGIOUS AND POLITICAL VALUES IN CANON

As national education developed in mid nineteenth-century Ireland, education in music was for the most part synonymous with the teaching of songs. The

---

63 *Appendix to nineteenth report* (1852), p. 164. **64** *Sixteenth report* (1849), p. 229; *Twentieth report* (1853), p. 132. **65** Donald H. Akenson, *Between two revolutions: Islandmagee, County Antrim, 1798–1920* (Don Mills, Ontario: T.H. Best Printing Co., 1979), p. 174. **66** 'The Christian Schools,' *The Standard*, 9 June 1928, 12. **67** Christian Brother, *A century of Catholic education*, p. 126.

presence of this activity varied across school types and areas of the country, but it is clear from the evidence cited that whenever singing was a feature of school life, its function and form were aligned to sociocultural, religious or political values. The nature of these values depended on the school type, the community, and the relationship of the school to the National Board of Education. The song recommended by the Board songs were aligned with the values of middle class, Anglo-Irish society, visible in the way Western art music defined 'good music,' the emphasis placed on the 'science of music' – music theory and sight-reading, and the promotion of Moore's *Irish Melodies* and other repertoire modelled on it. Although Irish in origin and content, Moore's *Melodies* expressed sentiments of Irishness that were not likely to instigate a nationalist movement. From the standpoint of high culture, the elegance of the lyrics and their harmonized melodies added to their value as school music. This song collection found an honoured place in the music curriculum of the schools because the songs were sufficiently flexible to suit all social classes and political groups.

Another genre of Irish song – the political ballad – did not find a place in the curriculum in this period. Considering the political and cultural goals of the Board, this exclusion is not at all surprising. Objection to their inclusion was evident in the *Report of Her Majesty's Commissioners on Endowed Schools in Ireland* (1857–58):

> Pupils who have received instruction in music of a higher kind, listen with distaste to the coarse and too often obscene performances of ballad-singers. Songs embodying noble and virtuous sentiments may be ranked among the most powerful agencies by which the moral nature is elevated and character is formed; and the influence of such music on the human heart is greatly enhanced when it is performed by many persons singing tunefully in concert.[68]

Neither did traditional song find a place in the canon of school music. The reasons are manifold: its association with the Irish language that was losing status in the lives of the native Irish, parents' attitude toward school music, and the international view of folk music as inferior to art music and not worthy of inclusion in the curriculum.

Religious song formed a central part of the canon of school music. This development ran contrary to the Board's intention to maintain nondenominational schools. The singing of religious song not only transmitted religious values and supported denominational practices, but it served to advance the movement toward denominational education. Singing as a communal activity created strong and tangible bonds between various denominations and the national schools that served their members.

---

68 *Report of Her Majesty's commissioners appointed to inquire into the Endowed Funds and actual condition of all schools endowed for the purposes of education in Ireland (1857–58)*, p. 216.

One of the principal insights gained through this study of song transmission in national schools is that social, political, and religious values are nested within each other in an institution such as schooling. They are typically in canon, interacting with each other and being shaped by those interactions. In many convent schools, the sisters negotiated the values of Catholic education with those of Victorian society; in model schools, singing served the purpose of maintaining good political relations with the Board of Education while reflecting the sociocultural values of local communities; the Christian Brothers united social, religious and national values when they included singing in the curriculum.

However, in whatever context singing occurred, the underlying belief was that song can convey values through lyrics and communal singing can assist in building group identity. Therefore, the content and context of singing in national schools came to be regarded by all educational stakeholders as significant and strategic. What this exploration reveals is that song transmission forms not simply one canon but rather several canons to serve the diverse political groups who are invested in education. It also confirms that the formation of identity through music in education is indeed a very complex and opaque process. The teaching of one of Moore's *Irish Melodies* may have underlying social, cultural, economic or political motivation; the teaching of a hymn could be placed on a continuum of motivation from religious to political; or sacred art music may be introduced for cultural or religious reasons. Social, cultural, religious, economic, and political identities are formed in canon within the institution of schooling, as teachers and administrators negotiate the role of personal, local and national values in the content and pedagogy of education. This was evident in the manner in which song functioned in national schools in mid nineteenth-century Ireland.

Singing and sobriety: music and the Temperance Movement in Ireland, 1838–43

MARIA McHALE

On 1 August 1842, the *Cork Examiner* contained details of two different sight-singing classes soon to be made available to the people of Cork. The first was organized by William Forde whose enterprise 'Voice of the People' was designed 'for the cultivation of choral music, sight-singing, time [and] intonation'.[1] Forde, a local teacher, had already begun advertising his venture the previous week in which he had urged interested parties, namely 'musical societies, religious congregations [and] heads of schools' to take note of the advantages of musical instruction.[2] But Forde was not the only one interested in securing the voices of Cork for his endeavour. Indeed, a competing venture appeared just below his second announcement, in which Joseph Mainzer, the well known German sight-singing instructor advertised his series of classes under the heading 'Singing for the Million'. In this announcement, Mainzer drew attention to his success in England:

> M. Mainzer feels some pride in having striven with unexampled success to raise the moral condition of the People. For the particulars of his success he begs to direct the Public to his 'Musical Times' published once a fortnight. Not 12 months ago he came to England a stranger to the country and its language. Now, he and his assistants are giving instruction in Music to 100,000 Pupils: and there have been sold in the last six months 200,000 copies of his little work, 'Singing for the Million'.[3]

The battle for the guardianship of the music and morals of the people of Cork had begun. Indeed, the month of August saw some fourteen separate notices appear in the Cork press for both ventures.[4] By the end of the month Forde, evidently under pressure, had resorted to advertising free classes. In a reworked scheme 'Grand Chorus of a Thousand People' he promised that he would 'teach singing to a thousand of you a month without any charge. I will then unite the thousand voices [...] in the performance of more than one mighty chorus'.[5] It would appear that Forde's ambitious plan went largely unheard since his chorus of a thousand (a newsworthy event if it had happened) remained unreported. Instead, he was

---

[1] 'Voice of the People – Singing Classes', *CE*, 1 August 1842. [2] 'Voice of the People – Mr William Forde', *CE*, 25 July 1842. [3] 'Singing for the Million – Sixpence a Month', *CE*, 1 August 1842. [4] The advertisements appeared 1–29 August 1842 in the *CE* and the *Southern Reporter*. [5] 'Forde's voice of the people', *Southern Reporter*, 30 August 1842.

usurped by the arrival in Ireland of Mainzer whose first official lecture in the Great Hall of the Corn Exchange in Cork on 26 August 1842 attracted a large crowd. The mood was exuberant as Mainzer, who had been invited to address the crowd by another philanthropist and head of the temperance movement, Father Theobald Mathew, proceeded to expound on the virtues of singing and temperance. The combination of Mainzer and Mathew proved to be a great success. It was their joint effort and not Forde's that made the pages of the Cork press. The confluence of these two great philanthropists served to promote both their respective causes: Mathew had long realized that his newly-converted teetotallers needed alternative amusements to keep them from indulging in alcohol; while it seemed likely that Mainzer's teaching methods in his native Germany, in France and most recently England, not to mention his accompanying primer *Singing for the Million* would be equally as popular in Ireland. The sight-singing phenomenon had arrived in Ireland, and alongside its sister movement, temperance, was hoped would enhance the morality, health and improvement of *The Nation*: the mood was wholly optimistic.

The importance of the temperance movement in Ireland, particularly in the pre-famine period cannot be underestimated. Indeed, in a recent investigation, Paul Townend argued that 'it must rank among the more unique and under-examined mass mobilisations of men and women in modern European history'.[6] With this in mind, the role of music within the movement is seminal to our understanding of popular culture and social improvement in nineteenth-century Ireland. The objective of this chapter is to illuminate the relationship between music and temperance in the years between 1838 and 1843. While temperance activity remained strong in some parts of Ireland into the 1850s, the years 1842–3 saw its popularity peak and then diminish as issues surrounding Repeal became increasingly prevalent. In discussing the period under study, my aims are threefold: firstly, to acknowledge the importance of temperance as the chief agent for social and cultural improvement at this time; secondly, to recognize the role of music within the movement; and finally to examine the music, and the debates surrounding the use of music for temperance and improvement in Ireland. My concern here is chiefly vocal music. While brass bands were an important temperance phenomenon whose role has been previously examined, the focus of this article is on singing, since it was a more inclusive and therefore more available option to a greater number of people.[7]

In attempting to chart the progress of the Irish temperance movement, in-depth accounts have been published in recent years by several historians.[8] However, and

---

[6] Paul A. Townend, *Father Mathew, temperance and Irish identity* (Dublin: Irish Academic Press, 2002), p. 1.   [7] Aiveen Kearney's 'Temperance bands and their significance in nineteenth-century Ireland', MA diss. (University College, Cork 1981) contains a thorough examination of the growth and repertoire of brass bands, in addition to the political and nationalist aspects of the movement in Ireland. Also, Richard T. Cooke's *Cork's Barrack street silver and reed band* (Cork: Quality Books, 1992) details the growth and history of that particular band throughout the nineteenth and twentieth centuries.   [8] In addition to Townend's *Father Mathew*, recent publications include Colm Kerrigan, *Father Mathew and the Irish*

not surprisingly, the role of music receives little attention in these publications. And yet, even a cursory glance at contemporary press reports discussed in this article reveals that music, and particularly singing, became increasingly important within the movement. Music had a multi-faceted function; while its moral worth and health benefits were extolled, it was also a vehicle for the dissemination of religious and political ideology, particularly by those seeking to promote nationalism. The following discussion of the growth of the temperance movement in its early years provides some understanding of the background to the phenomenon and to the role music would later play within it.

TEMPERANCE IN IRELAND

When Father Mathew was invited to become the president of the Cork Total Abstinence Society (CTAS) in 1838, temperance was of minor concern to most Catholics. It had Protestant associations and was regarded by many as a front for proselytising. Not surprisingly then, CTAS had only a few dozen members and was keen to bring the popular priest on board in a bid to rejuvenate the society. Under the leadership of Mathew, what had started out as a small local concern rapidly evolved into a mass national movement. The initial local campaign, which took place between April 1838 and November 1839, saw membership in Cork rise to over 50,000. From late 1839 to March 1840 Mathew focussed on regional expansion by travelling to Waterford and Limerick where he was reported to have 'dispensed the Temperance pledge to unexpected and unprecedented crowds, supposed to have numbered in the high tens if not the hundreds of thousands'.[9] By 1842, the total abstinence message had been disseminated nationwide thanks to his tireless and unrelenting travels around the country. Remarkably, Father Mathew administered the pledge to somewhere between three and five million Irish people.[10] In a period where the population numbered approximately eight million, it is astonishing to consider that half the country heard and directly responded to Mathew's message.

What was it then about Father Mathew and his mission that gripped a nation that had previously felt largely disenfranchised from notions of temperance? Father Mathew was certainly a popular figure in Cork prior to his association with CTAS, but popularity in one region would hardly be enough to mobilize millions throughout the country. The key to understanding the success of the movement lies perhaps in its message. While notions of moral improvement and health benefits common to previous temperance societies remained intact, under Mathew's leadership it was now promoted as a means for *national* regeneration.

---

temperance movement 1838–1849 (Cork: Cork University Press, 1992), and Elizabeth Malcolm, *'Ireland sober, Ireland free': drink and temperance in nineteenth-century Ireland* (Dublin: Gill & Macmillan, 1986). **9** Townend, *Father Mathew*, p. 4. **10** A more detailed analysis of these figures can be found in Townend, *Father Mathew*, pp 3–5 and 26–32.

A sober, upstanding people could free itself from the shackles of the past. As this article will demonstrate, the nationalist flavour of the crusade increased over time, and while the message of moral and national improvement was crucial the cultural shift brought about by temperance was central to the process of renewal. Reading rooms and coffee houses replaced pubs, and in many towns drunkenness became a thing of the past. Literature on temperance was published in the form of books and pamphlets as well as specialist newspapers. Music was used at meetings and festivals, and became increasingly important in spreading the message.

THE TEMPERANCE MESSAGE

There is an abundance of contemporaneous accounts of the various meetings and spectacles that took place throughout the country. The growth and size of the movement was such that two accounts of its progress were published within the period under study. The first of these was written by the Revd James Bermingham whose *A Memoir of the Very Rev. Theobald Mathew, with an Account of the Rise and Progress of Temperance in Ireland* (1840) was based on conversations with Mathew.[11] Only three years later, John Barclay Sheil, a doctor from Donegal, was prompted to write a history of the movement, *History of the Temperance Movement in Ireland*, again as it was occurring.[12] The fact that the temperance movement was already embedding itself into posterity indicates the perceived historical importance of the crusade as suggested by the title of Sheil's book. Sheil was encouraged to write the work by Mathew as is evident not only from the access he was given to Mathew's private correspondence, but is also clearly stated in the preface.[13] As with Bermingham's book, it can be regarded as a representation of the movement's 'official policy' thus demonstrating Mathew's approach towards the temperance movement and the message he propagated. A number of recurring themes abound, not only in the work of Bermingham and Shiel, but in the speeches and meetings reported in the press and in the temperance songs that were performed in public and private. These tropes frequently revolved around notions of providence, regeneration and national pride.

It is not surprising that the sheer success of the movement in terms of the numbers involved was regarded as nothing short of a providential act. In the introduction to his book, Bermingham reported that a 'mighty change' had followed the previously degraded state of the nation:[14]

---

[11] James Bermingham, *A memoir of the Very Rev. Theobald Mathew, with an account of the rise and progress of temperance in Ireland* (Dublin: Milliken & Son, 1840), p. xvi. [12] John Barclay Sheil, *History of the temperance movement in Ireland,* (Dublin: Samuel J. Machen, 1843). [13] 'In publishing the *History of the temperance movement in Ireland* [...] I have been induced to attempt it in consequence of the kind condescension and encouragement of the Very Rev. Theobald Mathew himself who has placed confidence in my disposition to serve the temperance cause', Sheil, *History of the temperance movement in Ireland,* Preface. [14] Bermingham, *A Memoir*, p. xvi.

Providence was pleased to regard their sufferings, to look down with pity on their faults [...] A mighty change has come over the land; the night of Ireland's degradation is past; the foul vapours are scattered which obscured our best prospects; bright and peaceful and happy days are opening upon us.[15]

This perceived God-given opportunity was a chance for improvement on both individual and national scales. While the official temperance line would suggest that it embraced every class, it was clearly aimed at the lower echelons of society: all of those eager to improve their situation and social position.[16] In short, the prospect of moral and material prosperity was key to the temperance message. This message of improvement for the individual was not new. Other temperance societies had preached the same message namely that individuals could better themselves by abstaining from alcohol and living a more industrious and moral lifestyle. However, the improvement of the nation was crucial to Mathew's movement. The evolution of the country from a state of degeneration to regeneration was, if anything, even more important than individual salvation. And yet Mathew was sensitive to the potential political associations of such large numbers of people converging in the name of abstinence, renewal and national pride. Keen to avoid any politicization of temperance, the point of being apolitical was almost obsessively driven home. Indeed, both Bermingham's and Shiel's books are littered with references to the non-party, non-sectarian nature of the movement. The strength of this rhetoric and the uniformity of the temperance message is evident not only from these books but also from temperance and other newspapers which indicate the growth of the movement. One such source is the informative, albeit short lived, the *Philanthropist and National Temperance Advertiser*, a weekly newspaper that was published in Dublin and ran for just under a year between March 1838 and January 1839. Importantly, even at this early stage, the non-sectarian, non-party affiliation of the paper was regularly stressed in its pages. A review of all the editions of the *Philanthropist and National Temperance Advertiser* reveals that for those in Dublin committed to total abstinence, there seemed to be little else in the meetings in the early days but motivational talks to keep them on the straight and narrow. By the following year, reports of gatherings elsewhere in the country, particularly in the southwest, Father Mathew's stronghold, indicate a somewhat livelier approach. There, meetings were supplemented by tea parties, festivals and processions, many of which were recorded in the *Dublin Weekly Herald – A Temperance, Agricultural, Commercial and Mechanics Journal*.[17] With its explicit aims and message, its

---

15 Ibid. **16** Sheil documented 'eye-witness' accounts of improvement. In one example, he quoted a letter from William Woolsey Simpson, 'a valuator and seller of estates' who reported: 'the gradual adoption of a better system of husbandry, whereby those small farmers who were formerly scarcely able to pay their rents or to procure the common necessaries of life, are now enabled to satisfy all the just demands of their landlords and procure for themselves and their families [...] comforts. [...] The better cultivation of the land too, and the moral improvement of the people have proceeded, *pari passu*'. Sheil, *History of temperance in Ireland*, p. 7. **17** This newspaper was first published in 1836 as the *Irish Temperance and*

nationwide reportage, not to mention a publication period spanning six years, the *Dublin Weekly Herald* is an invaluable source for charting the development of temperance in Ireland, and in particular, its increasingly nationalistic agenda, and the integral role played by music in the crusade. Reports on meetings and festivals, alongside the musical entertainment and stirring speeches delivered by temperance zealots make up much of the content of *Herald*. In June 1839 for example, a 'Temperance Soiree' [*sic*] was reported during which Mr Thomas Hogan addressed a group of Tipperary teetotallers.[18] In his opinion:

> Drunkenness was the besetting sin of the nation, all the foreign invasions, all the internal dissentions, all the bad laws, all the penal enactments, that had ravaged and desolated this country, had not entailed on her so many mizeries and sufferings as the detestable and ever to be lamented habit of drinking ardent spirits, so prevalent among his countrymen.[19]

Hogan's speech is entirely in keeping with the discourse of temperance which was one of campaigning, crusading and winning the battle for the future generations of Ireland. It fostered the idea that the strength of the nation had been annihilated through alcohol, more so than invasion, colonization and penal laws. The only way to fight this condition was through total abstinence. A survey of the numerous reports in the *Dublin Weekly Herald* reveals that the singing of 'temperance songs' was commonplace as a suitable pastime to replace the bottle and the public house; for example at the gathering mentioned above it was reported that 'several temperance songs having been sung, the happy group separated'.[20] Music was even more important at temperance festivals and concerts. These larger gatherings, as distinct from weekly meetings, gave members and their families an opportunity to enjoy tea, speeches and music in a community setting. Indeed, a substantial gathering of some 800 people in February 1839 was treated to 'twenty [male] singers performing the vocal part of the entertainment'.[21] Furthermore, the central role of music was revealed by one of the chorus, a Mr Moeran who said:

> [H]e was sure music was an ameliorating pleasure, and that it never stood so eminent in rank, as when it was made, as tonight, subservient to the advance of virtue, good morals, and rational happiness.[22]

'Virtue, good morals, and rational happiness' were all part of the improvement of the individual and of course, the nation. However, members were not simply entertained but were actively involved in the music making through local temperance bands or in singing at meetings, marches and festivals. A gathering in celebration of the Wexford Temperance Union in August 1839 is typical:

Literary Gazette under which title it ceased to exist from August 1838. **18** 'Nenagh temperance soiree (abridged from the *Nenagh Guardian*)', *Dublin Weekly Herald* [hereafter *DWH*], 1 June 1839. **19** Ibid. **20** Ibid. **21** 'Cork tea party and concert', *DWH*, 9 February 1839. **22** Ibid.

the attendance could fall nothing short of three hundred and fifty persons. [...] An excellent band of the members performed numerous national airs, and sang several original and appropriate songs during the evening.[23]

A similar festival in Cork was reported the following month:

A tea festival was held on Monday evening 26th August in the Globe Lane Temperance Reading Room, Cork: about 100 of the members [...] and their families being present. The company were entertained during a part of the evening by the performance of an excellent band belonging to the room; several temperance songs were also sung.[24]

These examples are representative of widespread reportage on temperance gatherings and demonstrate that the communal expression of temperance sentiments was crucial both for the internalization and dissemination of the message. Furthermore, the harmonious expression of temperance sentiments bound members to one and another and added to their sense of belonging to a community of teetotallers. Interestingly, the reporter of the Wexford meeting noted the use of 'numerous national airs', thus blurring the distinction between national airs and temperance tunes and emphasizing the idea that temperance was a national concern. The teetotallers of Ireland were rising with one voice to the challenge set for them by Father Mathew. However, while most of the articles indicate that music was integral to temperance gatherings, they fail to detail the actual music that was being sung. Yet the importance of music and the direction that it should take cannot be underestimated. In fact, Mathew was very proactive on this front also. In a speech given at a meeting in Naas he stated: 'It has been my wish to have music in our societies, as constituting a source of humble recreation and innocent enjoyment.'[25] Furthermore, he financed many of the instruments of the numerous temperance bands himself.[26] However, it was his invitation to Mainzer that proved to be a masterstroke in terms of mobilizing large numbers of temperance members to get involved in singing classes. As stated previously, singing was a far more inclusive pastime than band membership, and no doubt Father Mathew had this in mind as the temperance movement began to take pace. A constellation of events and publications in and around the years 1842–3 signal a marked increase in the use of music for the temperance cause: a trend accelerated by the arrival in Cork of Joseph Mainzer.

---

23 'Wexford Temperance Union (From the *Wexford Conservative*)', *DWH*, 10 August 1839. **24** 'Temperance festival in Cork', *DWH*, 7 September 1839. **25** *FJ*, 15 August 1840, quoted in Townend, *Father Mathew*, p. 100. **26** See Aiveen Kearney, 'Temperance bands and their significance in nineteenth-century Ireland', pp 32–3.

MAINZER AND TEMPERANCE

Mainzer's success in England was not only well documented, but was also promoted in the pages of his bi-monthly *Mainzer's Musical Times and Singing Circular*.[27] The massive sight-singing classes conducted throughout England could not fail to impress, with the claim that in London alone some 20,000 pupils were under the tutelage of Mainzer et al.[28] Indeed, armed with this information, not to mention the underlying ideology behind his cause, namely moral improvement for the lower classes, it is easy to see how Mathew and Mainzer regarded each other as mutually beneficial. Following much publicity in the local press in which he gained the competitive edge over local teacher, Forde, Mainzer arrived in Cork in August 1842. He began his campaign with an address to the members of the CTAS. According to the *Cork Examiner* following an introduction by Father Mathew, Mainzer was greeted with 'the most rapturous applause' by the teetotallers who had gathered to hear his message.[29] He went on to explain his work and the purpose of his visit to Ireland, adding that 'he had no other object in view than to improve [...] the moral condition of the poor and hard working'.[30] This would and could be achieved, he argued 'by giving the people a cheap, an agreeable and a delightful instruction, by teaching them the science of Vocal Music'.[31] With an understandably positive reception from CTAS (who had invited Mainzer to Ireland in the first instance), the next part of the process was to conduct an open meeting and sample lesson for the people of Cork. This came about the next evening with the arrival of a 600-strong paying crowd. The precise cost of attending the lecture is not detailed in the advertisements, but there is some indication of differing rates since a 'higher price' was charged for the reserved seats, chiefly occupied by 'professional gentlemen and distinguished musical amateurs [...] and respectable tradespeople' while a lower price ensured that 'many an honest unwashed learner' was in attendance also.[32] Again, following a warm reception, Mainzer went on to explain the benefits of singing and described the huge numbers he had taught, including one class in Paris that numbered 2,000 workmen. Mainzer then embarked on a sample lesson in which audience members were transformed into students. After some hesitancy, the previously timid 'pupils' found their voices and, according to a report in the *Cork Examiner*:

---

27 *Mainzer's Musical Times and Singing Circular* was taken over by Novello in 1844 and renamed *The Musical Times*. **28** '[I]t may be said that the number of pupils now receiving instruction From Mr Mainzer and his immediate assistants in London and the Provinces in not less than Twenty Thousand. But even this is but a partial view of the extent of the system [...] it is daily spreading itself all over the country, even in the small towns and villages, where multitudes of classes are taught', 'Introduction', *Mainzer's Musical Times and Singing Circular*, 15 July 1842, 1. **29** 'Popular Musical Instruction (From the *Cork Examiner*)', *Mainzer's Musical Times and Singing Circular*, 15 September 1842, 67–70: 68. **30** Ibid., 68. **31** Ibid. **32** Ibid., 69.

> In a short time [...] the sweet voices of the female portion of the audience blended with the rough energy of the male roar, harmony was restored between pupils, piano and instructor – who at last pronounced it to be "vary, vary goot", and whose only anxiety was then to restrain the generous and Irish obedience of the boy and men pupils, who generally sang more notes than they were desired, giving a supplementary tilly as a finish. Before one half hours practice the improvement was marvellous, fully proving the efficiency of the system [...] It was altogether a pleasant and satisfactory evening, in which real knowledge was quickly and happily received.[33]

After this positive start to his campaign, Mainzer continued in earnest. Indeed, the following day, some 1,200 children attended class at the South Monastery School. Furthermore, the same venue was besieged by between 1200 and 1400 adults that evening when Father Mathew accompanied Mainzer to introduce the man and his system to the crowd gathered at the school. Whatever Mainzer's successes in England, it is certain that Mathew's positive endorsement was central to the huge interest in sight-singing in Ireland. His encouraging words at the thronged evening meeting clearly indicate his desire to see the people fully engage with the system:

> the best way in which we can exhibit the gratitude we feel will be [...] by attending diligently the classes which he will establish (cheers). I am anxious that we should learn with diligence, in order that we may be able to join in singing at our great processions (tremendous cheering). We have been the first in the great Temperance movement, which gave health and happiness to so many; and we will be, or I mistake much, the first in our knowledge of Vocal Music of "Singing for the Million".[34]

Mathew was keen that the people adopt the system not only for their own benefit and for the purposes of healthy distraction and amusement, but also to enhance the temperance processions of which they were so proud. These processions were a public display and indeed, a celebration of sobriety. Many of these occasions were large and lavish affairs with huge numbers in attendance. Numerous temperance bands marched in their smart uniforms, while banners were paraded with messages of nationalism, sobriety and pride. They represented the emerging new face of Ireland, one that flouted the image of the lower classes as struggling, downtrodden and drunk. Father Mathew's idea that these should be further enhanced by huge numbers congregating with one voice in the name of temperance would surely have stirred an ardent teetotaller. Without doubt the amalgamation of Father Mathew and Joseph Mainzer, not to mention the timing of the sight-singing venture in Ireland when temperance was at its height, was masterful. Their reciprocal ideologies were summed up by Mainzer, who

33 Ibid. 34 Ibid.

proclaimed to loud cheering 'I hope that for the future the motto for your standard will be "Music and sobriety, sobriety and Music"' adding that 'Music will gain by being surrounded and supported by *sober millions*, and helped by your Friend and benefactor of the human race – Father Mathew'.[35] This union of the philanthropists and their causes was further summed up in one of the early editions of *Mainzer's Musical Times*. It is worth quoting extensively as it demonstrates several aspects of their shared interests:

> The rapid progress which Temperance has made in Ireland, once the land of poteen, has been observed by every well wisher of our race, and, more especially, of our country with unmingled satisfaction. The name of Father Mathew will be revered as long as the Emerald Isle lifts her green breast above the waves of the Atlantic. […]
>
> The only sound reason which we can perceive for doubting the Temperance Reform, lies in the circumstance that no general popular amusement has been hitherto provided as a substitute for that which is taken away. The demand for pleasure, in one shape or another which is inherent in the human mind, must have a corresponding supply. This supply was, till lately, found in ardent spirits […] When this is removed, and removed, too, by sudden effort, something else should be prepared, to fill up the vacancy […].
>
> The introduction of a simple method of imparting a practical knowledge of one of the most refined and captivating of the arts, affixes the stamp of permanency upon the reformation of the Irish people. Music and Temperance have met upon the shores of Cork, and from thence we hope these holy sisters will proceed hand in hand, upon their peaceful march throughout the lovely land of their adoption […]
>
> Father Mathew had, in fact, long ago perceived the advantages of such a union, and had endeavoured to cultivate a love for Music among his disciples by the formation of bands, which rude as they were, produced some good results, though necessarily limited in their sphere of action.
>
> The influence of Vocal Music, however, is of a far more extensive and powerful nature, and he therefore availed himself of the first opportunity of throwing his immense interest into the scale of favour of Mr Mainzer.[36]

The report acknowledged Mathew's progress in Ireland but also forewarned against the void created by the removal of alcohol. Not surprisingly, given the partisan nature of the magazine, the use of brass bands to fill that void was recognized as somewhat inadequate compared to the 'extensive and powerful' nature of vocal music. Nepotism aside, the fact was that vocal music did have a more sweeping appeal than band music by its inclusive nature and ability to be taught in large numbers. Mainzer continued his campaign and, using the same format of lecture and sample class, introduced his system to other groups around

---

35 Ibid. 36 Ibid., 67.

the country, in Limerick, Dublin and Belfast. However, if any one lecture encapsulated the Mainzerian philosophy, i.e. that of offering the lower classes an opportunity to engage with the most 'refined' of the arts, it was that given in Carrickfergus. Having made a detour from Belfast, he arrived in there in order

> [T]o establish singing classes among the men employed at the mills, and nine hundred of them, with their wives and children, formed his audience on the only occasion on which he could lecture there [...] These poor people, to whom musical training was entirely new, received him, nevertheless, in the warmest manner; and, delighted beyond measure by their first lesson, immediately formed themselves into a class for the purpose of obtaining further instruction.[37]

Following Mainzer's departure from Ireland, the Cork branch of the temperance movement moved quickly and a committee of twenty-four was set up to facilitate the establishment of sight-singing classes in the region. Barristers, doctors and clergy joined forces to found these classes in addition to a training school for teachers. The first teachers of the system were organists from the city's churches and cathedrals, and as early as 22 September 1842 the committee could report that eight classes had been established. This is remarkable considering that Mainzer had first arrived only a month before. Tuition was available morning and evening at several locations in the area, including the South Monastery and the Christian Brothers' schools, the Imperial Clarence Rooms and Mrs Sexton Baylee's College, described as 'one of the most eminent Ladies' Boarding Colleges in the South of Ireland'.[38] Meanwhile, the largest class of all, which numbered some 600 pupils, gathered in the evening at Batty's Circus. Given the availability of the classes and the locations, there seemed to be a concerted effort to make sight-singing a cross-class phenomenon. While the ongoing reportage and rhetoric suggested that those most in need of alternative recreation were the lower classes, it is interesting that a rather exclusive ladies' boarding college and a circus were both locations for the propagation of the same message. Although Mathew's utopian ideal – that temperance and its offshoots were of value irrespective of class or creed – clearly carried some weight, the general opinion was that the lower classes availed most from musical instruction as a report from the (London) *Inquirer* reveals:

> Amongst the lower classes in Ireland the entire social life is undergoing a blessed change. The lawless deeds of violence, for which the country was once infamous, are gradually disappearing – the intense wretchedness of habitation

---

37 'Music for the people (from the *Musical Times*)', *The Nation*, 19 November 1842, 83. **38** The details of the classes were outlined in a letter from William Keleher (chairman of the Cork committee) to the editor of the *Musical Times*. 'Popular musical instruction', *Mainzer's Musical Times and Singing Circular*, 1 October 1842, 83–7: 85–6.

and clothing, which characterised the Irish peasantry, are giving way to decency and comfort – their fairs and social meetings are no longer the scenes of revolting intemperance and savage rioting – reading rooms are springing up in all districts throughout the length and breadth of Ireland; a growing love of music is pervading all classes which is carefully fostered by the friends of the temperance cause and a worthy feeling of national pride and manly independence is beginning to arise in the popular mind.[39]

The speed with which singing classes were established was not exclusive to Cork. Others appeared around the country, including a cluster in Dublin where one instructor, Mr Gormley could report 'a class is now forming [...] and I have no doubt, from the manner in which the list is filling up, that it will quickly number 200 persons. At the Catholic church of St Andrew I have a class of 300; at the church of St Michael and St John I have another, containing upwards of 140 persons'.[40] While originating in *Mainzer's Musical Times* this particular report was reproduced in *The Nation*, the mouthpiece of Young Irelanders' Davis, Dillon and Duffy, and thus deserves special consideration in terms of its place in an overtly nationalist and popular publication.[41] *The Nation* had only begun its publication in the previous month but its initial print run of 12,000 copies sold immediately. Furthermore, its ongoing circulation of 10,000 (which was larger than any contemporary newspaper) meant that it had a massive readership of more than 250,000.[42] Readers of *The Nation* would have learnt how the system had been implemented at a number of locations in Dublin and Belfast. However, the aspect of the article that would have fallen in with the nationalistic agenda of the New Ireland group was the use of singing, in conjunction with temperance, to lead the Irish people into a bright new future:

> The Irish clergy [...] have looked beyond the immediate effects which singing is calculated to produce on the amusements and manners of the people, and have perceived the ultimate results which, in conjunction with the great temperance movement it will work out centuries hence, upon the whole nation. [...] it ought, therefore, to be universally employed in the important work of training the minds of infancy and youth.[43]

The use of music and verse as tools for promoting nationalist sentiment would become increasingly important to the editor and writers of *The Nation* with ballads and verses on nationalist themes regularly appearing in its pages. With this in mind, it is interesting to speculate how much the Young Ireland group was

---

[39] 'The temperance reformation in Ireland (from *The Inquirer*, a London weekly paper)', *The Nation*, 3 December 1842, 124–5. [40] 'Music for the People (from the *Musical Times*)', *The Nation*, 19 November 1842, 83. [41] *The Nation* was founded in October 1842 by Thomas Davis, John Blake Dillon and Charles Gavan Duffy. [42] The publication figures for *The Nation* are from James Lydon, *The making of Ireland – from ancient times to the present* (London and New York: Routledge, 1998), p. 297. [43] 'Music for the people', *The Nation*, 83.

spurred on to use song so extensively in their publication having witnessed such a large and organized movement to encourage public musical expression.

In terms of what was being sung at these early classes and indeed at the 'Mainzerian Festivals' that showcased various singing groups, it is reasonable to suggest that much of the initial material emanated from Mainzer's own *Singing for the Million*. While this series of graded vocal exercises was certainly popular, however, other music texts would come on to the Irish market in response to the temperance and sight-singing movements. The following examination of these publications reveals multi-faceted messages of pride, sobriety and nationhood.

TEMPERANCE MUSIC

In 1842, the year that Mainzer's primer *Singing for the Million* appeared in Ireland, *The Catholic Choralist* was also published. Dedicated to Father Mathew, *The Catholic Choralist* contained a number of hymns, twenty of which were specifically listed as 'Temperance Hymns'. Its subtitle *'for the use of the choir, drawing room, cloister, and cottage. Harmonized and arranged for the voice, band, piano-forte, and organ'* suggests that its compiler, William Young, envisaged its utilization in public and private spheres in urban and rural Ireland, and for church and civic music making. This clearly locates the book right at the heart of the temperance movement with its newly created interest in both choral and band music. The hymns themselves are verses on temperance themes set to suggested 'airs' from the works of 'the Masters including Haydn, Mozart, Pleyel, Webb, Beethoven, Spohr, Bach': music, as revealed in the preface, deemed appropriate for so elevated a subject.[44] Young's preface is notable for its length alone. In addition to an extensive dedication to Father Mathew, he addressed moderate drinkers to encourage their conversion to teetotalism, discussed the injurious effect of malt drinks, and promoted the ennobling effect of music and enthused over the regeneration of the country. This preface demonstrates how temperance rhetoric had become deeply ingrained across the board. The familiar themes of providence, regeneration and national pride reverberate throughout its twenty pages. Indeed, Young's statement that 'mysterious Providence' had brought about 'the most glorious revolution the world ever witnessed' was in keeping with familiar and popular ideas about temperance.[45] While this was admirable, a common concern was finding a replacement activity for newly sober minds, it was, as Young opined 'one of the greatest obstacles which had to be encountered'.[46] Musical expression satisfied a number of criteria as it provided suitable recreation in which temperance and religious sentiments could be promulgated. However, Young's concerns did not end at the spiritual and moral. He suggested that the promotion of widespread singing would benefit the nation's

---

[44] 'Preface', William Young, *The Catholic choralist* (Dublin: Catholic Choralist Office, 1842), p. viii.
[45] Ibid., p. iv.   [46] Ibid., p. xii.

health: 'The frequent exercise of the vocal powers strengthens the lungs, and thereby wards off consumption and spitting of blood; nay, even restores health in constitutions predisposed to consumption', the latter being the most feared of nineteenth-century ailments, tuberculosis.[47] If this were not enough for his readers to consider, Young's preface includes a reference to Germany, a nation of 'singing people' whose training in music was implemented from childhood, with the results that Germans were 'seldom or ever affected with these disorders'.[48] Young uses Germany as a template for what Ireland might be: a nation strong, upright, healthy and moral. Music, and especially singing was crucial to the nation's cultural and educational needs, not to mention the physical well-being of its citizens. The music, of course, had to be elevating in tone with worthy sentiments set to the works of the 'Masters'. Indeed, several 'airs' are suggested with each hymn, the verses of which are mainly based on themes of Ireland's moral victory as in 'Triumph of Temperance:

> Thousands now, intemp'rance dreading
> Bane of health, and joy, and peace
> Better principles are spreading
> See how temp'rance men increase
>
> Ev'rywhere the work is gaining
> In this highly favour'd land
> Drunkards now, from drink abstaining
> Spread the word with heart and hand
>
> Now the humble peasant's dwelling
> Once the scene of want and woe
> Rings with hymns divinely swelling
> Oh! What joys from temp'rance flow!
>
> Then let temp'rance ever flourish
> May it spread from shore to shore
> Drinking customs wholly perish
> Ireland's curse defame no more

---

47 Ibid., p. xii. Young's ideas are interesting in the context of contemporary attitudes to causes and treatments for tuberculosis. Indeed, his promotion of the idea that the practice of vocal music would aid the prevention of the disease is relatively early when considered in a broader context. In France, for example, between 1833 and 1872 a number of physicians who had close contact with singers published ideas relating to the perceived link between lung exercise and the reduction of respiratory problems. In America too, an article published in *Dwight's Journal of Music* in 1861 recommended singing as a preventative for tuberculosis. For discussion of these publications in the context of tuberculosis and vocal music see Katharine Ellis, 'The Fair Sax: women, brass-playing and the instrument trade in 1860s Paris', *Journal of the Royal Musical Association*, 124:2 (1999), 221–54, here 227–9. **48** Young, *Catholic choralist*, p. xiii.

The idea behind the hymns was entirely in keeping with the temperance ethic. In this example Young taps into the idea that the temperance movement was providential – 'highly favoured land' – and that the sinful drunkenness of the past – 'Ireland's curse' – had been replaced by the 'joys' of temperance. Musically speaking however, it is questionable as to how broadly the temperance hymns appealed to those they were meant to inspire. While it is difficult to measure the popularity of the hymns, the opposite is true for another temperance music book that was published the following year.

Much of the success of *Temperance Melodies for the Teetotallers of Ireland* by William MacNamara Downes was due to the music since the sentiments expressed in the songs were not entirely dissimilar to those in *The Catholic Choralist*.[49] Indeed, the choice of music was central to their nationalistic character. At the request of Father Mathew, Downes set about creating a book of temperance songs that was both appropriate in subject matter and appealing to its intended audience. His decision to rework a selection of Moore's *Irish Melodies* by setting them to temperance-inspired verse was the key to the book's success. The project was not only endorsed but positively encouraged by Father Mathew as Downes' letter to Mathew in the preface reveals:

> I feel much pleasure in dedicating to you the following songs on Temperance, which have been written at your suggestion, and I could wish they were more worthy of that exalted theme, the mighty moral movement which, under your venerated and sacred guidance, has happily sprung up in my native land.
>
> As I have endeavoured to commemorate in my verses, the triumph of moral worth among Irishmen, I thought the design would be the more appropriately national by associating the words with Irish Airs.[50]

With Mathew's encouragement, Downes had set about producing an overtly nationalistic collection of temperance songs. In contrast to Young's use of music from the continental art music tradition, Downes turned to Moore to underpin the familiar rhetoric of temperance with music that unequivocally conveyed Irishness. In attempting to read Downes' *Temperance Melodies* in context, it is necessary to overstep revisionism and assess Moore's *Irish Melodies* in their cultural framework.[51] When viewed from the perspective of their specific cultural milieu in the first part of the nineteenth century, Moore's *Irish Melodies* abound in contemporary nationalist aspirations, albeit expressed through a romanticized voice.

Notwithstanding the nationalist import of the *Irish Melodies* they were deemed a suitable, as well as an extremely popular choice by Downes and Mathew. Against this backdrop, Downes' and Mathew's decision to set temperance verses to

---

49 William McNamara Downes, *Temperance melodies for the teetotallers of Ireland*, 3rd edn. (Cork: 1843). All three editions are from that year. **50** 'Letter to the Very Rev. Mr Mathew' in Downes, *Temperance melodies*. **51** The beginning of this critique of Moore's *Irish melodies* has been located by Harry White to the latter part of the nineteenth century: see White, *The keeper's recital*, pp 44–5.

twelve of the *Irish Melodies* was a clear signal to recognize and promote a particularly nationalist slant to the movement. Downes' *Melodies* was a commemorative collection intended to encourage on-going teetotalism in Ireland and also to recognize and celebrate the transformation of the people. The collection is something of a monument to the 'moral revolution' that had rejuvenated the nation. The principles and ideas that informed a movement of national importance required a musical setting of equal national significance, and for that reason Moore's *Irish Melodies* were suitably fitting for the task. Indeed, a reviewer for the *Limerick Chronicle* concurred:

> There is much beauty of idea, and sweetness of versification in the Temperance Songs, – they are adapted to Mr Moore's imperishable melodies, and while the principles of Temperance are venerated by the masses of the people, it is not going too far to say that the New Melodies will be imperishable also.[52]

The description of the music as 'imperishable' indicates an understanding of the *Melodies* as a permanent fixture on the cultural landscape: sentiments entirely in accordance with the hopes for the lasting success of the temperance movement. Through these twelve songs, Irish teetotallers could celebrate their achievement in an explicitly national way. Interestingly, only the words to the songs were printed in Downes' *Melodies*. While this would no doubt have curbed printing costs, it might also suggest that there was no need to reproduce the music as it would seem that knowledge of Moore's *Irish Melodies* was assumed. Since the temperance movement largely drew on the lower classes for its membership, it begs questions of the dissemination of Moore's *Irish Melodies* and of course, of Downes' volume. It might be the case that either the *Temperance Melodies* were bought by middle and upper class teetotallers and then disseminated to their lower class fellow-teetotallers, or indeed, that familiarity with Moore's *Irish Melodies* had spread across the classes.[53] Since Downes' *Temperance Melodies* went through three editions in one year, they were certainly popular. Indeed, the preface from the third edition suggests that they were intended for all social classes:

> The sentiments expressed in the foregoing productions may well be adopted by the many thousands who have been rescued from vice, misery and death, and among whom there were not a few of the more exalted classes of society.[54]

---

52 'Opinions of the Press' in Downes, *Temperance melodies*. **53** My examination of the primary sources has yet to clarify either of these possibilities. However, in *Songs of Irish rebellion: political street ballads and rebel songs, 1780–1900*, 2nd edn (Dublin: Four Courts Press, 2004 [p. 63]) Georges Denis Zimmerman comments that 'Let Erin Remember', 'The Minstrel Boy', 'Remember the Glories', and 'She is far from the Land' were frequently reprinted in pedlars' garlands and also found on some broadsheets apparently issued between 1840 and 1870. **54** Downes, *Temperance melodies*, Preface.

A number of tropes, common to the official temperance doctrine as promoted in texts endorsed by Mathew, proliferate in Downes' verses thus indicating, as previously discussed, the extent to which certain ideas were ingrained. These were largely expressed in dualities of sin and redemption; stain and purity; degradation and rejuvenation; darkness and light, and often included praise for Father Mathew. Downes' selection of Moore's *Irish Melodies* is interesting too. His choices range from settings of spirited, march-like tunes, to beautiful and melancholic ballads. The following examination of three of Downes' *Temperance Melodies* provides something of an overview of the collection.

'Oh swell the song of fame' is Downes' setting of Moore's 'Song of the Battle Eve' or 'Tomorrow, Comrade, We' (the air of which is 'Cruiskeen Lawn'). Moore indicated that it should be performed 'With martial and melancholy spirit, not too slow'.[55] It is not too difficult to see how a rousing martial number might stir teetotallers, especially if intended for performance at Temperance parades alongside marching bands. In the original setting, the central theme is Ireland's freedom, as troops of patriots prepare themselves for a battle they are doomed to lose. In Downes' version, the battle cry is of course, for Ireland's sobriety. In some cases he draws on Moore's imagery, in others, he turns it on its head. In the original, for example, as the 'morning star' rises, the weary soldiers seek solace in wine:

> But there's still wine in the cup
> And we'll take another quaff,
> Ere we go boy
> We'll take another quaff, ere we go

In Downes' version, there is only one star, and that is Mathew: 'The star of our career, to his native land so dear'. The refrain calls upon teetotallers to re-pledge their allegiance to Mathew and his cause:

> To him and to our pledge we'll be true!
> We'll be true;
> To him and to our pledge we'll be true

In this march the figure of Mathew is one of biblical and indeed, messianic proportions. In the second stanza, his 'coming' is recorded in verse as the dawning of a new era for the country. Like the Israelites, the Irish are called upon to find their way towards the light of the Promised Land: 'He's like the pillar'd light, That through the gloom of night; Led Israel in ages that are gone'.

While Moore's warriors take up their weapons – 'grasp thy sword and away, boy away' – in the temperance version of the song, we are reminded that this is a peaceful struggle. Unlike Moore's patriots, Mathew's teetotallers are fighting and

---

55 See, for example, *Moore's Irish melodies with music* (Dublin: M.H. Gill & Son, 1909), p. 240.

winning a battle that causes no suffering, and yet the Temperance movement is presented as a battle of equal patriotic importance to the bloodshed of the past:

> But where our leader led
> Nor blood nor tear was shed
> The standard that he spread, has no stain,
> Has no stain,

While some of the *Temperance Melodies* were intended as uplifting and inspirational, others function as a warning through which Downes paints a woeful picture of the past and Ireland's degeneration through alcohol. Such is the intention of 'Away, away with the Poisoned Draught', Downes' reworking of Moore's 'The Minstrel Boy'. In the original, which steeped in the nationalistic symbolism of the harp, Moore's young bard dies a hero. The youth in Downes' verses know no such glory, as they are doomed to a life of misery. The emotional poignancy of 'The Minstrel Boy' is used as a backdrop to Downes' portrayal of the effects of alcohol on young people. The future generation is presented as neglected, orphaned and even dead:

> Ah, many an orphan strays forlorn,
> O'er his parents folly weeping;
> And many a youth from kindred torn,
> In an early grave is sleeping!
> All victims of that fatal bowl
> Whose dregs too long we've taken
> Oh never more shall taint the soul
> That vice we have forsaken

In 'Green Isle of our Fathers' Downes uses another stirring melody, this time Moore's 'The valley lay smiling before me' (to the air of 'The pretty girl milking her cow'). In the original, Moore's verses speak of the O'Ruark's unfaithful wife whose actions symbolize a traitorous conspiracy with the enemy. For Downes, the culpability for the past, lies solely with the intemperance of the nation. Drunkenness alone is responsible for the degraded state of the nation prior to the Temperance revolution. No blame is accorded to war, to an enemy or to colonization, a view made abundantly clear in the second verse:

> Oh what could so deeply degrade her,
> Or fix on her sons such a stain?
> It was not the hostile invader
> It was not the sword or the chain.
> Ah no – but the rank dregs of madness
> She drain'd – and that ill-fated bowl
> Brought on all the woes and the sadness
> That chill'd the pure fire of her soul!

Clearly, Father Mathew's ideal of a non-political, non-sectarian movement was strictly adhered to in speeches, in the published histories and pamphlets, and here, in song. The revolution that had swept the nation from a state of darkness was effectively de-politicized by inferring that the sins of the past were self-inflicted. Foreign invasions were not to blame; Ireland's own citizens had fallen prey to drunken degradation. By setting the Temperance movement's success story to Irish music, the 'revolution' took on a nationalist slant. However, the type of nationalism promoted was in accordance with Mathew's views in that it should be patriotic and celebratory in nature, rather than aggressive and political. While patriotism was harmless, its proximity to notions of uprising and reform was not. The potential political problems that might arise out of the temperance movement remained an underlying concern. Indeed, Sheil's *History* records several incidences of the perceived political and militant threat of temperance marches, and in some places reads as an apology for this 'misunderstanding'.[56]

Indeed, the need to find a balance between improving the state of the nation while largely maintaining the status quo was a concern addressed by another clergyman, Alexander King, pastor of the Independent Church in Cork who entered the discourse on music and morals in the latter months of 1842. King initially aired his views in the Cork press with lengthy open letters to Daniel O'Connell, Father Mathew and Dr Murphy (Bishop of Cork). His letters were collected and published in 1843 in London, Dublin and Cork in a fifty-two page pamphlet.[57] While he addressed many problems concerning contemporary Irish life, most of his opinions however, were reserved for the subject of music, and more specifically music and morals. King positively encouraged the progress of music in Ireland through the combined efforts of Mainzer and Mathew but he was concerned as to what direction it should take. From the paternalistic tone of his correspondence King saw himself, and others of his class and rank, as moral guardian of the masses. He was complimentary of the great strides made in the temperance movement. However, refinement was not enough to improve the moral condition of the nation. In King's opinion, singing and temperance needed to be wedded to religious sentiment, otherwise there was an implicit danger of simply attaining 'mere accomplishments' with neither communication with, nor understanding of, religious and moral values. Furthermore, King feared that a nation content to practise music for its own sake without any moral direction or association was in danger of emasculation:

> Unless the rational and moral character be improved, mere accomplishments will often do more harm than good. As music tends to awaken feeling, and elevate the imagination, if the formation of reflective habits, and of sound

---

[56] See Sheil, *History of the temperance movement in Ireland*, pp 10–11. [57] Alexander King, *The might and the right of the people: letters on popular education, temperance, political reform, etc. addressed to Right Rev. Dr. Murphy, Very Rev. T. Matthew and Daniel O'Connell, Esq. M.P.* (London, Dublin and Cork: 1843), pp 21–2.

moral principles be neglected, its influence must be to produce a frivolous sentimentalism, or a gross effeminacy [...] On the other hand, when adequate information is enjoyed, and correct religious principles are formed, the cultivation of a refined taste, and especially a love of music, gives that charm of sentiment, that elevated purity of emotion, which is the very finish of social character, the guardian and the grace of social intercourse.[58]

While praising Father Mathew's encouragement of music, King simultaneously forewarned against a weakening of the people by associating their practice of music with effeminacy, an idea that contravened Mathew's vision of a nation strengthened and invigorated by the temperance crusade. For King, the new 'arable mental territory' secured by temperance was ready to be implanted with fresh ideas. Music alone could not promote the moral ground necessary to stabilize the nation, but if allied with Christian teachings, it was possible. King's tone reveals a desire to police the minds of the masses. However, his fears were not only confined to the prospect of widespread effeminacy, but more worrying still, to political instability; and while encouraging improvement on one hand, he warned of rebellion on the other. Using revolutionary France as an example, he described a situation whereby a nation whose 'ancient religion [...] was attacked with irreverence', had resulted in public opinion becoming 'deeply tainted with destructive dogmas':[59]

The intellect that has long been degraded and depressed, if stimulated to vigorous action and not rightly directed, may run into moral anarchy: and, using its broken fetters as rude weapons against authority, it may, perhaps in its blind fury, destroy the only guardians of its freedom and its peace. The history of a neighbouring nation affords an appalling lesson on the infidel tendencies of excited ignorance, and shows how easy it is for elegant frivolities and superficial refinements, to associate with ferocious passions and bloody despotism.[60]

In King's view, the minds of the masses had to be harnessed for fear of insurrection. Such views on the possible outcome of temperance might seem extreme, however, his political concerns were not entirely unfounded. Daniel O'Connell pronounced 1843 as the great 'Repeal Year' and as the months progressed temperance and repeal became increasingly interconnected. Reports of temperance gatherings in *The Nation* for example were usurped by those on the so-called 'Monster Meetings'. O'Connell's arrival in numerous towns was greeted with music provided by local temperance bands, and many of the temperance halls were used for the subsequent 'banquets'. *The Nation* could report that in Skibereen, the temperance hall 'was elegantly fitted up for the important occasion of entertaining the Liberator'.[61] Similarly, a room in Dundalk

---

[58] Ibid., p. 23. [59] Ibid., pp 44–5. [60] Ibid., p. 31. [61] 'Repeal demonstration at Skibereen', *The Nation*,

was adorned with decorations and with the words 'Temperance – Religious Equality – Success – Onward to Victory' painted on the walls.[62] In fact, the perceived link between the two movements was enough for the journalists of the *Mail* to refer to O'Connell's massed gatherings as 'Repeal-teetotal' meetings. Father Mathew's wish for a non-political crusade was banished by the repeal movement.[63] In terms of music, while the bands continued to accompany O'Connell, *The Nation* continued publishing its nationalist verses and ballads which were cumulatively published as *The Spirit of The Nation* (1843). In the preface Davis stated that 'Most of the original airs are of a proud and fierce character, and peculiarly fitted for bands and chorus singing',[64] thus continuing the on-going link between music in *The Nation* and the temperance movement. However, in an even more explicit appeal to teetotallers, he requested: 'Will not the temperance bands learn to play these airs, and the young men, ay, and the young women learn to sing our songs, and chorus them till village and valley ring?'[65] Whether or not repeal sounded the death knoll for the Temperance movement is difficult to ascertain but it certainly coincided with the decline of Father Mathew's crusade. Whatever the causes, it is certain that the Great Famine would have eventually hastened its demise.[66]

Interest in temperance was resurrected in post-famine Ireland and indeed throughout the century, however, the peaks and troughs of the phenomenon and its music are beyond the scope of this article. In terms of a single concentrated effort to marshal a huge proportion of the population for the cause, Father Mathew was without doubt, the most successful. As a social and cultural phenomenon, temperance created a sense of mass community across the country and brought about a real sense of national pride. For those inscribing Temperance rhetoric, it was accorded a totemic place in the history of the nation as evidenced in the songs of the movement. In a period of Irish history that witnessed the intersection of nationalism, Temperance and Repeal, the music of the cause is of great social and cultural significance. Key figures engaged in music and ideas about music so as to propagate their messages. Questions surrounding the suitability of music as a partner of Temperance engendered debates on issues concerning morals, health, politics and nationalism. Moreover, it was Temperance music that helped to mobilize the multitude of teetotallers in Ireland, who marched with their bands and raised their voices in the name of nationhood and sobriety.

---

1 July 1843, 594–5; here 595. **62** 'O'Connell in Dundalk', *The Nation*, 1 July 1843, 604. **63** Malcolm, '*Ireland sober, Ireland free*', p. 132. **64** Preface to First Edition (1843), *The spirit of the nation: ballads and songs by the writers of "The Nation" with original and ancient music arranged for the voice and piano forte* (Dublin: William Duffy & Sons, 1845). **65** Ibid. **66** A number of suggestions have been put forward to explain the decline of the temperance movement, the most common reasons cited include: Repeal, the famine, the increasing debt of CTAS and Father Mathew in particular, as well as a lack of interest and support from the Catholic Church.

For the purpose of public music education: the lectures of Robert Prescott Stewart

LISA PARKER

Robert Prescott Stewart's career as a multi-faceted musician in Dublin in the latter half of the nineteenth century incorporated his role as a lecturer and music critic of repute.[1] He delivered over fifty public lectures between 1862 and 1893, mostly in his capacity as Professor of Music at Trinity College, Dublin. He also wrote programme notes for the 1886 Chamber Music Recitals at the Royal Dublin Society,[2] entries on Irish Music, Thomas Moore, and O'Carolan in *Grove's Dictionary of Music and Musicians*,[3] entries on Bach, Berlioz and Sterndale Bennett in *Cassell's Biographical Dictionary*,[4] and articles in various Irish journals and newspapers.[5]

A small selection of the lectures written by Stewart will be examined in this chapter including the 1862 lecture entitled 'Music: (with illustrations) a lecture' (published in the following year), a set of six lectures called 'Natural Music and its Relation to Modern Musical Art' delivered in 1876 and a paper penned for the 1881 Social Science Congress entitled 'Musical Education, by what means can national education in Music be best promoted'. Although the 1876 and 1881 lectures were not published, contemporary newspaper reports and references in the writings of Olinthus Vignoles and James Culwick provide the only remaining sources for information on these lectures.

I will explore the extent to which Stewart's lectures reflect contemporary views and ideas in areas including how music can affect the emotions, the origins of music, descriptive music and orientalism. Stewart's opinions on the current state of the music education system in Ireland in the latter half of the nineteenth century will also be examined.

---

1 For an overview of Stewart's career and compositions see Lisa Parker, 'Robert Prescott Stewart (1825–1894): an assessment of his compositions and contribution to musical life in Dublin', MA diss. (NUI Maynooth, 2000). 2 *Programme of the afternoon recitals of chamber music, autumn course, 1886, with analytical notes by Sir Robert Prescott Stewart* (Dublin: Ponsonby & Weldrick, 1886), NLI, item P935. These concerts included the music of Beethoven, Mendelssohn, Schubert, Bach, Rubinstein, Tartini, Mozart, Haydn, Brahms and Saint-Saëns. See also in the same item *Royal Dublin Society recitals of classical chamber music, session 1898–99* (Dublin: Ponsonby & Weldrick, 1899): programmes for 16 January, 13, 20 and 27 March 1899 containing programme notes by Ebenezer Prout and previously written notes by Stewart. 3 The 1906 and 1907 volumes were edited by J.A. Fuller Maitland. 4 *Cassell's biographical dictionary containing original memoirs of the most eminent men and women of all ages and countries* (London: Cassell, Petter and Galpin, 1867–69). 5 These articles include: 'Swift and Handel', *Irish Builder*, 16:344, 15 April 1874, 112, 115; 'The Wagner Festival', *DE*, 1, 2 and 4 September 1876; 'A New Work by Balfe', *DE*, 19 October 1881; 'Organs', *Irish Builder*, 30:676, 15 February 1888, 55; 'The Clarseach', *DE*, 23 December 1889; 'Irish Church Music', *Ulster Journal of Archaeology*, 2nd series, 1 (1895), 128–32.

Illustration 10.1: Sir Robert Prescott Stewart in 1875 from 'Our Portrait Gallery, Second Series, No. 14 – Sir Robert Prescott Stewart', *Dublin University Magazine* (March 1875).

Stewart lectured on a large variety of subject areas and topics including church music, Irish music and musicians, the harp, the bagpipe, the preludes and fugues of J.S. Bach, the life and works of Handel, stringed-keyed instruments, the history of the piano, Eastern music, the lyric drama, Wagner, Mozart and Palestrina,[6] indicating the diversity of knowledge required of a music professor. His lectures were sometimes delivered as a single lecture on a subject but between 1873 and 1877 his professorial lectures consisted of five sets of six afternoon talks delivered to the public in the Examination Hall at Trinity College, Dublin.

PUBLIC LECTURES

As Professor of Music at Trinity College from 1862 to 1894 Stewart was not obliged to teach or lecture because Trinity, in a similar vein to Oxford, Cambridge, Edinburgh and London, did not contribute anything to the training of music degree candidates.[7] His predecessor at Trinity College, John Smith taught

[6] Despite the number of lectures written by Stewart there is no surviving evidence to suggest that any plans were made to publish them. [7] Deborah Rohr, *The careers of British musicians, 1750–1850: a profession*

pupils in a private capacity, examined the candidates for music degrees and did not receive a salary as Professor of Music.[8] Stewart's annual salary of £100 contracted him to examine the 'exercises' of the music degree candidates at Trinity College at that time[9] and allowed him to compose music for noteworthy occasions at Trinity College such as his *Ode for the Installation of the Earl of Rosse as Chancellor of the University of Dublin*[10] and his *Tercentenary Ode*. This salary was reasonable considering that full professorships at Trinity College carried an income of £200 or less,[11] that Stainer received £120 a year from Magdalen College Oxford in 1860 for playing the organ and training the choir, and that by the 1890s few organists and choir masters received an income much higher than £300.[12] Weekly lectures were offered at Trinity in subjects such as Mathematics, Classics, Greek, Hebrew and other science subjects but because music students were external at this time, it was not obligatory for them to attend classes and therefore Stewart's professorial lectures were open to the public and were usually free of charge.[13]

Public lectures on an enormous variety of subjects 'flourished abundantly' during the nineteenth century and were given by societies, institutions, professionals and 'local worthies'.[14] The *Irish Times* remarked that Stewart's desire in giving his lectures 'was not merely to amuse the public, but to make them better',[15] reflecting a popular attitude of educators in Victorian times who attempted to pass on some 'useful' information to improve the 'taste' of their audience and to enhance their appreciation of art and music. This was certainly the case with Stewart's first recorded lecture delivered in 1862.

'Music: (with illustrations) a lecture' was delivered at a Dublin Young Men's Christian Association Meeting in March 1862.[16] The Dublin YMCA had as its aim the 'spiritual, mental and moral uplift of young men'[17] in an effort to dissuade the workingmen from visiting 'unsuitable' establishments such as taverns for their enjoyment. Lectures on literary, scientific and religious subjects organized by the association became popular with the admission fee proving to

---

of artisans (Cambridge: Cambridge University Press, 2001), p. 66.   **8** R.B. McDowell and D.A. Webb, *Trinity College Dublin 1592–1952: an academic history* (Cambridge: Cambridge University Press, 1982), p. 194.   **9** During the period of Stewart's professorship at least sixty BMus and thirty DMus degrees were conferred at Trinity College Dublin (not including honorary doctorates). See *Dublin University Calendar* (Dublin: Hodges, Smith & Co.; London: Longman, Brown, Green, Longmans & Roberts, 1862–95): Appendix I at the end of this chapter records some of those graduates.   **10** Composed in 1863, it remains unpublished. The remaining vocal and instrumental parts are in the possession of the University of Dublin Choral Society.   **11** McDowell and Webb, *Trinity College Dublin*, p. 160.   **12** K. Theodore Hoppen, 'The business of culture', *The Mid-Victorian generation 1846–1886, The new Oxford history of England*, ed. J.M. Roberts (Oxford: Clarendon Press, 1998), p. 400.   **13** It was not until the introduction of an Honour School at Trinity College in 1974 that the role of the music professor included teaching duties. Brian Boydell, 'Dublin', *GMO* (accessed 20 October 2003).   **14** Geoffrey Best, *Mid-Victorian Britain, 1851–75* (London: Weidenfeld & Nicolson, 1971), p. 212.   **15** 'Sir Robert Stewart', *IT*, 26 March 1894.   **16** Robert Stewart, 'Music: (with illustrations) a lecture', *Lectures delivered before the Dublin Young Men's Christian Association* (Dublin: Hodges Smith, 1863), Preface.   **17** *A century of service: 1849–1949*, ed. Walter H. Godden and William N. Maslin (Dublin: Earlsfort Press, [1949]), p. 27.

be a useful source of revenue. The preface to the publication that included Stewart's talk refers to the 'instruction and advantage' of the lectures conveyed to the young men, once again echoing the attitude among the wealthier classes and the religious agencies that they were associated with in relation to the education and salvation of the less fortunate classes.

This lecture comprises different topics relating to music including harmonics, temperament, the effect of music on the body and mind, the use of music as a cure for diseases and descriptive music. The talk briefly describes the origin of music and provides a synopsis of the chronological development of western art music from ancient times to the nineteenth century, with particular reference to the main composers of each epoch up to and including Spohr and Mendelssohn and the Irish composers Balfe and Wallace.

Explaining the different role played by music in the life of a rich and poor person, Stewart remarks that to the rich person music 'furnishes a refined and intellectual pursuit' and to the latter, it provides a 'relaxation from toil that is more attractive than the haunts of intemperance'.[18] The Victorian belief in the ability of music to 'soften and purify the mind' is also reiterated by Stewart who informs his audience that music was incapable of suggesting a malicious thought or of corrupting the mind, except perhaps when speech was added to it.[19] The continuation of this opinion well into the second half of the nineteenth century is apparent when we read a paper written by George Alexander Osborne in 1885 which states: 'We may have specimens of painting, poetry, and sculpture which we would not exhibit in our family, not so with music, it may be trivial, it never can be offensive'.[20] From a letter written to Revd Dr George Bell in 1890 we see that Stewart retained this opinion throughout his career:

> I am quite at one with you on the wisdom of rescuing the lower classes from their dismal surroundings, and from brutal amusements. Music of all arts is the purest, and what evil thoughts can be engendered by it?[21]

This statement reinforces the view held by the middle-class Victorian that music should be 'more than a mere artistic experience or a form of amusement' because it is the 'indirect means of aiding worship, temperance and culture, of holding young men and women among good influences, of reforming character, [and] of spreading Christianity'.[22] The alleged ability of music to affect the emotions of the listener ensured that it was 'uniquely suited to the task of shaping men's thought and actions'.[23] Music was described as 'an object of social utility and

---

18 Stewart, 'Music', p. 110.   **19** Ibid.   **20** G.A. Osborne, 'The emotional aspects and sympathetic effects of the sister arts: poetry, painting, and music', *Proceedings of the Musical Association* (11th session, 1884–85), 92.   **21** Letter from Stewart to Revd Dr George Bell, 9 March 1890 in Olinthus J. Vignoles, *Memoir of Sir Robert P. Stewart* (Dublin: Hodges, Figgis & Co.; London: Simpkin, Marshall, Hamilton, Kent & Co. 1898), p. 184.   **22** Ronald Pearsall, *Victorian popular music* (Newton Abbot: David & Charles, 1973), p. 119.   **23** Dave Russell, *Popular music in England, 1840–1914: a social history* (Worcester: Manchester University Press, 1987), p. 18.

balm for society's many evils', an opinion that lasted into the early years of the twentieth century. This thinking centred on the middle-class wish to 'destroy the potentially "dangerous" elements within working-class culture and to create a respectable, self-reliant collaborationist working class'.[24] These views also echo Charles Darwin's *The Descent of Man*, which describes the effects of music and its ability to arouse various emotions. These feelings are not the 'terrible ones of horror, fear [and] rage' but instead are the 'gentler feelings of tenderness and love, which readily pass into devotion'.[25]

When referring to the use of music to cure diseases, Stewart discusses how in the days of the music historian Charles Burney, a French physician believed that music could cure sciatica and how, according to another source, flute music could cure rheumatism. He further quotes Burney in relation to his discussion of the effects attributed to the music of the ancients who believed that Terpander was able to calm a sedition at Lacedaemonia 'by singing to the mob'.[26] Stewart claims that much of the effect of music on the mind was attributed to the power of association and incorporates the Swiss national melody 'Ranz des vaches' as his case in point. When Jean-Jacques Rousseau referred to it in his *Dictionnaire de musique* of 1768 he commented that it was 'so generally beloved among the Swiss, that it was forbidden to be play'd in their troops under pain of death, because it made them burst into tears, desert or die, whoever heard it; so great a desire did it excite in them of returning to their country.'[27] It is quite probable that Stewart borrowed his references to the 'Ranz des vaches' from Rousseau's dictionary because Burney does not mention this tune in his writings and when William Stafford refers to it in his *A History of Music*,[28] he does not discuss it in the context of the Swiss soldiers deserting their post as Rousseau did.

Stewart's discourse then discusses the bird song, the whistling of the wind, the rolling of thunder and the tolling of bells that are illustrated in the music of Handel and Beethoven. Yet to 'descend to particulars' and to write passages descriptive of scourging, as Stewart claimed Pergolesi is said to have done in his *Stabat Mater*, or passages that emulate the creeping of worms in Haydn's *The Creation*, or the rocking of a cradle in 'For unto us a child is born' from Handel's *Messiah* is described by Stewart as 'overstepping the fair limits of expressive art'. Stewart is convinced that the composers in question never meant these effects.[29] Praising the effect produced by the deep sustained notes in the 'Darkness Chorus' and the *staccato* basses and rattling scale of the 'Hailstone Chorus' from Handel's

24 Ibid., pp 17–18.   **25** Charles Darwin quoted in Peter Kivy, 'Charles Darwin on Music', *Journal of the American Musicological Society*, 12:1 (Spring, 1959), 44.   **26** Stewart, 'Music', pp 121, 132–3; and Charles Burney, *A general history of music from the earliest ages to the present period* (London: Payne & Son; Robson & Clark; G.G.J. & J. Robinson, 1789), i, 172 and 173.   **27** Anonymous, 'Ranz des vaches', *NG*, xv, 586. Stewart is more likely to have read one of the English translations of Jean-Jacques Rousseau's book such as Rousseau, *A complete dictionary of music consisting of a copious explanation of all words necessary to a true knowledge and understanding of music*, trans. William Waring, 2nd edn. (London: printed for J. Murray Fleet St & Luke White, Dublin, 1779).   **28** William C. Stafford, *A history of music* (Edinburgh: Constable & Co.; London: Hurst, Chance & Co., 1830).   **29** Stewart, 'Music', pp 124–6.

Israel in Egypt, Stewart also enforces the point that if he and his audience were to hear these choruses for the first time in a language that they did not understand 'not one in a thousand listeners would recognise it as conveying the impression of darkness in one case, or of a hailstorm in the other'.[30]

These comments are interesting in light of the ongoing debate between those in favour of programme music and those who held that absolute music was the purest form of music. The issue of programme music started to gather momentum from around 1840 as the essays and compositions of Berlioz and Liszt began to gain in popularity.[31] The conservative critic Eduard Hanslick considered the idea of absolute music as the 'quintessence of "genuine" music', and founded a line of aesthetic thought that rejected emotional and programmatic interpretations of music.[32] In contrast to this, Franz Brendel's writings favoured the new German school and proclaimed programme music and the music drama to be musical progress.[33] While Stewart criticizes the analysts who claim that the composers listed above incorporate more devices of descriptive music than actually intended by them, he is not 'anti' programme music as the synoptic instrumental overture to his cantata, *The Eve of St John*, demonstrates. The overture to this work, composed in 1860, includes the musical portrayal of mischievous fairies, knights and guardian angels that later re-appear throughout the cantata.[34] Stewart wrote a biographical entry on Berlioz for *Cassell's Biographical Dictionary* so he was no doubt aware of the attitudes towards his music at the time. Stewart also met Liszt at the Bayreuth Festival in 1876.[35]

Promising not to inflict upon his audience any stories of 'Mercury's discovery of a dead tortoise or the hammers of Pythagoras', Stewart attributes the origin of music to the speech of man, which, 'by a little raising of the sound, and prolonging it, at once becomes a song',[36] reflecting his awareness of some of the writings on the subject including Stafford's *A History of Music* and Herbert Spencer's essay 'The Origin and Function of Music'.[37] In his lecture, Stewart dismisses the theories that the origin of music should be attributed to 'man imitating the birds' and the 'winds whistling in hollow reeds on river banks', two theories according to Stewart that are 'equally stale and untenable'.[38] This statement demonstrates that he did not agree with the opinions of Diodorus Lucretius and other authors that Stafford refers to in his *A History of Music* who 'attribute the invention of wind instruments to observations made on the whistling of the wind in reeds, and in the pipes of other plants'.[39] The similarity in language

---

30 Ibid., p. 125. **31** Ralph P. Locke, 'Cutthroats and casbah dancers, muezzins and timeless sands: musical images of the Middle East', *19th-Century Music*, 22:1 (Summer 1998), 29. **32** Carl Dahlhaus, *Nineteenth-century music*, trans. J. Bradford Robinson (Berkeley: University of California Press, 1989), p. 250; Vincent Duckles and Lydia Goehr, 'Musicology, §II, 8: Disciplines of musicology: aesthetics and criticism', *GMO* (accessed 28 April 2006). **33** Dahlhaus, *Nineteenth-century music*, p. 250. **34** Stewart, *The Eve of St John* (London: Blockley, 1884). **35** Letter from Stewart to Lily Hutton, 29 September 1884 in Vignoles, *Memoir*, p. 157. **36** Stewart, 'Music', pp 127–8. **37** Herbert Spencer, 'The origin and function of music', *Style and music* (London: Watts & Co., 1857/1950). **38** Stewart, 'Music', p. 127. **39** Stafford, *A history of music*, p. 2.

here suggests that Stewart referenced Stafford's book when writing his section on the origin of music for his lecture but unfortunately Stewart does not seem to have written or discussed his thoughts on the origin of music in greater detail. His lecture proceeds with a discussion of 25 composers from Josquin des Prez to Mendelssohn.

MUSIC IN IRELAND: CLASSIC VERSUS MODERN

Of the composers treated in Stewart's lecture, Mendelssohn was referred to as 'the greatest musician of the present day'. According to Stewart, Bach and Mendelssohn were the only composers of 'real' organ music and Beethoven, who had 'few imitators' was 'free from those mannerisms by which we can at once distinguish a work by Handel, Mozart or Mendelssohn'.[40] Motets by Tallis and Palestrina, the preludes of Bach, excerpts from Handel's *Messiah*, from Haydn's *The Creation*, Mozart's Piano Sonata in C minor and Spohr's *The Last Judgment* are some examples of the music that accompanied Stewart's lecture. Under the heading of 'antient music' Stewart remarks that nothing dating before the fourteenth century is worthy of the name music[41] but it is difficult to conjecture whether Stewart reflected the opinion of those who favoured the music of the 'Renaissance-Baroque polyphonists' or the 'modern Italian opera and the new instrumental and symphonic style'.[42] His cathedral training as a chorister at Christ Church Cathedral, Dublin, may suggest a preference for the former. Stewart referred only to the 'different epochs' which marked the progress of music in this lecture.[43]

Stewart concluded his lecture with an examination of the present state of music in Dublin. Pointing out that Ireland had neither the wealth to reward or encourage a composer, nor a resident aristocracy to patronize and protect him, Stewart criticized his fellow countrymen for not supporting performances by resident musicians:

> It has been proved again and again by the surest test, – pounds, shillings, and pence, – that an oratorio or cantata, properly performed, with full chorus, full orchestra, and the best resident singers, has no attraction for our citizens when compared with an *olla podrida* of music executed by strangers.[44]

Pessimistically illustrating that Ireland was not a 'paradise of musicians', he continued to explain that the Irish public was far behind that of London, 'who sit out and warmly applaud those grand choruses and symphonies, of which people here scarcely take pains to conceal their dislike'.[45] His frustration is obvious as he complained about the inferior quality of music in Dublin's churches despite

---

[40] Stewart, 'Music', pp 149, 159, 160–1. [41] Ibid., p. 127. [42] Leanne Langley, 'Criticism, §II, 3(i): Britain: To 1890', *GMO* (accessed 4 May 2006). [43] Stewart, 'Music', p. 137. [44] Ibid., p. 166. [45] Ibid.

the number of people who can sing or play an instrument and urged the congregational members to attend rehearsals 'without which there can be no decent performance'.[46] As we shall see later in this chapter, Stewart continued to despair two decades later when in 1881 he delivered a talk on the status of music in Ireland to the Social Science Congress.

Stewart found it difficult to determine the direction that mid-century European art music would take, and commenting on the current developments in Germany, he had the following to say about Wagner's music:

> With the new German school, of which Richard Wagner is the apostle, I have no sympathy. This music not only lacks the melody essential to please the general ear; but is deficient in *form* which is an important element in the works of the great composers. Notwithstanding the partial success which has attended the efforts of the Wagnerites in Germany, and among some of the Germanized Americans, they have numbered very few converts in our own country.[47]

Who are the 'great composers' that Stewart refers to in this quote and what does it indicate in relation to Stewart's opinion on classic versus modern composers? Composers such as Bach, Handel, Purcell and Mendelssohn were held in extremely high regard by Stewart. He explained to his audience how he was reared in the 'very strictest school' of the English cathedral writers and 'taught from childhood to believe in Handel, and Handel alone'. But he did concede that Bach's organ fugues allow him to 'tower' above all other musicians, 'even Handel'.[48] Stewart's openness to contemporary music is demonstrated when he stated 'I have yet learned to enjoy the music of all the modern writers of ability down to Verdi – a man of true talent and individuality of style'.[49] Although Stewart had formed a harsh opinion of Wagner's music at the time of this lecture, his opinions changed quite dramatically after his first visit to the Bayreuth Festival in 1876, after which he became an ardent protagonist and defender of Wagner and his music. The history paper which he set for the Royal Irish Academy of Music examinations of 8 December 1888 was devoted to Wagner.[50] The favourable stance towards Wagner is implicit in the questions, and the knowledge required of his students could have been gleaned from the newspaper notices in the Dublin newspapers, some of which Stewart famously authored.[51] It can be surmised that Stewart was neither a classicist nor a modernist but recognized the merits of both schools of composition.

Stewart's professorial lectures continued sporadically over the next decade but between the years 1872 and 1877 Stewart's annual lectures established him as an erudite scholar of local repute and ensured his prominence as one of the primary musical figures in Dublin.

---

[46] Ibid., p. 169. [47] Ibid., p. 126. [48] Stewart, 'Music', pp 164, 148. [49] Ibid., p. 164. [50] Appendix II at the end of this chapter records the history examination paper. [51] See note 5 above, and see also Michael Murphy's and Joachim Fischer's chapters in this volume for Wagner reception in late nineteenth-

ORIENTALISM

The 1876 group of lectures entitled 'Natural Music and its Relation to Modern Musical Art' no doubt proved very popular with Stewart's Dublin audience as it introduced an exotic, mysterious and exciting element to his conservative Dublin audience by referring to the music of the untamed 'savages' of other countries. The indigenous music of Africa, Australia, China, Egypt and Russia was explored and the vocal and instrumental illustrations, taken from a number of sources, were provided by a group of performers from the University Choral Society (of which Stewart was the conductor). Examples of music performed throughout the six weeks included an Aboriginal Corroboree song,[52] a traditional Eskimo song,[53] a Burmese boat song and Arabic love songs. Microtones, instruments, drones, snake charmers, cannibals, folk music incorporated into art music and writings on Eastern music were all discussed at length in the lectures.

The subject matter of Stewart's lectures indicates that the 'oriental' element in music was a well-known concept in the latter half of the nineteenth century. By the middle of the nineteenth century a 'virtual epidemic of Orientalia' affected poets, essayists, philosophers and musicians. Victor Hugo even recorded in 1829 that 'Au siècle de Louis XIV on était helléniste, maintenant on est orientaliste'.[54] The 1830s and '40s saw a 'sudden burst in production' of compositions such as operas and ballets that portrayed the Middle East in a serious and imaginative way.[55] The medium of opera with its exotic characters, libretto, stage sets, costumes and musical language proved to be 'the most effective vehicle for embodying Orientalist images'.[56]

So what enticed Stewart to compose these lectures in the first instance? In the first lecture he recorded how it was his communications with former members of the University Choral Society working abroad that had sparked his interest in the native music of other countries and was the reason why he decided to research the subject further. Some of the members of the University Choral Society may have been students of oriental languages at Trinity, who hoped upon graduation to work in India with the Civil Service. The reforms in the British civil and colonial service recruitment procedures introduced in the mid-nineteenth century recommended that the Indian Civil Service should be recruited by competitive examination, and Sanskrit and Arabic were among the recommended subjects. The first chair in Arabic was introduced at Trinity in 1855 and the chair in Sanskrit in 1862.[57] After the introduction of these chairs at Trinity a number of students became attracted to the prospect of adventure and travel to distant lands that a career in the Indian Civil Service offered. Throughout the set of six

---

century Ireland. **52** *NG II* defines the term corroboree as 'an aboriginal occasion on which singing and dancing take place'; Alice M. Moyle, 'Corroboree', *NG II*, iv, 804. **53** According to Stewart, Captain William Edward Parry heard the Eskimo song referred to in this lecture on his 1821 voyage to the Arctic; 'Lecture on music', *IT*, 13 March 1876. **54** Victor Hugo quoted in Edward Said, *Orientalism* (London: Routledge & Kegan Paul, 1978), p. 51. **55** Locke, 'Cutthroats and casbah dancers', 29. **56** Ibid., 41. **57** McDowell and Webb, *Trinity College Dublin*, p. 232.

lectures, Stewart examined the aborigines of 'still uncivilized countries', with a view to 'tracing the connection between these aboriginal musical efforts and the best music of modern times in Europe'.[58]

It could be suggested that it was the environment that existed at Trinity College, consisting of the intellectual discipline of orientalism and the possible links with India through the Civil Service, that instilled in Stewart a sense of affiliation to, and familiarity with the exotic lands of the East and Far East. Having visited the Great Exhibition in 1851, Stewart had seen and heard the many exhibitions and performers who had travelled to London for the event, and so had some idea of the concept of westernized versions of eastern music that were performed in the West. Stewart as a member of the establishment Protestant class in Dublin felt that he was at the centre of colonial expansion (as a 'colonizer' and not one of the 'colonized'), a section of society that also considered themselves 'full citizens and redoubtable defenders of the Empire'.[59] The stimuli for the huge interest in the Orient during the 1870s included the visit of the Prince of Wales to India in 1876 and the title of Empress of India that was bestowed upon Queen Victoria in January 1877. These events in particular illustrate that a sense of India was certainly in the air.

In his first lecture, Stewart referred to the University Choral Society as 'a sort of musical missionary association', and listed the foreign experiences of some of the past members of the society. Apparently one former member had played the harmonium for a native Hindu choir; another had 'drilled four "black fellows", Queenslanders, in C.F.W. Müller's little glee, *Spring's delights*'; and a third sent home a 'queer' Burmese instrument [a wooden harmonicon], which had been taken from two natives who were fighting over its possession. With such an intriguing opening Stewart's audience knew that they were in for an interesting and entertaining lecture.[60]

Stewart's lecture continued by describing accounts of the music of the South Pacific. The 'horrid din' of drums and gongs of a 'cannibal's song' that was performed at the lecture illustrated the music of a 'savage degraded race'. Stewart then read portions of a letter referring to the cannibals of Fiji and the 'peculiar beat of drums with which they invariably accompanied their horrid rites'.[61] This emphasizes a point made by Rana Kabbani in *Imperial Fiction: Europe's Myths of Orient* where the East has been described as 'a place of lascivious sensuality, and … a realm characterised by inherent violence' since medieval times.[62] As the travel writers of the eighteenth and nineteenth centuries maintained this stereotype, it is not surprising to find references to this opinion in Stewart's lectures.

A number of sources were referred to by Stewart in his talks, including essays on oriental music by writers such as Thomas Edward Bowdich (*c*.1719–1824),

---

[58] 'Lecture', *IT*, 13 March 1876.   [59] David Fitzpatrick, 'Ireland and the Empire', *The Oxford history of the British empire*, iii, ed. Andrew Porter (Oxford and New York: Oxford University Press, 1999), p. 508.
[60] 'Lectures on music', *DE*, 13 March 1876.   [61] 'Sir R. P. Stewart's lectures', *DE*, 20 March 1876.
[62] Rana Kabbani, *Imperial fictions: Europe's myths of orient* (London: Pandora, an imprint of Harper

Charles Burney (1726–1814), William Chappell (1809–88), Jean-Benjamin de La Borde (1734–94), François-Joseph Fétis (1784–1871), Edward William Lane (1801–76), Carsten Niebuhr (1733–1815) and Guillaume-André Villoteau (1759–1839). When speaking of the music of Africa, Stewart used the musical examples from Thomas Edward Bowdich's *A Mission from Cape Coast Castle to Ashantee*.[63] On his visit to Africa, Bowdich met with members of the Fanti and Ashanti tribes of Ghana and recorded the society and culture of these people. The Fanti dirge performed was described by the *Daily Express* as 'a few mournful thirds on flutes, followed by strokes on a gong and a drum', and the vocal Ashanti song as 'music, consisting first of local dialogue and harmony of the voices, also in thirds'.[64]

La Borde and Lane[65] were Stewart's trusted sources on the music of the Egyptians and Arabs, having written *Essai sur la musique ancienne et moderne* and *An account of the Manners and Customs of the Modern Egyptians* respectively.[66] Stewart quoted from La Borde in relation to the unfavourable opinions with respect to music held by the upper classes of the East:

> the higher class of Turks and Arabs deem it beneath their dignity to study music or dancing; just so the Chinese, seeing a dance of the officers attached to Lord Macartney's Embassy, enquired 'Could you not let your servants do all this for you?'[67]

La Borde also wrote how music, deemed profitless if not dangerous among Orientals, was condemned by the prophet Mahomet.[68] When discussing the call to prayer used in the Egyptian cities of Aleppo and Cairo, Stewart paraphrases Lane with reference to the Cairo style:

> The manners and customs of its inhabitants are peculiarly interesting, being a combination of those which prevail in the towns of Arabia, Syria, and the whole of Northern Africa; customs which not all the Frankish proclivities of Mehemet-Ali were quite able to destroy.[69]

The 'Cairo Call to Prayer' from Lane's book and an excerpt from the Koran were then performed by one of the tenor singers in attendance.

That Islam has been treated with caution by the West over the centuries cannot be doubted; Islam was judged as a 'fradulent new version of some previous experience, in this case Christianity', and Europe tended to view it with caution,

---

Collins, 1986), p. 6. **63** Thomas Edward Bowdich, *Mission from Cape Coast Castle to Ashantee* (London: John Murray, 1819). **64** 'Lectures', *DE*, 20 March 1876. **65** Lane was the great-uncle of Stanley Edward Lane-Poole (1854–1931) who was Professor of Arabic at Trinity College Dublin from 1898 until 1904. **66** Jean-Benjamin de La Borde, *Essai sur la musique ancienne et moderne* (Paris: 1780) and Edward William Lane, *An account of the manners and customs of the modern Egyptians* (London: 1836). **67** 'Lectures', *DE*, 20 March 1876. **68** Ibid. **69** 'Sir R. Stewart's lectures on music', *DE*, 27 March 1876.

scepticism and even hostility.[70] While the nineteenth-century missionary and orientalist shared a common thought that Islam might be transformed through 'westernization' or 'modernization', or 'reformation',[71] attitudes that viewed Muslims as the intellectual inferiors ruled by the Westerner in his role as enlightener (not exploiter) were commonplace and exemplified by Lord Cromer, England's Representative in Egypt (1882–1907) in his *Modern Egypt*:

> Let us, in Christian charity, make every possible allowance for the moral and intellectual shortcomings of the Egyptians, and do whatever can be done to rectify them.[72]

This missionary tone is not unusual for the time and echoes the opinion of Stewart and his audience towards the music of the indigenous countries that he refers to in his lectures. To Stewart, this music was simplistic because it originated in cultures that were far behind the West in terms of artistic merit, culture and development and the music performed was a subject of interest and amusement.

Villoteau is also employed by Stewart as an expert source on Egyptian music as he accompanied Napoleon to Egypt in 1798.[73] Stewart quoted some interesting remarks by the French writer on the absence of the 'sensible', or semitone at the top of the scale in Oriental music.[74] Villoteau 'describes with much gusto the difficulties he experienced in making the Orientals sing the scale of C major, with the semitone of B to C at the top'.[75] This proved an all but insuperable barrier to these people and Stewart quoted from Villoteau's account before the choir sang a transcription of an air sung for Napoleon at Cairo in 1799:

> I have had occasion to convince myself of this in Egypt while endeavouring to make Greek, Egyptian, Arabian, Ethiopian, Persian, Armenian, or Syrian musicians sing it; and truly the grimaces and contortions that these good people were obliged to make in order to reach with their voices to our B natural (which they tried, however, and with the best faith in the world to sound, but always unsuccessfully), appeared to me so singularly laughable that I believe it would have been impossible for me to look at them unmoved if the motive which determined me to make the experiment had not then occupied all my attention.[76]

---

70 Said, *Orientalism*, p. 59. **71** A.L. Tibawi, 'English-speaking Orientalists', in *Orientalism: a reader*, ed. A.L. Macfie (Cambridge: Edinburgh University Press, 2000), p. 60. **72** Lord Cromer, *Modern Egypt* (London: 1908), quoted in Kabbani, *Imperial fictions*, p. 43. **73** Guillaume-André Villoteau's writings include *Mémoire sur la possibilité et l'utilité d'une théorie exacte des principes naturels de la musique* (Paris: 1807) and *Recherches sur l'analogie de la musique avec les arts qui ont pour objet l'imitation du langage* (Paris and Geneva: 1807). **74** 'Sir Robert Stewart's lecture on music', *IT*, 27 March 1876. **75** 'Lectures', *DE*, 27 March 1876. **76** Villoteau, *Recherches*, ii, 46–7 quoted by Stewart in his lecture; 'Lectures', *DE*, 27 March 1876. Stewart added a note to confirm that this semitone is not completely absent from Eastern music in his lecture.

Sir Frederick Ouseley, a 'learned and talented friend' of Stewart, also featured in this lecture in relation to an essay on Oriental music that he presented to the Church Congress in 1863. According to Stewart, Ouseley remarked that Oriental music is 'so over charged with ornament and minute variations of pitch and pace, that the air is well nigh lost' and considered ornamentation to be of Oriental origin whereas beauty was more modern and European. These opinions that Stewart cites also reflect the views of writers such as Villoteau and Fétis[77] with respect to the excessive ornamentation of Eastern music.

In the last three lectures, Stewart introduces examples of art music that incorporate indigenous music from Eastern and Arabic countries. The main composers that Stewart focuses his attention on include Beethoven and his incorporation of Russian folk music in the Razumovsky Quartets, and the 'Turkish Dance' and 'Chorus of Dervishes' in his *Die Ruinen von Athen*, Félicien David's incorporation of the Arabic air 'Ikki Belbol' in *Le Désert*, the employment of eastern music in Weber's *Oberon, Preciosa, Der Freischütz* and *Turandot* and the appearance of an Eastern chant in Macfarren's *The Sleeper Awakened*.

The Arabic air 'Ikki Belbol' was performed in Stewart's third, fourth and fifth lectures. Stewart heard this song for the first time in London in 1851 performed by a group of Arabs who travelled to the Great Exhibition and performed at the Egyptian Hall at Piccadilly,[78] where they had coffee, pipes, and a little hump-backed storyteller pacing up and down and reciting tales in genuine Arabic.[79] As the dulcimer was the main instrument of this group of musicians, Stewart displayed two diagrams – one of the modern instrument and the other of the ancient Assyrian dulcimer.[80] In the fourth lecture, Stewart pointed out that David had used this tune in his symphonic ode *Le Désert* of 1844. This piece in three movements contains sections entitled 'desert storm', 'prayer to Allah', 'caravan', '*rêverie du soir*' and 'the muezzin's call'.[81] According to Stewart, the silence of the desert is imitated in the long sustained notes on the violins and violas in the orchestral introduction that precede the *Ikki Belbol* tune played on the horns.[82] In David's composition, the strings copy the Kemengeh, 'a rude sort of fiddle with three strings and a horsehair bow'[83] and Stewart had a drawing of the instrument by the German traveller and writer Carsten Niebuhr on display. According to Niebuhr who refers to the instrument as a 'Semenge', a 'cocoa nut-shell' is attached to a long-bodied viol in order to increase the resonance of the instrument.[84] Stewart compares this instrument to the Tingadee (an instrument that has three gourds), and showed a picture of it from the *Illustrated London News*.[85]

77 'Sir R. Stewart's lecture on music', *DE*, 10 April 1876.   78 'Lecture', *IT*, 27 March 1876.
79 'Lectures', *DE*, 27 March 1876.   80 Ibid.   81 John M. MacKenzie, *Orientalism: history, theory and the arts* (Manchester and New York: Manchester University Press, 1995), p. 149.   82 Stewart is the only source to mention this tune in relation to David's *Le Désert*.   83 'Sir R. Stewart's lectures on music', *DE*, 3 April 1876.   84 Carsten Niebuhr, *Travels through Arabia, and other countries in the East*, trans. Robert Heron (Dublin: Gilbert, Moore, Archer & Jones, 1792), p. 134.   85 The picture entitled 'A strolling minstrel at Madras playing the tingadee' was included in the *Illustrated London News*, 29 January 1876;

Weber, who Stewart noted enriched his works with Spanish, Bohemian, and Arab airs, was discussed in relation to his employment of folk music in classical composition.[86] According to Stewart, Weber endeavoured to impart a local colour to the Oriental adventures of Sir Huon of Bourdeaux in *Oberon* by introducing into the first finale in C major 'Now the evening watch is set' an Arabic melody notated in Niebuhr's *Voyage en Arabie*.[87] The other Arabic air introduced into *Oberon* is played on the magic horn, 'and by thus compelling the black slaves to dance to its sounds, Sir Houn and his lover Rezia are enabled to effect their escape'.[88] According to Stewart, this air is to be found in La Borde's *Essai sur la musique ancienne et moderne* and in *Specimens of Various Styles of Music referred to in a Course of Lectures* by William Crotch as 'Danse Turque'.[89] 'Now the evening watch is set' and the finale to the third act, 'Hark! What notes are swelling' containing the second Arabic air were then performed.[90]

Weber's *Preciosa* is another example of a composition in which national tunes had been interwoven, and Stewart performed the 'Gipsy March' air that is present throughout the Allegro section of the overture to demonstrate this technique. Similarly, *Der Freischütz*, set in Bohemia, illustrates Weber's incorporation of Bohemian airs in the bridesmaid's song; 'the wafts in the first scene may or may not be a dance tune of that country' according to Stewart.[91] Stewart concludes his section on Weber's music by referring to the Chinese influence in his *Turandot*. Briefly describing the pentatonic characteristic of Chinese music Stewart deferred the performance of the Chinese air from *Turandot* by wind and string instruments until the end of the lecture because the March was 'simply grotesque' and would only excite laughter.[92]

The language employed in Stewart's lectures to describe the natives of various countries is interesting to examine. It was of course representative of the attitudes of the time held by western countries towards the indigenous people of non-western countries (especially those countries that were colonized by the British) who were seen as savages. The Australian Aborigines were reported to have been described by Stewart as 'the aborigines of still uncivilized countries',[93] as 'black fellows' and 'savage tribes',[94] and the music recorded in the South Pacific Islands was referred to by Stewart as the music of a 'savage degraded race'.[95] The recitations of the Arabs were reported as 'the vain repetitions of the heathen'[96] which illustrates the western attitude towards Muslims as a demonic people of 'hated barbarians'.[97] However, as MacKenzie reminds us, the word 'barbaric' should be read not in its modern one-dimensional meaning but in its nineteenth-century context 'with its suggestions of the sublime, lack of restraint, an attractive

---

see 'Lectures', *DE*, 3 April 1876.   **86** 'Lecture', *DE*, 10 April 1876.   **87** Stewart is referring to the 'March of the Harem Guards' at the end of Act I.   **88** 'Lectures', *DE*, 3 April 1876.   **89** La Borde, *Essai sur la musique*, and William Crotch, *Specimens of various styles of music referred to in a course of lectures* (London: R. Birchall, [*c*.1807–15]).   **90** 'Lectures', *DE*, 3 April 1876.   **91** 'Lecture', *DE*, 10 April 1876.   **92** Ibid. This Chinese air was taken up by Hindemith at a much later date for a series of variations, see MacKenzie, *Orientalism*, p. 154.   **93** 'Lecture', *IT*, 13 March 1876.   **94** 'Lectures', *DE*, 13 March 1876.   **95** 'Lectures', *DE*, 20 March 1876.   **96** 'Lecture', *IT*, 27 March 1876.   **97** Said, *Orientalism*, p. 59.

colourful and dramatic approach, liberating new sensations on a grand scale'.[98] Yet for citizens of nineteenth-century Britain and France, empire was a major topic of unembarrassed cultural attention.[99] Stewart also shared this thinking of 'belief and pride'[1] in the Empire that included 'the notions about bringing civilization to primitive or barbaric peoples',[2] that the Empire was 'the embodiment and expression of a British character comprising of individuality, stoicism, a sense of duty, a sense of humour and a sense of superiority' and ultimately that Britain was in the Empire 'for the good of its native peoples'.[3]

Despite his interest in the indigenous music of countries of the East, Stewart did not incorporate any elements of orientalism into his compositions. His allegiance to the British Empire manifests itself in his composition of a song called 'The Saving of the Colours (Isandula)' to words by Mrs M. Gorges.[4] This song was written in memory of the members of the 24th Regiment who were killed by the Zulus at the Battle of Isandhlwana on 22 January 1879. So what orientalist compositions would Stewart have been familiar with before 1876? In a time before Puccini's *Madama Butterfly* and *Turandot*, and Rimsky-Korsakov's *Schéhérazade* he was certainly familiar with the works of Weber and David's *Le Désert* that were performed in Dublin by the University Choral Society, and the Antient Concerts Society with Joseph Robinson as conductor.[5] That Stewart was also familiar with Verdi's operas is evident from Hercules MacDonnell's remark: 'Thus when Verdi's operas were first introduced, he was the only professional musician in Dublin who agreed with me in my high estimation of the composer's gifts'.[6] Stewart may also have known Bizet's *Carmen* and Delibes' *Lakmé*. Other compositions displaying elements of the exotic and performed at University Choral Society concerts included Verdi's *I Lombardi alla prima crociata*, Beethoven's *Die Ruinen von Athen* and Macfarren's *The Sleeper Awakened*.

Stewart's lectures educated his audiences on the indigenous music of 'savage' cultures and the current trends in European art music. His lectures were almost always reported as having been densely crowded by a 'numerous and most respectable audience,' an expression employed by many reporters in relation to lectures held at Trinity College at the time. Most of the reports from the various daily Dublin newspapers introduce their critique of Stewart's lectures by describing how 'every nook and corner [was] seemingly occupied by eager listeners'.[7] The fellows, professors and students of Trinity College also attended

---

98 John M. MacKenzie, 'History, theory and the arts', in *Orientalism: a reader*, ed. Macfie, p. 331. **99** Edward Said, *Culture and imperialism* (London: Vintage, 1994), pp xi–xii. **1** Jeffrey Richards, *Imperialism and music: Britain, 1876–1953* (Manchester and New York: Manchester University Press, 2001), p. 14. **2** Said, *Culture and imperialism*, pp xi–xii. **3** Richards, *Imperialism and Music*, p. 16. **4** This song was published by John Blockley of London [1879]. **5** Selections from Weber's *Der Freischütz*, *Oberon* and *Preciosa* appeared in the University Choral Society concerts between 1847 and 1862 and *Oberon* and David's *Le Désert* were performed by the Antient Concerts Society on 1 February 1856; see *FJ*, 2 February 1856. **6** Quoted in Vignoles, *Memoir*, p. 209. **7** 'Professor Stewart's lectures', *IT*, 23 April 1864.

Stewart's lectures, and occasionally a guest such as the wife of the Lord Lieutenant would also attend adding to the social status of the occasion. In fact, sometimes it was impossible for the reporters themselves to gain entry as the following anecdote from the *Irish Times* demonstrates in relation to one of Stewart's lectures on Handel in 1874:

> There was a crowded attendance. A representative from the *Irish Times* applied for admission *before* the hour announced for the lecture, and was refused admission by a College porter on the ground that the hall was full. It might be worthwhile for Sir Robert Stewart or the College authorities to consider whether it would not be well to reserve a place for reporters on such occasions.[8]

In the 1880s it is evident that Stewart was becoming frustrated with the refusal of his Dublin audiences to come to lectures which involved an entrance fee in order to raise funds for memorials to other Dublin musicians. In a letter dating from 1883 Stewart wrote:

> but after delivering about six annual sets of lectures – 36 in all, I got disgusted with the Dubliners, who flocked in great crowds to *gratis* lectures, but attended very badly when I wanted to raise funds for my two memorial windows to Stevenson and Balfe, although I kept the tickets so low that 6d. admitted to hear my lectures, illustrated by specimens of the best musicians and full of local chat of days gone by, without any political or religious tint (or *taint* if you prefer the word). Feeling after this that it was only whiskey and furious political harangues that the Irish want, I made a resolution never to give them another free lecture, and I won't![9]

Stewart no doubt softened in his opinion as time went by because he did deliver up to seven lectures in Cork and Dublin during the next decade.

MUSIC EDUCATION

One of Stewart's notable papers on education was undoubtedly that written for the Social Science Congress that took place at Trinity College Dublin in October 1881. Entitled 'Musical Education: By what means can native education in music be best promoted', Stewart examined the present state of music in Ireland and discussed systems of music teaching and a plan for promoting the national education of music in Ireland. By dividing music into three sections, historic, scientific and social, Stewart lists nine reforms and improvements that would ensure the best possible way of promoting music education in Ireland.

---

[8] 'Sir Robert Stewart's musical lectures', *IT*, 16 March 1874. [9] Letter from Robert Stewart 'To his pupil Miss – [Edith Oldham]', dated 24 November 1883 in Vignoles, *Memoir*, p. 147.

He began with a discussion of the patronage of music. Citing works such as Handel's *Acis and Galatea*, Haydn's symphonies and quartets and Beethoven's Mass in D as examples of music that would not have been composed but for the support of patrons, Stewart emphasized how important it was for artists to be nurtured and protected in order for their craft to be encouraged. However, Stewart could not see where funding of this nature could come from and only wished that there were more 'gentlemen' with the same generosity as Henry Roe, who had given £250,000 to restore Christ Church Cathedral, Dublin (between 1871 and 1878).

Stewart then went on to make nine suggestions about how music education could be structured both in terms of how music is taught and performed in the public and private institutions:

(1) The introduction of historical concerts and lectures to teach the history of the art and the instruments of past times by examples. Dividing the History of music into three subsections, 'History of the Art', 'National music and its influence on society', and 'Invention, structure and use of musical instruments', Stewart calls for the introduction of lectures or concerts on the history of music 'as had been lately done at Düsseldorf by the Bach Society, where specimens ranging from the ancient Greek music down to the works of Wagner had been produced in October 1879'. He also encouraged the collection of music of all countries and nations similar to *Specimens of Various Styles of Music referred to in a Course of Lectures* by William Crotch at Oxford[10] and lectures and catalogues on musical instruments, similar to those by Carl Engel in relation to the instruments held at the South Kensington Museum.[11]

(2) Lectures on the scientific and philosophical aspects of music. Stewart believed that the introduction of these lectures would lead to an increased appreciation of music among the Irish concert audience. The scientific aspect of music was divided into two subsections by Stewart, 'Acoustics' and 'The physical effects of music in the treatment of diseases'. Lectures to the public on acoustics should be given free of charge (or at a nominal fee) and the talks given by the Royal Dublin Society and other similar organizations in Ireland should be better promoted and encouraged. The second subdivision on how music could be used in the treatment of diseases was also an interesting one, worthy of further research according to Stewart.

(3) A better style of pianoforte teaching, embracing a knowledge of musical form, and increased attention to playing at sight.

(4) To include sight-singing (not singing by ear) at every school in the country. Stewart suggests this in order to improve the sight-reading ability of the church-

---

10 See note 89 above. **11** Stewart borrowed photographs of instruments from the South Kensington Museum for his lectures on stringed keyed-instruments.

going public which would in turn improve the standard of church music in Ireland.

(5) The establishment of a resident orchestra in Dublin of sixty instruments, to refine and guide the taste of the public which he believed was incapable of comprehending instrumental music of large calibre.

(6) A good concert hall, with a really fine organ, on which public performances could take place at stated times, and at low admission fees.

Stewart recorded that the absence of a resident orchestra in Dublin had been noticed by Henry Chorley of the *Athenaeum* and by Charles Hallé. This was attributable to 'political economy rather than ... music'. Apparently many musicians in Dublin had left the capital because they earned more money in Manchester or London. Stewart had researched the matter and believed that for £4,000 a year (a sum which was not a third of what some of Dublin's merchants had given to the city) a full orchestra could be maintained perennially, resident in Dublin, but available at a nominal cost for service in the provincial towns such as Cork, Limerick, and Belfast. According to the *Daily Express*, Stewart criticized current policy in the following terms:

> But if £4,000 a year seemed an extravagant sum to indoctrinate a nation in the noblest format that music could assume, in the symphony, the concerto, the oratorio, what should be said of the £100,000 a year devoted by the Government at present to encourage music in elementary schools, of which some was merely given to encourage singing by ear, and was therefore little better than thrown away?[12]

It cannot be doubted that Stewart had a valid point here and he continued with the remaining reforms in his schedule:

(7) The inclusion of music as a voluntary subject in the *curriculum* of the Universities.

(8) An authorized qualification for teachers of music, whereby 'quacks' would be discountenanced.

(9) Some means whereby the works of young composers might be adequately produced in public.[13]

---

[12] 'Social Science Congress, "Art Section"', *DE*, 8 October 1881.   [13] Ibid. and 'Social Science Congress, "Art Section"', *IT*, 8 October 1881

Under these new terms and conditions, the musical public would benefit culturally from the frequent opportunity of hearing the great works of classical music performed by a competent orchestra and this would in turn introduce a 'refining influence on public taste similar to that exhibited by the arts of sculpture and painting'.[14] The writings of John Larchet and Brian Boydell indicate that recommendations made by Stewart including his suggestion in relation to the establishment of a resident symphony orchestra and a good concert hall did not come to fruition during his lifetime.[15]

Stewart was of course not the only musician in Ireland who lectured on music. James Culwick and Annie Patterson for example wrote as many if not more lectures and articles than Stewart.[16] In Culwick's case, the majority of his lectures were delivered and published in the 1880s when Stewart was lecturing less frequently and Patterson's writings (including her numerous articles for the *Weekly Irish Times*) and books were published quite some time after Stewart had died. Ebenezer Prout (Stewart's successor at Trinity College Dublin) and William Henry Grattan Flood were other figures lecturing and writing on music and perhaps if Stewart was not so caught up with his day to day duties, he might have attempted larger scale writings or books that may have been more successful in standing the test of time than his lectures.

Stewart was a popular, distinguished figure with a reputation as an erudite scholar, and Harry White describes his 'profound' influence as an educator of music in Ireland.[17] Culwick respected and revered Stewart and held him in high regard as a lecturer; he recognized that he was 'no retailer of second-hand knowledge ... following another man's lead' and referred to Stewart's views as broad and many-sided.[18] A man of much literary culture, Stewart was also aware of the negative effects that insularity could bring and made a conscious effort to visit the continent at least once a year after 1851. Stewart himself said 'nothing is so narrowing, contracting, hardening, as always to be moving in the same groove, with no thought beyond what we immediately see and hear close around us'.[19] His annual trips to music festivals on the continent proved a vital link to the current developments that were taking place in England and Europe.

The topics of Stewart's lectures discussed above demonstrate his awareness of the shortcomings of the music education system in Ireland and the lack of a proper support system for the musical infrastructure of the country. His lectures on indigenous music are representative of the elements of exotica and orientalism

---

14 'Social Science Congress', *IT*, 8 October 1881.   **15** See White, *The keeper's recital*, p. 130ff.   **16** For more information on the writings of James Culwick see: *The Culwick Choral Society celebrates one hundred years, 1898–1998*, ed. Jane Clare, Magdalen O'Connell, and Ann Simmons (Dublin: The Culwick Choral Society, 1998) and Annie Patterson, 'Dr James Culwick', *Weekly Irish Times*, 4 August 1900, 3. Further information on Annie Patterson and her writings is found in William H Grattan Flood/Patrick F. Devine, 'Annie Patterson', *GMO* (accessed 19 January 2006), and Jennifer O'Connor, 'Fanny Arthur Robinson and Annie Patterson: the contribution of women to music in Dublin in the second half of the nineteenth century', MA diss. (NUI Maynooth, 2003).   **17** White, *The keeper's recital*, p. 101.   **18** James C. Culwick, *Fifty years in the life of a great Irish musician* (Dublin: Chadfield, 1903), p. 9.   **19** Vignoles, *Memoir*, pp 57–8.

that he undoubtedly came into contact with at Trinity College. The 1862 lecture demonstrates his familiarity with some of the eighteenth- and nineteenth-century writers on music such as Burney, Rousseau and Stafford and shows us how Stewart reflected the attitudes and opinions that were common in England and Ireland during the latter half of the nineteenth century. His intention as a music educator was to 'raise the musical taste of his fellow-citizens'[20] and although Stewart was little known outside of Ireland as an educator, his presence and influence in Dublin certainly calls for further consideration.

APPENDIX I

Recipients of music degrees at Trinity College Dublin (1862–94) (based on the entries in the *Dublin University Calendar*).
Asterisks after name indicate a biographical note below.

Bachelor of Music	Date
Revd Edward Synge	30 June 1869
Arthur Wolfe Hamilton	15 December 1869
John William Hinton	6 July 1870
George William Röhner	14 December 1870
Revd George Fortescue Reade	21 February 1871
Revd David Henry Ellis	13 February 1872
Henry Dawson Stanistreet	26 June 1872
Duncan Thackeray	25 June 1873
Revd John Harpur	24 June 1874
Thomas Osborne Marks	24 June 1874
Stephen Henry Edward Chamier	16 December 1874
Revd Savile Richard William L'Estrange Malone	16 December 1874
T.R.G. Jozé*	30 June 1875
William Hodgson Telford*	30 June 1875
Albert Frederick Otho Hartmann	15 December 1875
Revd George William Torrance*	25 June 1879
Robert Henry Allen	15/16 December 1880
Francis Bates	15/16 December 1880
Benjamin Hobson Carroll	15/16 December 1880
Arthur Hamilton Collyer	15/16 December 1880
Walter Peake Fairclough	15/16 December 1880
John Francis Fitzgerald	15/16 December 1880
Revd John Bulmer	10 February 1880
Thomas Gick	30 June 1880

20 'A distinguished Irishman, Sir Robert Stewart', *Pittsburg* [sic] *Chronicle*, 1872, quoted in Vignoles, *Memoir*, p. 105.

Bachelor of Music (continued)	**Date**
Frederick William Haydock	30 June 1880
William Henry Smart	30 June 1880
Joseph Smith	30 June 1880
Revd Frederick Augustus Glover	30 June 1881
George Bell	29 June 1882
Robert Malone	2 May 1883
Ebenezer Goold	29 June 1883
Charles Edward Allum	26 June 1884
William Alexander [Houston] Collison*	26 June 1884
Charles George Marchant*	26 June 1884
Edward Cooney	25 June 1885
John Edward Green	9 March 1886
Henry Theodore Brunard	9 March 1886
John William Jackson	9 March 1886
David John Jeduthin Mason	1 July 1886
Revd Henry George Bonavia Hunt*	30 June 1887
Revd Ernest Hamilton Whelan	15 December 1887
John Warriner	15 December 1887
Frank Merrick	28 June 1888
Arthur Thomas Froggatt	9 December 1888
Revd Samuel James Rowton	27 June 1889
Albert Ham*	18 February 1890
Samuel McBurney	26 June 1890
Henry Crane Perrin	18 December 1890
Bartholomew Warburton Rooke*	26 June 1890
William Henry Barrow	17 December 1891
George Henry Pugh	17 December 1891
Joseph Seymour*	23 June 1892
Robert Henry Earnshaw	15 December 1892
Edward Emmanuel Harper	15 December 1892

Doctor of Music	**Date**
Revd Edward Synge	30 June 1869
George William Röhner	14 December 1870
Henry Dawson Stanistreet	26 June 1872
Lewis James Watters	6 July 1872
Duncan Thackeray	25 June 1873
Thomas Osborne Marks	24 June 1874
John William Hinton	24 June 1874
Albert Frederick Otho Hartmann	15 December 1875
T.R.G. Jozé	28 June 1881
Revd George William Torrance*	25 June 1879
Joseph Smith	30 June 1880
Thomas Gick	29 June 1882

Doctor of Music (continued)	Date
Benjamin Hobson Carroll	18 December 1884
Francis Bates	26 June 1884
William Henry Gater*	1 July 1886
John Edward Green	1 July 1886
Charles Edward Allum	30 June 1887
Edward Cooney	30 June 1887
Revd Henry George Bonavia Hunt*	30 June 1887
Revd George Bell	28 June 1888
Revd Samuel James Rowton	26 June 1890
William Alexander Houston Collison	18 December 1890
Samuel McBurney	18 December 1890
Frederick William Haydock	10 February 1891
William Henry Barrow	17 December 1891
John William Jackson	17 December 1891
John Warriner	23 June 1892
Robert Henry Earnshaw	15 December 1893
Albert Ham*	15 December 1893
Arthur Thomas Froggatt	6 February 1894

William Alexander Houston Collison Collison was organist at St Patrick's, Trim, and St Paul's, Bray, and in 1885 he became organist and director of the choir at Rathfarnham Church. He collaborated with Percy French on compositions such as *The Irish Girl: A Comedy Opera*, and songs 'Are ye right there, Michael?', 'Father O'Callaghan' and 'Tullinahaw'. His only book, *Dr Collinson in and on Ireland: a diary of a tour, with personal anecdotes, notes autobiographical and impressions,* details his many concerts around Ireland in 1907 (London, 1908).

William Henry Gater Gater received organ lessons from Robert Stewart and was organist of Christ Church, Bray, 1871–3. He was the organist at the Dublin Exhibition Palace in 1872–3. From 1873 to 1876 he was organist of St Andrew's, Dublin, and also held the post of organist of St Stephen's Church for over fifty years. Gater was deputy conductor to Stewart at the Dublin University Choral Society and also conducted the Bray Choral Union. He composed some church music and a cantata entitled *The Passions*.

Albert Ham Ham was a choirboy at Bath Abbey and studied the organ with James Kendrick Pyne. He moved to Canada in 1897 and remained there until 1935. Ham retained the post of organist and choirmaster of St James' Cathedral, Toronto for thirty-six years and he was the president of the Canadian College of Organists for over ten years. His compositions include several anthems and two cantatas. He authored several books including *The rudiments of music and elementary harmony* and *outlines of music form, with analyses from well-known works.*

Henry George Bonavia Hunt Hunt was born in Malta in 1847 and was the founder of the Trinity College of Music, London. Hunt edited several popular magazines and journals including the *Quiver* (1865–1905) and *Cassell's Magazine* (1874–96) and contributed articles to the *Guardian*. Between 1900 and 1906 Hunt was lecturer in music history at London University and his *Concise History of Music* (1878) reached its nineteenth edition in 1915. His compositions include a motet *The Blessed Dead* and a Magnificat and Nunc Dimittis in B♭.

Thomas Richard Gonsalvez Jozé Jozé held several positions within the RIAM including professor of singing, organ and chamber music and teacher of harmony and composition and piano. His compositions include a comic opera, *Les Amourettes* (1885), and a cantata, *The Prophecy of Capys* (1877), to words by Macauley.

Charles Marchant Marchant became a chorister of St Patrick's Cathedral in 1865 and was appointed organist of Holy Trinity, Rathmines (1874), Christ Church, Bray (1876), St Matthias' Church, Adelaide Road (1879, where he remained for one week) and organist and choir-master of St Patrick's Cathedral. He was also conductor of the Dublin University Choral Society and organist of Trinity College Chapel. Marchant was engaged as an assistant to Stewart at the RIAM in 1880 and he was appointed organ professor there following Stewart's death in 1894. He became senior professor of organ at the Academy upon Jozé's resignation. From 1892 to 1899 Marchant taught chamber music at the academy and from 1894 to 1899 he taught choir. He received an honorary MusD from Trinity College Dublin in 1911.

Bartholomew Warburton Rooke Rooke held several positions at the RIAM including professor of piano and harmony and composition. Rooke and Hewson succeeded Charles Marchant to become professors of organ at the academy. In 1898 he became a member of the Board of Studies at the academy and Vice-Chariman of the Board of Studies in 1908. He was also an examiner for the local centre examinations from 1918.

Joseph Seymour Seymour was appointed organist of SS Peter and Paul, Cork in 1878 and this was followed by the position of organist of St Andrew's, Westland Row in 1881. He founded the Tonic Sol-Fa Society in 1896 and was associated with the Dublin Glee Singers. He edited *Lyra Ecclesiastica* from 1884 to 1891 and was an examiner at the RIAM. His compositions include four masses, an operetta called *An Irish May-Day* and numerous motets and part-songs.

William H. Telford Son of organ-builder Henry Telford and brother of Edward Henry Telford. William Hodgson Telford was the founder and conductor of The Orchestral Union and also conducted the Dublin Amateur Orchestra Union. He is listed in *Thom's Directory* as an organist living at 109 St Stephen's Green, the same address as the Telford organ-building firm up until 1875, after which he appears in as 'William H. Telford, Mus. Bac. TCD'. William joined with his brother Edward to carry on the organ-building business as 'Telford and Sons'.

George William Torrance Torrance was a chorister at Christ Church Cathedral Dublin from 1847 to 1852 and was organist at Blackrock (1851), St Andrew's (1852) and St Ann's (1854) in Dublin. He went to Leipzig to pursue his musical studies in 1856, was ordained in 1865 and moved to Australia in 1869 where he received an honorary MusD from Melbourne University in 1880. Torrance composed several oratorios including *Abraham* (1855), *The Captivity* (1864) and *The Revelation* (1882). He returned to Ireland in 1898 and settled in Kilkenny where he was appointed chaplain to the bishop of Ossory and bishop's vicar choral at St Canice's Cathedral, Kilkenny. Torrance edited a collection of Chants and Responses with Jozé and is known for his opera *William of Normandy* (1858). He also composed hymns, anthems, songs and madrigals.

APPENDIX II

Royal Irish Academy of Music History Paper
8 December 1888

Modern Music

When was Richard Wagner born?
What are his chief works?
What was his theory of Opera and Drama?
What were his objections to the operas existing before his time?
Was Wagner celebrated for anything but his musical compositions? Give details.
What was that department of the Musical Art in which even his enemies admit his supremacy?
What are his claims as a vocal composer?
In what departments is he generally admitted to have been excelled by Mozart, Beethoven, and even Weber?
What famous musician was Wagner's great helper?
What phrase was devised by Wagner's opponents to prejudice the world of music against him, and what was in reality, the expression used by Wagner himself?
When and where did Wagner die?

The Society of Antient Concerts, Dublin, 1834–64

PAUL RODMELL

> This Society [has] for its object the cultivation of Vocal Music, especially the Choral compositions of the Antient Masters.[1]

This 'mission statement', to use a distinctly un-Victorian term, encapsulates the function of perhaps Dublin's most important musical society of the early Victorian period. After discreet beginnings, the Society of Antient Concerts became, within five years of its foundation, a leading light in the city's music scene. Its concerts were attended by Dublin's social elite, acclaimed for their quality, and included several notable first Irish performances. Perhaps most importantly, the society provided Dublin with a highly-regarded concert venue which remained in use for over a century. This paper presents a brief history of the society, its repertory and performances, social function, and contribution to the musical life of Dublin.

The main sources of information concerning the Antient Concerts are contemporary directories, and newspaper articles and announcements; no business records of the society are known to survive. Some printed programmes are held by Trinity College Library, Dublin, and the National Library of Ireland.[2] A substantial archive of music is owned by the Royal Irish Academy of Music.[3] A number of private memoirs have also been used.[4]

Assuming one came from an acceptable social background, and had an adequate income, there was ample opportunity to make and listen to music in early Victorian Dublin. Given the city's relative isolation from Britain until the 1850s, the greater part of musical life depended upon a small group of resident professional performers and talented amateurs. Professional musicians did, of

---

[1] *Dublin Almanac and General Register of Ireland* (Dublin: Pettigrew & Oulton, 1839), p. 175. [2] IRL-Dtc, call nos. OLS L–2–728 and OLS 198.q.67, and IRL-Dn call no. Ir 780 p 104. Twenty-six programmes survive altogether, but six are duplicates. The two collections cover most concerts given between 1844 and 1851; TCD also possesses programmes for 22 March 1838 and 1 February 1856. See also note 43. [3] I am very grateful to Philip Shields, Librarian at the RIAM (IRL-Dam), for allowing access to the collection, which is currently being catalogued by Catherine Ferris, postgraduate student at NUI Maynooth, to whom thanks are also due for valuable co-operation. The archive comprises some 5,000 items, mainly printed music, but also some manuscript material, most of which appears to have been bought by the Antients but some of which was acquired from other sources, most notably the Sons of Handel. The archive was bought by the RIAM from Joseph Robinson in 1872. [4] See Charles Stanford, 'Joseph Robinson', in *Studies and memories* (London: Archibald Constable, 1908), pp 117–27; Patrick J Stephenson, 'The Antient Concert Rooms', *Dublin Historical Record* [hereafter DHR], 5 (1942–3), 1–14; [Anonymous] *Recollections of Dublin Castle and of Dublin Society* (London: Chatto & Windus, 1902).

course, travel to Dublin from outside Ireland and rich pickings were to be had. As a proportion of Dublin's musical activity, though, such events were a minority, although improvements in transport resulted in a steady increase in visits by performers such as Thalberg, Joachim, Arabella Goddard, Charles Hallé and a host of singers, mostly in visiting opera companies. Compared to the latter part of the nineteenth century, however, Dublin's musical life in the early Victorian period was distinctly self-sufficient.

These activities were 'codified' by the presence of a variety of (often transient) musical societies. When the 'Antients' was founded, the longest-standing was the Hibernian Catch Club, founded some 150 years earlier by the Vicars Choral of the two Anglican cathedrals (St Patrick's and Christ Church) for the singing of glees, catches and madrigals. Focussed on orchestral music, another long-running society was the Anacreontic. Of more recent genesis were the Dublin Philharmonic Society (refounded in 1826 and also dedicated to orchestral works), the Festival Choral (1830–36), the Dublin Choral (1836–41, replacing the former), the University Choral (founded 1837 and based in Trinity College), the Metropolitan Choral (1842–7), Amateur Harmonic (founded 1842), the Amateur Melophonic (founded 1845) and the Madrigal Society (founded 1846). Some of these outlived the Antients, others did not. Part of the problem, it seems, was that many performed the same music and drew their membership and audiences from the same social group, Dublin's Anglican middle and upper classes; to compound this most societies permitted only men to be members.[5] Only occasionally were other demographic groups targeted: the Dublin Choral noted that it was 'the only [one] in Dublin to which ladies are admissible as members',[6] while the Sacred Harmonic, founded in 1841 with the aim of achieving 'the improvement of psalmody and the cultivation of sacred vocal music',[7] was run by and based in the Presbyterian Scots' Church on Ushers' Quay, thereby focusing on Dublin's small non-conformist population.[8]

Most societies were organized on similar lines: acquisition of membership required proposal by one or two current members, thus ensuring social exclusivity. Committees were elected annually although, in many cases, the same men served in successive years. A significant distinction was made between amateurs and professionals (almost literally 'gentlemen' and 'players'); this did not, however, imply so much of a difference in social status as of roles within the society. Professional members were expected to organize the musical activities, conduct and take solo roles, while amateurs were business managers, chorus members or back desk players in the orchestra.[9] It is unclear whether or not professional

---

[5] Some societies, such as the Antients, allowed women to participate as performers (discussed below), but many others, such as the Hibernian Catch Club and Dublin University Choral Society, were exclusively male. [6] *Dublin Almanac and General Register of Ireland* (Dublin: Pettigrew & Oulton, 1837) [hereafter *DA* 1837], p. 163. [7] *Dublin Almanac and General Register of Ireland* (Dublin: Pettigrew & Oulton, 1843) [hereafter *DA* 1843], p. 178. [8] In the early 1840s Dublin's dissenting church membership formed about 2.5% of the total population, Anglicans 25.5% and Roman Catholics 72% (see *DA* 1843, p. 583). [9] The social separation between amateur and professional members was not nearly so pointed in Dublin

members were paid; conversely, amateurs occasionally appeared as soloists, their status being invariably and significantly mentioned in press reviews and in some printed programmes (the demarcation implicitly inviting a more sympathetic hearing). A distinction was also made between performing and non-performing members: the latter were guaranteed a fixed number of free tickets for each concert plus the opportunity to buy extras. Tickets were on public sale only exceptionally, so societies were not only able to control the social makeup of their membership but also of their audiences (consequently there are almost no surviving records of ticket prices, although annual membership was typically around £1).[10] The Antients conformed to these general precepts: its membership was founded upon and, so far as can be deduced, drawn from the Anglo-Irish middle and upper classes. Its Patron, President and Vice-Presidents were invariably drawn from the same elite and the cachet supplied by association with such men undoubtedly exemplified the respectability which was a prerequisite for success and flourishing membership.[11]

Unlike some of its contemporaries, the society was founded discreetly. It was initiated by an eighteen-year-old, Joseph Robinson, the youngest of four brothers who all played prominent roles in Dublin's musical life.[12] The brothers came from a musical background: their father, Francis, had founded another Dublin society, the Sons of Handel, in 1810, and his sons formed a well-known vocal quartet (their voices ranging from John's high tenor to William's low bass) until John's premature death in 1844. John (b. 1812) served as organist at both St Patrick's and Christ Church and was joint conductor of the Metropolitan Choral upon its foundation, while Francis (b. 1799) also served briefly as organist at St Patrick's. Francis, William (b. *c*.1805), and Joseph were all Vicars Choral at both Anglican cathedrals. According to the *Dublin Daily Express*, there were three sisters, two of whom became professional musicians; this article also relates that

---

as in London. Whereas, in the latter, the most important distinctions arose out of social class (aristocracy, professions, trade, etc.), in Dublin religion was an important distinguishing factor and, due to the overall smaller population, and relative lack of resident aristocracy, an accomplished Anglican whose money was made through trade gained access to social strata which his London contemporary could not have done. For discussion of this issue as regards London, see William Weber, *Music and the middle class* (Aldershot: Ashgate, [2nd edn.], 2004), pp 71–80. It is significant that of the four Robinson brothers mentioned in this article, at least three were engaged in mercantile activities: Francis and Joseph were partners in a music shop in Westmoreland Street and William appears to have owned an iron foundry; clearly being 'in trade' was not in itself a barrier to musical or social advancement. **10** A rare exception took place on 21 January 1847 when the Antients gave a charity concert in support of the RIAM and tickets were put on public sale at 7*s*. for a single ticket and 1 guinea for a 'family' ticket for up to four people (see *SN*, 14 January 1847, 3). **11** For almost all of its existence the society's patron was George Whateley (Anglican archbishop of Dublin, 1831–63); its first president was Charles Dalrymple Lindsay (dean of Christ Church and bishop of Kildare). Lindsay was succeeded by Francis Blackburne, a former vice-president who was, successively, Master of the Rolls, Chief Justice of the Queen's Bench, Irish lord chancellor, and lord justice of appeal. Henry Pakenham (dean of St Patrick's and Christ Church), Viscount Monck, Field Marshal Viscount Gough, the earl of Dunraven, David Pigot (lord chief baron of the Court of Exchequer), and Viscount Adare were also sometime vice-presidents. **12** Brief biographical information on the Robinson brothers can be found in *NG II*, xxi, 471; see also Stanford, 'Joseph Robinson'; Joseph Robinson's obituary in *MT*, 1 September 1898, 609; and 'The career of Joe Robinson', *DDE*, 27 August 1898, 4.

Francis and Joseph in particular were well-travelled; Joseph met Rossini in Paris, Mendelssohn in Birmingham, and possibly Spohr in Norwich. All were members of the Hibernian Catch Club, and while William's activities seem to have been largely confined to Trinity College and the cathedrals,[13] Joseph and Francis were involved in many of Dublin's musical societies and were active performers for most of their lives. While Francis always confined his public performances to singing, Joseph's ambitions lay elsewhere and he soon became known primarily as a conductor, this ambition having sprung from his attending the Royal Musical Festival at Westminster Abbey in 1834.[14] It was also this visit which inspired him to found the Antient Concerts on his return to Dublin, its name and role clearly based on the Concerts of Antient Music founded in London in 1776.

At first the society seems to have been as much a social as musical organization and its early activities remain obscure. According to Hercules MacDonnell, the earliest meetings were held in 1834 at Francis Robinson's house at 85 Lower Mount Street, and the society also met at the house of one John Scoales (4 Fitzwilliam Square) and another later occupied by the Royal Irish Academy (Dawson Street).[15] MacDonnell gives 10 December 1835 as the date of the first public concert,[16] while another source claims that the work given was Handel's *Samson*, the performance of which left 'such an impression of the resources of the society and the ability of the conductor, that the latter was looked upon as the pioneer of progress, and the former as the field for his display'.[17] No contemporaneous reviews have been traced but, notwithstanding the flattering comments quoted above, this is perhaps unsurprising, as the society had not courted popularity.[18] The earliest confirmed concert took place on 9 February 1837; unfortunately and ironically, the content of the programme is not known since, while some 57 individuals were named as being among the audience, no comment whatever was made on the performance, rather emphasising that the social function of Dublin concerts could be as great as the musical.[19] The society

---

13 He appeared as a soloist with the Antients in the 1840s but not subsequently. 14 *MT*, 1 September 1898, 609. The Royal Musical Festival was held to mark the fiftieth anniversary of the first Handel Commemoration, which had been a significant turning-point in London's musical life. Both Francis and William appeared as soloists; Joseph was later similarly employed by George Smart at the Gentlemen's Concerts in Manchester (see *DDE*, 27 August 1898, 4, and John Parry, *An account of the Royal Musical Festival held in Westminster Abbey, 1834* (London: 1834), GB-Lbl pressmark 7896.cc.3). 15 Hercules MacDonnell, *A book of dates, operatic, dramatic and musical, compiled for The Strollers* (Dublin: Browne & Nolan [for private circulation only], 1878), p. 11. 16 Ibid. (but see note 18 below). 17 'Music past and present in Ireland', *Musical World* [hereafter *MW*], 10 July 1875, 462. No date for the concert is given in this article, whose author is unnamed. It is possible that MacDonnell and *MW* are referring to different events; the first known performance of any music from *Samson* is 1 February 1838. 18 Stephenson suggests that MacDonnell's date may be erroneous as no review could be found, and cites other proven inaccuracies in MacDonnell's book in support (see Stephenson, 'The Antient Concert Rooms', 2); additionally, no advance announcements of the concert have been traced, suggesting that the first performance was a private affair. Stephenson may be right, but concert reviews in the 1830s were sporadic for the Antients and other Dublin societies so lack of newspaper commentary does not prove MacDonnell's date to be incorrect. As Stephenson points out in support of MacDonnell, the concert programme for 4 June 1844 (in IRL-Dtc) declares the Antients to be in their tenth season, implying that the first concert did take place in 1835. 19 See *SN*, 11 February 1837, 3; the same review appeared in the *DEM*, 13 February 1837, 3.

is listed in the *Dublin Almanac* for the first time in 1838, in which the barest details – the names of the committee and a contact address – are given.[20] This entry fits with MacDonnell's claim that the society was instituted formally in 1837.[21]

Another concert was given in early June 1837, and this is the first for which partial programme details survive: Handel was the composer most prominently represented, by *Zadok the Priest*, selections from *Acis and Galatea* and *Judas Maccabaeus*, and brief extracts from *Jephtha* and *Solomon*. More strikingly, part at least of Purcell's incidental music to *The Tempest* was given,[22] as were the Dies Irae, Tuba Mirum, Rex Tremendae, and Hosanna from Mozart's *Requiem*.[23] The concert was reviewed by the Dublin correspondent of the *Musical World*:

> This society has closed the season brilliantly. The annual concert was held in the Rotundo [*sic*] and went off in a most excellent style ... The room was full, without being unpleasantly crowded, not more than 500 tickets being ever issued. The style in which the choruses were given, showed a marked improvement in the members ... The system used by the very able conductor, Mr Joseph Robinson, in frequently practicing the voices without any accompaniment whatever, must ensure a greater degree of confidence in the members than could be attained if they were accustomed to rely on any instrumental aid.[24]

Already the significance of Joseph Robinson's role in and concept of the society is apparent and subsequent reviews rarely fail to mention the importance of his contribution; a review of the concert given on 1 February 1838 remarked that the society was indebted to Robinson 'for its original formation and subsequent success and to this gentleman's high musical talent and continued attention must assuredly be attributed in a great degree the excellence to which, in so short a period, it has advanced.'[25]

In social terms the Antients 'arrived' on 23 March 1838 when a charity concert to raise funds for 'the distressed poor of this city'[26] was attended by the Lord Lieutenant.[27] Any event patronized by the monarch's representative in Ireland immediately gained immense social cachet, and so, implicitly, did the society which organized it.[28] A printed programme survives,[29] and this is therefore the first concert for which the society's approach to programming can be seen *in toto*

---

20 *DA*, 1838, p. 171. **21** MacDonnell, *A book of dates*, p. 12. **22** With the exception of one song, this is now thought to be by John Weldon. **23** The reference in the review (see next note) to the Hosanna is obscure, but the implication is that either the Sanctus or Benedictus was also performed as the two Hosannas run straight on from these items. **24** *MW*, 9 June 1837, 199. The date of the concert is not given. **25** *DEM*, 7 February 1838, 3. A rather different view of Robinson is to be found in the gossipy and anecdotal volume [Anonymous], *Recollections of Dublin Castle* in which he is described as a 'singular original ... he was but an ordinary teaching musician, but was much inflated by self-importance', p. 276. **26** *SN*, 19 March 1838, 3. **27** Constantine Henry Phipps, 6th Earl Mulgrave; according to newspaper announcements (see previous note) the Lord Lieutenant directed that the concert should begin at 8.30 pm. **28** For extensive satirical commentary on the social role of the Lord Lieutenant, see *Recollections*, especially pp 3–7. **29** In IRL-Dtc (see note 2 above).

Table 11.1: Antient Concerts Society programme, 23 March 1838

Composer	Work	Items performed (if a selection) and comments
Handel	*Esther*	Overture
Handel	*Judas Maccabaeus*	No. 8 'Oh Father whose almight power' No. 10 'Arm, arm ye brave' No. 11 'We come, we come in bright array' No. 19 'Come ever smiling liberty' No. 20 'Lead on, lead on' No. 60 'Sing unto God'
Handel	*Jephtha*	No. 49 'Deeper and deeper still' No. 53 'Waft her, angels'
Marcello	'Qual anelante cervo che fugge da fieri'	A setting of Psalm 42, probably by Benedetto Marcello (1686–1739) and contained in his *L'estro poetico-armonico* (8 volumes, Venice, 1724–26)
Mozart	*Requiem*	Dies Irae, Benedictus
Haydn	*The Creation*	No. 13 'In splendour bright' No. 14 'The heavens are telling'
Morley	'Now is the month of maying'	
Handel	*Acis and Galatea*	No. 2 'Oh, the pleasures of the plains' No. 13 'Happy, happy, happy we' No. 28 ''Tis done' No. 30 'Galatea, dry thy tears'
Pepusch	*Alexis*	Also known as 'See, from the silent groves', first published in Pepusch's *Six English Cantatas*, book 1 (London, 1710).
Festa	'Down in a flow'ry vale'	'Quando ritrovo la mia pastrorella' by Constanzo Festa (c.1485/90–1545).
Haydn	*The Seasons*	No. 4 'At last the bounteous sun' No. 5 'With joy the impatient husbandman' No. 20 'In mute and list'ning fear' No. 21 'Hark the awful tempest comes' (extracts from 'Spring' and 'Summer')
Handel	'God save the Queen'	An adaptation of part of *Zadok the Priest*

(see table 11.1). The event attracted a good review and raised £110 for the Mendicant Society:

> We were gratified at finding the attendance upon the occasion not only highly fashionable, but also numerous. Those who were present upon the occasion enjoyed a musical entertainment of a superior order; and the feeling of satisfaction must have been heightened by the consciousness that the interests

of charity were advanced through the same agency which conferred individual pleasure ... The orchestra, which comprised in it some eminent performers, was effective, particularly in the choruses. The principal vocalists were Messrs F[rancis] and W[illiam] Robinson, and the Misses Searle. Mr F[rancis] Robinson was encored in the air from Pepusch's cantata 'Charming sounds that sweetly languish' and the exquisite manner in which it was given rendered any other result impossible. The violoncello accompaniment of Mr Pigott materially contributed to the delight with which the air was heard. A madrigal, composed in 1541 [by Festa; see table 11.1], also met with an encore, and the quaintness of the strain, together with a forcible simplicity, rendered it a composition of interest. The choruses were well sung, although in one of Haydn's, 'The arm of the Lord is upon them', some of the voices were too prominent.[30]

While the society had clearly scored with this concert, the action which placed it at the heart of Dublin's musical life for the next twenty years was audacious, and had beneficial implications for cultural activity in the city well into the twentieth-century. Hitherto the main venue for concerts in Dublin had been the Rotunda in Rutland Square.[31] The Antients turned this convention on its head. Probably late in 1842, the society obtained the premises of the former Dublin Oil Gas Light Company on Great Brunswick Street;[32] it carried out substantial modifications to the building and gave its first concert there on 20 April 1843, performing a substantial portion of *Messiah*. The new venue attracted positive press attention:

> The building is still in an unfinished state, owing to the short time that has elapsed since the works were commenced; but, when completed, will not be inferior, for the purposes for which it was constructed, to any other in Europe.
> The principal room (in which the concert was given) is in the Ionic style, and beautifully proportioned, being nearly a double cube of 43 feet, or 86 feet long, exclusive of the recess for the organ at the back of the orchestra, and is calculated to accommodate between 900 and 1000 persons. At the extremity of the hall, and facing the orchestra, supported on metal pillars, is a light

---

30 *SN*, 24 March 1838, 2. The Haydn chorus (usually known by the Latin title, *Insanae et vanae curae*) is not listed in the printed programme. A financial statement on the result of the concert (income from tickets £165 12s.6d., donations £7 6s. expenses £62 10s.2d., net contribution to the Mendicity Society £110 2s.4d.) was published in *SN*, 5 April 1838, 3.   **31** Now Parnell Square, at the north end of O'Connell Street. The Rotunda was the circular function room of the Dublin Lying-In Hospital (usually known as the Rotunda Hospital, founded in 1745 by Bartholomew Mosse) built in 1748. It later became the Ambassador Cinema and is now largely unused, awaiting restoration.   **32** See Stephenson, 'The Antient Concert Rooms', 2, who states that the building was vacated when the company merged with another local gas supplier and relocated to the Grand Dock. Robert O'Byrne asserts, however, that the building was erected in 1824 and vacated when the company went bankrupt in 1834 after fish oil (which was converted into gas using a process pioneered by two engineers, Gosling and Taylor) became prohibitively expensive; see <www.ireland.com/newspaper/property/2001/0222/prop3.htm> (accessed 14 February 2005), a reproduction of an article from *IT*, 22 February 2001. Great Brunswick Street is now Pearse Street; the building is almost opposite Pearse Street station.

looking elliptical gallery, capable of holding two hundred persons. The massive scroll brackets, supporting the gas pendants, from the foundry of Mr William Robinson, are particularly elegant, and the remainder of the fittings for the lighting, by Millner and Co. of Fleet Street, are equally so. The room, besides being lofty, is well ventilated by admitting warmed or cold air diffusedly round the bottom of the room, and carrying off the foul air through ornamental openings in the ceiling and thence, by inverted funnels in the roof, out of the building.

The seats are supported on light-looking cast iron framing with scroll arms, and backed with mahogany, affording altogether a degree of comfort that was not known in any music room in Dublin before. We may fairly say that when the seats are cushioned, a new organ put up, and the painting and decorations completed, it will display an appearance presenting architectural beauty, combined with comfort, such as no other hall in this country possesses ...

Of the style in which the several portions [of *Messiah*] was performed, we might be satisfied to say that it was equally worthy of the society and the music. The choruses were executed with a degree of precision and steadiness which reflected the highest credit on the conductor, Mr Joseph Robinson, and the performing members of the society: and with respect to the solos – where all were excellent from the first, sung by Mr Francis Robinson, to the last 'The Trumpet Shall sound' by Mr William Robinson, which was most ably accompanied by Mr G Eschrich on the trumpet, we should be silent, did we not feel compelled to observe, that we have seldom been more gratified than by Miss McDermott's execution of that exquisite air 'He was despised'.

The effect of this new hall, as a music room, must have surpassed the most sanguine expectations of all the lovers of harmony and melody who were present. The most delicate sound uttered in the songs and recitatives was heard with the utmost distinctness, and the fullest choruses had a crispness and clearness which we have never heard excelled and we congratulate the city of Dublin on having at length acquired, through the instrumentality of the Antient Concert Society, what has been so long a desideratum – a good concert room.[33]

Additionally, the hall's proximity to the fashionable squares and terraces of the south-east quarter gave it a huge advantage; the relocation of the Philharmonic Society from the Rotunda soon after the building's opening was the first instance of a trend followed by most of Dublin's musical societies, and the Antient Concert Rooms soon became the city's most important concert venue.

In later years further improvements were made. An organ by Telford was installed in 1847, a dining room added in 1850,[34] and in 1853 the hall enlarged:

[33] *DEM*, 21 April 1843, 3. *SN* was also impressed, although it did not review the opening concert, and made its positive comments when reviewing a Philharmonic Society concert a couple of weeks later, see *SN*, 6 May 1843, 2. Elsewhere, the rooms had been described as 'a rather shabby tenement in Brunswick Street, about the size and proportions of a moderate Dissenting chapel; but it justly boasted that it was the "finest thing of the kind in Ireland"', [Anonymous], *Recollections of Dublin Castle*, p. 3. [34] MacDonnell,

the roof has been raised nine feet, the hall has been lengthened seven feet at the sides and ten feet in the centre, so that the present dimensions are ninety-six feet long in the centre, forty-one feet wide, and forty-two feet high to the ceiling. The orchestra, which before was very confined, is now large, and all the performers point to the conductor, which is a matter of very great importance [!] The extra accommodation for the public will be sixty seats, so that the hall will accommodate over one thousand persons. The lighting is brilliant but perfectly cool, and if the temperature should become disagreeably hot provision is made for an ample supply of cool air. The decorations of the room are pure Roman Corinthian, from the design of Mr N. Jackson, architect of this city.[35]

In 1859 further improvements were contemplated, including the erection of new entrances, cloakrooms and reception rooms, plus a further extension to the hall and its gallery, although it is unknown whether or not these alterations were made.[36]

From about 1838 the society gave two or three public concerts per year (plus perhaps unadvertised members-only concerts), rising steadily after 1843 to up to six per year, although the nature of the concerts changed significantly in the late 1850s (see below). Only limited information is available regarding the society's size, and this implies that it grew steadily, at least until the late 1840s.[37] In 1838 the *Musical World* reported that:

[The Society] is limited in number to thirty performing members, and thirty non-performers ... The performing members consist of eight *alti*, ten *tenori* and twelve *bassi*. As the rules of the society do not admit of the presence of ladies at the weekly meetings, where treble voices are required, the boys from the cathedrals of Christ Church and St Patrick are usually called in; but on occasions when it is desirable to produce an increased effect, the committee have found it necessary to engage the assistance of female voices.[38]

The use of cathedral choristers, exemplifying the implicit Anglican basis of the society, was not unusual but, as in 1835 there were only twelve boys at the two cathedrals,[39] it seems certain that women were increasingly involved (and, presumably, rehearsed separately from the men, perhaps only coming together at

---

A book of dates, p. 15. **35** *SN*, 2 February 1853, 2. It is unclear why the dimensions given here do not agree with those in the *DEM* (see note 33 above). **36** See *SN*, 8 March 1859, 3. **37** Surviving programmes contain no references to participants and do not, therefore, clarify this aspect. **38** *MW*, 22 March 1838, 202. The number of singers is similar to that claimed by the Metropolitan Choral Society in 1844 (six altos, ten tenors, twelve basses); see *SN*, 25 November 1844, 3. Quite probably several singers were in both choirs. **39** See W. Harry Grindle, *Irish cathedral music: a history of music at the cathedrals of the Church of Ireland* (Belfast: Institute of Irish Studies, 1989), p. 62. The Metropolitan Choral and Dublin University Choral also employed boy trebles (see next note regarding the latter); the former advertised for up to twelve choristers in 1844, promising them payment of £1 for the season, subject to fines for lateness and non-attendance; it is also implied that choristers could be loaned to other societies; see *SN*, 25 November 1844, 3.

Table 11.2: Examples of 'early' music (pre-1700) performed by the Antient Concerts Society (see also Table 11.1)

Composer	Work	Total	First known performance
Bennett	'All creatures now'	2	15 April 1847
Bennett	'My mistress is as fair'	3	1 June 1848
Dowland	'Come again sweet love'	6	15 April 1847
Edwards	'In going to my lonely bed'	3	31 May 1849
Farrant	'Lord for thy tender mercies sake'	2	17 April 1845
Ford	'Since first I saw your face'	3	31 May 1849
Locke (now attrib.)	Incidental music to *Macbeth*	4	31 May 1849
Morley	'Now is the month of maying'	5	23 March 1838
Palestrina	'Alla trinita'	5	21 January 1847
Palestrina	'I will give thanks to thee O Lord'	2	21 January 1847
Purcell	'Behold I bring you glad tidings'	1	1 April 1852
Purcell	'O give thanks unto the Lord'	1	1 April 1852

Due to the scarcity of printed programmes, many of these works may occur more frequently and earlier than stated here.

Table 11.3: Examples of large works performed by the Antient Concerts Society

Composer	Work	Total	First known performance and comments
Handel	*Israel in Egypt*	7	1 February 1838
Handel	*Judas Maccabaeus*	5	June 1837
Handel	*L'Allegro e il Penseroso*	6	20 February 1846
Handel	*Samson*	5	17 April 1845 (but see footnote 17 on the date of the first concert)
Haydn	*The Creation*	9	1 February 1838
Haydn	*The Seasons*	12	23 March 1838 (usually only one season per concert, although all seasons were eventually performed)

the final rehearsal). Solo soprano and alto roles were always taken by local female professional singers so while women could never be members their involvement in essential capacities was never shunned.[40] A review in the

---

[40] Unlike the Dublin University Choral which was wholly male; here only cathedral choristers sang the soprano line and annotations on surviving programmes in IRL-Dtc indicate that senior boys sang complex solos from works such as Handel's oratorios, suggesting that performances were adequate, although it is

Table 11.4: Selections from Handel's Jephtha, 4 June 1844

Item	Type	Incipit
2	Recitative	'It must be so, or these vile Ammonites'
3	Air	'Pour forth no more'
4	Chorus	'Chemosh no more'
15	Recitative	'What mean these doubtful fancies of the brain?'
18	Chorus	'O God! Behold our sore distress'
23	Recitative	'Such, Jeptha, was the haughty king's reply'
24	Chorus	'When his loud voice in thunder'
32	Recitative	'Zebul, thy deeds were valiant'
33	Air	'His might arm'
34	Chorus	'In glory high, in might serene'
41	Recitative	'Why is my mother'
45	Quartet	'Oh! Spare your daughter'
49	Recitative	'Deeper and deeper'
50	Chorus	'How dark, O Lord'
53	Air	'Waft her, Angels'
71	Chorus	'Ye house of Gilead'

Freeman's Journal refers to an orchestra of just over forty in 1849,[41] while the same newspaper's review of the society's first performance of *Elijah* (discussed below) gives precise figures for the whole ensemble: nine vocal soloists, a choir comprising 25 sopranos, 16 altos, 26 tenors and 33 basses (100 in total), and a complete orchestra (37 in total) including four first violins, six seconds, three violas, three cellos and three basses; the figures for the choir imply that the presence of women as chorus members was by then a given.[42]

For repertory it is impossible to provide a comprehensive survey or statistical analysis as printed programmes survive for only a small proportion of the concerts; all remaining information has been gleaned from newspaper reviews, but these rarely mention all of the items performed. Furthermore, some concerts, especially in the early 1840s, were not reviewed at all and it is probable that, for the earlier years of the society, not all events have been traced.[43] To compound this difficulty, the Antients rarely gave complete performances of any substantial work (see below), which further undermines statistical analysis. Consequently it is only possible to isolate broad trends in programming and to note important events.

difficult to believe that they were of sufficient strength to give a really confident performance. **41** *FJ*, 24 February 1849, 2. **42** *FJ*, 9 December 1847, 2. The nine vocal soloists arise because some character roles were divided between two people. It is unclear whether or not the chorus alto line was mixed. No further traced reviews mention the size of the chorus so it is unclear if this size was maintained in future years. **43** In total 100 concerts have been recorded; of these there are printed programmes for 20, and newspaper reviews with partial programme information for a further 69, leaving 11 concerts for which there is no known programme. It seems likely that before 1840, when newspaper commentary was sparse, there may be up to about six concerts which took place neither announced nor reviewed.

The model for the society's programming policy was clearly its London namesake, which only performed music at least twenty years old. In spirit and in practice, however, Dublin's approach was different: here the music of the 'antient masters' (preferring therefore a subjective rather than objective temporal definition) was only to be 'especially' rather than exclusively performed, and there was to be as much emphasis on choral music as on music of any particular era.[44] As exemplified in table 11.1, the society performed a mixture of sacred and secular music, the former preponderating, while the latter generally comprised shorter items such as glees and madrigals. In later years, however, the society gave selections from operas,[45] and performed such overtly secular works as Mendelssohn's *Die erste Walpurgisnacht*. 'Lofty' secular works such as Haydn's *Seasons*, Handel's *L'Allegro, il Penseroso ed il Moderato* (Parts 1 and 2 only) and Mendelssohn's cantata 'Sons of Art' (*Festgesang an die Künstler*, op. 68) were also popular. All works were performed in English, with the exception of mass settings and some motets, which were given in Latin;[46] opera selections were performed in Italian unless, as in the case of *Oberon*, the original was in English.

Overall, Handel, Haydn and Mendelssohn dominate, with Mozart and Beethoven some way behind; despite the growing interest in England and Germany, Bach barely appears.[47] Pre-Baroque music appears only sporadically and is mainly represented by the recurrence of certain madrigals, motets and other short works (see table 11.2); on the one known occasion when a programme with a notable proportion of early music was attempted, it received a mixed reception in the local press.[48]

Selections from substantial works were preferred.[49] The society gave *Messiah* at least nine times, but never complete (all available evidence points to a seasonal

---

[44] The latter policy may have existed as much to avoid conflicts with the primarily orchestral Philharmonic and Anacreontic Societies as to show an especial preference for choral music, although, as Joseph Robinson's primary musical expertise was as a singer, this emphasis is unsurprising.   [45] For example Weber's *Oberon* (1 February 1856), Act I of Rossini's *La gazza ladra* (5 February 1858), Meyerbeer's *Dinorah* (25 November 1859), and Rossini's *Semiramide* (29 May 1857 and 18 January 1860).   [46] The society adopted an erratic policy towards Latin motets, probably dictated by the edition it owned: Hummel's 'Quodquod in orbe revinctum est' (from *Graduale*, op. 88, first given on 18 December 1845), and Mozart's 'Ne pulvis in cinis' (an adaptation of 'Ihr Kinder des Staubes', No. 7 from *Thamos, König in Aegypten*, K. 336a, first given on 8 June 1847) were always given in Latin. Conversely, Haydn's *Insane et vanae curae* was always given in English as *The arm of the Lord is upon them*.   [47] Only three occurrences: in some unspecified items (27 May 1859) and an unnamed Prelude and Fugue (2 June 1862), all for violin solo, played by Joachim, and in a performance of 'There is a calm for those who weep' (30 March 1855), a poor arrangement by William Shore of the chorale 'Wie schön leuchtet der Morgenstern' from the cantata of the same name, BWV1, and ironically not by Bach at all, but by Phillipp Nicolai and dating from 1599; see GB-Lbl, pressmark H.1771.q.(28).   [48] The programme included works by Purcell, Pergolesi, and Palestrina, as well as Greene, Mendelssohn and Beethoven. *DEM* stated that 'if it was not a concert to gratify an audience as much as the former ones given by this society during the season, it certainly was an instructive one, and will do much in conveying a proper idea of the grandeur of our cathedral music, when properly performed' (5 April 1852, 2) while *FJ* referred to 'this extremely difficult, though not very effective concert' (2 April 1852, 3). The performance was, incidentally, the only one not conducted by Joseph Robinson before his resignation in 1862, the baton being taken on this occasion by James Wilkinson.   [49] A similar situation pertained at the London Concerts of Antient Music, and at the Royal Musical Festival, although, in the case of the former, each selection was much smaller.

Table 11.5: Running order of selection from Israel in Egypt, 4 June 1846

Item	Type	Incipit
1	Recitative	'Now there arose a new king over Egypt'
2	Chorus	'And the children of Israel sighed'
5	Air	'Their land brought forth frogs'
6	Chorus	'He spake the word'
7	Chorus	'He gave them hailstones'
8	Chorus	'He sent a thick darkness'
19	Duet	'The Lord is my strength'
12	Chorus	'He rebuked the Red Sea'
14	Chorus	'But the waters overwhelmed their enemies'
10	Chorus	'But as for his people'
22	Duet	'The Lord is a man of War'
23	Chorus	'The depths have covered them'
34	Air	'Thou shalt bring them in'
35	Chorus	'The Lord shall reign for ever and ever'
36	Recitative	'For the horse of Pharaoh'
37	Chorus	'The Lord shall reign for ever and ever'
38	Recitative	'And Miriam the Prophetess'
39	Solo and Chorus	'Sing Ye to the Lord'

distinction with Parts 1 and 2 being performed in Advent, and Parts 2 and 3 during Lent and Eastertide); further examples of repertoire are given in table 11.3. The size of these selections varied greatly: sometimes a single recitative and aria might be given (for example nos. 19 and 20, 'And there was a disciple' and 'I praise thee, O Lord my God', from Mendelssohn's *St Paul*, 17 February 1848), while a selection from a classical mass might comprise three movements (for example the Kyrie, Gloria and Benedictus from Mozart's 'Coronation' Mass, K. 317, 21 December 1848). A larger selection of sixteen items from Handel's *Jephtha* was given on 4 June 1844 (see table 11.4) and is a typical quantity for a larger work. The sole exception was the works of Mendelssohn, which were almost always performed complete, no doubt partly due to his revered position, but also because his works were comparative novelties and unfamiliar to many: the performances of *Elijah*, for instance, were major musical occasions in a way that those of Haydn and Handel had long since ceased to be.

Adaptation also took place: *Israel in Egypt* was not only subjected to the selection policy, but the order of items in the middle was sometimes altered, possibly to inject variety into an otherwise long run of choruses (see table 11.5). In another form of adaptation, *Zadok the Priest* was performed at least once with altered words (6 June 1851, reflecting the pro-Union membership):

Table 11.6: Antient Concerts Society performances of works by Mendelssohn

Work	Total	First performance
Antigone	1	1 June 1848 (selection)
As the hart pants (Psalm 42)	6	4 June 1844
Athalie (incidental music)	6	8 February 1850 (a)
Concerto in G minor for piano and orchestra, op. 25	1	25 March 1858
Elijah	7	9 December 1847 (a)
Die erste Walpurgisnacht	3	19 February 1852
Hear my prayer, O Lord (Psalm 55)	7	21 December 1848 (d)
Hymn of Praise	5 (b)	18 December 1845 (selection) 21 December 1845 (complete)
Lauda Sion	1	26 March 1860
A Midsummer Night's Dream (incidental music)	2 (e)	1 June 1848
My God, my God, look upon me (Psalm 22)	1	1 April 1852
O come, let us sing unto the Lord (Psalm 95)	1 (c)	1 June 1846
Piano Trio in C minor, op. 66	2	10 May 1858
Piano Trio in D minor, op. 49	1	27 May 1859
St Paul	3	23 February 1849 (a)
Son and Stranger (*Heimkehr aus der Fremde*, op. 89)	3	26 January 1855
'Sons of Art' (*Festgesang an die Künstler*, op. 68)	2	15 April 1847

(a) first performance in Ireland
(b) two of these performances were selections
(c) printed programme claims this was the first performance in the United Kingdom
(d) first performance of the orchestral version
(e) both of these performances were selections

> Queen of the isles, Victoria reigneth,
> The glory of all nations.
> Let all the people rejoice and say,
> 'God save the Queen,
> May the Queen live for ever'.
> Amen. Hallelujah.

The society's most significant contribution to Dublin's musical life in terms of repertory was its promotion of Mendelssohn. It was not the only body which supported him,[50] but the Antients' resources afforded it frequent opportunities to

---

[50] The University Choral also performed much Mendelssohn, although its exclusive use of boys on the soprano line limited its facility.

perform Mendelssohn's music, which were probably also the best renditions in the city. This was a taste acquired only in the mid-1840s, and Mendelssohn's domination of the society's programmes arose only in the second half of its existence (see table 11.6; in terms of 'performance hours' Mendelssohn represents 20–25 per cent of the society's total output). While his music appeared on 4 June 1844 with a rendition of Psalm 42, it was the society's first Irish premiere of *Elijah* which cemented the association. Poignancy was added as the Antients' concert took place on 9 December, only a month after Mendelssohn's death on 4 November. A black-bordered biography appeared in the programme, describing him as 'the greatest composer and most accomplished musician of the age' and adding that he had been 'seated on the throne of musical fame, vacant since the death of Beethoven'.[51] The *Freeman's Journal* declared that *Elijah* was '*the* work of the age',[52] arguing that not since Dublin had mounted the first performance of *Messiah* over a century earlier, had there been a musical event of such significance in the city. Clearly, while Mendelssohn was not an 'antient master', he was the inheritor of the crown in this mythical line of succession. The concert turned into a laudatory memorial service:

In respect to the memory of Mendelssohn, the organ and the orchestra were, last night, hung in black, whilst in the centre of the black drapery on the organ, a laurel wreath tied with white ribbon was suspended ... Long before the usual hour for opening the doors, Brunswick Street, from one end to the other, was one line of vehicles. At five minutes to eight, every available space in the concert room was filled. At eight o'clock precisely, Joseph Robinson, attired in deep black, mounted the conductor's chair. Mr Stamford [*sic*] as Elijah, stepped forward, and the oratorio commenced.[53]

Saunders' Newsletter was impressed,[54] and the *Freeman's Journal* paid the unequivocal compliment, 'we do not think Mendelssohn could have found a more conscientious or more able interpreter of his ideas than Joseph Robinson'. In subsequent performances (six more up to March 1864) both composer and society were invariably eulogized, with the work always drawing a large audience.

A second Mendelssohn work with which the society was even more closely associated was his setting of a paraphrase of Psalm 55, 'Hear my prayer'. Robinson asked Mendelssohn to orchestrate it when they met at Birmingham in 1846, and the Antients gave the first performance of this version on 21 December 1848.[55]

Although the presence of Mendelssohn most obviously belies the literal definition of the word 'antient', the society showed a recurrent interest in contemporary music. Early on this was exemplified by its short-lived composition

---

51 Concert programme for 9 December 1847, IRL-Dtc (see note 2 above).   52 *FJ*, 10 December 1847, 2.
53 Ibid. 'Stamford' was, in fact, John Stanford.   54 See *SN*, 9 December 1847, 2.   55 See Stanford, 'Joseph Robinson', pp 122–3, and *DDE*, 27 August 1898, 4. The work was composed in 1844, and first performed in London on 8 January 1845. The score was received by Robinson from Mendelssohn's executors some months after his death.

Table 11.7: Performances of post-Beethoven works by the Antient Concerts Society*

Composer	Work	First performed	Antient Concerts first performance
Spohr	*The Last Judgment* (selection)	1827	15 February 1844
Spohr	*God, thou art great*, op. 98	1836	17 April 1845
David	*Le Désert*	1844	1 February 1856
Horsley	*David* (selection)	1850	7 February 1851
Lindpaintner	*The Widow of Naïn*	1853	14 December 1855
Macfarren	*May Day*	1857	6 February 1857
Benedict	*Undine*	1860	25 January 1861

* excluding selections from operas and works by Mendelssohn (see table 11.6)

prize, awarded after an open competition, of ten guineas and a performance by the society. The first competition was announced in the concert programme for 23 March 1838,[56] with a closing date of 1 October 1838 and a choice of texts from either *Joel* or *Lamentations*;[57] entries were to be submitted anonymously. Thomas Walmisley's setting, 'Remember thou, O Lord' (from *Lamentations*), won and it is notable that the work contains a prominent quartet for four male voices, surely aimed at the Robinson brothers.[58] The competition did not stand the test of time. In its second year the prize was not awarded, the money being held over to 1840 when 20 guineas was awarded to Henry J Gauntlett.[59] After this, the competition appears to have been abandoned. In subsequent years the society gave performances of works by a diverse selection of nineteenth-century composers, many of which were probably first performances in Ireland (see table 11.7). Joseph Robinson may have heard these pieces on his travels abroad, so while the society never commissioned music, it often promoted new works in Ireland.

Gauging the standard of performance is difficult since almost all contemporary reviews are positive and criticism is usually discreet. Amateur soloists are dealt with delicately but professionals, especially men, are more directly treated; the *Dublin Evening Mail* once commented:

[56] And in the press; see, for example, *MW*, 22 March 1838, 205. [57] Either *Joel*, chapter 3, vv. 9, 14, 15, and 16, or the *Lamentations of Jeremiah*, chapter 5, vv. 1, 7, 15, 17, and 19. [58] No review of the first performance of this work has been found. Given the date of the award the concerts on 21 February or 8 May 1839 are most likely (these events were announced in *SN* but no reviews have been traced). Third place was awarded to the thirteen year-old Robert Stewart; see Laurence O'Dea, 'Sir Robert Prescott Stewart', *DHR*, 17, (1961-2), 77–93. The autograph manuscript of Walmisley's anthem is in IRL-Dam. [59] This unnamed piece was described as 'a very beautiful composition, consisting of four movements, including a bass solo of great power and expression, a soprano solo of exceeding beauty, and two choruses – the last movement, especially, seizes the ear, enchanting with its great simplicity of melody and richness of harmony. The entire composition is one which reflects the highest credit on Mr Gauntlett, as well as on the society whose spirit has elicited the work. There were fifteen other compositions sent in, several of which were of very great merit.', *DEM*, 29 January 1841, 3. No work of this description survives in IRL-Dam and no other reference to it has been traced.

> Mr Frank Robinson was scarcely equal to the recitative 'Men, Brethren, and Fathers', lacking sufficient physical power to convey the intentions of the author, but in 'Lo I see the heavens opened' and the aria, 'Be thou faithful unto death' he amply compensated, singing with great purity of tone and expression.[60]

Of instrumentalists relatively little is said; a poorly balanced orchestra (for example, the numbers of stringed instruments, and disposition of strings in relation to woodwind and brass, cited in the first performance of *Elijah*), attracted no comment, but brass players are sometimes singled out, for varying reasons:

> Mr [Richard] Smith sang Spohr's 'Love and courage' ['Was treibt den Waidmann'] capitally, and the horn accompaniment was miraculously accurate. We never before heard in this country a solo horn who did not break on his upper notes and so spoil the whole piece; but, on this occasion, both Mr Smith and his obbligato were worthy of each other.[61]
>
> 'The Trumpet shall sound' [was] magnificently sung by Mr R[ichard] Smith. We could have wished the trumpet to have been somewhat more perfect, and deal less in cracked notes.[62]

A consistent trend in all newspaper reviews is admiration of Joseph Robinson, both for his musicianship and for his organizational and choir-training skills.

In 1858 an apparent change in programming policy represents the first sign of decline. Choral music was downplayed while instrumental music, both orchestral and especially chamber, gained a strong foothold. The first instance of this, a performance of the slow movement from a Haydn symphony (probably no. 97 in C) on 5 February, was discreet but, on 25 March the concert was dominated by Mendelssohn's Piano Concerto in G minor, op. 25, played by Joseph Robinson's wife, Fanny. The *Dublin Evening Mail* commented:

> This combination of Antient Concert and Philharmonic elements was not exactly according to rule, seeing that the society was established for the cultivation of vocal music only, but no musical red-tapist could object to an irregularity which gave him the pleasure of hearing Mrs Joseph Robinson ... [who] exceeded herself on this occasion; and we trust that the constitution of the Society of Antient Concerts may be frequently violated in the same manner hereafter.[63]

On 10 May, the change was even more marked: Tartini's 'Devil's Trill' Sonata, Mendelssohn's Piano Trio in C minor, op. 66, and Beethoven's 'Kreutzer' Sonata, were played by Fanny Robinson, Joseph Joachim and Wilhelm Elsner. Perplexity, though not disapproval was evident:

60 *DEM*, 25 April 1851, 3, on the previous evening's performance of *St Paul*.   **61** *DEM*, 8 December 1858, 3, on the concert of 6 December.   **62** *FJ*, 28 March 1851, 2, on the concert of the previous day.   **63** *DEM*, 26 March 1858, 3.

> This society gave a concert on last Monday evening, but we should be in error were we to call it an Antient Concert. There was nothing Antient about it, Tartini's sonata excepted ... The absence of the usual chorus, too, made it even less like an Antient concert than a Philharmonic, while the absence of an orchestra made it less like a Philharmonic concert than an Antient ... Whether it was Antient or Philharmonic, it was a brilliant and successful concert ... The Antient concerts of this season, or, to speak more correctly, the concerts given by the Antient Society, have, without any exception, been excellent but perhaps it is to the concert of last Monday that people will look back with the greatest pleasure.[64]

On 6 December the chorus reappeared, but the programme was still infiltrated by instrumental items, performed by Charles Hallé. The *Dublin Evening Mail* was restive:

> We were glad to see in the programme an advertisement that this society will perform the *Elijah* at their next concert ... Only three years ago the committee made declaration that 'As long as the Antient Concerts Society continued in existence, it would keep steadily in view the *sole* object for which it was original founded, viz., the cultivation of classical *vocal music*, especially the *choral* compositions of the Ancient masters'. When we remember the great benefits which this society has conferred upon Dublin, and consider the loss music and musicians would sustain were it definitively to abandon the legitimate object of its labours, we trust that in future it will always confine itself within its own channel, doing only what it was intended to do, and what no other society can do better.[65]

The change was not wholly new; the society had, for example, given two 'soirées musicales' in 1855 with violinist Bernhard Molique as guest soloist,[66] reflecting a wider trend toward engaging visiting professional artistes rather than Dublin-based ones.[67] In 1858, though, this trend became much more pronounced. Public speculation did not reach the newspapers, although it was later assumed that audience preference drove the change (see below); it seems certain that financial pressures were significant. Whether or not Joseph Robinson approved or not is unknown, though he probably exploited his many international connections to encourage famous performers to appear with the Antients,[68] in the hope that their presence would secure full houses.[69]

---

[64] *DEM*, 12 May 1858, 3.   [65] *DEM*, 8 December 1858, 3, on the concert of 6 December, the principal items of which were: Mozart, Overture to *Le nozze di Figaro*; Rossini, Overture to *La gazza ladra*; Weber, *Concert-stück*, op. 79; various Mendelssohn partsongs; and Moscheles, *Hommage à Handel* for piano duet.
[66] See *SN*, 1 May 1855, 2, and 4 May 1855, 2, on the concerts of 30 April and 3 May respectively.
[67] Including Louisa Pyne (19 December 1850), Victoire Balfe (19 December 1852), and Catherine Hayes (19 December 1856).   [68] Stanford recalled that Robinson's house was a major musical social centre in Dublin, and that many famous artistes stayed there; see Stanford, 'Joseph Robinson', pp 123–4.   [69] An interesting manifestation of this use of star performers arose in 1860 when Clara Novello appeared with

The change of policy was sustained during 1859,[70] but then programming drifted; choral items made a strong return in 1860,[71] and in 1861 the sides balanced, but with many visiting soloists.[72] On 3 February 1862 Mendelssohn's *Athalie* and a selection from Handel's *Samson* with vocalist Hermione Rudersdorff were performed. In anticipation the *Freeman's Journal* reflected on the previous years' programming, while the *Evening Mail*'s positive review contained a sting in the tail:

> For some seasons past it had been a source of regret to the lovers of the great choral compositions – for the production of which the Antient Concert Society was founded – that it had been forced to deviate (in obedience, we presume, to some inevitable necessity) from its legitimate course, and undertake occasionally the production of … music not demanding large choral resources and altogether independent of orchestral aid. It would be profitless to engage in any speculation as to the reasons for such a change, but of this we feel convinced, that the responsibility does not rest with the clever and energetic conductor of the society, Mr Joseph Robinson.[73]

> Here was a goodly programme, well prepared and given with feeling and power – showing that, were the musical public of Dublin to encourage grand choral concerts, there is to be found in this city material for a choir little inferior to that of the large towns in England, or even London itself … [Is] it not much to be lamented that such a decadence in public taste has taken place that our better educated classes would now rather hear 'nigger melodies' or a third-rate itinerant concert party from London, than listen to the lofty choruses of Handel, Mendelssohn, Mozart and Haydn? But such is the fact, and if the subscribers do not rouse themselves, we shall be without a trained band of singers equal to the works of the above-named composers … The whole performance brought back memories of the palmy days of the Antients – days which, we hope, are now to return with performances such as formerly of the finest works of the greatest oratorio composers.[74]

Despite the return to form, unease remained. Previewing the concert of 13 May 1862 the *Freeman's Journal* wrote:

---

the Philharmonic Society on 7 November in a secular programme, and on the following night with the Antients singing selections from *The Creation* and *Messiah*. **70** Joachim and Hallé appeared again on 27 May 1859; the programme included the 'Kreutzer' Sonata and Mendelssohn's Piano Trio in D minor, op. 49. On 25 November 1859 a predominantly orchestral programme included Mozart's 'Jupiter' Symphony, the overtures to *Der Freischütz* and *Fidelio* and a selection from Meyerbeer's *Dinorah*. **71** Mendelssohn's *Festgesang an die Künstler* on 18 January; his *Lauda Sion* and selections from Handel's *Samson* and Haydn's 'Nelson' Mass on 29 March; Mendelssohn's settings of Psalms 42 and 55, and Beethoven's Mass in C on 11 May; selections from *Messiah* and *The Creation* on 8 November. **72** Catherine Hayes (25 February); Louisa Pyne (10 May); Prosper Sainton and his wife Charlotte Sainton-Dolby (8 November). Of the last concert *SN* commented 'The Antients have begun well, to say the least, if not altogether in the manner they used … Orchestra there was none, but a band of singers varied the performance, now and then with unaccompanied choral pieces', 9 November 1861, 2. **73** *FJ*, 3 February 1862, 3. **74** *DEM*, 4 February 1862, 3.

> Latterly rumours have been afloat in musical circles that this [society] ... has been gradually but surely declining in prosperity, and consequently in influence – and that before many seasons passed, if not become altogether effete, [it would] certainly cease to occupy the high position which it had heretofore deservedly maintained ... For some seasons past, the society has, to a great extent, deviated from its original 'platform' ... and pandered to the craving for novelty, which is the besetting sin, intellectually speaking, of 'the general public'. This was certainly a great mistake, and had it been persevered in the career of the society must have inevitably come to an untimely end. Happily such has not been the case, better counsels seem latterly to have prevailed, and the recent performances of the Antients have been consistent with the purpose for which the society was founded and worthy of the men by whom it was originated.[75]

This concert was effectively, however, Robinson's last. The programme was an archetypal one: Mendelssohn's *Hear my Prayer* plus selections from *Israel in Egypt* and the 'Nelson' Mass. An additional concert was given on 2 June when Joachim was the star turn, but the choral section, comprising some Mendelssohn and Bishop partsongs, was minimal. No formal announcement of Robinson's resignation has been traced, although when the next concert, on 19 December, was presided over by George Torrance,[76] Robinson's successor, there was only passing comment in the newspapers.[77]

Torrance, though, conducted just six concerts. Programming reverted to the old format and he received good reviews, but they hint that the Antients was still in difficulty:

> The production of [a selection from Handel's *Judas Maccabaeus*] manifested on the part of the committee of the Antients a desire to present the subscribers with the best and most elevating compositions – and all now required is encouragement from those outside to place the society foremost as an exponent of the choral works of the great masters, as it had been heretofore, and restore it to the prestige of its palmiest days ... The performance of last evening ... did great credit to the conductor Mr Torrance, whose zeal and energy throughout is deserving of all praise.[78]

---

[75] *FJ*, 13 May 1862, 4. [76] Born in Kilkenny in 1835, Torrance was something of a prodigy; a chorister at Christ Church (and therefore almost certainly one of the boys who sang for the Antients in the 1840s), he became organist at Blackrock in 1851 and studied briefly in Leipzig (1856–57) before returning to read divinity at Trinity in 1859. An oratorio, *Abraham* (1855), and an opera, *William of Normandy* (1858) were both premiered in Dublin. He also appeared regularly as the Antients' organist. See also note 83. For further biographical information see *MT*, 1 September 1907, 609, *Dictionary of national biography*, ed. Sidney Lee (London: Smith, Elder, 1912), 2nd supplement, iii, 531, and *Grove's dictionary of music and musicians* ed. John Fuller Maitland (London: Macmillan, 1910), 2nd ed, v, 130–1. [77] See *FJ*, 20 December 1862, 3, and *DEM*, 20 December 1862, 2. [78] *DEM*, 21 February 1863, 3, on the concert of the previous day.

> Mr Torrance, as conductor, acquitted himself with great credit. He possesses all the qualifications for so important a post and it will not be his fault if the Antient Concerts do not maintain their old pre-eminence.[79]

'A real "Antient Concert"!'[80] declared the *Freeman's Journal* of the society's last performance, on 27 May 1864, the programme of which included Mendelssohn's setting of Psalm 42 and the society's first performance of Rossini's *Stabat Mater*. There was no sign that the Antients' end was imminent but a Special General Meeting was called on 13 December, adjourned, and resumed nine days later.[81] Almost certainly the event which precipitated these meetings was Torrance's resignation due to his impending ordination and his consequent decision to give up professional musical activities.[82] Even if Torrance had wanted to remain with the Antients this would have been impossible as his first curacy was in Shrewsbury, where he moved in 1865.[83]

His resignation appears to have thrown the society into a state of limbo from which it never emerged. Why Joseph Robinson did not resume his role as conductor is a mystery, and it is tempting to speculate that some fracture took place earlier which precluded him from doing so, although there is no evidence to support this hypothesis. Previously quoted reviews, however, show that the Antients had, due to changing tastes, been in difficulty for some years; Torrance's departure may simply have hastened the inevitable. A later article corroborates and extends this:

> Many are the reasons assigned for the dissolution of this society … That there may have been some errors in the administration is likely; but it is unlikely that they would have had the effect of dissolving the society. We have inquired a good deal into the subject, and after all are obliged to come to the conclusion that the Antient Concerts died from a decadence in taste amongst our better classes – those who supported the institution from the beginning, and under whose influences it grew and prospered. We have no under-middle class here as in England, and all fostering of art must emanate from the educated and upper citizens. If these fall away, the cultivation of art must languish. Our musical societies are exclusive, and the members invite audiences and bear the expenses of performances. The general public have nothing to do with them. That the best promoters of art should be found amongst the cultivated, and those with leisure to study, is true. But may not this eclecticism lead to cliqueism?[84]

79 *SN*, 21 February 1863, 2. **80** *FJ*, 28 May 1864, 3. **81** See *FJ*, 12 December 1864, 1, and *SN*, 21 December 1864, 3. **82** Between these two meetings, on 19 December, Torrance's second oratorio, a setting of Goldsmith's *The Captivity*, was premiered by a specially formed choir and orchestra in the Antient Concert Rooms; in its review *SN* lamented Torrance's departure from the musical scene, while praising his commitment to serve in the church; see *SN*, 20 December 1864, 2. **83** Torrance returned to Dublin in 1867, but emigrated to Australia in 1869 where he remained until 1898 before returning once more to Kilkenny. He continued to compose and to be involved in church music. **84** 'Music past and

Apparently, therefore, the society fell victim to its own exclusivity. In common with its London namesake, and the London Philharmonic Society, the social makeup of the Antients played a major role.[85] Reviews refer to the 'fashionable' nature of the audience, always mentioning the presence of the Lord Lieutenant and, often, the names of other dignitaries, especially of the judiciary and Anglican church, the twin pillars of Dublin's social establishment in the post-Union era.[86]

The division between the Anglo-Irish and Catholic communities seems to have been reflected in the society's membership; local Catholic singers, for example, do not appear to have been involved in the society's concerts.[87] Notably, the Catholic and pro-Repeal *Freeman's Journal* does not appear to have reviewed any of the society's concerts before 1847; a year later, when tensions were running high due to the combined impact of rural famine, revolutions across Europe, and the aftermath of the death of Daniel O'Connell, the *Freeman's Journal* admitted that 'in what are called politics we believe most of the gentlemen of the Antient Concerts differ from ourselves', before adding that 'if every institution in Ireland manifested the same practical patriotism ... Ireland would, in many respects, be advantaged.'[88]

Religion and politics, it would seem, were inescapable and inextricable in musical affairs. Whether or not the society considered broadening the social base of either its membership or audience is unknown. The zigzagging programme policy of the late 1850s indicates acknowledgment of a problem, but it would appear that social exclusivity remained a *sine qua non*. Perhaps, had the membership criteria been altered and the audience broadened by selling tickets publicly, the Antients would have survived, albeit in a modified form.[89]

In comparison to many contemporary choral societies in Dublin, the Antients lasted a long time, imbuing it with an enviable status. Although press reviews are discreet in making any adverse comments on the society's performances, the Antients clearly set a new standard both in terms of quality of performance and breadth of repertoire. Especially from the late 1840s the society's programmes were often innovative, bringing new works to Dublin audiences by well-known figures such as Mendelssohn and much less famous composers such as Lindpaintner and Horsley. Undoubtedly it is with the performances of Mendelssohn that the society achieved its greatest feats, and the society's devotion to his music is an excellent exemplar of how it took hold in the British Isles. Over the longer term,

---

present in Ireland', *MW*, 10 July 1875, 462. See also [Anonymous], *Recollections of Dublin Castle*, p. 279.
85 See Weber, *Music and the middle class*, pp 71–80.   **86** See, for example, *DEM*, 24 January 1845, 3, and 2 February 1859, 3; *SN*, 22 January 1847, 3; *FJ*, 15 June 1849, 2.   **87** The anonymous author of *Recollections of Dublin Castle* states that 'The ordinary Catholics were altogether looked down upon by the High Protestant set. A few of them were just recognized as worthy persons ... otherwise the barriers were stoutly guarded', pp 180–1.   **88** *FJ*, 14 April 1848, 3. O'Connell died on 15 May 1847, but *FJ* had been one of his strongest supporters and blamed the English establishment for his death on the grounds that his imprisonment in 1844 had fatally undermined his health.   **89** As new members had to be proposed by existing members, exclusivity was maintained; the society could, for example, have considered admitting women, or overtly reaching beyond its core Anglo-Irish membership to embrace the growing Catholic professional classes. The level of subscription would have ensured a residual level of social exclusivity.

however, the Antients' greatest achievement was a material one: the creation of Dublin's best and most widely-used concert room. The Antient Concert Rooms continued in use, and to be known under that name until the early 1920s. Joseph Robinson himself returned there as conductor of the Dublin Choral Society in the mid-1870s; later the rooms were used for the first productions of the Irish Literary Society,[90] and were mentioned by James Joyce in *Ulysses* and several other works. In the early 1920s the concert rooms began doubling as a cinema, and were wholly converted to this purpose in April 1956. The building fell into disuse in the early 1980s and for some time appeared to have no future; not without some controversy, planning permission was given for the building to be extended and converted into offices. At the time of writing this work was ongoing.

---

90 W.B. Yeats' *The Countess Cathleen* was first performed there on 8 May 1899.

Concert auditoria in nineteenth-century Belfast

ROY JOHNSTON

Towns such as Belfast, which in the early nineteenth century lacked the ready-made spaces associated with ancient ecclesiastical establishments, a university or a resident aristocracy, and which were not centres of government like Dublin or places of fashionable resort like Bath, suffered from a lack of auditoria when concert life began in the eighteenth century. The Thomas Phillips ground plan of Belfast in 1685 (see illustration 12.1) shows a small town of some 600 inhabitants,[1] with only three substantial buildings: a church at one end of High Street, the castle of the earls (later marquises) of Donegall at the other, and near the castle a building with a tower, which was the market house, serving also since the mid-seventeenth-century as town hall and court house.

When concert life began some half-century later two of those three properties were out of commission; the church, in a state of dilapidation, was to be demolished in 1774 and the castle, vacated by the family after a disastrous fire (in 1708), was never to be rebuilt. Concert life was to set up the basic questions of where performers were to perform and where people were to listen. There would be the churches; but non-devotional music would be frowned on in churches for many years to come. Theatres provided secular auditoria, but although there was a great deal of music in the eighteenth-century theatre, the internal design and ambience – pit, gallery, boxes, stage, scenery – militated against the evolving concept of a public concert. They would be used for concerts, but a theatre was not felt to be a satisfactory concert auditorium.

As the discourse develops, so do the participants. The performers, at the early stage of this evolution, may be gentlemen amateurs playing together in private and occasionally inviting their friends and womenfolk to come and hear them play 'in concert'. Later, they may be visiting professionals of established national reputation performing in large halls to large audiences. The audience, for its part, may have begun as the friends and womenfolk of the performers; by the time they comprised the big audience in the big hall they have changed not only in numbers but in social range and class.

In the summer of 1750 a small party of London-based professional musicians, passing through Belfast *en route* between Dublin and Edinburgh, gave concerts in the market house.[2] There is no indication of a concert life in Belfast at this time, but by the late 1760s evidence begins to appear of the Belfast Musical

---

[1] A census of 1659 had shown Belfast as having 589 inhabitants, see Jonathan Bardon, *A history of Ulster* (Belfast: Blackstaff Press, 1992), p. 146. [2] Roy Johnston, 'The pleasures and penalties of networking: John Frederick Lampe in the summer of 1750', *Concert life in eighteenth-century Britain,* eds Susan Wollenberg and Simon McVeigh (Aldershot: Ashgate, 2004), pp 231–3, 237–40.

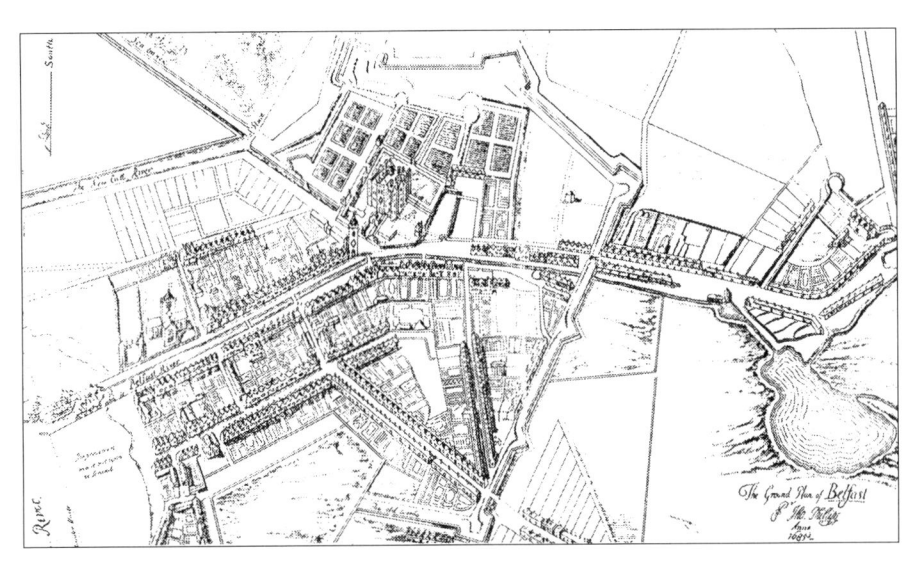

Illustration 12.1: Thomas Phillips' ground plan of Belfast in 1685 has south at the top of the page and north at the foot. The Farset appears as the 'Belfast River', flowing down what is now High Street to its junction with the Lagan.

Society, a gentlemen's club whose members met at regular intervals to play together and have supper afterwards, both activities of equal importance. For these meetings an inn had initially sufficed. But as time went on the Society moved its meetings to the market house, by then an old and shabby, if commodious, building. By the final quarter of the century, however, one building had been built which offered superior amenity for the giving of concerts. After the destruction of their castle, the Donegall family had gone to live in England. The fifth earl came into his inheritance in 1757, and set about instigating improvements in his town, if at a distance, and facilitating the initiatives of others by making land available. A new market house was built on a new site, providing also, in the growth of the town's mercantile life, the function of an exchange. A few years later an upper floor of considerable amenity was provided by the earl.[3] It comprised a room of 60ft x 30 (20.45m x 10.22) and two smaller rooms of 30ft x 30 (10.45m x 10.45). From its inception in 1776, this suite of rooms, which became known as the Exchange Rooms, was in great demand in the social as well as the commercial life of the town. The Musical Society began to hold its meetings there.

An aristocrat had provided the Exchange Rooms; another would recognize their potential for concerts. John O'Neill of Shane's Castle near Antrim, later a viscount, had formed a private band 'by making it a *sine qua non* in the appointment of a servant that he should play upon an instrument'.[4] He and his

---

[3] C.E.B. Brett, *Buildings of Belfast, 1700–1914* (Belfast: Friar's Bush Press, 1967, revised edn. 1985), p. 4.
[4] John Bernard, *Retrospections of the stage* (London: 1830), i, 321.

wife, notable patrons of the arts, had built a private theatre on their estate; they had also entertained professional musicians from the Rotunda concerts in Dublin. O'Neill, no stranger to Belfast, saw in the Exchange Rooms a better concert auditorium than Shane's Castle could provide, and put on concerts there with his band including such artists as Ashe, Mahon and the Weichsells.[5] William Ware, organist of St Anne's parish church, also recognized the potential of the Exchange Rooms for subscription series of professional concerts. In the turbulent Ireland of the 1790s, however, concert life languished in Belfast, as did the theatre and other forms of public entertainment.

In the new century, the Belfast Musical Society had not survived, and O'Neill had died in the attack on Antrim by the insurgents of 1798.[6] The old market house would be demolished in 1812.[7] Belfast, now a busy market town, would soon, with the manufacture of cotton, enter its industrial era. Edward Bunting, of Belfast Harp Festival fame[8] and formerly Ware's organ apprentice, proved himself a good keyboard performer with a flair for concert promotion. Most of his subscription series took place in the Exchange Rooms. In 1807 he pulled off a coup, when he persuaded Catalani, on her visit to Dublin, to come north, with the band of the Theatre Royal, Dublin and their conductor Tom Cooke. Bunting, to meet Catalani's notoriously exorbitant fees, was having to charge high prices to the biggest possible audience; he took advantage of the Theatre season not having begun, by having Catalani and her company give two concerts in the Theatre.[9] When she agreed to come again the following year the Theatre was not available, and so her concerts took place in the smaller Exchange Rooms.[10]

Although Bunting had been out of his apprenticeship to William Ware for some time he had no base as an organist in Belfast. The only church in Belfast with an organ was St Anne's, and Ware, far from retirement, remained the incumbent. But the young William Drummond, who had become the minister of Second

---

[5] Andrew Ashe (b. Lisburn, County Antrim 1759, d. Dublin 1838): flautist and composer of flute concertos; played at the Rotunda concerts in Dublin for several seasons; engaged by Salomon for the Hanover Square concerts in London; took over direction of the Bath concerts after the death of Rauzzini. John Mahon (1749–1834), violinist and clarinettist; member of a musical family of Irish origin who lived in England in the eighteenth century; debut 1772 in the Holywell Music Room, Oxford playing a clarinet concerto. Carl Weichsell, German oboist established in London by the 1750s, came to Dublin to play in the Smock Alley theatre orchestra 1783; father of Charles Weichsell (c.1766–post-1805), violinist and conductor of several Rotunda concert seasons. [6] A.T.Q. Stewart, *The summer soldiers: the 1798 rebellion in Antrim and Down* (Belfast: Blackstaff Press, 1995), pp 111–12, 116, 117. [7] Marcus Patton, *Central Belfast: an historical gazetteer* (Belfast: Ulster Architectural Heritage Society, 1993), p. 186. [8] It is worth noting in the interest of historical accuracy that what has become generally known as a festival was described in the contemporary handbill, in the note of the subsequent meeting of the subscribers, in the contemporary newspaper reports and in the minutes of the Belfast Society for Promoting Knowledge, as a 'meeting'. For that matter, each of its predecessors at Granard, County Longford had been described as a 'ball', and the Three Choirs annual meetings in England were not described as festivals until the nineteenth century. Bunting still calls the 1792 festival a 'meeting' in his 1840 volume, and it is not called a festival in George Petrie's valedictory article on Bunting in the *Dublin University Magazine* of January 1847, 64–73; see Roy Johnston, *Bunting's 'Messiah'* (Belfast: Belfast Natural History and Philosophical Society, 2003), p. 48n. [9] *Belfast News-Letter* [hereafter *BN*], 18 September 1807. [10] *Belfast Commercial Chronicle* [hereafter *BCC*], 26 October 1808.

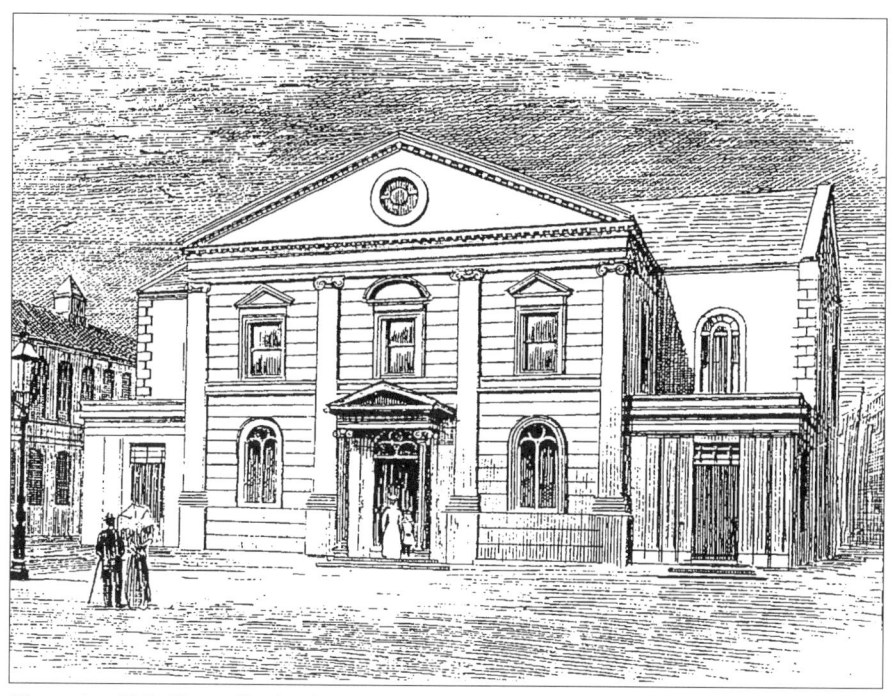

Illustration 12.2: The auditoria of Bunting's festival. Second Presbyterian Church in Rosemary Lane (now Rosemary Street) was opened in 1790 and demolished in 1964.

Illustration 12.3: The Theatre in Arthur Street (now Arthur Square) was opened in 1793 and demolished in 1871. Private Collection.

Presbyterian church in Rosemary Lane (now Rosemary Street), had set his heart on having the first organ to be installed in a Dissenting church, and he enlisted Bunting's help in designing it and having it built by 'Mr White, an ingenious mechanic from London'.[11] In 1806 Bunting became Dr Drummond's organist, and a creative partnership developed. In May 1813 the Belfast newspapers carried the announcement of an ambitious musical event, a sacred-and-secular festival on the lines of the Three Choirs and other English festivals.[12] There would be secular concerts on three nights and 'sacred' events (the term 'concert' was not used for churches) on three 'mornings' (commencing at noon). With Bunting playing on an instrument in the design of which he had participated, and with the encouragement of Dr Drummond, the sacred events took place in Second Presbyterian church (see illustration 12.2). The Exchange Rooms would have been the expected venue for the secular concerts. But not only were they almost impossible to book, for preliminary setting-up, three consecutive nights and rehearsals, they were by then too small. As an alternative there was only the Theatre (see illustration 12.3). There were postponements of the original starting date, and the festival began on Tuesday 19 October, uncomfortably close to the opening of the Theatre season; however, as with the two Catalani concerts, every event in the festival took place.[13] But it had shown the woeful lack by now in Belfast of auditoria fit to accommodate its concert audience. The church had given the festival three substantial 'sacred events', including the first complete performance (for its time) of Handel's *Messiah* in Belfast;[14] but the secular concerts had exposed the serious faults of the Theatre as an auditorium. Bunting had pushed the auditorium situation to its limit and beyond.

By the end of the second decade of the nineteenth century Bunting had gone to live for the rest of his life in Dublin. The Exchange Rooms were harder to book than ever, held only a fraction of the potential concert audience and had become shabby; too small for an exchange and unsuitable in design, they were for commercial purposes in dire need of replacement. There would be no munificent latter-day gestures like those of the fifth earl; his son, the second Marquis of Donegall and his family had returned to live in their town in the final years of the eighteenth century, but they were in flight from their London creditors.[15] Not for the first time, the Belfast mercantile community was thrown back on its own resources. A new building was opened in Waring Street in 1820, a few yards away from the Exchange Rooms, of much greater space and flexibility, known as the Commercial Buildings. There was a newsroom, an assembly room and 'numerous offices for merchants or others';[16] one side of the complex was to consist of shops, and there would be a hotel 'on the most extensive scale'; an area

---

11 *BCC*, 6 September 1806. 12 *BN* and *BCC*, 7 May 1813. 13 For the festival, see Johnston, *Bunting's 'Messiah'*, pp 74–97, 114–35. 14 The complete *Messiah* now expected by audiences is a fairly recent phenomenon. The same substantial cuts were accepted in Bunting's time until well into the twentieth century; ibid., pp 84–6. 15 W. A. Maguire, 'Lords and landlords – the Donegall Family', in J.C. Beckett et al. (eds), *Belfast: the making of the city, 1800–1914*, (Belfast: Appletree Press, 1983), p. 27. 16 George Benn, *The history of the town of Belfast* (Belfast: Mackay, 1823), pp 90–1.

Illustration 12.4: The façade of the Commercial Buildings of 1820 still stands in Waring Street.

in the interior, and 'a piazza, supported with metal pillars', would be for the use of merchants who assembled on 'change days' to transact their business. The commercial community had designed and built it themselves; the outlay would be recouped by 'the subscriptions to the news-room, the rents of the different shops and offices, and the superior accommodations for mercantile affairs which the place affords'.[17] There is no mention of hirings or lettings, and the strong impression given is of a group of buildings conceived, designed and built for the use of businessmen only. It would be several years before concerts would take place in the Commercial Buildings (see illustration 12.4). Outmoded the Exchange Rooms might now be, but their function as a concert auditorium was, *faute de mieux*, to continue. The pressure at first, however, was not heavy; very few concerts took place in the 1820s.

No successor to Edward Bunting as concert promoter came forward in those years, but there had been one potentially benign portent. In 1814 there had come into being the Belfast Anacreontic Society. It had many of the features of the Musical Society of the previous century; supper afterwards was an essential element of the new Society's evening. It was composed of playing members (including the president, the marquis of Donegall) and a few non-playing members who were designated as 'associates'. It had a professional leader, Vincenzo Guerini, who

[17] Ibid.

had arrived in Belfast from Naples via Dublin in 1806 to teach violin, piano, singing and the Italian language.[18] The Society patronized the concerts of a visiting soprano in 1815 and in 1817 put on a charity concert of its own with local soloists.[19] A series of three subscription concerts took place in the 1819–20 season. All the concerts took place in the Exchange Rooms (which were, as it happened, in the ownership of the Society's president).

The 1820–1 concerts were to commence in December[20] but none was separately advertised or reported in the press. If some Anacreontic Society members were in favour of giving public concerts, there were those who preferred it to be a private music club. The latter now entered on a long period of ascendancy. When Kalkbrenner came to play with them in September 1824[21] it was the first indication of an Anacreontic public concert since 1820. It was in the private-music-club frame of mind, and without regard to external influences, that the Society approached the question of a place of their own. In 1825 it decided 'to adopt immediate measures for building Rooms suitable for the meetings of the Society' and set up a committee and a subscription list;[22] for the first time, a musical society had taken on the provision of a place for itself without regard to its use by other bodies. A few years later, when the Belfast Saving [sic] Bank was building new premises for itself in King Street, the Anacreontic Society persuaded the bank to provide a room on the first floor for the Society with its own staircase. The Society moved in in December 1829. It was delivered from vexatious hirings and the shabbiness of the Exchange Rooms; but nothing shows the private-club mentality more clearly than the dimensions of the King Street room,[23] which at 42ft by 31 (12.80m x 9.45) were substantially smaller than the 60ft by 30 of the Exchange Rooms.

The 1820s came to an end without the emergence of a regular framework for the promotion of public concerts in the town. There had been a low average of four concerts a year, and in one three-year period there had been only one concert. The concerts in the Exchange Rooms had nearly all been given by local musicians and minor visitors. The Theatre had been the most frequently used auditorium for concerts, and for the performances of such major figures as the tenor John Braham who did at this stage of his career sing in the concert room. The Theatre, however, had lost the patronage of the nobility and gentry, and had not won the taste of a public from the expanding middle classes. Successive managers of the Theatre had diagnosed music as an attraction for such a public, and the decade was marked by the engagements of a line of good singers. But they played to small houses; and even the efforts of one manager, Seymour, in bringing Caradori and Catalani (on her farewell tour)[24] failed both to bring back the old public or attract significant numbers of the new. Those of the burgeoning

---

18 *BN*, 8 August 1806.   **19** *BN*, 3 March 1815, 28 January 1817.   **20** *BN*, 5 December 1820.   **21** *BN*, 16 September 1824.   **22** *BN*, 20 December 1825.   **23** Anacreontic Society Minutes [hereafter ASM], meeting of 4 February 1829.   **24** *Northern Whig* [hereafter *NW*], 16, 21 May 1829 (on Caradori), 25, 29 June 1829 (on Catalani).

middle classes who were prepared to spend some money on evening entertainment had shown that they were not interested in the theatre.

Before the end of the third decade of the century, however, a small number of concerts were given in the Commercial Buildings, including those given in 1828 by a notable touring ensemble, the Brothers Herrmann.[25] Sparse provision was now to be followed by a decade of relative profusion; by the mid-point of the 1830s as many concerts had taken place as in the whole of the previous decade. There were abundant signs that there would be more and more visiting artists; from Dublin, from across the Irish Sea and the continent of Europe, that there would be welcoming concert audiences for them – and that they would perform where they could. The Exchange Rooms, in their faded state, were still available, but of the new travelling virtuosi only Giulio Regondi the guitarist appears as using them; his farewell concert took place there in November 1835.[26] A few months later, in March 1836, on the occasion of a charity concert given by the Belfast Amateur Band, use of the rooms was granted by 'Mr Scott'. A ground plan in a lease of 4 November 1840 shows the ground floor as occupied by 'Mr Scott, seedsman' and 'Graham and Co., hat shop'.[27] Bar a trickle of bookings up to December 1837 the era of the Exchange Rooms as a concert auditorium was over; by 1845 the building had become a bank.[28] The Theatre was still available, and would so continue for several decades; Paganini played two of his three concerts there in 1831[29] and Ole Bull played a series of four concerts in the Theatre in 1837, his performances interpolated into the theatrical bill of fare.[30] Thalberg gave a concert and a matinée there over the new year 1838/9.[31] Bochsa and Mrs Bishop chose the theatre for their week of concerts in 1839.[32] Under pressure from the growing concert world, the Commercial Buildings had at last come into more frequent use as a auditorium. Paganini gave a matinée there in 1831.[33] In the final three years of the decade the management found themselves swamped with applications; in the year 1839 concerts were given by Thalberg on his retirement tour,[34] by the Johann Strauss band (twelve players under Schallehn),[35] and by the Distins,[36] the first of many visits to Belfast by this famous family of brass players. No less than ten users gave concerts in the years 1838 and 1839.

Once the Anacreontic Society retired from concert promotion, they virtually vanished also from the newspapers. Fortunately, their minute book survives for the period from late November 1828 to October 1845, a valuable primary source.[37] However content the private-music-club people were with the King Street room (visiting virtuosi were sometimes invited to supper), the membership

---

25 *BCC*, 12, 15 March 1828. For information on this pioneering string quartet, who were not brothers and none of whom was called Herrmann, see 'Zeugheer' in *A dictionary of music and musicians*, ed. George Grove (London and New York: Macmillan, 1890), iv, 507. **26** *NW*, 16 November 1835. **27** S. Shannon Millin, *Additional sidelights on Belfast history* (Belfast: Baird, 1938), p. 162. **28** Ibid., 161. **29** *BCC*, 10 October 1831. **30** *NW*, 11, 14 March 1837. **31** *NW*, 2, *BN-L,* 5 January 1838. **32** *NW*, 4, 8 and 9 May 1839. **33** *BCC*, 10 October 1831. **34** *BN*, 11, 15 October 1839. **35** *NW* and *Ulster Times* [hereafter *UT*], 12 November 1839. **36** *NW* and *BN*, 10 December 1839. **37** The bound single volume is held in the Linenhall Library, Belfast. No minutes of the Society for other periods have been found.

Illustration 12.5: The Music Hall in May Street. Long disused for its original purpose, it was demolished in 1983 (despite being a listed building).

at large found it increasingly difficult to ignore the burgeoning concert scene beyond its doors. The decline and impending disappearance of the Exchange Rooms had brought the paucity of auditoria into sharpest relief. Since a building capable of being used as a concert hall was plainly not going to be provided by any outside body, those of its membership who saw the Anacreontic as primarily a concert-promoting body began to gain ground. There was a proposal to hold a public concert in January 1837.[38] it proved abortive, but it was followed by sweeping changes in the membership of the Society's committee. The minutes of the new secretary, John Cameron, record a scene of enterprise and energy differing greatly from his predecessors' laconic chronicle of genteel stagnation. Two public concerts took place, in December 1837 and March 1838.[39] Cramming 200 people into the King Street room proved extremely inconvenient, but by then the Society, prepared in its new mood to grasp nettles, had decided to erect a new building of its own (see illustration 12.5). It continued with its new policy of promoting concerts and put on several concerts in the Commercial Buildings

38 ASM, meetings of 3, 10 January 1837. **39** *UT*, 23 December 1837, 3 March 1838.

while the new hall was being built in May Street.[40] The Music Hall had its opening concert on 26 March 1840.[41] The Anacreontic Society had fended for itself for a second time, and where before it had been beholden to the Savings Bank, this time it had bought the site and employed an architect and builder on its own. The new hall had a floor area of 86ft by 35 (26.22m x 10.67); it had a capacity of some 700, outstripping all predecessors except perhaps the Theatre, which it utterly outdid in amenity. The leader in the project had been Dr Samuel Smith Thomson (1778–1849), a founder-member of the Anacreontic Society, its vice-president for eight years and president for twelve. Mentions of him are few in the newspapers; it is in the Society minutes that the value of his membership can be appreciated, not least in the sheer number of its meetings and committee meetings that he attended. It was by no means his only interest. Described by the medical historian Andrew Malcolm as the 'father of the medical profession in Belfast', he was closely associated with the foundation in 1815 of the Fever Hospital, later the Belfast General Hospital (today's Royal Victoria Hospital) of which he was consulting physician; he also put his talents at the service of philanthropy and of his church. It is perhaps curious that the memorial tablet to him in First Presbyterian church pays tribute to him in these fields but does not mention the Anacreontic Society.

The face of concert life was changed by the new hall. Among the first and most distinguished visitors was Liszt in the January after it opened, at the end of the Irish section of his British tour.[42] Dr Thomson, having found himself learning the skills of securing the necessary finance and bringing a new auditorium into being, now had to learn those of the impresario. Roads had improved, railways were being built, access to Belfast from Britain was improving as the scheme to excavate, straighten and deepen the river Lagan began to move forward.[43] Audiences at first were delighted to encounter so many of the best artists from Dublin, but Dr Thomson and his colleagues soon found that Music Hall audiences wanted the big names from London and Europe. The supply of such artists would in the course of time become the specialty of such London-based impresarios as Willert Beale, and the efforts of the Anacreontic management would be directed at ensuring that a Beale-type concert party of big names would include Belfast on its itinerary of the cities and towns of the British Isles. Concert promotion and the maintenance of a big hall had become a much more expensive operation than had been imagined: the capital debt on the erection of the building, so far from being reduced, remained static. There had been unforeseen hazards. Dr Thomson, on the occasion of a very severe storm in the Irish Sea, had had to appear before a packed audience in the Music Hall to apologize for the fact that the ship, with Thalberg and others on board, had had to flee back for safety into Liverpool.[44]

---

40 For its building, see Roy Johnston, 'Concerts in the musical life of Belfast to 1874', PhD diss. (Queen's University, Belfast, 1996), pp 336–340. **41** *NW* and *UT*, 28 March 1840. **42** *NW* and *BCC*, 16 January 1841. **43** See Robin Sweetnam, 'The development of the port', in Beckett, *Belfast*, pp 57–62. **44** ASM, meeting of 27 January 1845.

It had not been long before, supply creating demand, other local concert promoters began to appear in Belfast who were keen to hire the Music Hall for their concerts. The Anacreontic Society were glad to comply, on their own terms. They refused to allow an organ to be installed; it would take up too much room and incommode the orchestra.[45] The refusal had an interesting and ultimately disconcerting outcome. If the Anacreontic, putting on concerts in its own hall with major invited soloists and its own orchestra, felt that it had cornered the market, it was to encounter, on the contrary, competition which would challenge and in a few years take over its hegemony.

The nineteenth-century choral societies in Belfast arose not in mainstream concert life but from the desire of the churches to improve the singing of their congregations. In February 1839 the Belfast Choral Society attracted an audience of 300 to its 'public night' which was held in the parochial school room of St Anne's.[46] The proceedings began and ended with prayer by Anglican and Presbyterian clergy as did the Society's second public appearance a few months later in the school room of the Fisherwick Place Presbyterian church at which an even bigger audience of 500–600 attended.[47] The music at both consisted of anthems and oratorio choruses as well as psalms and hymns, and accompaniment consisted of two pianos and a 'seraphine' (a keyboard reed instrument, with bellows and swell but a 'harsh and raspy' tone, which appeared in 1833 in London and by 1852 had been superseded by the harmonium). The guiding spirits were the organists John Willis and Charles Dalton. Encouraged by this reception, they were aware also that the school rooms of the churches were far from being secular auditoria. Within the next two years they succeeded, with skill and diplomacy, in using hirings of the Music Hall to get the choral movement out from under the aegis of the churches and into the public domain.

Other choral societies came into being. The Classical Harmonists, formed in 1851, achieved leadership in these new ventures. Unlike the Anacreontic Society, they were outward-looking, with their collective finger on an important social innovation; membership was open to all, including women. It was outstandingly well managed: the link with the churches was retained and valued; the Donegalls and other nobility and gentry were welcomed. The most important link, in business terms, was with the higher ranks of industry. The Classical Harmonists brought them in as vice-presidents – by the 1860s they had twenty. It was also fortunate in its first two conductors. William Vipond Barry, from Bandon in County Cork, a pupil of Liszt with degrees from Göttingen, had appeared first in Belfast as a piano soloist styling himself 'the Beethoven of Ireland'. One would hardly have expected from so flamboyant a beginning the careful way in which he guided the Classical Harmonists in their formative years to, first, a competence in choral singing, and then a familiarity with individual choruses and the shorter works of the canon, resisting the clamour of the newspapers for a complete and premature *Messiah*. When he had to retire, owing to ill health, he was succeeded

---

[45] ASM, meetings of 2, 13 April 1840. [46] *UT*, 2, and *BN*, 5 February 1839. [47] *BN*, 14 May 1839.

by George Benjamin Allen, a vicar choral of Armagh cathedral with a London background and considerable relevant experience behind him. Building on Barry's foundation, Allen developed a most creditable track record. In his six years the Classical Harmonists gave twenty-one performances of ten complete works, including six of *Messiah* and four of *The Creation*.

Oratorio, however, cried out for the noble sound of the organ, and this choral development was not achieved in the Music Hall. In 1854 the Classical Harmonists acquired a concert hall of their own on the second floor of a building in the new Victoria Street,[48] which became known as the Victoria Hall; its dimensions are not known, but the capacity was roughly the same as that of the Music Hall. The Classical Harmonists took the hall on a lease, not loading themselves with a capital debt as the Anacreontic had done. They readily persuaded the owner to let them install an organ. Thus, after so many years of under-provision, Belfast found itself with two concert halls with a joint capacity of at least 1,400.

The Anacreontic season in the Music Hall would include concerts built around the star touring groups, with, to save money, a concert or two using local and/or Dublin soloists; the Anacreontic orchestra played at all concerts. Barry had not encouraged the Classical Harmonists to go for big-name oratorio soloists until they acquired choral expertise; Allen was now in a position to invite the best. The Classical Harmonists would also augment their organ accompaniments with the Anacreontic players. But there was an inbuilt instability. The Music Hall was as large, and larger, than the Anacreontic could afford, but in building it the Society was more concerned to get out of the King Street room than to look far enough ahead. Level-headed as the Classical Harmonists were, they cannot have looked on the Victoria Hall as their long-term base. It had as many seats as the Music Hall, but the concert audience in a very short time was demanding more from both auditoria. For the elderly component of the Victoria Hall audience, and the infirm and the pregnant, there was the inconvenience of its second-floor location. When the Commercial Buildings opened in 1820 Belfast's population was 35,000; when the Music Hall opened in 1840, 70,000; by the mid-1850s the town's population was 110,000, and the existing auditoria, whether relatively young like the Music Hall and the Victoria Hall or much older like the Theatre (all three shared much the same audience capacity), were far too small. It affected both musical societies, too, that the major artists were becoming accustomed to larger halls elsewhere on the touring circuit. The Commercial Buildings, having proved in their turn too small and out of date, had not been extended but, with the separation of the needs of commercial life into the building of individual exchanges, of which the Corn Exchange was an example, sidelined.

The big secular, centrally placed hall was an important feature of the mature town of the Industrial Revolution. It was temple to Mammon, status symbol, auditorium and money-maker. By 1851 Belfast, a late developer in the Revolution, had taken its place in the list of the twelve biggest British towns outside London

---

48 *Belfast Daily Mercury* [hereafter *BDM*], 2 November 1854.

and Dublin, and become the world centre for linen and for manufacture of linen-making machinery. On Thursday 12 February 1857 a meeting was held 'of those persons who feel interested in the erection of a new concert hall suited to the present and prospective wants of the town'.[49] A resolution was carried that a company be formed to erect a building.[50]

A newspaper gave dimensions of halls erected in recent years in industrial towns in England to show how far Belfast lagged behind.[51] The oldest and smallest, in Birmingham, had a floor area more than three times that of the Music Hall, while that of Bradford, the town nearest in population to Belfast, was nearly four times the size. In February 1859 the Ulster Hall Company (Limited) issued its prospectus.[52] The object of the Company was to erect in Belfast 'a spacious Hall, with the necessary minor apartments, affording accommodation for between 2,000 and 3,000 persons, and suitable for Concerts ... and all other public purposes to which such buildings are generally applied'. There would be 'a large Organ, by the aid of which Grand Musical Festivals and Cheap Popular Concerts may be given'. A site was obtained in Bedford Street and the design of the new hall put out to competition (see illustration 12.6). No single moving spirit such as Dr Thomson dominated the Ulster Hall project. The names of a small number of directors of the Company appeared more frequently than the others in the newspaper reports, but they are representative of the substantial number of directors, perhaps the majority, who were or had been members of the Anacreontic Society and/or the Classical Harmonists. Some were or had been office-bearers, and some had playing and/or singing experience. However varied the pie-chart of uses for which the new hall was intended, concerts would be a large slice, and this was reflected in the interest and knowledge of the directors. It was not a parochial interest. Familiarity with the concert and opera worlds was a required attribute of the mercantile elites in Britain, Europe and farther afield with whom the Belfast merchants did business.

Conspicuous by their absence in the deliberative process were George Benjamin Allen of the Classical Harmonists and Leo Kerbusch, conductor of the Anacreontic Society. The Company wanted a free hand; directors had visited Manchester, Bradford, Birmingham and London, inspecting halls and gathering information. The commitment to an organ had in mind a solution adopted in some other towns. A splendid organ had recently been installed in St George's Hall, Liverpool, and William Thomas Best, the organist, had by his arrangements and his playing used it in such a way as almost to make it serve as substitute for a municipal orchestra. By early 1862 (rather late in the day) an anonymous donor had promised to provide an organ for the Ulster Hall. He proved to be Andrew Mulholland, doyen of the town's linen magnates and a former mayor. The

---

[49] *BN*, 13 February 1857. [50] For the Ulster Hall project, see Roy Johnston, '"Here will we sit": the creation of the Ulster Hall' in Christina Bashford and Leanne Langley (eds), *Music and British culture, 1785–1914: essays in honour of Cyril Ehrlich* (Oxford: Oxford University Press, 2000), pp 215–32. [51] *BDM*, 10 September 1858. [52] *BN*, 9 February 1859.

Illustration 12.6: The Ulster Hall, an uncompromising shoebox. The architect's perspective view of the interior, from his own designs (in watercolour, *c.*1860). The gas chandeliers and the ceiling decoration had to be omitted from the completed building for economic reasons. Members of the orchestra are posed decoratively in front of the organ, the depiction of which is conjectural.

instrument would not be ready for the opening concerts in May 1862; for those, the Classical Harmonists would transfer their organ from the Victoria Hall for the occasion. The Classical Harmonists promoted themselves with a barrage of advertisements for the first performances in the new hall. *Messiah* and a concert version of *Der Freischütz* had been chosen. The chorus and orchestra were augmented: Allen conducted both concerts; it was a personal triumph. Downstairs in the Ulster Hall, it was thought, 1,500 persons could sit and the gallery would hold 500. The platform could accommodate 200–250 singers and players. The main auditorium was 138ft long, 63ft wide and 63ft high (42.01m x 19.20 x 19.20).[53] Estimates of the first-night audience varied between 1,800 and 2,000, in addition to orchestra and chorus of 200. The audience for the second concert was even larger.[54]

53 *BN*, 13 May 1862. **54** *NW*, 14 May 1862.

There was to be a second 'opening' in December, comprising a festival to celebrate the installation of the magnificent Mulholland organ. But any expectation that Allen would also preside at that event was premature. The organist was a vitally important appointment to the new hall. The directors, ranging widely, were attracted by the skills, reputation and personality of Edmund Thomas Chipp; he was a former chorister of the Chapel Royal and had been a violinist in the Queen's Private Band for twelve years; he also held a doctorate of music from Cambridge and had been organist at the Panopticon in London. Chipp knew his market value and was not readily lured away from his native London. When he arrived in Belfast in the autumn of 1862 he was not only the organist of the Ulster Hall but the appointed conductor of both the Anacreontic Society and the Classical Harmonists (Allen and Kerbusch were summarily sacked), and organist of St George's parish church. In the festival of inauguration in December he played a full part as organist, conductor, and composer. His first concerts with the Anacreontic and the Classical Harmonists left audiences and his new employers in no doubt of his energy, abilities and high standards and, moreover, attracted rave notices in the press.

An auditorium with nearly three times the seating capacity of the Music Hall secured for Belfast a place on the visiting and touring itineraries of the wider musical world. The local musical scene proved less happy. Chipp, after only three seasons, left Belfast to become for the rest of his life organist and master of the choristers of Ely Cathedral. The sheer size of the Ulster Hall auditorium had a daunting effect on the two musical societies, and by the end of the 1860s, when the Anacreontic Society had withdrawn from the scene and the Classical Harmonists were struggling, the local contribution to concert performance in the Ulster Hall looked to be seriously in danger of vanishing. Recovery began in 1872 with the formation of a new instrumentally-based Belfast Musical Society. It gave concerts, supplying a counterbalance to the Classical Harmonists, who against this competition revived somewhat. In 1874, the two societies formally amalgamated, becoming the Belfast Philharmonic Society.[55] The model proved, as elsewhere in Europe, to be the consolidation of concert life in its modern form: a town's concert life having at its apex a single society with its own chorus and orchestra and access to a large modern concert hall.

It is a good place to stop tracing the discourse. The population of Belfast was to go on increasing with the development of another major industry, shipbuilding. The 1857 reference to the 'present and prospective wants of the town' embodied an acknowledgment of the short space of time it had taken for the Music Hall to become too small. In building even as large a hall the Ulster Hall Company were deferring to their grandchildren, rather than their children, the need to build an even larger one. The rising graph of population, it was evident, required a *pro rata* increase in the capacity of the town's main auditorium. But there was an unforeseen bonus. What the Company were not to know was that they were

---

55 *BN*, 2 September 1874.

building the Ulster Hall at the very time the capacity curve was flattening. The concert public had kept rising: the size of auditoria had risen to meet it, aided by technological improvements in the carrying power of instruments, by louder singing technique, and by larger orchestras. But the apogee of this composite phenomenon was at hand. There was a limit to the productivity the performer and the instrument could achieve.[56] Once it had been reached, those who wished to admit bigger audiences had to resort to amplification, from the early stunts with megaphones to present-day electronic technology. The potential of audience growth might be limitless, but for the concert repertoire, played live to a live audience, auditoria could be larger than the Ulster Hall but not infinitely larger. In this may lie part of the secret of the longevity of the mid-nineteenth-century big civic halls. It is only in relatively recent years, when the twentieth century had brought so many new musics and so much essential technology associated with them into the discourse, that the need has been felt for a new generation of big halls. The Belfast example, the Waterfront Hall which opened in 1996, has greater flexibility, versatility and comfort but its seating capacity is not much in excess of 2,000, which is the same as the Ulster Hall's in 1862, when it was built for a catchment area one-fifth of the size. Not that the day of the older halls is totally over; the old shoebox Ulster Hall, with its ambience and its remarkable acoustic for orchestral music, will not lightly be abandoned by concert audiences.

Where, however, would the post-Ulster-Hall audiences of the nineteenth century sit? There would come into being a proliferation of other spaces capable of being used as concert auditoria. St Mary's Hall in Bank Street came into being in the 1870s, the Wellington Hall in Wellington Place in the 1890s, the Grosvenor Hall in Grosvenor Road in 1925. Both the new City Hall and Queen's University had Great Halls, over the years becoming available for concerts. None rivalled the Ulster Hall. The old Theatre would be replaced, and accompanied by the end of the century by several more theatres; the basic perception remained, however, that theatres did not make good concert auditoria. The greatest proliferation of auditoria, however, came about through the growth of the suburbs, with their demand for neighbourhood entertainment; and the relaxation of the stance of the churches. Local halls of various allegiances sprang up, and the city became dotted with church halls in which largely secular entertainments, including concerts, could be held; secular concerts in the churches themselves had to wait until the following century. The 'apex' which the Ulster Hall represented was not to be challenged, however, and rested eventually on a very broad base indeed.

In retrospect, the entire nineteenth-century discourse had taken place against a background of constant population increase, itself a function of the growth of Belfast from a market town of modest size at the beginning of the century to a

---

[56] See W.J. Baumol and W.G. Bowen, 'Anatomy of the income gap', in *Performing arts: the economic dilemma: a study of problems common to theater, opera, music and dance* (Boston: Massachusetts Institute of Technology, 1966), pp 161–72. I am obliged to the late Cyril Ehrlich, when he was at Queen's University, Belfast for drawing my attention to this chapter.

major industrial city at its close (Belfast became a city in 1888). The Exchange Rooms remain the only auditorium in this survey in which the nobility and gentry participated in provision and exploitation. If the eighteenth century bequeathed a concert audience, the business community did not take it into consideration in designing the Commercial Buildings, the successor to the Exchange Rooms; its discourse was between the business community and the growth of business. The concert audience lacked a voice of its own; it could have been provided by the Anacreontic Society, but that body had turned its back on the discourse when it provided itself with a room of its own which was smaller, not larger, than the Exchange Rooms. But it could not resist for ever the increase of the concert audience, especially when performers of international reputation, with their own demands, came into the equation by including Belfast on their travels. When the Anacreontic Society did return to the promotion of public concerts, the Music Hall they built was primarily for concerts. The business community could hire it for its own purposes; with the Exchange Rooms and the Commercial Buildings it had been the other way round. There was an identifiable and growing concert audience which deserved inclusion at the planning stage of new buildings. The concert audience and the commercial community were not, of course, mutually exclusive bodies; a good many businessmen attended concerts and helped run the musical societies. When the Classical Harmonists took on a hall of their own, the Victoria Hall, it was by no means a King-Street-room withdrawal. On the contrary, the Classical Harmonists, whose management were very much at home in the market-place, were taking their Society into an important and growing part of the musical mainstream ignored by the Anacreontics. The Classical Harmonists, also, had kept with them the churches, who bore them no ill-will for their part in secularizing the oratorio and who continued to provide the proving-ground for the Classical Harmonists chorus. In the mid-century clamour for bigger auditoria, there came into view an additional element in the discourse which put the solution beyond the resources of the concert audience on its own. It was the *amour propre* of a town which insisted on buildings worthy of its place in the bigger picture. If the Ulster Hall Company Limited had not come forward when it did, it would have been necessary to invent it. Not the least of the achievements of the Ulster Hall project was that it involved so many of the people and agencies which had taken part at one time or another in the discourse stretching back into the previous century. The nobility and gentry, if they were not to be movers and shakers like the fifth earl and John O'Neill, were present in the management of the Classical Harmonists, lending their presence to the essential respectablility of the enterprise.

There are, however, contemporary voices which are not heard in the narrative. The university, founded in 1849, had a choral society, but town-and-gown initiatives were not yet to be found in Belfast. With all the town's prosperity, the only example of a tycoon participating in the discourse is Andrew Mulholland who provided the Ulster Hall with its organ. The political voice was not part of the discourse.

Looking back twenty years, say, after the Ulster Hall opened, it must have seemed to the musical fraternity that things, after all, had worked out well. The musical societies had recovered from their lean years even before the 1874 amalgamation. All three of the professionals most affected in the traumatic early years – Allen, Kerbusch and Chipp[57] – had continued elsewhere with congenial musical careers. After using a good deal of imported help, the Philharmonic gradually built up an orchestra of its own composed of the more able of its members and other local amateurs, with a stiffening of local and invited professionals. The only long-term losers were the shareholders of the Ulster Hall Company (Limited). After four decades in which no money had been made for them or would be, there stepped into the proceedings, in the role of saviour, a major new participant. The Ulster Hall was sold to the city council in 1902 (for rather less than it cost to build), and has remained in public ownership since.

[57] George Benjamin Allen (b. London 1822, d. Brisbane 1897), composer of songs, singer, conductor; trained in Westminster Abbey, vicar choral (bass) Armagh cathedral 1843; conductor of Belfast Classical Harmonists 1856–62; thereafter, posts in London before going to Australia where he ran opera companies which toured widely in the southern hemisphere; after a further spell in Britain he returned to Australia where he died. Leo Kerbusch (b. Düsseldorf 1828), conductor and composer; studied with Spohr and Richter; conductor of Belfast Anacreontic Society 1858–62; thereafter promoted chamber concerts in Belfast; Mus. Doc., TCD 1869; an active member of the Cecilian Society on its formation, his Mass for St Cecilia (1879) was called by Bishop Donnelly 'the first fruit of the Cecilian plant in Ireland'. Edmund Thomas Chipp (b. London 1823, d. Nice 1886), composer, organist, conductor; chorister in Chapel Royal; member of HM private band as violinist 1843–55; organist in several London churches (including St Olave's, Southwark, succeeding Gauntlett) and at Royal Panopticon (succeeding W.T. Best); Mus. Bac., Cantab 1859, Mus. Doc. 1860; organist Ulster Hall, Belfast 1862–6; conductor Belfast Anacreontic Society 1862–4, Classical Harmonists 1862–4, Vocal Union 1864–6; organist Kinnaird Hall, Dundee and St Paul's Edinburgh 1866; organist and master of the choristers, Ely Cathedral 1866–86.

The musical press in nineteenth-century Ireland

MICHAEL MURPHY

> Criticism is out of the question. The audience had merely to record by their applause a succession of triumphs, as they recognized each favourite air, and heard the wonderful productions of Bellini derive a new charm from the artiste.
>
> *Cork Examiner*[1]

This epigraph is taken from a notice of Catherine Hayes' performance in *La Sonnambula* in Cork's Theatre Royal in the middle of the nineteenth century. As a typical encomium it represents most readers' worst impressions of musical criticism in the daily and weekly newspapers of the nineteenth century, which is to say there is no attempt at criticism in any sense of that term, a problem that was repeatedly lamented in the same era.[2] Moreover, it reminds us that the majority of the notices were preoccupied with Anglo-Italian opera, the genre that dominated classical musical life in Ireland for the majority of the century. The operas by Balfe, Wallace, Verdi, Bellini and Rossini *inter alia* were funded by the lessees of the theatres, and were performed by visiting companies from England under the management of an impresario who sometimes may have been one of the singers or conductors. The majority of musical criticism was an adjunct to that model of music making. It was only in the final three decades of the century that this model of musical criticism was eroded notwithstanding the continued popularity of Anglo-Italian opera. Indeed, notices were remarkably similar over the decades. Also, they typically reflected the style of the British press, a pervasive presence in Irish newspapers until the advent of national ideals. It is important to see such notices as a reflection of the 'corporate' vision of the editors and patrons of the newspaper. Consequently we must engage with a range of issues that are at once extra-musical but nevertheless seminal to the production

---

I gratefully acknowledge the funding provided by the College Research Directorate at Mary Immaculate College, University of Limerick for enabling me to engage a research assistant, Ruth Stanley, who undertook much archival work for this chapter. **1** 'Miss Catherine Hayes in Cork', *CE*, 15 March 1850. **2** For discussion on this point see Leanne Langley, 'Music', *Victorian periodicals and Victorian society*, ed. J. Don Vann and Rosemary T. VanArsdel (Aldershot: Scolar Press, 1994), p. 103. Langley's work is a seminal source for work on the musical press in Britain in the nineteenth century. See op. cit. for a bibliographical essay on the topic. See also, Simon McVeigh, 'London newspapers, 1750 to 1800: a checklist and guide for musicologists', *A handbook for studies in 18th-century English music*, 6, ed. M. Burden and I. Cholij (Oxford: Oxford University Press, 1996); see also <www.concertlifeproject.com> (accessed 20 October 2006) the website for the *Concert Life in 19th-Century London Database and Research Project* which has been reported on in Rachel Cowgill, Christina Bashford and Simon McVeigh, 'The concert life in nineteenth-century London database project', in *Nineteenth-century British music studies 2*, ed. Jeremy Dibble and Bennett Zon (Aldershot: Ashgate, 2002), pp 1–12.

and consumption of music. Only in the final three decades of the century, with the advent of the Cecilian movement and the Feis, do we find articles on musical subjects *per se*: church music and musical nationalism respectively.

The sources for the musical press in nineteenth-century Ireland are overwhelming and no systematic bibliographic work has been done in relation to this material. This chapter does not attempt to remedy this lacuna, nor does it present a systematic guide to sources.[3] Rather, I have focused on a number of topics and particular historical moments, a strategy which allows us to see the press conducting its business in a variety of contexts. This thematic approach provides useful points of comparison and contrast both synchronically and diachronically. The topics selected are as follows: the hegemony of Anglo-Italian opera, problems in the standards of musical criticism, inter-press rivalry, Wagner reception, and nationalism. These will be dealt with in a number of case studies such as the 1831 Festival, Catherine Hayes' tour of Ireland, Bayreuth and Carl Rosa's productions of Wagner in Dublin.

THE CRITICS

> ... the living, breathing, erring, human, nameable and addressable individual who writes criticism.
>
> GBS[4]

Irish newspapers did not employ full-time music critics until the final three decades of the century, relying instead on the occasional use of critics when a major event necessitated it, and frequently using generalist reporters who were cheaper to employ. Because of the pervasive practice of anonymity, which was current in all British periodicals and newspapers until the mid century, we cannot identify the majority of these critics.[5] It was only towards the later part of the century that certain individuals can be identified either by name, initials or pseudonym. On occasion critics are identified in other sources: Stanford famously identified Robert Prescott Stewart and Hercules MacDonnell as critics of the first Bayreuth Festival of which I treat in detail below. A less well-known critic such as Frank Sullivan was identified by *Ireland's Eye* as the critic for the *Freeman's Journal* in 1874 (see illustration 13.1).

3 However, Ite O'Donovan is completing a PhD entitled 'Music in Irish periodical literature, 1770–1970' at UCD, and I am grateful to her for sharing her resources with me in preparation for this chapter. Some readily available resources include: <www.irishnewspaperarchives.com> (accessed 10 October 2006) which contains a searchable database of the *Freeman's Journal inter alia*; the website of the National Library of Ireland contains information on the 'Newsplan' project; the *Waterloo directory of Irish newspapers and periodicals, 1800–1900* ed. John S. North (Waterloo, Ontario: North Waterloo Academic Press, 1989) is an important source; the *Irish Times* (29 June 2006) announced plans to digitize and make available its entire microfilm archive by late 2007. 4 George Bernard Shaw, 'On musical criticism', *The World*, 13 June 1894. 5 See Ruth Solie's chapter, '*Macmillan's Magazine* in the Grove years', in her book *Music in other words: Victorian conversations* (Berkeley: University of California Press, 2004) where she examines the issue of anonymity and music criticism with respect to Grove's editorship of *Macmillan's*

For much of the century, the question whether the writer did or did not have the skills to critique musical performance was secondary to the fact that the newspaper had an editorial policy that dictated the style and rhetoric of the review. An analysis of this style over a period of time can demonstrate editorial intervention when the prospect of 'diminished receipts' threatened the manager.[6]

It is important to distinguish two types of writer on musical affairs: the 'critic', an expert who was musically knowledgeable and capable of articulating musical terminology; and the 'penny-a-liner' who would have been assigned to report on circuses, court proceedings as well as opera. The difference between the two is registered in the language and use of musical terminology, and in some cases the critic would announce his credentials by referring to his familiarity with opera houses in Italy and London. When a 'star' came to town, newspapers usually opted for a critic who would typically write an article in advance of their appearance and then follow up with the notices.

Critics had free access to all performances of Italian opera even when ticket prices were inflated for special occasions and when all other patrons had their entitlements suspended. In other words, music criticism was sponsored by the theatre managers and the paying public. Its function was to mediate audience participation in musical life, and therefore musical considerations typically took second place to economic necessity. As tax on advertising revenue was high in the first half of the century, the critic, as an employee of the paper, was under pressure to provide a return on the theatre manager's speculation by way of positive notices. Audiences were frequently reminded of their debt to the theatre managers whose name was kept before the public eye along with that of the state representative, usually the lord lieutenant and his entourage.

THE POLITICS OF THE 'PLAUDITS'

> Praise is lavishly dispensed because the system pays.
> *Irish Builder*[7]

It is rare to find any overt negative criticism of operatic performers, and the use of superlatives was customary. Applause and encores were always recorded to the benefit of the artists and the audience alike: it praised the former for their artistry and the latter for demonstrating their ability to appreciate it. As a mode of social

---

Magazine, a publication which pioneered the abolition of anonymity. *The Wellesley index to Victorian periodicals, 1824–1900*, v, ed. Jean Harris Slingerland (Toronto: Toronto University Press, 1989) enables scholars to identify certain anonymous authors: but one should also consult Eileen M. Curran, 'The Curran index: additions to and corrections of *the Wellesley index to Victorian periodicals*' which is published at <http://victorianresearch.org/curranindex.html> (accessed 7 November 2006) and which is part of the *Victorian Research Web* <http://victorianresearch.org> which is itself a very useful resource for nineteenth-century periodical research. **6** See *CE*, May to November 1855 for a controversy over the boisterous behaviour of the gallery occupants. See also below. **7** 'Our "musical festivals" and "musical" critics', *Irish Builder* [hereafter *IB*], 15 January 1873.

Illustration 13.1: Cartoon of Frank Sullivan, music critic with the *Freeman's Journal*, in *Ireland's Eye*, December 1874, with a short article (p.116) given here below.

'The gentleman who is the subject of our Cartoon this week is well known to many who have never seen him. He has long been connected with *The Freeman's Journal*, and his writings have formed a notable feature in the columns of that newspaper. The position of dramatic, musical, and art critic, which he now occupies, is one which his experience, knowledge, and artistic tastes eminently qualify him to fill. Mr. Sullivan's humorous and satirical reports of Police Court proceedings used to attract much attention. Ridicule is a powerful weapon, when directed against the minor failings of humanity, and Mr. Sullivan always wielded it with good effect.'

flattery, reporting on applause was an important part of the currency of the musical economy because the notices reassured the middle and upper classes of their status in society, a condition that both necessitated their presence at such social luxuries as opera and on which the entire enterprise depended.

Throughout the century one finds more thoughtful and critical commentaries in contemporary journals whose writers were not under pressure to meet frequent deadlines, and, perhaps more significantly, whose editors did not rely on advertising from the impresarios who staged Italian opera. Early nineteenth-century journals typically avoided the criticism of opera, opting instead for analysis of instrumental works by Irish composers. The *Monthly Museum* consistently reviewed new music by Irish composers such as Stevenson, Blewitt, Cooke and Bishop who were often subjected to 'a sedulous examination.'[8] While that journal occasionally commented on performances or events, it concerned itself primarily with giving advice to composers on their most recent works. The critic was knowledgeable and commented on such detail as modulations, enharmonic changes, dissonances, and typically deplored such solecisms as consecutive parallel fifths. Clearly, this magazine set a high standard and established such a demand for criticism that omission from its purview was a fate worse than the dreaded 'sedulous examination' itself.[9] The tradition of analytical scrutiny was continued by the *Dublin Magazine* as evidenced in its review of two symphonies by Paul Alday. While the critic was happy to acknowledge the beauties and ideas in the work, the predominant criterion was academic correctness, and praise was reserved for those passages that evinced 'a deep knowledge of science' and 'a thorough knowledge of theory'.[10] Typically, musical composition was treated as a craft rather than an art.

As the newspaper industry gathered pace in Ireland in the late nineteenth century, the quality of material was often sacrificed to the exigencies of providing copy, and it is not surprising, therefore, that problems multiplied in the standard of music criticism. However, these sins did not go unnoticed or unpunished by professional journalists. One of the most important trade journals, the *Irish Builder: Architectural, Archaeological, Engineering, Sanitary, Arts and Handicrafts*, took a tough stance on problems in contemporary music criticism in the 1870s. In the first of two substantial articles on musical criticism it asked if there was 'such a thing as independent dramatic or theatrical criticism, or aught else in this line, by the Press of Dublin?'[11] The answer was in the negative as the majority of 'fulsome notices' were written 'to order' and 'consequently bad, good, and middling singing and acting come in for systematic praise.' In condemning these 'slap-dash' notices as 'dishonest, shameful, utterly unworthy, and a scandal to

---

8 See the review of Cooke's 'Sonata Fugata' in *Monthly Museum*, November 1813, 164, quoted in Ita Hogan, *Anglo-Irish music, 1780–1830* (Cork: Cork University Press, 1966), p. 118.   **9** See for example *Monthly Museum*, January 1814, 230. I am grateful to Ite O'Donovan for drawing this to my attention. **10** *Dublin Magazine*, February 1820, quoted in Hogan, *Anglo-Irish music*, p. 119.   **11** 'Our "musical festivals" and "musical" critics', *IB*, 15 January 1873, and continued in 15 February 1873.

journalism and Ireland' it identified the economic imperative that motivated these 'unscrupulous' penny-a-liners who knew that an impresario was more likely to pay for advertising space on Monday if his investment received fulsome praise on Saturday. The practice of critics hobnobbing with 'stars' was also exposed, as were the double standards of those critics who damned performers privately while extolling them publicly. In the second article under that title, the *Irish Builder* exposed some of the other immoral tricks of the trade: the '*sub silentio* move' was explained whereby some performers were ignored by the press because they had offended the critical fraternity.[12] Also, the practice of critics reviewing performances that they had not attended seemed to be widespread, and the *Irish Builder* cited four recent examples. It claimed that only one Dublin newspaper had a *bona fide* music critic, and that other critiques were supplied by penny-a-liners or 'clippers' i.e. a sub-editor who clipped extracts from other sources so as to 'enliven and diversify the contents of their own papers.'[13] The *Irish Builder* hoped that by exposing such shameful practices the dailies would adhere to higher standards. (I shall return to this issue below.)

INTER-PRESS RIVALRY DURING THE 'GRAND MUSICAL FESTIVAL'

The Triumph of Faith is a splendid composition.
Freeman's Journal[14]

The Triumph of Faith may be fairly esteemed a failure.
Dublin Evening Mail[15]

While political polemics between newspapers is a *sine qua non* of nineteenth-century Irish history,[16] antagonism between newspapers could manifest itself in any quarter, and the musical columns were not innocent of such inter-press rivalry. The 'Dublin First Grand Musical Festival for the Benefit of the Mendicity Association and Sick and Indigent Roomkeepers' Society' generated much controversy in the Dublin press.[17] Although the Festival (held between 29 August and 5 September 1831) is chiefly remembered today for the presence of Paganini and Dragonetti, the inter-press rivalry it generated is worthy of the attention of music historians.

12 *IB*, 15 February 1873, 58. For a specific instance of the '*sub silentio* move' exposed see 'Madame Daviez – music and criticism', *IB*, 1 March 1873, 61.   13 'A Nut for Figaro', *IB*, 1 February 1873, 43: this article demonstrated how its own material had been recently plagiarized by *Figaro*.   14 'The Dublin Musical Festival', *FJ*, 1 September 1831.   15 'Musical festival', *DEM*, 2 September 1831.   16 See Maire-Louise Legg, *Newspapers and nationalism: the provincial press, 1850–1892* (Dublin: Four Courts Press, 1998).   17 For details of its organisation see Derek Collins, 'Music in Dublin, 1800–1848', in *To talent alone: the Royal Irish Academy of Music, 1848–1998*, ed. Richard Pine and Charles Acton (Dublin: Gill & Macmillan, 1998), pp 15–16. I am grateful to Ita Beausang for drawing my attention to the following two sources: *Dublin musical festival: programme, books of the words etc the first Dublin musical festival with ms. notes by Sir George T. Smart* (Dublin: W. Underwood, 1831) which is in the British

The *Freeman's Journal* offered its full support to the festival and affected to take the high moral ground in the attendant 'politico-religious controversy' by vilifying 'certain journals' who bickered over 'whether this lord or that earl is on the committee' or whether it was appropriate to have sacred works performed in a secular venue.[18] Its main target, the *Dublin Evening Mail*, which it styled 'the *soi-disant* organ of the *beau monde*', continued to rant against the festival even after it had ended and was declared a success by all other sources.[19] Notwithstanding the impressive forces mustered for the occasion – an orchestra of 300, the Dublin Festival Choral Society, the Liverpool Choral Society, and the choirs of the principal Cathedrals in Ireland, conducted by such notables as George Smart and Ferdinand Ries – the *Freeman's Journal* nevertheless chided the organising committee for not having engaged expert international singers: its main argument was that no expense should have been spared to ensure the quality of the performances. While reminding readers of its patriotism through its encouragement of 'native talent', the *Freeman's Journal* regretted that none of the great vocalists of the day were engaged (e.g. Pasta, Malibran, La Blache), and consequently that justice would not be done to the 'sublime productions of genius' in the programme by Handel, Mozart, Haydn, Beethoven and Ries.[20] It was for this reason that the *Freeman's Journal* claimed that it was 'lunacy' to engage Paganini, the 'lion of the cat-gut scrapers', at a cost of 1000*l*.[21] However, as with the English press which had initially vilified Paganini, the *Freeman's Journal* executed a sudden U-turn and lauded the Italian virtuoso immediately after his first concert. Subsequently, the reception of the core sacred works was eclipsed by the mania for Paganini.

In the early stages of the festival the initial commitment of the *Freeman's Journal* to musical standards was reflected in the detail and quality of the notices of the performances. The style of these notices was singularly poetic, and might be said to be mimetic of the sublime nature and 'mighty grandeur' of the music itself. In one particular notice of Ries' *The Triumph of Faith* the critic detailed how the 'spirit of the listener becomes almost celestialised [*sic*] beneath its influence ... it is a moment before you recover from the trance of ecstasy'.[22] All doubts about the success of the festival were dispelled in this review. But the success was not only musical; it had political implications also. The notice

Library (C.61.g.8.); and a volume of newspaper cuttings about the festival in the National Library of Ireland. It was not the 'first' such festival, as the lord mayor and Dublin Corporation had organized a 'Dublin Grand Musical Festival' in 1814. **18** 'The Musical Festival', *FJ*, 10 August 1831, 2. See also the 'Musical Festival; to the Editor of the *Freeman's Journal*', *FJ*, 29 August 1831, 3. **19** 'The Musical Festival', *FJ*, 8 September 1831. **20** These included Mozart's arrangement of *Messiah*, extracts from *Jeptha*, *The Mount of Olives* and *The Creation*, and the first performance in the United Kingdom of *The Triumph of Faith* by Ferdinand Ries which was composed for the Lower Rhine musical festivals. It seems that the exhortations by the *Freeman's Journal* were taken seriously by the committee as on the next day the usual front-page advertisement contained an extra line: 'The Committee are in treaty with several other principal Vocalists, whose names will speedily appear.', 'Dublin First Grand Musical Festival' [advertisement], *FJ*, 11 August 1831, 1. **21** 'Theatrical Mems [*sic*]', *FJ*, 25 August 1831, 3. **22** 'The Dublin Musical Festival', *FJ*, 1 September 1831.

concludes with a patriotic evocation of 'the days of her [Ireland's] ancient glory' when she was proverbially 'the home of the minstrel, and nurse of song'. This is of course a veiled reference to detriment caused by the Union, a frequent theme in the reviews of the festival, a topic to which I will return subsequently.

As the days passed, more and more newsprint was devoted to Paganini in inverse proportion to the space allotted to the sacred works. The notice of his first concert dispelled the antipathy that had hitherto preceded his actual appearance: his valetudinarian 'physical configuration' was described in detail, and it was intimated that his wizadry was related to his otherworldly configuration. (Even though the *Freeman's Journal* was quick to criticize other papers that plagiarized its own political reports, that particular pen portrait was itself reprinted verbatim and unacknowledged from a contemporary English newspaper.[23]) Moreover, initial concerns about the appropriateness of mixing the sacred and the secular evaporated when Paganini expressed his desire to support the Festival by performing at one of the oratorio concerts – up to that point sacred and secular concerts were held on separate days, but Paganini interspersed his solos between movements of *The Creation*. Instead of taking offence at this daring departure from protocol, the critic employed imagery from Greek myth and quotations from Byron in an attempt to capture the magic of his 'spell-fraught bow'.[24] By the end of the festival not only had the *Freeman's Journal* defended Paganini from vitriolic attacks in the English press,[25] it even attempted to draw parallels between Paganini's art and Irish folk music: 'There is in some of his productions that plaintive sweetness and that luxurious strain of melancholy so peculiar to Irish melody'.[26] The *Freeman's Journal* finally admitted to sacrificing 'minute notice' of the oratorios to make room for eulogizing the 'modern Orpheus'. The standard of criticism had declined in direct proportion to the Paganini mania.

If the *Freeman's Journal* supported the Festival for political reasons, i.e. that the Hudson brothers, who were staunch supporters of O'Connell, were on the organizing committee, the *Dublin Evening Mail*, which was virulently anti-Catholic, initially attacked the enterprise on religious grounds. After quoting at length from a sermon by 'that most faithful servant of God, the Rev. John Newton', in which the author condemned the decline in 'the tastes and desires of men', referring to Ries' *The Triumph of Faith* in particular, the *Dublin Evening Mail* added its voice to the moralizing and declared that Ries' work was 'profane' and 'derogatory to God's glory'.[27] Warming to his subject, the critic then intimated that the day of judgment was at hand, and that any citizen of Dublin who would attend such a base entertainment when they should instead be preparing their souls to meet God was guilty of 'insanity'. In a subsequent article the

---

[23] Compare 'The Dublin Musical Festival', *FJ*, 31 August 1831, 3, with the extract from an unidentified Liverpool newspaper quoted in John Sugden, *Paganini: The illustrated lives of the great composers* (London: Omnibus Press, 1980), p. 103.   [24] 'The Dublin Musical Festival', *FJ*, 3 September 1831.   [25] 'Birmingham morality on Paganini's prices', *FJ*, 31 August 1831, 4.   [26] 'The Dublin Musical Festival', *FJ*, 5 September 1831.   [27] 'The First Grand Musical Festival', *DEM*, 24 August 1831, 4.

Dublin Evening Mail defended itself against the charge of being a 'foe' of both music and public charity, and vilified the 'nameless and disreputable' persons on the organising committee, their unaccountability, their poor decision making, their squandering of money, etc.[28] While a derogatory tone pervaded any mention of the organizational logistics (from the 'conduct of the ruffians who were placed as door-keepers' to the lack of ventilation), high praise was reserved for individual performers, notably Dragonetti. Remarkably, however, the *Dublin Evening Mail* declared itself lost for words when it came to praising Paganini, and instead reproduced a eulogy from one of the morning papers, citing it as an example of 'fine' writing worthy of Lady Morgan. Having condescended to worship the 'Devil riding upon a *fiddle-stick*', it further criticized the oratorio by the 'obscure' Ries, which it had nick-named the '*Triumph of Dullness*'. This time its fault was that it was a failure as a work of art and could not compare with the 'inexhaustible beauties of the established writers, the *Classics*', namely Haydn, Mozart and Beethoven, in particular the latter's *The Mount of Olives* which should have been the centrepiece of the festival in its opinion.[29] Despite the various *ad hominem* attacks and repeated condemnation of the festival, the writer was an able music critic and wrote engagingly on the purely musical features of the various works, especially *The Creation*.[30]

Perhaps the *Dublin Evening Mail* was correct in its assertion that Paganini was the reason for the festival's popular success. Ultimately, it was the work of another Italian, Bellini, whose *Norma* and *La Sonnambula*, both composed in that year, which had a greater impact on Irish musical life for the next fifty years when 'absolute' music took a distant second place to opera in the public mind.

THE 'TWIN CULTURES' OF MUSIC AND MUSICAL CRITICISM

> It may be, perhaps, that Beethoven sometimes did not understand his own thoughts; or it may be that sometimes there was really nothing in them to understand ...
>
> *Dublin Evening Mail*[31]

Dahlhaus' notion of the 'twin cultures of music', Franco-Italian opera on the one hand and German instrumental music on the other, specifies 'a dichotomy [which] extended to the very roots of the nineteenth-century concept of music, far transcending differences of genre or national style.'[32] Time and again that dichotomy was reinforced in the Irish musical press.

In 1841 the *Dublin University Magazine* published an extensive theoretical essay on 'modern scientific music' by which the author meant the works of

28 'The Musical Festival', *DEM*, 31 August 1831, 3.   **29** 'Musical festival', *DEM*, 2 September 1831, 3.
30 'The Musical Festival', *DEM*, 5 September 1831.   **31** 'Philharmonic Society', *DEM*, 21 January 1856.
32 Carl Dahlhaus, *Nineteenth-century music*, trans J. Bradford Robinson (Berkeley: University of California Press, 1989), p. 13.

Mozart, Spohr and Weber.[33] The article was an appeal for greater representation of classical music in contemporary concert programmes. The Antient Concert Societies of Dublin and Cork were the main vehicles for this genre, the reviews of which tended to be laudatory of their efforts to improve musical taste.[34] Good intentions, however, were no match for social entertainment, and implicit in nearly all music criticism was the popularity of the secular (opera and ballads) over the sacred. In a notice of Haydn's *The Seasons* performed by Cork's Antient Concert Society in 1850, the *Cork Examiner* argued that 'grandeur and majesty become tiresome in a short time' and 'ordinary mortals' long for 'the feelings of the heart'.[35] Ironically, *The Seasons* was the exception that proved the rule because 'the music was light, agreeable, and much diversified'. Five years later the *Freeman's Journal* disapproved of Lindpaintner's oratorio *The Widow of Nain* which was performed by the Dublin Antient Concert Society while nevertheless praising 'the concert [which] was one calculated to do much to increase the growing taste for the works of the great composers which we are happy to find is rising amongst us.'[36] The Viennese masters and Mendelssohn were again elevated as the artistic *ne plus ultra* of musical taste.

The first Irish performance of Beethoven's 'Grand Choral Sinfonia' on 18 January 1856 by the Dublin Philharmonic Society under the direction of Henry Bussell brought the issue of instrumental music into sharp focus.[37] The critics employed a variety of techniques to variously cajole and chastise the audience into appreciating high-quality instrumental music. The *Freeman's Journal*, while praising the performance, all but apologized for the singularity of the work. While the well-worn excuse of the composer's deafness was proffered as the chief cause for its defects, the reader was assured that the 'wayward, eccentric, and curiously beautiful burden' of the music exhibited 'all the science' of modern instrumentation.[38] The critic in the *Saunders' Newsletter* brought some historical perspective to his notice by recounting the London Philharmonic's rejection of the work on account of its 'unintelligibility', a strategy employed to praise Bussell and the 'capabilities' of the Dublin orchestra. He then marshalled a passage from Moscheles' translation of Anton Schindler's biography of Beethoven in explicating the meaning of the work.[39] By contrast, the critic for the *Dublin Evening Mail* scorned the 'upper classes' of Dublin for their ignorance and intolerance of instrumental music, and confronted them with the fact that, while a tuneful ballad or chorus would elicit an *encore*, instrumental music was

33 'An apology for harmony', *Dublin University Magazine* [hereafter *DUM*], 17 (May 1841), 570–84. The *DUM* devoted relatively little attention to musical matters apart from sporadic reviews of recent compositions, and no notices of Italian opera.   34 See Paul Rodmell's chapter in this volume.   35 'Antient Concert', *CE*, 5 April 1850.   36 'Antient Concert Society', *FJ*, 15 December 1855.   37 This was the Second Grand Concert of the season and was held in the Concert Rooms in Great Brunswick Street (see Paul Rodmell's chapter in this volume for that venue). It is worth noting that with regard to the necessary choral and orchestra forces, Ireland could have had a performance of Beethoven's Ninth as early as 1831 when Ries, Beethoven's champion in London, came to Dublin for the Grand Musical Festival. On that occasion, of course, all the choral works were sacred.   38 'Dublin Philharmonic Society', *FJ*, 19 January 1856.   39 'Philharmonic Society', *SN*, 19 January 1856, 2.

habitually received with 'weariness and inattention'.[40] However, he noted that in this instance the 'instrumental dulness [*sic*]' commonly associated with symphonies was relieved by the unique nature of the Ninth, a fact which accounted for the sustained attention of the audience on this occasion. Dispensing with the rhetoric of persuasion, the critic took for granted the greatness of this 'very powerful work' and asserted the need for careful study and multiple opportunities of hearing it if one were to understand it. That particular notice could only have been written by an independent and authoritative critic who did not baulk at annoying his readers and editor alike. As we shall see presently, he overstepped the mark with the claim that the '"rank, beauty and fashion" would rather hear the noisiest and most commonplace polka by Jullien than the best symphony which has ever been conceived by genius.' This was a particularly pointed reference to Jullien because over the next five days that charismatic maestro presented a series of 'Grand Vocal and Orchestral Concerts' in the Rotunda.[41]

The light 'classical' concert, modelled with aplomb by Jullien, had become a firm favourite in the Dublin musical and social calendar by this time.[42] Jullien's programmes contained solo vocal items, in addition to arrangements of *bel canto* favourites, alongside his own dance suites such as the programmatic quadrille, *The Fall of Sebastopol*. It was in this context that 'classical' works, usually the slow movements from symphonies by Beethoven, Haydn and Mendelssohn, were presented, but as the *Cork Examiner* had commented in the previous year, they were 'selected with a view to popularity rather than to the comprehension of classic music.'[43] A 'Grand Concert' of Jullien's was first and foremost a social event that had more in common with the opera business than with well-intentioned attempts at promulgating the Austro-German canon of instrumental music.

Just how important Jullien's presence was in Dublin can be estimated from the eulogistic tone, detailed content and increased length of the press notices whenever he appeared. The *Freeman's Journal*, for example, extended effusive welcome to the 'talismanic' Jullien while offering fawning gratitude to the gentry for coming out of their comfortable homes in the inclement winter weather.[44] On the same day, 23 January, the *Saunders' Newsletter* proffered a detailed account of Jullien's celebrated quadrille, and lavished abundant praise on the musicians and audience alike.[45] Most remarkable of all was the review in the *Dublin Evening Mail* which reproduced verbatim extracts from the notices in both the *Freeman's Journal* and the *Saunders' Newsletter* of the same date.[46] Clearly, editorial intervention replaced the critic (see above) with a 'clipper' probably due

---

40 'Philharmonic Society', *DEM*, 21 January 1856, 3. 41 The Round Room, Rotunda, Dublin, 22–26 January 1856. The advertisements highlighted the difference between his considerable orchestral resources and the more usual substitution of a piano for the orchestral part. See, for example, *FJ*, 18 January 1856, 1. 42 For details of Jullien's previous visits to Ireland see Derek Collins, 'Music in Dublin', pp 19–20. 43 'M. Jullien's Concert', *CE*, 2 March 1855, 2. 44 'Music &c.', *FJ*, 21–28 January 1856. 45 'M. Jullien's Grand Concerts', *SN*, 23 January 1856, 2. 46 'Mons. Jullien's Concerts', *DEM*, 23 January 1856, 3.

to the pressure from Jullien, not to mention complaints from some of Dublin's 'rank, beauty and fashion'. It seems most likely that the *Dublin Evening Mail* waited to see what its contemporaries had to say and then followed suit. It was into this climate that the *Irish Times* launched its first salvo at its rivals three years later.

HIGH STANDARDS

> ... we shall not indulge in the vague and stereotyped panegyrics at present so much in vogue; panegyrics that neither deceive the reader nor benefit the artist, but have only the effect of retarding the public appreciation of works of real merit.
>
> *Irish Times*[47]

The editorial in the first edition of the *Irish Times* (just quoted), committed the paper to providing quality notices on the creative arts. A reader familiar with the writings of Leigh Hunt or another reformer might have hoped for criticism in the best sense of that word.[48] Unfortunately, the first review in the first edition confined itself to stating the obvious: 'Italian Opera and its leading artistes continue to exercise an increasing powerful influence upon all classes of the citizens'.[49] While subsequent articles maintained the high moral tone of the first editorial, little intellectual effort was expended over the rest of that very busy musical year.[50] A comparative study of the *Irish Times* and the *Freeman's Journal* shows they both said the same thing but with a different accent.[51] With reference to Verdi's *Macbeth*, the *Irish Times* complained about the 'noisy instrumentation', the 'superabundance of chorussing [sic], some of which is indifferent' and the absence of 'sweet melody', while the *Freeman's Journal* engaged with the dramatic nature of the music itself, and indicated that the audience acknowledged 'that the intense dramatic interest of Shakespeare's tragedy was now conveyed through a medium which more powerfully than words pourtrayed [sic] the workings of human passions.' By contrast the *Irish Times*' review of the final performance of *Macbeth* merely complimented the singers who 'sustained' their parts with their 'usual talent', with most attention given to the presence of the lord lieutenant and the Countess of Eglinton, and the embarrassing uproar in the

---

[47] 'Editorial', *IT*, 29 March 1859, 2. [48] See Theodore Fenner, *Leigh Hunt and opera criticism: the 'Examiner' years, 1808–1821* (Lawrence: University Press of Kansas, 1972). [49] 'Italian opera', *IT*, 29 March 1859, 4. [50] There were at least 32 operatic nights between March, April, August, and October in the Theatre Royal. In addition, all the 'stars' *inter alia* Lind, Garcia, Mario, Grisi and Titiens sang with the Philharmonic Society in the Antient Concert rooms. Moreover, the season boasted a number of Irish premieres including Verdi's *Macbeth* on 30 March and Flotow's *Martha* on 9 April. And on 27 October Lind performed for the benefit of Mercer's Hospital and the Irish Musical Fund Society. See R. M. Levey and J. O'Rorke, *Annals of the Theatre Royal, Dublin* (Dublin: Joseph Dollard, 1880), 201. [51] Compare for example the notice of Verdi's *Macbeth* in 'Italian opera', *IT*, 31 March 1859, and 'The Italian opera', *FJ*, 31 March 1859.

gallery.[52] Equally disappointing was the cursory coverage given to a performance in May of that year of the 'Kreutzer' sonata which was described as 'Beethoven's lovely sonata for piano-forte and violin ... a work so replete with melody ... as to be the delight of all lovers of classical music.'[53] The performance itself drew a mere mention of the 'celebrated violinist Herr Joachim, and the equally famous Mons. Halle'.[54] The lack of interest in instrumental music is indicated in the same article which announced a London piano recital containing works by Bach, Beethoven, Hummel, Mendelssohn, and 'the gifted but eccentric Chopin.' As in other papers, sub-editors in the *Irish Times* were happy to cut and paste from the English newspapers, and consequently sustained some of Davison's worst blunders.[55]

The quality of the musical coverage in the *Irish Times* varied over the years. For example, the initial years of the *Irish Times* featured an article every other day entitled 'The Drama, Music &c' (later expanded to 'Dramatic, Musical, and Literary' on 21 April 1859). In addition to announcing local musical events, often repeating the advertisements on the front page, a lot of space was devoted to musical news from London. One was also likely to find news and gossip about the private lives of popular singers and composers. Mention was also made of recent musical publications on the continent, and concerts and festivals in European centres. It occasionally included reviews of performances, often quoting from foreign newspapers (e.g. *Gazette Musicale*). After an absence of some years it was revived and greatly extended by 1875 when it appeared under the heading 'Gossip' and was penned by someone styling himself 'Faust'. In addition to that informal and intriguing column, the *Irish Times* also engaged an anonymous expert music critic who reviewed performances. His reviews of sacred music, no less than opera or symphonies, were scholarly, technically detailed, and contained quotations from historical texts, for example biographical information on Bach and Beethoven.[56]

A number of factors converged to elevate standards of criticism at this time: the vigilance of the *Irish Builder*, the Royal Irish Academy of Music in its contribution to the increase in musical literacy and theoretical and historical knowledge; and we should also note Hugh Oram's claim that theatrical criticism in Dublin was revolutionized by Bram Stoker's notice in the *Dublin Morning Mail* of *She Stoops to Conquer* which was staged on the opening night of the Gaiety Theatre on 27 November 1871.[57] However, despite these developments, one of the most seminal influences on critical standards was the advent of Wagner's music in Ireland.

---

52 'Italian opera', *IT*, 7 April 1859, 2.   53 'Dramatic, Musical, and Literary', *IT*, 24 May 1859, 4.
54 Ibid.   55 J.W. Davison was music critic for *The Times* and *Musical World*. See Charles Reid, *The music monster: a biography of James William Davison, music critic of 'The Times' of London, 1846–78, with excerpts from his critical writings* (London: Quartet Books, 1984).   56 See, for example, 'Music in Dublin churches', *IT*, 7 August 1877.   57 See Hugh Oram, *The newspaper book: a history of newspapers in Ireland, 1649–1983* (Dublin: MO Books, 1983), p. 75.

CRITICISM OF THE MUSIC OF THE FUTURE

> Ireland has not reached the Wagnerian stage yet: I have been there and I know.
>
> GBS[58]

When *Lohengrin* was performed in Dublin in October 1875 the dailies recorded the failure of the reception despite the quality of the performance.[59] The *Irish Times* began its notice by quoting one of the 'denizens of the top gallery' who shouted for all to hear 'We don't like Wagner, and we don't want him!'[60] The critic, however, refused to make any value judgments, preferring instead to narrate the libretto and comment on the performance. By contrast, the *Freeman's Journal* offered its own reasons why Wagner was too difficult for the audience, and concluded in a tone that was to characterize its attitude to Wagner for years to come: 'On the whole, we think this generation will rest satisfied with the music of the past, and leave Wagner willingly to posterity'.[61] Notwithstanding the various shadings of reticence and antipathy to Wagner among the public and the press, a substantial body of critical material emerged over the concluding decades of the century and brought about a sea change in Wagner reception and musical criticism in Ireland.[62]

While the Bayreuth Festival was widely reported in the Irish dailies, most of the articles, of variable length and quality, were reproduced from English and continental papers.[63] However, it would be a mistake to assume that the Irish critical reception merely recycled foreign opinion. The independence from British influence of the Irish critical reception is signalled by Robert Prescott Stewart's assertion that 'Wagner is not so bad as the English press will have him, nor so good as his own ... pretend to consider him'.[64]

Thus one could divide the 1876 reportage into two categories: the many second-hand social and gossip articles that reported on the doings of Wagner and the nobility on the one hand, and the few lengthy music criticisms by Irish writers on the other.[65] Predictably, pro- and anti-Wagnerian trends were immediately

---

[58] George Bernard Shaw, 'Voices and Registers', *The Star*, 11 October 1889.   [59] 11 October 1875, the Royal Italian Opera under Julius Benedict in the Theatre Royal, in a season that featured *Rigoletto*, *Don Giovanni*, Gounod's *Faust*, *inter alia*.   [60] 'Theatre Royal – *Lohengrin*', *IT*, 21 October 1875.   [61] 'Wagner's new opera', *FJ*, 12 October 1875.   [62] See Joachim Fischer's chapter in this volume for an exploration of Wagnerism in Ireland in the wider literary, cultural and political contexts.   [63] For example, on 17 August 1876 the same one-sentence bulletin reporting the presence of County Andrassy appeared in the *CE* and *FJ*; similarly, the *FJ* (18 August) and *Limerick Chronicle* (19 August) carried the same brief report on the performance of *Siegfried*. By contrast a lengthy summary of *The Ring* originating in the *Daily News* entitled 'The Wagner Festival at Bayreuth' appeared in the *DE* and *FJ* on 18 August and again in the *CE* on 22 August 1876. The *DE* carried two further articles, one, unattributed, on 22 August and another on 25 August reproduced from *The Times* which was penned by Davison; see Reid, *The music monster*, pp 114 and 202–4 for extracts from that article (the article on 22 August was probably taken from Davison also judging from the style and content).   [64] Letter of 19 September 1876 to Vignoles in O.J. Vignoles, *Memoir of Sir Robert P. Stewart* (Dublin: Hodges, Figgis, 1898), p. 117, quoted in Lisa Parker, 'Robert Prescott Stewart (1824–1894): an assessment of his compositions and contribution to musical life in Dublin', MA diss. (National University of Ireland, Maynooth, 2000), p. 67.   [65] The *CE*'s reportage

apparent. Stanford mentioned Robert Prescott Stewart and Hercules MacDonnell, both Wagnerians, writing in the *Daily Express* and the *Irish Times* respectively.[66] However, Stanford greatly exaggerated the quality and significance of MacDonnell's article claiming it was 'far the best which appeared; scholarly, brilliant, and unbiassed [sic].'[67] As Wagnerian criticism goes, MacDonnell's article is disappointing as it provided little more than a scene-by-scene summary of the 'wild, strange, legendary drama', in addition to some vacuous speculation as to how Wagner might have felt about the success of the whole enterprise.[68] And while Stanford mentions that MacDonnell 'put his clever finger on the weak spot of the work, when he said that the underlying mischief was the composer being his own librettist'[69] there is no indication of any negativity in his *Irish Times* article. Stewart's article, on the other hand, was scholarly in its attention to the musical score, giving many details of orchestration, harmony, texture and staging.[70] Stewart defended Wagner against the charge of dispensing with melody by pointing out passages such as the love scene between Sieglinde and Siegmund. And with a characteristic sense of civic duty, he was aware that he was writing for a home audience, and while not patronising his readers' lack of knowledge, he wrote in a familiar style: for example, he criticized the 'ugly, droning, utterly unvocal stuff, against which both my ears rebelled, albeit long trained to dissonance by a life devoted to teaching!'

Stanford's commendations of MacDonnell's and Stewart's articles noted that they were 'Written far away from the clash of party, and the intrigues of the foreign stage'.[71] While undoubtedly invoking the 'ultra-Tory critics', Davison, Joseph Bennett of the *Telegraph* and Charles Lewis Gruneison of the *Athenaeum*,[72] this is also a veiled reference to the *Freeman's Journal*. If in 1875 the *Freeman's Journal* played to the gallery, as it were, in 1876 the anti-Wagnerian line was championed by the Paris correspondent in his regular column, 'Continental Gossip', wherein he took his cue from 'one of the most pungent Parisian critics', Albert Wolf, who wrote for the *Figaro*.[73]

The next body of Wagner criticism were the notices of Carl Rosa's productions of *The Flying Dutchman* in 1877. In an unsigned article, which was presumably by MacDonnell (judging by the style) the summary of the drama was succeeded by some observations on Wagner's significance for musical taste.[74] The rest of the article attempted to educate the reader on the terminology associated with the 'Wagnerian school': the role of the music in conveying the drama, the leitmotif,

---

appeared under the general heading 'Latest Telegrams' which carried brief items from all over the world. **66** C.V. Stanford, *Pages from an unwritten diary* (London: Edward Arnold, 1914), p. 50, 169–70; and Stanford, *Interludes, records and reflections* (London: John Murray, 1922), pp 143–4. **67** Stanford, *Interludes*, p. 144. **68** MacDonnell's unsigned article, 'The Wagner Festival at Bayreuth', was published in two instalments in *IT* on 21 and 24 August 1876. **69** Stanford, *Pages*, p. 169. **70** Stewart's unsigned article, 'The Wagner Festival', appeared in three instalments in *DE* on 1, 2 and 4 September 1876. **71** Stanford, *Pages*, p. 50. **72** See Stanford, *Interludes*, pp 143–4 where he describes George Osborne defending Wagner against those named critics during the interval at the festival. **73** 'Continental Gossip: A word about Wagner', *FJ*, 24 August 1876. **74** 'Gaiety Theatre – English operas: *The Flying Dutchman*', *IT*, 10 August 1877.

the 'music of the future', the summative meaning of the overture, chromaticism etc. It would seem that this was necessary as the 'audience did not appear exactly to comprehend its scope or meaning'. The *Freeman's Journal* ran an equally long article on the same date.[75] Despite the customary ambivalence, high praise was forthcoming for the melodic beauty of the music, reminiscent of Weber and Rossini.

In 1878 Carl Rosa returned for another short season which again featured *The Flying Dutchman*. The inclusion of Wagner in the programme drew a substantial notice from the *Irish Times* but this time signed by 'Faust' (who was not MacDonnell), and, moreover, not under the heading 'Gossip'. The article is notable for its equivocation: although Wagner's music will never be as 'popularised' as Italian opera, one cannot deny the 'many remarkable beauties' in his music, and 'Without any profession of faith in the composer or his school ... there is ample evidence of surpassing ability'.[76] And while 'Faust' conversed on Wagner's theories he rather supposed that producing Wagner in Ireland did not represent value for money for the 'great paying public' who '[do] not care to go deeply into recondite theories of music' but who rather '[want] to be amused, not enlightened – diverted, not instructed.' Once again, the traditional dichotomy between the sublime and the diversionary was reinforced. Significantly, 'Faust' turned to a meditation on the nature of music criticism, and in particular the position of the critic *vis-à-vis* the public:

> From one point of view there is no more misleading pronouncement than to say that the critic who "knows what pleases himself and says so," is competent enough to judge of a great musical work. [...] But there is a higher function belonging to the office of a critic, and that may best be filled when one invites attention to such works as that which now claims our notice.

But for 'Faust' *The Flying Dutchman* was the culmination of Wagner's 'best period' after which

> he allowed himself to wander in the mazes of a fantastic and extravagant aestheticism which like all exaggerations, overshot the mark, and met the fate of him who held with too rash and daring a hand the reins which controlled the horses of the sun.

Having thus established the limits of Wagner's art, 'Faust' continued with unreserved praise for *The Flying Dutchman*.

By contrast the *Freeman's Journal* had nothing to say about this production of Wagner beyond listing the main performers and concluding with an apology: 'Pressure on our space prevents our noticing the merits of the performance.'[77] The

---

75 'English Operas', *FJ*, 10 August 1877.   **76** 'Theatre Royal – English operas', *IT*, 29 April 1878.
77 'English opera at the Royal', *FJ*, 27 April 1878.

pressure seemed to be coming from the Rathmines Ladies' Association whose 'public entertainments' were noticed in some detail beneath the Wagner item.

In the 1880s Wagner's presence was invoked by those who sought to improve musical taste in Ireland. The journal *Hibernia*, in the spirit of the *Irish Builder*, took up the challenge to the daily press as it lamented the impoverished repertoire and the equally impoverished public discourse on musical matters. The economic relationship between musical taste and imported opera was explicitly stated: 'Impressarii cannot and will not risk the experiment of teaching classical music at cheap prices, when they know that a profitable return cannot be expected.'[78] The omnipresence of Anglo-Italian opera was contrasted with the dearth of Austro-Germanic symphonies: the 'public vastly prefers Balfe and Wallace to Beethoven and Wagner' not for 'patriotic considerations or prejudices' but because 'The best music, like everything else, can only be got by paying for it, and we are not musical in the highest sense because we are poor.'[79] The second of these articles hoped that Carl Rosa would return and perform Wagner's music dramas, and thereby 'do much to compensate for the comparative dearth of artistic musical instruction in our city, and the utter absence of progress in our musical ideas and knowledge.'[80] The writer continued with an eloquent discourse on the 'twin cultures' and the nature of aesthetic value judgments:

> It is not a question of taste to like or dislike the *Flying Dutchman*. The grave reasons we have been laying down as art principles are conclusive in its favour, and in any case time will tell the truth, just as it has settled the relative merits of Rossini [and] Beethoven [...] In short, this certainty of final judgment, recognised as true by the awakened and developed faculties of all mankind, shows very plainly that there is no such thing as difference of taste in such matters, save in so far as there is the question of truth or falsehood, light or darkness, clearness of perfection, or the misty haziness of error.[81]

While musical education is ultimately blamed for the aesthetic lacunae in Ireland, these comments implicitly indict the press, the vehicle of the bourgeoisie, the 'taste-bearing stratum' to use Dahlhaus' phrase.

However, things did improve, Carl Rosa did return, and Wagner's oeuvre (some of it at least) became normalized in the eyes of the public and the press. The degree to which this happened can be best assessed by considering the *Freeman's Journal's* critical acclaim of *Tannhäuser* in its first Irish performance by the Carl Rosa Company in 1893.[82] In addition to an article dedicated to an explication of the overture (30 August), and two long notices of the performances (31 August and 5 September), Wagnerian ideals were contrasted with the other works in the season *inter alia* Gluck's *Orpheus*, Verdi's *Otello*, and Gounod's

---

78 'Music in Dublin 1', *Hibernia*, 2 January 1882, 6–8.   **79** Ibid.   **80** 'Music in Dublin 2', *Hibernia*, 1 April 1882, 63.   **81** Ibid.   **82** See the daily notices entitled 'The Carl Rosa operas' from 24 August to 8 September 1893, *FJ*.

Faust. Notwithstanding the critic's admission that he was not familiar with Wagner's later works,[83] coupled with his warning that Wagner's 'admirers are idolising him too much',[84] he nevertheless surrendered to Wagnerian theory and its musical realization: 'Song uniformly sustained so nobly is more effective than any succession of "tunes". To call such music "heavy" is impossible for anyone with music anywhere in his soul.'[85] Most significant, perhaps was the historicist tone of regret at the belated appreciation of Wagner in Ireland:

> How extraordinary it seems now that all through the days of Grisi and Mario, and Lablache and Cruvelli, and Viardot Garcia and Titiens, and all the other great vocal stars who have appeared here in succession, during that long interval the opera of the great German should never have found its way hither … Of course we know better than that now.[86]

In a curious reversal, the *Irish Times* devoted less space than the *Freeman's Journal*, and although staunchly in support of Wagner it sustained the factual tone of its previous coverage.[87]

Wagner's music had, over a period of two decades, gradually altered the benchmark of musical criticism. However, just as the achievements of German romanticism were assimilated into the mainstream musical press, Irish nationalism was in the ascendant, and had a decisive influence on musical criticism at the turn of the century.

MUSICAL IRISHNESS, NATIONALISM AND THE PRESS

> 'Mother dear, don't sing that song again; its makes me sorrowful,' whispered the little child, with broken voice, and eyes charged with tears. Here was the true poetic and musical temperament …
>
> *The Nation* on William Carleton[88]

The issue of 'Irishness' in music was present in the musical press throughout the century. Unsurprisingly it was inseparable from the relationship between England and Ireland, and the changing nature of that relationship had the profoundest effects on musical criticism and musical life in general.

On the occasion of Catalani's first visit to Ireland in 1807 the *Freeman's Journal* drew attention to the issue of national singing styles, and, moreover, the critic's role in making comparisons between native and visiting artistes: 'A hearer is apt to perceive the value of the music of other countries as they approximate to

---

[83] 'Wagner's *Tannhauser*', *FJ*, 5 September 1893.   [84] 'Wagner's *Tannhauser*', *FJ*, 29 August 1893.
[85] '*Tannhauser* at the Gaiety', *FJ*, 31 August 1893.   [86] 'Wagner's *Tannhauser*', *FJ*, 5 September 1893.
[87] '"Tannhauser" at the Gaiety', *IT*, 31 August 1893.   [88] 'Music, the interpreter of nationality and literature', *The Nation*, 2 February 1850.

his own.'[89] In 1831 the same newspaper considered how techniques associated with Italian opera and 'modern English' music were not suited to singing Irish melodies. Thus Mrs Wood's singing of 'the charming Irish melody, "Sa Vourneen Deelish" was a complete failure' because her 'scientific embellishments' destroyed the 'natural pathetic ease and softness of the Irish melody'. In a resonant phrase the critic claimed 'the old airs of Ireland, like natural beauty, are most adorned when adorned the least'.[90] It seems that Wood had learned her lesson for she was later praised for 'divinely' singing 'Though the last Glimpse of Erin' because her singing expressed the 'tender pathos of the plaintive Irish air'.[91]

At this time, due to Daniel O'Connell's attempt to repeal the Union after his success with Catholic emancipation, the press in Ireland was subject to extreme censorship from Dublin castle which retaliated to sedition with fines and imprisonment.[92] The chief secretary of Ireland considered the *Freeman's Journal* to be the most dangerous of all the Dublin newspapers and prosecuted the owner for publishing a letter by O'Connell who had been arrested in January 1831. Political commentary in the musical notices was therefore rare and potentially dangerous. In this context, the *Freeman's Journal*, in July 1831, used its musical notices as a weapon against the state, and blamed the decline in Irish musical life on the Union. Thus the poor attendance at Rossini's *The Maid of Judah* served as an opportunity for defiance of the lord lieutenant whose presence was customarily acknowledged in all opera notices:

> If the taste for splendid music, good scenery, and fine acting, which once rendered Dublin famous were not defunct, or what is a more probable cause, if the city had not been pauperised by accursed legislation, there would have been an overflow of fashion in the boxes, of easy trading, comfort in the pit, and of laughing artisans in the galleries last night.[93]

It was rare indeed for Italian opera to be associated in any way with Irish political independence, but wider political circumstances could engender unexpected results as we have already seen in relation to the Musical Festival of the same year.

A more conspicuous and familiar political reading of Irish music *per se* emanated from the academic journalists particularly from within the folds of Dublin University. While many notices praised Bunting's 1840 edition of *Ancient Music of Ireland*,[94] the *Dublin University Magazine* offered a conspicuously nationalist interpretation. The writer waxed eloquent on the power of native music to overcome the 'intemperate, and often disgraceful contentions of our sects and parties amongst our countrymen'. In the absence of 'a philosophical national spirit' music can provide a common ground on which all men can unite:

[89] *FJ,* 24 September 1807, quoted in Hogan, *Anglo-Irish music*, pp 117–18.   [90] 'The Theatre', *FJ*, 12 July 1831, 2.   [91] 'The Theatre', *FJ*, 25 July 1831, 2.   [92] See Brian Inglis, *The freedom of the press in Ireland, 1784–1841*: *Studies in Irish history*, vi (London: Faber & Faber 1954), pp 194ff.   [93] 'The Theatre', *FJ*, 8 July 1831, 2.   [94] See, for example, P[etrie], 'Ancient music of Ireland', *Irish Penny Journal*, i/1, 4 July 1840, 8, and 'Ancient music of Ireland', *The Citizen*, 2, (August 1840), 207–12.

Yes, the time shall come when we shall be a great, because a united, nation ... glorying in our ancient music, the common property of all.[95]

Davis famously made that very notion the seminal impulse of *The Nation* which had a profound influence his contemporaries and later generations of nationalists.[96] Davis' famous distain for the 'paltry scented things from Italy, lively trifles from Scotland, and German opera cries'[97] led him to crystallize an exclusive and prescriptive view of what music in Ireland should be. By placing Balfe and Rossini in the same category he was able to pit them both against an essentialist construction of native Irish art music that saw Carolan as its last great exponent:

> those [composers] we have do not compose Irish-like music, nor for Ireland ... Balfe is very sweet, and Rooke very emphatic, but not one passion or association in Ireland's heart would answer to their songs.[98]

For Davis, it was bad enough that these foreign imports should dominate the stage, but, woe of woes, even the Temperance bands included them in their arrangements.[99] It is not surprising, therefore, that *The Nation* did not concern itself with reviewing Italian opera, and its influence on its contemporary titles was slight in this regard.

The significance of *The Nation*'s perspective on the issue of Irishness in music is brought into sharp focus when we compare its musical journalism with that of the other dailies at the time of Catherine Hayes' tour of Ireland in the winter of 1849/1850. While the mainstay of Hayes' repertoire was drawn from Italian opera, she always included Irish ballads in her repertoire, notably 'Kathleen Mavourneen', 'Why do I weep for thee?' and 'Terence's farewell to Kathleen'. While these were usually performed as 'encores', on occasion they found their way into the opera itself, a phenomenon that was considered a triumph for Irish music. For example, during a performance of *Lucrezia Borgia*, Hayes acquiesced to the audience's calls for 'The harp that once':

> The progress of a serious opera stopped for the performance of an Irish ballad! It was, in truth, an incident without precedent, and equally without precedent were the roars of gratification that followed; one ardent gentleman in the middle gallery shouting with a voice that was heard above all the tumult, 'Musha! God bless you, Catherine darlin.'[1]

---

95 *DUM*, 17, (January 1841), 5. **96** See White, *The keeper's recital*, esp. p. 53ff. for a conspectus on Davis' three essays 'Irish music and poetry', 'Irish songs' and 'Ballad poetry of Ireland' which are anthologized in *Essays literary and historical by Thomas Davis*, ed. D.J. O'Donoghue (Dundalk: 1914). **97** Davis, 'Irish music and poetry', *The Nation*, 29 June 1844: see note 96. **98** Ibid. **99** Notwithstanding *The Nation*'s support for the Temperance movement, it was highly critical of the damage done to the airs in those arrangements. **1** *Dublin Evening Packet*, 5 November 1850, quoted in Basil Walsh, *Catherine Hayes, the Hibernian prima donna* (Dublin: Irish Academic Press, 2000), p. 158.

The press revelled in such patriotism. Moreover, rather than dichotomize European opera and Irish melody, the Irish papers revelled in the dignity which one could lend the other. In this regard, the dailies competed in their attempts to claim Hayes as an *Irish* operatic star: 'The Irish *prima donna*' (*Cork Examiner*), 'The Irish Queen of Song' (*Limerick Chronicle*), 'Irish Queen of Melody and Song' (Wexford Independent), 'The Irish Jenny Lind' (*Evening Packet*), the latter title which became a commonplace. Moreover, this branding of Hayes as 'Irish' was simultaneously a reaction to and an imitation of the English press who referred to her as an 'English *prima donna*' (*Daily News*) or 'English vocalist' (*Times*) which again rated her second only to Lind. The editor of the *Dublin Evening Packet* intervened in this discourse with a substantial article that addressed the comparisons with Lind. (Up to that point the *Dublin Evening Packet* was itself guilty of over-using the phrase 'The Irish Jenny Lind'.) It is a notable article for its sustained national tone and its return to the themes which had exercised the *Freeman's Journal* in 1807: the Irish are praised for their 'delight in the charms of perfect vocalism ... unlike our English neighbours, who invariably neglect their native singers'.[2] Where Lind's singing was 'like the mechanism of an instrument', by contrast 'the triumph of Miss Hayes is in the combination of sweetest sounds into a stream of melody, which gradually sheds itself into the heart.' Waxing eloquent he continued:

> Or we might compare the foreign artist to one of her native landscapes, basking in splendour, and clear in its outline and objects beneath a starry sky: Miss Hayes' beauties are those of our own clime, with its features of tenderness melting into light, or darkening into shade.

Undoubtedly the concurrent disaster of the Great Famine added an urgency to the appropriation of Hayes as 'Irish' both in her singing and her physical appearance. While the famine *per se* was scarcely mentioned in the notices of Hayes' performances it remained an unspoken presence. The *Cork Examiner* let the veil fall in a delicate reference to that calamity:

> The personal appearance of Miss Hayes is most attractive; and were we inclined to be at all poetical in this age of iron realities, we might regard her as the impersonation of the grace, and delicacy, and innocence of Irish modesty and Irish beauty.[3]

While someone so beautiful could hardly personify the present condition of a wretched nation, she could represent a vision of a glorious past or future, or of an Ireland that simply did not exist other than on the musical stage and in the public imagination. If, as Declan Kiberd has noted, Ireland after the famine was 'a sort

---

2 *Dublin Evening Packet*, 7 March 1850, reproduced in Walsh, *Catherine Hayes*, pp 141–2. **3** *CE*, 16 November 1849.

of nowhere, waiting for its appropriate images and symbols to be inscribed in it',[4] the Hayes mania was the first major national event that was conspicuously successful and cosmopolitan.

But the famine in Ireland is inseparable from the consequent emigration to America which was widely reported in the press. Thus Ireland's fascination with America was seminal to the success of Hayes' tour. By the time she had arrived in Ireland, newspaper readers were familiar with the reports of Jenny Lind's recent success in America, or rather with the success of T.P. Barnum's promotional techniques. It was through the press that the Irish learned how to overreact in the American style, and even allowing for exaggeration, it seems that Irish audiences exceeded all bounds of normalcy in encoring Hayes.[5] The pervasive sentimental pride at a time of national tragedy would have seemed more appropriate coming from Irish-American exiles than from those who stayed at home. But the Irish in Ireland distanced themselves from the surrounding disaster and shared in the euphoria of American prosperity through the newspapers, particularly through the activity of reading the reportage of their own behaviour. There were few other activities that allowed people to see themselves in such a good light at such a bad time. The musical press thus recorded a poignant time when the Irish became disembodied in their own country and were transported to another imagined Ireland personified in Hayes and expressed in her singing.

Unlike most of the notices of Hayes in the Irish press which contained nothing overtly political other than rivalry with England, the *Cork Examiner* approached the expression of cultural nationalism reminiscent of *The Nation*:

> It is a singular fact that Ireland, so essentially the land of song, whose bardic remains have obtained a world wide reputation – whose national melodies alternate from the touchingly simple to the thrillingly superb, being alike 'beautiful exceedingly' whether they breath the soul of pathos or glow with the fervour of martial enthusiasm – whose 'keens' express the very passion and abandonment of grief – whose war songs stir up the heart like the sound of a trumpet – it is a remarkable fact, we repeat, that our musical Island has given to the lyric stage but a single female vocalist within our memory capable of interpreting with success the highest order of dramatic music. Although in every other branch of art our country has given proof of that genius and talent which are the inalienable birthright of her children, as a vocalist, Irish by birth and Irish in heart, who has already achieved triumphs which place in the sake many of the proudest lyric victories of the Italian and German prima donnas, Miss Catherine Hayes stands alone.[6]

However, while the influence of Davis is evident here, the *Cork Examiner* did not disdain those perfumed Italian melodies. By contrast, *The Nation*, apart from

---

4 Kiberd, *Inventing Ireland: the literature of the modern nation* (London: Vintage, 1996), p. 115. **5** See, for example, the reports in the *Wexford Independent*, 6 November 1850, reproduced in Walsh, *Catherine Hayes*, p. 160. **6** 'Catherine Hayes', *CE*, 4 November 1850, 4.

advertising some of the musical merchandise associated with Hayes' repertoire,[7] all but ignored her presence in the country. Rather than attend Hayes' performances, *The Nation*'s reporter audited six lectures entitled 'National Music of Ireland' delivered by Mr William Murphy, B.Mus., in the Dublin Mechanics' Institution in December 1849.[8] While Murphy received some praise for his efforts, he was censured for performing English music as illustrative examples. This in turn prompted the critic to pour scorn on those audience members who encored those works.

The 'twin cultures' manifested itself in a specifically nationalist context in *The Nation* in two articles that were probably written by Henry Philerin Hudson or John Edward Pigot.[9] The author of these articles lamented the impoverishment of Irish intellectual life due to the pervasive ignorance of European art music: 'The unnatural divorce between Intellect and Music which exists in Ireland, is a bad symptom in the health of both.'[10] The sublime works of Beethoven were repeatedly referenced as the zenith of musical art, and due reverence was given to the modern romantic composers; Berlioz, Chopin, Liszt, Meyerbeer, and above all, Mendelssohn. The fact that Ireland could boast no composers of such genius was pitted against the threadbare claim that the Irish were a uniquely musical people. The 'hosts of minor artists' such as Balfe, Osborne and Catherine Hayes were merely 'gathering laurels, to be woven into a garland for our oppressor's brows.' In a sequel to that article, German romanticism was advocated as the epitome of European culture and therefore as a healthy model for Ireland's artists and intellects to emulate. Moreover, Ireland had lost contact with the 'electrical soil of Music' from which sprang the creative genius of the nation. In consequence Ireland's contemporary thrall to opera was a symptom, and thus a symbol, of its political oppression: 'A slave surrounded with luxury will sing, and the expression of his content will be sensual, joyous, voluptuous; such is Italian music.'[11] The solution to this problem was to foster 'National Music' in the peasantry and for composers to follow the example of Beethoven's 'pastoral symphonies [*sic*]' which painted nature in its various moods and expressed every nuance of sentiment in a truly poetic manner. This article was an extraordinary validation of the Austro-German canon at a time of national crisis (the famine) and national euphoria (Catherine Hayes), and it was a unique claim for mobilising the resources of European instrumental music as a vehicle for Irish national music. It was some time to come before such a discussion would permeate the mainstream press.

---

7 Namely, Richard Frederic Harvey's song 'Home of My Heart' and the 'La Bella Catarina Polka' advertised in *The Nation*, 12 January 1850.   **8** 'The National Music of Ireland', *The Nation*, 1 December 1849, and 'Irish national music', *The Nation*, 22 December 1849.   **9** Pigot, who had previously published an article on Mozart, and Hudson, and wrote for the *Citizen*, had translated Beethoven's *Christ on the Mount of Olives*. Both of them had prepared the music for *The Spirit of the Nation* (1845) and were committed to the preservation of Irish folk music: see Jimmy O'Brien Moran's chapter in this volume for their involvement with folk music collections.   **10** 'Modern music and musicians', *The Nation*, 12 January 1850.   **11** 'Music, the Interpreter of Nationality and Literature', *The Nation*, 2 February 1850.

Twenty years later *the Irish Builder* (in an article already examined above) regarded the issue of national music as contingent on a professional standard of music criticism:

> We have a national music, ancient and modern, sufficient to rouse the most lethargic natives, but why is not some noble or honest attempt made to give it an expression consonant with national desires and feelings? This will never be done until we have an independent Press proprietary in our midst, and critics who understand what they write about.[12]

However, the notion of an independent press was highly unlikely in a country where culture became increasingly nationalized. The remainder of this chapter contrasts one of the established regional newspapers, the *Cork Examiner*, with one of the new national papers, *The Leader* with regard to their treatment of musical topics at the end of the century.

God save the Queen ... and Ireland
The *Cork Examiner* was one of the many provincial newspapers that Dublin Castle subscribed to in its scrutiny of dangerous politics.[13] In the final decades of the century there would have been little to worry the British with regard to the *Cork Examiner*'s coverage of national music. The mainstay of musical criticism involved detailed reports of local musical activities,[14] and while support for the Gaelic League was evident, the British presence was never criticized. At its most pungent, the critic would target the products of the English music hall while praising conspicuously Irish musical efforts. In a substantial and supportive notice of the Gaelic League's first concert in Cork on St Patrick's Day 1895, the writer expressed the opinion that it was

> a pleasant departure from the everyday concert with its tasteless doses of the tra-la-la of the Roeckels and the Pinsutis and the other drawing-room minstrels known to young ladies – and a hopeful sign of the times from every point of view.[15]

Unsurprisingly, the *Cork Examiner* was as enthusiastic as all the other dailies in reviewing Stanford's *Shamus O'Brien* in the following year. *Shamus* received almost twenty performances in November 1896 in Belfast, Limerick, Waterford, Cork and Dublin and engendered a popular response that was as 'national' as

---

12 'Our "musical festivals" and "musical critics"', *IB*, 15 January 1873.   **13** For the list of newspapers subscribed to by Dublin Caste see Legg, *Newspapers and nationalism*, p. 126, n6.   **14** The Cork School of Music, the Cork Amateur Orchestral Society, the Cork Amateur Opera Company, the Cork Musical Club. See for example, 'Concert at the Imperial Hotel', 3 February 1890; 'Theatre Royal: The Sultan of Mochal' 7, 8 and 11 February 1890 which reviewed the efforts of the Cork Amateur Opera Company. Also, frequent attention was given to concerts in Mallow, Cappoquin, Valentia, Midleton, and Lismore.   **15** 'The Gaelic League Concert', *CE*, 18 March 1895.

Catherine Hayes' mid-century tour. The Irish papers eulogized its 'realism', which is to say its faithful representation of Irish costumes, speech (the brogue), music and dancing, the latter which impressed the *Freeman's Journal* as 'far more captivating than that French kick-up called 'ballet', and also far more 'dacent.'[16] During its first run, the opera was seen as concurrent with the ideals of the Gaelic League. However, despite the theme of 1798 and the theme of betrayal of the hero by the local traitor, the reception was notable for its avoidance of political meaning. The *Cork Examiner* implied that dangerous politics had no place in art: 'The lyrics for 'Shamus' are boldly written, are in fact, stirring war songs *minus* vulgar effects.'[17] While the majority of the Irish dailies, including the northern papers, gave it extensive coverage, *The Nation* was the only paper not to review it because of Stanford's dispute with the Feis committee of which he was President and from which he had resigned in that year. While acknowledging that Stanford 'had rendered Ireland sufficiently lasting and useful service',[18] his plan to invite the Hallé orchestra to perform at the opening and closing concerts at the inaugural Feis was seen as an act of betrayal: 'There is, at any rate, something to be grateful for in the fact that if, in too many cases, we have to allow the Saxon to make our boots he shall never make our music.' There was plenty of 'Saxon' music-making in Cork city at the turn of the century. For example, in 1900, the Moody-Manners Opera company was offering *Tannhäuser*, *Carmen*, *Maritana* and *The Lily of Killarney*, 'Fashionable Concerts' were devoted to popular English ballads, and 'attractive' Queenstown (Cobh) Promenade concerts were regularly given by the various British army bands. All of this co-existed with the Incorporated Society of Musicians which promoted classical repertory, and the churches and cathedrals which provided both venerable and recently-composed scared music, not to mention the Feis and the 'Gaelic Leaguers' who promoted Irish music that was both 'high class' and 'racy of the soil'.[19] The *Cork Examiner* reported on all these musical events and did not attempt to mediate between them in terms of musical taste or political or religious allegiance. In plain terms, if a 'selection of Irish airs' was performed at either the Munster Feis or by the Fourth Battalion of the King's Royal Rifles it received equally favourable comment. More significantly, if one concert concluded with 'God save the Queen' and another with 'God save Ireland' no political loyalty was hinted at by the critic. The Crosbies were all things to all Corkonians.

At the other end of the spectrum lay D.P. Moran's *The Leader: a review of current affairs, politics, literature, art and industry* which was established in 1900 just as *The Nation* was coming to an end. Taking the essentialist claims of the Gaelic League to extreme conclusions, *The Leader* kept a close eye on its contemporary titles for any hint of West Britishisms, notably 'her ladyship' the *Irish Times*. Extensive space was devoted to musical matters, and the

16 '"Shamus O'Brien". Dr Stanford's opera at the Gaeity', *FJ*, 22 November 1896.   **17** *CE*, 17 November 1896, 5.   **18** *The Nation*, 20 June 1896.   **19** 'The Munster Feis: an attractive and thorough Irish programme', *CE*, 18 September 1900.

predominant perspective was that of the Irish Ireland movement. Indeed, *The Leader* was less a 'newspaper' than a political institution. Unsurprisingly, it attacked the *Cork Examiner*, not only for its cosmopolitanism, but more pertinently for its claim to be The Only Nationalist Newspaper' published in Cork: one correspondent, 'Oisin', responded to that claim with the memorable phrase 'The Devil preaching Christianity!'[20]

In the spirit of a truly national newspaper, *The Leader* dispensed with anonymity and we are thus able to read the opinions of such notables as Edward Martyn, Heinrich Bewerunge, Heinrich Tils, and Charles G. Marchant. Equally innovatory was its sponsorship of lively correspondence on musical matters. The exchanges between the quasi-anonymous 'IMAAL', 'An Irish Musician', 'Oscar', 'Ceólán', 'Cloyne', 'Cormac', and 'G minor' and the aforementioned notables centred predominantly on the issue of native Irish music: for example whether Field was an 'Irish' composer, the 'West-British' nature of the Royal Irish Academy of Music, and the lack of a truly Irish style of singing at the Feiseanna. Other topics included the issue of women singing in church and the practice of secular music (usually operatic favourites) finding its way into the liturgy. These debates were a welcome relief from the musical journalism in the other nationalist titles (e.g. *The United Irishman*) which tended to report on the Feis and Oireachtas concerts to the exclusion of wider issues.

From this overview of music criticism in nineteenth-century Ireland, it is clear that the musical press is more than just a primary source for the study of concert life, performance practice, *inter alia*, and that it can be more profitably treated as a substantive part of musical life in Ireland and not merely its reflection.

---

20 'Oisin', 'The only nationalist Cork paper', *The Leader*, 27 October 1900, p. 135.

Musical national traditions in Ireland and the Czech lands in the nineteenth century: similar roots, creative divergences

JAN SMACZNY

In an era in which nationalism was, if not always burning, certainly an issue at the forefront of the political and cultural agenda for many areas dominated by an Imperium, comparisons between a number of groups in Europe aspiring to nationhood can readily be made. Signal congruities between the situation of the Czech lands[1] and Ireland provide on the one hand grounds for mutually illuminating comparison and on the other equally illuminating divergences. Neither Ireland nor the Czech lands were operatively independent nations in the nineteenth century despite possessing political institutions which, in the right circumstances, might have served a proto-national agenda for government. Both were dominated politically, culturally and linguistically by powerful neighbours, each of which was an imperial power.

In an ingenious examination of the Czech situation 'from an Irish point of view',[2] Harry White makes many pertinent observations concerning the similarities between these two geographical units. One of the more poignant of White's comparisons concerns 'The parallels between Dublin and Prague [which] are comparatively easy to discover: both were 'second cities' in relation to an imperial capital'.[3] Both were, indeed, substantial provincial centres in population terms in the nineteenth century, and indeed beyond, second only to the imperial capitals. Furthermore both cities at various stages had enjoyed far more exalted status than they possessed in the nineteenth century, Dublin as capital of Ireland for centuries before the Act of Union of 1800, and Prague effectively as the imperial capital of the Holy Roman Empire notably during the reign of Charles IV (elected king of the Romans in 1346 and crowned emperor in Rome in 1355) and during the major part of the reign of Rudolf II (from 1583 to 1608).[4] In addition to sociological, political and economic parallels, inevitably there were cultural similarities, not least in terms of self image and the impact of Enlightenment thinking, that may be addressed fruitfully.

---

[1] These are understood to comprise the lands of the Bohemian crown and the Margravate of Moravia, in the nineteenth century, and effectively since the Battle of the White Mountain in 1620, the possessions of the Habsburg monarchy.   [2] Harry White, 'Art music and the question of ethnicity: the Slavic dimension of Czech music from an Irish point of view', in Harry White, *The progress of music in Ireland* (Dublin: Four Courts Press, 2005), pp 68–86.   [3] Ibid., p. 73.   [4] For an engaging English-language account of the history of Prague, its triumphs and vicissitudes see Peter Demetz, *Prague in black and gold* (London: Allen Lane, the Penguin Press, 1997).

INSTITUTIONS AND EMIGRATION

Notwithstanding size and the pronounced good will of the citizenry and minor aristocracy, the advantages of full metropolitan status were not to be had in either Dublin or Prague during the nineteenth century. The cultural institutions necessary for the development of music-making on an appreciable scale were slow to emerge and often halting in delivery. In an age where patronage was to a large extent dependent on the aristocracy, historical accident conspired to deprive both cities of an appreciable volume of potential patrons. Dublin's musical 'golden age', as Brian Boydell typified it,[5] was played out through the eighteenth century and contingent on extensive aristocratic patronage; notwithstanding evident highpoints, such as the premiere of *Messiah* at the Great Musick Hall in Fishamble Street, its character was remarkably sustained and durable enough to ensure a moderate degree of musical immigration. Even during the uncertain years at the turn of the eighteenth century over 'a quarter of the concerts … in this period [1792–1806] were promoted by visiting performers'.[6]

The musical life of Prague in the eighteenth century has tended to be seen more as a story of emigration. Although certainly not entirely bereft of musical incomers, notably Italian singers and opera impresarios, it is telling that Mozart's landmark visits between 1787 and 1791, variously for performances of *Le nozze di Figaro* and the premières of *Don Giovanni* and *La Clemenza di Tito*, were highlights that have, in the informed popular imagination, almost entirely eclipsed other musical activities in the Bohemian capital.[7] While Prague was far from being a musical desert, many of the institutions crucial to a flourishing cultural life were simply not present.[8] Aristocratic patronage, notably that of Count Franz Anton Sporck[9] (1662–1738) ensured a reasonable amount of operatic activity, but it was not until Count Franz Anton von Nostitz-Rhineck opened his one thousand capacity 'National Theatre' on 21 April 1783 that Prague had an opera house. Although the major nobility maintained residencies in Prague, some of a very extensive nature, in addition to their palaces in Vienna, the presence of many in the Czech capital was distinctly seasonable in nature. Thus opportunities for the abundant talent produced by the excellent musical education available in the Czech lands had little opportunity to flourish at home, as Burney observed 'now and then, indeed, a man of genius among them becomes an admirable musician, whether he will or no; but, when that happens, he generally runs away, and settles

---

[5] In 'Dublin', *NG II*, vii, 624. [6] Derek Collins, 'Concert life in Dublin in the age of revolution', PhD diss. (Queen's University, Belfast, 2001), pp 27–8. [7] See Jan Smaczny, 'Prague', in *The Cambridge Mozart encyclopaedia*, ed. Cliff Eisen and Simon Keefe (Cambridge: Cambridge University Press, 2006), pp 397–402. [8] For an English-language account of music in Prague and the Czech lands in the eighteenth century see Christopher Hogwood and Jan Smaczny, 'The Bohemian lands', in *The Classical era: from the 1740s to the end of the 18th century*, ed. Neal Zaslaw (London: Macmillan, 1989), pp 188–212. [9] See Daniel Freeman, *The Opera Theater of Count Franz von Sporck* (New York: Pendragon Press, 1992); for a more general account of opera in Prague in the eighteenth century see John Tyrrell, *Czech opera* (Cambridge: Cambridge University Press, 1988), pp 13–17.

in some other country, where he can enjoy the fruit of his talents'.[10] Thus from St Petersburg to Dublin, Czech musicians could be found readily in the courts and musical establishments of Europe. (Interestingly, the somewhat mysterious and decidedly raffish Bohemian musician, František Kocžwara (c.1750–91) worked in Ireland in the 1780s, probably as an orchestral viola player, and his greatest compositional success, the sensationally popular *The Battle of Prague*, was published in Dublin in 1788.)

The tendency toward emigration was hardly less marked in the nineteenth century with figures of the stature of Jan Václav Kalivoda (1801–66) leaving Prague for a career as a conductor in Donaueschingen. Even Smetana, frustrated by the slowness of progress after the revolutionary year, 1848, toward political liberalization and the growth of effective musical institutions, in particular a Czech theatre, was prompted to seek his fortune in Göteborg in Sweden in 1856 and likely would not have returned to Prague but for the opening of the Provisional Theatre (see below). Inevitably, comparison can be made with the career trajectories of Balfe and Wallace whose success was contingent on their work abroad. Unsurprisingly, given his Europe-wide popularity, Balfe's music was known in Prague with *The Bohemian Girl* given in Czech in the Prague Provisional Theatre seven times between 1863 and 1864[11] before being more or less swept from the stage by the overwhelming popularity of the operettas of Offenbach. Wallace's *Maritana* was given its Prague premiere in German in 1851, but not in Czech in the Provisional Theatre. Nevertheless, at least its overture was known to the Czech-speaking community since Dvořák spoke about it as 'a favourite' in an interview given to the *Sunday Times*.[12]

MUSICAL LIFE AND THE ARISTOCRACY

For all its significance as a political and cultural caesura, the Act of Union of 1800 certainly did not put an end to musical activities in Dublin. The departure of much of the aristocracy and the political turbulence occasioned by the rebellion of 1798 and subsequent risings, such as that of July 1803 with its consequent eight o'clock evening curfew, had, of course, a deleterious effect on concert life.[13] Nevertheless, aristocratic patronage, headed by the crown's representative, the lord lieutenant, played a considerable part in helping maintain what concert life there was; in the period 1794 to 1806, no less than one hundred

---

10 *Dr Burney's Musical tours of Europe*, ii, ed. Percy A. Scholes (London: Oxford University Press, 1959), p. 138.   **11** See Jan Smaczny, *Daily repertoire of the Provisional Theatre Opera in Prague* (Prague: Miscellanea musicologica, 1994), pp 13 and 116; *The Bohemian Girl* was premiered in German in Prague in 1847 and given for the first time in Czech the following year. The title of the opera was changed in the Czech translation from *The Bohemian Girl* to *The Gypsy Girl* (Cikánka), presumably owing to local sensitivities.   **12** *Sunday Times*, 10 May 1885, 6; reprinted in *Rethinking Dvořák: views from five countries*, ed. David R. Beveridge (Oxford: Clarendon Press, 1996), pp 281–8.   **13** See Collins, *Concert life*, pp 42–3. Collins identifies the years 1802–4 as an 'all-time low' in concert activity in Dublin in the

and thirty one of the greater and lesser nobility and senior prelates were counted among the patrons of the Irish Musical Fund Society.[14] The Czech nobility, while often absent from Prague, nevertheless were avid patrons of music and Mozart counted a number of them among the subscribers for his Lent season concerts in Vienna in 1784.[15]

In nineteenth-century Prague, the role of the aristocracy was played out in a more evidently civic arena. A member of the leading noble family, the Schwarzenbergs, was a founder of the Prague Organ School in 1830, an establishment designed to improve standards of church music which had suffered noticeably in the decades following the abolition of the Jesuits in 1773. In 1818, the 200th anniversary of the year in which the Czech Estates rose against the Habsburg crown precipitating the start of the Thirty Years War, a national museum was established in Prague, an idea fostered by three of the nobility, Counts Šternberk, Klebelsberk and Kolovrat, the last being the Supreme Burgrave and effectively the equivalent of the lord lieutenant.[16] As the national revival got underway after the middle of the century, the involvement of the aristocracy was once again clearly to the fore. As far as music was concerned, the opening of the Prague Provisional Theatre,[17] the forerunner of the National Theatre, in 1862 was by far the most significant event. This attractive, though decidedly small-scale building, was designed to provide a home for opera and plays, exclusively in the native tongue for the growing Czech speaking population of Prague. Embarrassingly, the existing repertoire of operas in Czech was so slight that in the early years of the theatre performances were almost entirely of foreign works in translation; indeed, the first opera to be given in the theatre was Cherubini's *Les deux journées* (the Czech title was given on the posters as *Vodař*, a translation of the opera's alternative designation, The Water Carrier).[18] To stimulate the composition of a repertoire of native operas, a competition for new scores and libretti was unveiled by Count Jan Harrach on 10 February 1861.[19]

OPERA AT THE HEART OF THE NATION

Superficially there were similarities between the way in which opera was delivered in Ireland in the middle of the nineteenth century and in the Prague Provisional Theatre. Italian opera, which dominated the foreign repertoire in nineteenth-century Dublin[20] was strongly represented in the Provisional Theatre,

---

early nineteenth century.   **14** Ibid., pp 342–5.   **15** Smaczny, 'Prague', p. 398.   **16** See Derek Sayer, *The coasts of Bohemia: a Czech history* (Princeton, NJ: Princeton University Press, 1998), pp 53ff.   **17** In Czech, prozatímní divadlo; its original official title in Czech was Královské zemské české divadlo (the Royal provincial Czech theatre); it was replaced briefly by the much larger National Theatre in 1881, but owing to a fire which destroyed the new theatre's auditorium, was brought back into service until the second opening of the National Theatre in 1883.   **18** See Smaczny, *Daily Repertoire*, pp 11 and 115.   **19** For a translation of Harrach's competition instructions see Tyrrell, *Czech opera*, pp 126 and 209.   **20** See Brian Boydell, 'Dublin' in *The new Grove dictionary of opera*, ed. Stanley Sadie (London:

particularly in its early years. More colourfully, there could, even in the context of Italian opera, be a place for demonstrations of national enthusiasm. Catherine Hayes' singing of 'The harp that once' during Donizetti's *Lucrezia Borgia* in the winter season of 1849–50[21] finds an echo in a similar practice in Prague: on 6 April 1864 František Škroup's patriotic song to words by the popular playwright, Josef Kajetan Tyl, 'Where is my home?' (Kde domov můj?), now the Czech national anthem, was introduced into the singing lesson in the second act of Rossini's *Il barbiere* and became a firm favourite in this context.[22] The demotic dimension in the presentation of opera in the early years of the Provisional Theatre was something which Smetana in his incarnation as the critic of the Prague daily, *Národní listy* often decried, notably, when according to the musical director, Jan Maýr, the finale of Vaccai's *Giulietta e Romeo* was unceremoniously appended to the end of Mozart's *Don Giovanni* 'by popular request'.[23] An even more remarkable manifestation of the extent of populist tendencies on the part of the management of the Provisional Theatre were the guest appearances of the one-legged Spanish ballet dancer, Juliano Donato (his limb loss had occurred during an earlier career as a toreador). He was a huge favourite with audiences as a star attraction between the acts of a number of operas in 1864 including the Grand Operas *La Juive* and *La Muette*.[24]

The populist nature of the presentation of opera in the Provisional Theatre was in large part driven by commercial concerns given that the management were on time-limited renewable contracts. But there was also something of a desire to promote a kind of popular interaction between audience and stage embedded in the instructions for the writing of comic operas in Harrach's competition rules. In addition to encouraging composers to a study of folksong in order to ensure a 'truly national character', Harrach added the following advice 'Choruses, especially in a comic opera, should not be a mere diversion for the audience, but by providing a living echo of folksongs, should encourage the audience's lively participation'.[25] This notion of the sing-along night at the Provisional Theatre was certainly resisted by the generation of Czech composers who were to provide a new national repertoire, notably Smetana, who became musical director of the Theatre in 1866 until the rapid onset of deafness forced him to step down in 1874.

However, the fundamental difference in the nature of operatic production by the Irish and the Czechs is also to a considerable extent enshrined in Harrach's rules. While all of them were not followed to the letter by either the composers or librettists who took part in the competition, they set an agenda and to an extent affected the composition of opera for well over a generation. Comedies were to reflect national stereotypes up to and, most notably in the case of Weinberger's *Svanda the Bagpiper* (Švanda dudák), even beyond the turn of the century

Macmillan, 1992), i, 1261.   **21** For an account of this see Michael Murphy's chapter in this volume. **22** Smaczny, *Daily Repertoire*, pp 14 and 116.   **23** *Národní listy*, 16 July 1864; reprinted in V.H. Jarka, *Kritické dílo Bedřicha Smetany* (The critical writings of Bedřich Smetany) (Prague: Nakladatelství Pražské akciové tiskárny, 1948), pp 90–1.   **24** See Tyrrell, *Czech opera*, p. 27.   **25** Translation taken from Tyrrell, *Czech opera*, p. 209.

(although the use of folksong clearly favoured by Harrach was relatively rare in this period).[26] Serious operas were to be based on the history – usually read as the historical mythology – of the Czech crown lands.[27] Thus parameters were set and to a large extent adhered to in the twenty years of the Provisional Theatre's existence. All three of Smetana's serious operas, *The Brandenburgers in Bohemia* (Braniboři v Čechách), *Dalibor* and *Libuše* are set firmly within the confines of these precepts. Of the nineteen serious operas by Czechs staged in the Provisional Theatre a majority of twelve were of the historical-mythological Czech type. The most notable exception among composers was Dvořák whose two grand operas staged in the theatre, *Vanda* and *Dimitrij*, were respectively based on Polish and Russian subjects. Even in later generations where Wagnerian experiment, in the shape of Fibich's *The Bride of Messina* (Nevěsta messinská) or the growing fashion for verista subject matter in the 1890s, the historical and mythological could surface with surprising regularity, for example in the *Šárka* operas of Janáček and Fibich, and Ostrčil's *The Death of Vlasta* (Vlasty skon).

But for all the cultural, and to an extent political, underpinning the agenda for Czech opera, a still more fundamental driving force was the whole question of language. And here lies a profound difference in the situation between Ireland and the Czech lands. As Tom Garvin so pertinently observes of the Irish situation in relation to more general trends in Europe:

> In Western Europe, the political mobilisation of general populations coincided with urbanisation and industrialisation. In Ireland, the usual European sequence was reversed; intense political mobilisation occurred long before substantial industrialisation or even commercialisation has occurred. In fact, the Ireland of 1790–1840 was being 'de-urbanised', as the rural population was growing faster than the town population.[28]

The situation in Prague was an almost complete reverse and while it certainly had important political ramifications through the nineteenth century, it was if anything more significant in turning Czech into the predominant urban language. The cultural, political and linguisitic domination of Austria subsequent to the Battle of the White Mountain in 1620 meant, effectively, that Czech was reduced to a rural, non-literary language. The industrial revolution certainly did much to change this.

Economic matters improved steadily for both the German and Czech speaking inhabitants of Bohemia and Moravia through the early decades of the nineteenth century. Parisian and Viennese investment in mining led to the systematic exploitation of the country's rich mineral deposits providing the basis for considerable industrial strength.[29] The financial circumstances of city dwellers

---

26 An exception was Janáček who, having had extensive experience of folksong collecting during the late 1880s, incorporated a number of folksongs into his opera *The Beginning of a Romance* (Počátek romanu) of 1892. **27** See Tyrrell, *Czech opera*, p. 126. **28** Tom Garvin, *The evolution of Irish nationalist politics* (Dublin: Gill & Macmillan, 1981), p. 49. **29** In the 1860s, Emil Škoda took over the engineering works opened in Plzeň by Count Wallenstein.

were further advanced by the abolition of guild monopolies in 1859 and the removal of trade tariffs between Hungary and the Czech lands. The consequent importation of cheap corn created economic difficulties in the Czech countryside, but it furthered the intensification of industrial prosperity in towns. There were certainly benefits from the changing political situation in the Habsburg empire, not least Austrian defeats in Italy and Franz Joseph's renunciation of absolutism in October 1859 which led to a constitutional agreement for the Czechs within the space of a few months. But culturally, the demographics of the language were more decisive as a guarantee of the national revival. The inevitable consequence of the need for labour prompted an inexorable drift toward urban industrial centres from the predominantly Czech-speaking countryside. In all of this, Dvořák's early career makes an interesting test case. Although he came to Prague in the autumn of 1857 in order to study at the Organ School, the uncle with whom he lodged, Václav Dušek, was a railway worker. This influx of a Czech speaking population into Prague and other industrial centres ensured the ascendancy of the language.[30]

The growing confidence of the Czech-speaking classes, and it should be remembered many of them had to learn Czech as a second language,[31] led to the founding of cultural institutions which often mirrored those of Prague's German-speaking community. Alongside the Provisional Theatre a Society for Artists (umělecká beseda) was set up in 1863 with Smetana as the first president of its music division. While there is something of a more unified look to the Czech musical organizations of Prague as opposed to those of Dublin, this was by no means a guarantee of excellence. For most of its existence the Provisional Theatre orchestra only fielded a string section of four first and four second violins, two violas,[32] two cellos and two double basses.[33] Furthermore, standards were not always of the highest since many of the players were more used to playing for commercial balls, the basis of the orchestra having been Karel Komzák's dance band, as Dvořák later reminisced 'I must leave you to imagine how we dance-music players got on during our opening season with such operas as Bellini's *Montecchi e Capuletti* and *Norma*, Rossini's *Otello* and Cherubini's *Deux Journées*'.[34] In many ways, Hamilton Harty's comments concerning the Dublin Orchestral Society, founded by Esposito in 1899, have some resonance with Dvořák's experience: 'The worst of musical life in Ireland is that there are practically no orchestras. ... At Dublin I was admitted into the local orchestra as a violist, and a very inferior violist I was; but the orchestra itself was no superlative'.[35]

---

30 According to Demetz the German-speaking population of Prague 'quickly decreased (in 1880 to 15.5 percent, and in 1900 to 7.5 percent)', *Prague in black and gold*, p. 317.   **31** The linguistic background of the two greatest composers of the Czech national revival exemplify the class-based nature of who was likely to speak German or Czech: Smetana, from a relatively prosperous middle-class background was a German speaker who had to learn Czech and was always more at ease with his first language; Dvořák, from a very poor rural background, was a Czech speaker who, more or less as a matter of course, learned German.   **32** Between 1862 and the summer season of 1871 when he left the orchestra, Dvořák was the senior of the two players.   **33** See Jan Smaczny, '*Alfred*: Dvořák's first operatic endeavour surveyed', *Journal of the Royal Musical Association*, 115, part 2, 83.   **34** *Sunday Times*, (see note 12 above), 286.   **35** *MT*, 61 (1920), 228.

'... FOREIGN INFLUENCE, FOREIGN INTONATION,
FOREIGN RHYTHM AND MELODY'[36]

Harry White's discussion of the difficulties which attended developing a link between the Irish language and music in *The Keeper's Recital*[37] reveals how fundamentally problematic the establishment of a union of these two vital elements was for art music in Ireland. Once again, a near completely opposite state of affairs pertained in Prague. Among the Czechs of the national revival, language, as we have seen even for first-language German speakers, was not an issue, as it had been for the Irish League and the National Literary Society, and that music as far as the Czech-speaking community was concerned never became as White puts it 'a symbol of sectarian cultural discourse'.[38] While there were what might be described as political sectarian divisions within the Czech national revival, notably that between old- and new-Czech political activists, music *per se* was rarely a battle ground in the nineteenth century. Something of an exception was the critical attitude toward Wagnerian influence which was seen as militating against the 'Czechness' of the native product, though, as Tyrrell points out this could be as trivial as the presence of slightly thicker orchestration in an opera.[39] In the twentieth century, it might be argued that musicological attitudes toward Smetana and Dvořák crystallized along quasi sectarian lines with the former being seen by one camp, led by the highly influential Zdeněk Nejedlý, as leader of the true line of modernist descent for the Czech tradition and the latter as its negator.[40]

A major battle for the Czechs where music and language was concerned, however, was the vexed question of finding a satisfactory accentual basis for setting the language to music. For nearly two hundred years after the Battle of the White Mountain of 1620 Czech effectively ceased to be a literary language. There were some specialist exceptions, such as the libretti for small-scale operas often based on trade occupations, such as Karel Loos' the *Chimney Sweep* (Opera Bohemica de Camino) from the late eighteenth century. Thus, the securing of the integrity of the Czech language was the prime prerequisite for the health of the national revival, a task which fell largely to academic philologists. The major figure in the awakening of interest in the language was Josef Dobrovský (1735–1829). A cleric, and formerly a Jesuit before the abolition of the order in the Habsburg empire by Josef II, he was also a humanist and, significantly, an

---

[36] From Eliška Krásnohorská, 'O české deklamaci hudební' [concerning Czech musical declamation], *Hudební listy*, ii, nos. 1–3. (1, n8, 15 March 1871). All translations from this article are by the author. See also Tyrrell, *Czech opera*, pp 253–98, and Jan Smaczny, 'Dvořák's *Cypresses*: a song cycle and its metamorphoses', *Music & Letters*, 72:4 (1991), 560–5. [37] See in particular 'Music and the Literary Revival', pp 194–224. [38] Ibid., p. 97. [39] Tyrrell, *Czech opera*, p. 213. [40] This view was promulgated in Zdeněk Nejedlý, *Zdenko Fibich: zakladatel scénického melodramatu* [Zdenko Fibich: the founder of the scenic melodrama] (Prague: 1901), pp 172–3. Nejedlý pursued this campaign against Dvořák and his adherents with considerable virulence throughout his career variously as a critic and writer, and finally as Minister of Education and Culture in the Communist government of Czechoslovakia from 1948.

enthusiastic propagator of Rousseau and Hume. Ironically, much of his voluminous writing on Czech and other Slavic languages was in German and even his greatest successor, Josef Jungmann (1773–1847) was pessimistic that the language would survive. Thus it should not be an object of surprise that František Palacký (1779–1876), widely regarded as the father of the growth of Czech consciousness in the nineteenth century, published the first volumes of his monumental history of Bohemia (Geschichte von Böhmen, 1836–1847) in German (the volumes printed between 1848 and 1867 were issued in Czech).

The practical consequence of the slow development of Czech as a literary language for composers as the national revival moved up a gear in the 1860s was difficulty over accentuation. A poignant example of the frustration felt by composers was voiced by Dvořák in a note at the end of his song cycle *Cypresses* of 1865 in which he stated baldly 'When I played these songs with Mr Bendl he told me that the declamation was wrong in many places; after a year, when my prematurely-born offspring came back to my hands, I realised that his criticism was entirely justified'.[41] The situation was compounded by metrical approaches to setting Czech, a language in which the accent invariably falls on the first syllable in words prompting a firm tendency toward a downbeat character further enhanced by the lack of definite or indefinite articles (in strong contrast to the dominant local language, German). Thus, while many writers attempted to incorporate standard metrical schemes into their poetry and libretti, the complexity of these very same schemes cut across the natural accent of Czech. This had a knock on effect in musical settings since a composer could easily conflict with the metrical patterns in the verse while faithfully reproducing the correct accent of the spoken word. Although Dvořák was a first-language Czech speaker, the style of his word setting at this stage was affected profoundly by German models and thus inappropriate upbeat patterns abound in settings of verse that are for the most part fundamentally accentually downbeat in nature.

Coming to the rescue of Dvořák, and even more seasoned composers among his contemporaries, notably Smetana, was a remarkable young woman poet, Eliska Krásnohorská (1847–1926), who produced one of the formative articles of the national revival where music was concerned: published serially in three editions of one of the most prominent Czech musical periodicals, *Hudební listy*, the article was entitled 'Concerning Czech musical declamation',[42] and in it she analysed with startling clarity the problems faced by composers attempting to deal with their own language:

Let every Czech say: '*přilítlo jaro*', every musician will sing: '*přilítlo jaro*'. This is the consequence of foreign influence, foreign intonation, foreign rhythm and melody, to which we have become accustomed. So, above all, let

---

[41] See Smaczny, 'Dvořák's *Cypresses*', p. 560. For the Czech original see Jarmil Burghauser, *Antonín Dvořák: Thematický Katalog* [Antonín Dvořák: Thematic Catalogue] (Prague: Bärenreiter/*Editio* Supraphon, 1996), p. 62. [42] Krásnohorská, 'O české deklamaci hudební'.

the composer guard against declaiming the first syllable of a multi-syllable word weakly or as an upbeat: there is not a single multi-syllable word in Czech which is weakly accented, since each is pronounced with an accent on the first syllable; whether it is long or short, this strong syllable must be sounded on a strong beat.[43]

Although Otakar Hostinský, one of the chief aestheticians of the national revival, pursued the same subject at greater length and in greater depth some thirteen years later,[44] Krásnohorská's article was the key rallying call. A major consequence of her rise to prominence was that she became the librettist of the last three of Smetana's operas *The Kiss* (Hubička), *The Secret* (Tajemství) and *The Devil's Wall* (Čertova stěna). For Dvořák, the consequence of her article was also far reaching. Having not set Czech for six years after his experience with *Cypresses*, within a month of the article's appearance he was at work on his second opera, *The King and the Charcoal-Burner* (Král a uhlíř) – his first opera, *Alfred*, composed some four years after *Cypresses* was to a German libretto – setting its Czech text with every indication of greater confidence. Thus, what might be described as 'the battle for the idiomatic setting of Czech' had been won and the national revival could proceed on its way with a coherent approach to the treatment of language within a musical frame.

FOLKSONG AND THE HERDERIAN DESCENT

In a sense, the point of closest convergence between the music of the Czech national revival and the development of music in Ireland comes at the start of our long nineteenth century. In the background to both is the presence of Enlightenment thinking from France, Germany and Scotland. The association of music with the national profile was, of course, well established before the main tenets of Enlightenment philosophy were set in place. In the case of Ireland, the credentials for musical excellence are attested to by Giraldus Cambrensis as early as the twelfth century who painted a near prose poem to the art of Irish harp playing.[45] If the association of the nation with music is not as ancient in the Czech tradition, Czech musicians were certainly valued throughout Europe from the seventeenth century onwards. Moreover, music was both celebrated and symbolized as a national characteristic in a number of operas, notably Smetana's *Dalibor* and even more explicitly in Dvořák's *The Jacobin* (Jakobín).[46] In this tale of a prodigal's return to his native Bohemia after the travails of the French Revolution a central figure is Benda, an embodiment of the village musician

---

43 Ibid., 3. Author's translation. **44** Otakar Hostinský, 'O české deklamaci hudební', *Dalibor*, iv, nos. 1–8, 10–12, 18, (1882); reprinted by Urbánek in ed. Emil Chvála, *Rozpravy hudební*, ix (1886). **45** See Gerald of Wales, *The history and topography of Ireland*, trans. J.J. O'Meara (St Ives: Penguin Books, 1982), pp 103–4. **46** See also Tyrrell, *Czech opera*, pp 162–70.

schoolmaster. Throughout the eighteenth century and well into the nineteenth century, the musical schoolmaster was a crucial figure in the community and the village school a place associated with music as Burney attests:

> I went into the school, which was full of little children of both sexes, from six to ten or eleven years old, who were reading, writing playing on violins, hautbois, bassoons, and other instruments. The organist had in a small room of his house four clavichords, with little boys practising on them all: his son of nine years old, was a very good performer.[47]

A key moment in Dvořák's *The Jacobin* comes when the prodigal Bohuš wins over the initially sceptical Benda with an aria rich in sentiment: 'We wandered long in foreign lands, ah, for long years ... only in [Czech] song did we find sweet relief'.[48] If no single instrument in the Czech national revival has quite the iconic status of the harp[49] in Ireland, one instrument, as representative of the musicality of the common folk, was certainly important, the bagpipe. As Tyrrell attests 'Švanda the bagpiper, a Czech village Orpheus whose instrument has magic powers, personified the musicality of the Czech people'.[50] Where Švanda was celebrated in plays and a number of operas by Bendl and Weinberger among others, the bagpipe itself was often called upon to fix musically the typical village location for Czech comedies of the national revival with notable orchestral imitations of the instrument shortly after the rise of the curtain in the first acts of Smetana's *The Bartered Bride* (Prodaná nevěsta) and Dvořák's *The Devil and Kate* (Čert a Káča), as well as setting the scene for the celebrations at the end of the first act of Dvořák's *The King and the Charcoal-Burner*.

Certainly, the belief that both the Irish and the Czechs were 'innately musical' informs many aspects of cultural discourse in both countries. Alongside this trope as part-validation is the celebration of the ancient excellence of the nation's music, expressed on behalf of the Irish most resoundingly in the prefaces to Bunting's collections of 'The Ancient Irish Music'.[51] If the Czech tradition does not resonate with these kinds of exordia, recourse to ancient excellence, whether real, in the case of religious reform and the flowering of culture in the late sixteenth and early seventeenth centuries, or imagined certainly took place. In pursuit of the latter one need look no further than two manuscript sources heralded in the early nineteenth century as evidence of the excellence of the

---

47 *Dr Burney's musical tours*, p. 132: it is interesting to note that Dvořák's musical education in the 1840s and 1850s, including his years at the Prague Organ School, was not materially very different from that of his eighteenth-century Bohemian predecessors.   **48** See Antonín Dvořák, *Jakobín*, vocal score (Prague: Orbis, 1952), pp 212–18.   **49** Interestingly, the folk harp, often associated with itinerant musicians, is encountered quite frequently in the musical iconography of the Czech lands; see Jiří Kleňha, *Harfenictví v Čechách* [Harping in the Czech lands] (Prague: Granit, 1998).   **50** Tyrrell, *Czech opera*, p. 163.   **51** See variously the prefaces to *A general collection of the ancient Irish music* (Dublin: 1796), *A general collection of the ancient music of Ireland* (London: 1809) and *The ancient music of Ireland* (Dublin: 1840) reprinted in facsimile (Dublin: Walton Manufacturing, 2002).

Czech language from the middle ages (the first from before the year 1,000 and the second from the thirteenth century). The Green Mountain Manuscript (Zelenohorský rukopis), which in part supplied the material for Wenzig's libretto for Smetana's opera *Libuše*, and the Queen's Court Manuscript (Rukopis Královédvorský) were, somewhat in the manner of James Macpherson's *Ossian*, creative realizations of old Czech texts produced mainly by Václav Hanka (1791–1867) in 1818, a pupil of Dobrovský and a talented translator of a number of Slav languages.[52]

Numerous Czech composers, including Dvořák, duly set them in good faith. Not only did these forgeries supply the raw material for some of the operas of the national revival, the trope of medieval excellence they represented contributed to evocations of a heraldic past, not unreminiscent of the bardic qualities looked to in so many commentaries concerning Ireland's past.[53] Smetana's image of *Vyšehrad*, the founding fastness of Prague, the first symphonic poem of his cycle *My country* (Má vlast, a celebration of the history, mythology and countryside of Bohemia) begins with a flourish on the harp in frank allusion to the chants of ancient bards. Smetana's own verbal introduction to *Vyšehrad*, recorded in a letter to the Prague publisher Urbánek, records the intended programmatic content of the symphonic poem which is rich in nostalgia for an imagined past: 'The harps of the bards begin; a bard's song tells of the events at Vyšehrad, of its glory, splendour, tournaments and battles, finally of its downfall and ruin. The work ends in elegiac tone.'[54]

So much of this pervasive nostalgia, and its broader consequences in both traditions, is energized by the writing of Johann Gottfried Herder (1744–1803). Comerford quite rightly refers to the significant proximity of Herder's *Treatise on the Origin of Language* (Abhandlung ueber den Ursprung der Sprache) of 1772 to the Belfast Harp Festival of 1792.[55] The effect of Herder's brand of German Enlightenment philosophy was far reaching in both Ireland and among the Czechs. What might be typified as the Herderian descent may be traced through the work of the early philologists and writers, such as Dobrovský and Jungmann, scholars such as Šafařík, poets such as Kollár and founding historians such as Palacký to the 'father' of the new nation of Czechoslovakia, Tomáš G. Masaryk.[56] Herder's jaundiced view of contemporary France as representative of European decay and his enthusiasm for the Slavs in general and Russia in particular as a vitalizing force proved seductive as a means of underpinning the philosophical roots of the Czech national revival. These emerged most strongly

---

[52] See Tomáš G. Masaryk, *The meaning of Czech history*, ed. René Welleck, trans. Peter Kussi (Chapel Hill: University of North Carolina Press, 1974), p. 153. [53] See for example Richard Vincent Comerford, *Ireland: inventing the nation* (London: Arnold, 2003), pp 181–5. [54] Reprinted in the introduction to the Smetana collected edition, ed. František Bartoš, vol. xiv (Prague: Národní hudební vydavatelství orbis, 1958). Smetana added in German the word Bardengesang after 'The bard's song' and at the end 'Nachgesang des Barden'. Author's translation. [55] Comerford, *Ireland*, p. 184. [56] See Frederick M. Barnard, 'Humanism and Titanism: Masaryk and Herder' in *T.G. Masaryk (1850–1937): vol. 1, Thinker and politican*, ed. Stanley B. Winters (London: Macmillan, 1990), p. 23.

in Herder's influential consideration of the Slavic people found in his major work, *Ideas on the philosophy of the history of mankind*, 1784–91.[57] Translated into Latin in 1795 by Václav Durych and finally into Czech by Jungmann, the essay was full of assertions that found a powerful resonance with the Czechs of the national revival. More specifically culturally, it promoted a tendency toward the idealization of the Czech and Slavic character reflected at an early stage in the literary works of Kollár and the scholarship of Palacký and Šafařík. In part this was managed by portraying the adversaries of the Slavs in an exaggeratedly gloomy manner, while, conversely, the Slavs were depicted as peaceful, moderate in their actions and, in the case of the Czechs, of course musical.

This distortion of history, which flows directly from Herder, led to an idealized image of the Slavic character which finds its way into musical portrayals in particular in opera. Peaceful and pastoral is very much the melos projected in parts of Smetana's *Libuše*, notably at the start of the third scene in act one where the harvest is being gathered in, and at an allegorical remove in Dvořák's *Vanda* where the Poles of the story can easily be read as Czechs in a story in which they withstand an invading German army.[58] The inevitable cult of 'victimhood', again whether real or imagined, and the two come together with considerable force in such poems as Hálek's poem of 1869, *The Heirs of the White Mountain* (Dědicové bílé hory),[59] attaches with unselfconscious ease and has no better illustration than in the titles of signal operas from the pioneering years of the national revival such as Smetana's *The Brandenburgers in Bohemia* or J.N. Škroup's *The Sweeds in Prague* (Švédové v Praze) in both of which you can be sure that neither Brandenburgers nor Sweeds are up to any good. Though written on a far larger scale, the sentiments in these operas accord well with those projected in so many of Moore's melodies, not least 'Erin Oh! Erin' with its reference to 'long ages of darkness and storm' and the 'long night of bondage', not to mention 'The full noon of freedom shall beam round thee yet', all to be delivered 'With Feeling and Solemnity'.[60] Even the iconography adopted by Moore for this same publication seems to lean heavily on images of the peaceful and implicitly violated, with shield and helmet at rest upon the greensward on the frontispiece of the 1810 publication, and the pastoral in the crowning of the bard amid rural surroundings as a masted ship sails away in the 1811 publication.

To return to Comerford's suggested coordination of Herder and the Belfast Harp Festival, the force of Herder's philosophy, in which as A. Gillies remarks 'They [folksongs] provide the practical example in support of his general theories'.[61] Much of the folksong collecting that went on among the Slav peoples,

---

57 *Ideen zur Philosophie der Geschichte der Menschheit*, ed. Bernhard Suphan (Berlin: Weidmannsche Buchhandlung, 1909): 'The Slavic Peoples' is found at pages 277–80 of volume xiv of the complete works. **58** See Smaczny, 'Grand opera among the Czechs' in *The Cambridge companion to grand opera*, ed. David Charlton (Cambridge: Cambridge University Press, 2003), p. 378. **59** Set by Dvořák as a cantata in 1872 (B 27), the same year as his settings of poetry from the Queen's Court Manuscript. **60** See Thomas Moore, *A selection of Irish melodies* (Dublin, 1810), p. 7. **61** A. Gillies, *Herder* (Oxford: Basil Blackwell, 1945), p. 75.

notably František Ladislav Čelakovský's formative three-volume *Slavonic national songs* (Slovanské národní písně, 1822–27), owed much to Herder's ideas and practices. Of the Slavs, the Czechs were somewhat behind their fellows such as the Russians, Poles, Ukranians and Slovenians in beginning formal folksong collection and were in fact prompted by the Viennese Gesellschaft der Musikfreunde which charged provincial governments in all parts of the Austrian empire with the fostering of folksong collecting. The chief monuments of this collecting activity were František Sušil's 2,500 *Moravian folksongs with tunes included with the text* (Moravské národní písně s nápěvy do textu; publication complete in 1860) and Karel Jaromír Erben's *Czech folksongs and nursery rhymes* (Prostonárodní česke písně a říkadla; the melodies were published in 1862 and the texts in 1864). Erben's presentation of the melodies separately from the texts is significant (not least for composers such as Dvořák who frequently made recourse to the poetry for art-song settings, but did not use the melodies as any kind of resource for composition) since it made sense simply to provide a single melody line rather than adding an elaborate accompaniment in the manner of Moore and others. This formal, one might suggest, academic approach to the publication of the Czech folksong repertoire is perhaps the fundamental difference between the Czech and Irish understanding of the folk resource. It is noticeable that both Smetana and Dvořák were resistant to the explicit quotation of folksong, although the aesthetics of symmetry and simplicity certainly underpin their composing manner when playing the national card. For the Czechs these monuments of folksong collecting appeared to be just that, monuments, and there is no broad adoption of folksong in an art-music context until the late 1880s and early 1890s, pioneered notably by Janáček. The quite different approach adopted by the Irish, albeit as profoundly influenced by the same Enlightenment philosophical currents, marks one of the most significant differences in attitude to the national accent.

An ironic tail-piece concerning this divergence is exposed by the curious interface between Dvořák and Irish cultural-musical practice in the shape of Hamilton Harty's *An Irish Symphony* (1904). Given the nature of some of Dvořák's own public comments on the potential for folksong in the art music repertoire, any reader might be forgiven for imagining him to be enthusiastic in his quotation of native material. In fact he made only two explicit quotations of folksong in the entirety of his voluminous output: a popular song of Polish origin, 'Hej, Slované', in the scherzo of the early string quartet in D major (B18) and the Czech folksong 'Na tom naše dvoře' in the incidental music to the play *J.K. Tyl* (op. 62, B125) by František Šamberk where the melody is specifically called for by the text. A number of comments attributed to Dvořák during his first stay in America might seem, if not to flatly contradict his own unwillingness to use folksong, to at least belie a dislike of borrowed material:

> When I was in England one of the ablest musical critics in London complained to me that there was no distinctively English school of music, nothing that

appealed particularly to the British mind and heart. I replied to him that the composers of England had turned their backs upon the fine melodies of Ireland and Scotland instead of making them the essence of an English school. It is a great pity that English musicians have not profited out of this rich store. Somehow the old Irish and Scotch ballads have not seized upon or appealed to them.[62]

Notwithstanding the ethnographic confusion, these comments seem clear enough in providing guidance to fellow composers in search of an identity, and while Dvořák himself was not of a mind to follow them himself, plenty of others were. The belief, widespread in the musical press, that the symphony *From the New World* was based on existing plantation melodies,[63] had considerable ramifications abroad, not least in Ireland. After the symphony's Dublin premiere in 1901, the committee of the annual Feis Ceoil initiated a competition for the composition of a symphony based on Irish traditional songs and folk melodies presumably in imitation of Dvořák's supposed practice in his sensationally successful 'American' symphony; Michele Esposito was the first to win the prize in 1902 followed by Hamilton Harty in 1904. Harty's *An Irish Symphony*, while vigorous, superbly orchestrated and ingenious in its use of popular melodies certainly recognizable to his audience, has never approached the popularity of Dvořák's last symphony. One might advance qualitative reasons for this state of affairs, but also surely to be taken into account must be the local dimension represented by melodies with a clear significance only to a limited audience. Thus the misreading of Dvořák's own practices as a composer in general, admittedly in part prompted by such comments as the above, and as the composer of the symphony *From the New World* in particular led to products that were not just founded on, but trapped by their locality.

---

62 From an interview printed in the *New York Herald*, 21 May 1893, reprinted in *Dvořák in America: 1892–1895*, ed. John Tibbetts (Portland, OR: Amadeus Press, 1993), p. 356.   **63** Dvořák himself stated in another interview with the *New York Herald*, printed on 15 December 1893, the day before the symphony's premiere that 'I have not actually used of the [plantation] melodies', reprinted in Tibbetts, *Dvořák in America*, p. 363.

Wagner, Bayreuth, and the Irish image of Germany

JOACHIM FISCHER

In previous research I have concerned myself with the Irish perception of Germany, in particular during the period 1890–1939.[1] Scholars working on national images and their function in Ireland, in particular literary scholars, sometimes forget that on the cultural side – not only during these years – music and musicians have shaped the image of Germany in Ireland at least as much as its literature. While Handel, Bach, Beethoven and indeed Wagner continue to mean much to the ordinary Irish citizen, it is less likely that many will have heard of Goethe, Schiller, Lessing, or Günther Grass and Heinrich Böll. Richard Wagner, as will become clearer in the course of this contribution, was an integral part of the Irish perception of Germany during the period I examined. Indeed it can be argued that this particular composer, his music and his world are close to the core of what Irish people associated with Germany then and perhaps still do. National images are remarkably stable and many go back a long way; not a few Irish stereotypes about Germany still at large today have their origin in the decades I intend to look at here in more detail: the time when Wagnerism was in its heyday in the world and in Ireland, more precisely the period from the 1880s to World War I. Wagnerism in Anglo-Irish literature has already received attention in a number of insightful studies.[2] The literary angle is, however, of less interest in this context and will only be touched on. My aim is to set the scene and place Irish interest in Wagner in a broader cultural and political context and relate it to Irish nationalists' growing interest in Germany from the 1890s onwards, an affinity which ultimately led to the German arms shipment in support of the Easter Rising in 1916. Germany was a significant reference point in political and cultural discourses of the time as was Wagner and his works.

I will begin at the close of the long nineteenth century. Illustration 15.1 shows the frontispiece of a book entitled *What Could Germany Do for Ireland?* by the American-Irish nationalist James K. McGuire. It was published by the Wolfe Tone Co. in New York in 1916 and was subsequently distributed secretly in

---

1 Joachim Fischer, *Das Deutschlandbild der Iren 1890–1939: Geschichte – Form – Funktion* (Heidelberg: Winter, 2000). **2** For example, William F. Blisset, 'George Moore and literary Wagnerism', *George Moore's mind and art*, ed. Graham Owens (Edinburgh: Oliver & Boyd, 1968), pp 53–76; Raymond Furness, 'Richard Wagner und Irland', *Richard Wagner, 1883–1983: Die Rezeption im 19. und 20. Jahrhundert. Gesammelte Beiträge des Salzburger Symposions* (Stuttgart: Heinz, 1984), pp 277–89; Patrick O'Neill, *Ireland and Germany: a study in literary relations* (New York, Berne, Frankfurt: Lang, 1985), pp 194ff; Timothy Peter Martin, *Joyce and Wagner: a study of influence* (Cambridge: Cambridge University Press, 1991).

Illustration 15.1: Frontispiece in J.K. McGuire, *What Could Germany Do For Ireland?* (1916).

Ireland by radical separatists in order to drum up support for German-Irish cooperation. Roger Casement was in Germany at the time trying to secure German military help for a full-scale rising in the *soi disant* backyard of Britain, Germany's enemy in the Great War then in its second year.

In the image we see a tall Germanic goddess in full battle armour, her long blond hair flowing, wearing a spiked helmet, holding in one hand the shield with the German Imperial eagle and with the other pointing towards the sun rising over a landscape of smoking chimney stacks. To us this seems like a grim prophesy about the effects of industrialisation, at the time this was to be taken at face value and was meant positively: Germany was to bring Ireland into the new age in which as Æ (George Russell) was to put it in the 1920s, Ireland's political and economic problems were to be solved 'in the big modern way.'[3] The little black haired Cathleen Ní Houlihan seems excited about these prospects and is clasping her hands in delight while turning her back to what lies in the shade: little thatched cottages, intended as a symbol of Irish backwardness. Where did this image of the Germanic warrior goddess originate, and why did Irish separatism consider it useful and consequently appropriate it for its ideological purposes? Germany had been on the minds of Irish nationalists ever since

3 *Irish Statesman*, 28 March 1925, 70.

Herder's idea of basing national identity on cultural traditions, on language, literature and national myths had impacted on the Young Irelander Thomas Davis in the 1840s. The Young Irelanders, however, were less interested in ancient myths than in the actions and words of German nationalists in their successful fight against Napoleon and their continued struggle for German unity and nationhood. The two mythical figures in the illustration were largely creations of the second half of the nineteenth century, of Standish James O'Grady and the Celtic Renaissance on the Irish side, and more than any other of Wagner and his works on the German side. Wagner's operas, which became increasingly more influential from the foundation of the German Reich in 1871 onwards, spread the image of the powerful and dominating German gods and goddesses all over the world. Musically and visually they illustrated the Kaiser's drive towards a place in the sun, the attempt of a late-comer to establish Germany as a world power and to rival the British Empire. In Ireland Wagner impacted not only on the musical world. Within Irish literary circles, Yeats and Edward Martyn acted as important transmitters of Wagner's creative use of national myths and his ideas of the *Gesamtkunstwerk* as evidenced by their contributions to the debate in the *Daily Express* about the literary ideals of 1899. For example, a parallel was drawn between Wagner's Siegfried and the Irish model hero Cú Chullainn.[4]

We have to view the Wagner reception in Ireland against the backdrop of debates in Irish nationalism. The political debate centred around the questions of what strategy to pursue to obtain the much desired independence and which allies to co-opt in the struggle against the British overlord. Against the parliamentary strategy of the Parliamentary Party the more radical sections of Irish nationalism grouped around Arthur Griffith and his Sinn Féin banner. Their disillusionment with their erstwhile ally France grew steadily, especially after the latter concluded the *Entente cordiale* with Britain in 1904. In these circles Germany got an increasingly better press. Irish nationalists applauded Germany's attempts to stand up to the British, however bungled her efforts were. The fact that some Irish separatists fought alongside German soldiers in the Boer War further improved the image of Germany among the separatists:

> The Germans and Irish are shoulder to shoulder
> The Teuton's War eagle, the harp of the Gael
> [...]
> For Freedom! For freedom! From Rhine and from Shannon,
> As they stood against Caesar, years thousand ago

we read in Frank Hugh O'Donnell's poem 'For the free Republics!' published in Griffith's *United Irishman* of 21 October 1899. Ancient links are constructed here which go back even further than the Irish monks who went to Germany in the

---

[4] Republished as John Eglinton et al., *Literary ideals in Ireland* (Dublin: 1899); see also William Irwin Thompson, *The imagination of an insurrection, Dublin, Easter 1916: a study of an ideological movement* (West Stockbridge, MA: Lindisfarne Press, 1982), pp 49ff.

early Middle Ages, delving into the dark mists of history when Germans and Celts fought mythical battles against the Roman invaders.

Around the same time, nationally-minded Irish Catholic clerics, who were gaining an increasing influence in Irish nationalism, showed themselves impressed by the victory their German co-religionists had scored against Bismarck in the *Kulturkampf* and looked to Germany rather than secularized France for solutions to the problems the new industrial age and the resultant social questions posed. Some of the German models for Irish Catholics were also of a musical nature. The Irish Cecilian movement for Catholic church music tried to follow the example set by the movement in Germany, with the German Heinrich Bewerunge, appointed Professor of Church Music in Maynooth in 1888, further encouraging close contacts with his home country.[5] There was strong support from this side for Wagner, as evidenced by articles on his music in the journal *Lyra Ecclesiastica*. A commentator in the 1888 volume noted with satisfaction that Wagner 'was thoroughly in accord with the principles of the Cecilian Society' because of its focus on choral singing; he noted that the Kaiser supported the movement as well.[6] Other Germans also came to Ireland to revitalize musical life. The English-based opera company of Carl Rosa, a German by the name of Carl Rose, was responsible for many opera performances in Dublin during the period in question, among them not a few Wagner operas. There were German organists whose appointment Bewerunge had supported,[7] and in Cork Aloys Fleischmann (senior) and the Swiss Theo Gmür were active in reinforcing the notion of Germany as a musical model at the very time political developments brought German Imperialism into view for Irish nationalists. The ground was fertile for Wagner's musical images of the heroic Germanic and Celtic mythical past.

It is true, of course, as Harry White has shown in his contributions to the social history of Irish music, that opera and indeed art music did not play a major role in the debates around the turn of the century about the creation of a new Irish culture.[8] Compared to other European countries, there was little classical music available, there was no resident symphony orchestra, only travelling companies from Italy and Britain, such as Rosa's, brought opera to Dublin a few times a year. Opera was clearly and demonstrably a 'foreign' art form and additionally associated with the Anglo-Irish establishment in the Irish capital. Irish nationalists were therefore unlikely to have much time for it, which makes Wagner's relative success stand out even more.[9]

Throughout most of the nineteenth century Italian opera was more popular than German opera,[10] and it was largely due to Wagner that this situation changed

---

5 See Kieran Anthony Daly, *Catholic church music in Ireland: the Cecilian Reform Movement* (Dublin: Fourt Courts Press, 1995). 6 'The Emperor William II of Germany, Bismarck, and Church Music', *Lyra Ecclesiastica*, 11 (1899), 63ff. 7 See Paul Collins' chapter in this volume. 8 White, *The keeper's recital*, pp 94ff. 9 I am stating all of this tentatively since little work appears to have been done on the cultural (rather than musical) history of opera and its audience during the time in question. A long-standing nationalist bias it seems has favoured research into indigenous 'traditional' music rather than into 'foreign' forms such as opera. 10 See T.J. Walsh, 'Opera in nineteenth-century Dublin', *Four centuries of music*

towards the end of the century. His operas had started to make an impact in Dublin from the 1870s onwards. In 1875 the opera-going public was introduced to *Lohengrin* sung in Italian. Three years later *Der fliegende Holländer* was given in English by the Carl Rosa Opera Company. That Wagner and his music must have meant something to the Irish educated middle classes is evidenced by the Irish newspapers of the time. The Irish dailies, the *Daily Express*, the *Freeman's Journal*, the *Irish Times* and the *Cork Examiner*, all contain detailed reports over several days about the opening of the Opera House in Bayreuth with the first complete performance of the *Ring* in August 1876.[11] The fact that the German Emperor Wilhelm I was present, thus underlining both the importance of the event and the link between Wagner and Germany's political establishment, was stressed by the commentators. When Wagner died in Venice on 13 February 1883, all papers marked his passing with extensive obituaries, despite the fact that the event had to compete for space with the Phoenix Park murder trials which inevitably grabbed the headlines. Interestingly, and a good indicator of the composer's fame, one of the longest obituaries appeared in the *Limerick Chronicle* of 17 February 1883, a reprint of an article in the English paper the *Standard*. *The Freeman's Journal* wrote at the time:

> The events at Bayreuth, a small town in Central [*sic*] Germany, are so recent as not to require recital. The spread of German literature and the influence of German political ascendancy no doubt assisted Wagner of late years. Nowhere is Wagner's musical genius unrecognized, and nowhere will the announcement of his death fail to evoke expressions of regret as at the news of the decease of a familiar, a favourite, and a friend.[12]

Wagner was recognized as part of a growing attention worldwide to Germany and its culture, or *Kultur*.[13] Although, as in all obituaries, there is a good deal of *de mortuis nihil nisi bene*, in these articles there can be little doubt that Wagner was at the time of his death, perhaps after the Kaiser and Bismarck one of the best-known Germans in Ireland.

There were a small group of Irish Wagnerians who had the means to travel to the home of their hero, Bayreuth. The fact that Bayreuth was in Catholic Bavaria helped: the Catholic majority in Ireland, in particular those of a nationalist persuasion had since the days of Catholic emancipation developed a particular affinity with that part of Germany which had supported O'Connell and his policies.[14] An equally positive image existed of another Catholic part of Germany, the Rhineland. Because Wagner's works used myths associated with the Rhine

---

in Ireland: essays based on a series of programmes broadcast to mark the 50th anniversary of the BBC in Northern Ireland, ed. Brian Boydell (London: BBC, 1979), pp 45–9.   **11** See Michael Murphy's chapter in this volume for a consideration of these reports.   **12** *FJ*, 14 February 1883.   **13** M.F. Egan's article 'Kultur and our need of it', *Studies*, iv (1915) proves the importance of the German concept of *Kultur* for Ireland; see also Fischer, *Das Deutschlandbild der Iren*, pp 534–36.   **14** See Geraldine Grogan, *The noblest agitator: Daniel O'Connell and the German Catholic movement, 1830–50* (Dublin: Veritas, 1991).

they fitted neatly into preconceived (Romantic and positive) notions and indeed travel habits and in turn reinforced them. Bayreuth of course had to compete with the ultimate Catholic spectacle at Oberammergau. The first major Irish travel account about Oberammergau appeared a few years before those about Bayreuth,[15] but there was never a real competition between the two destinations, since the Passion Plays took place only every ten years.

Tickets for the 1876 opening festival in Bayreuth were £15 for the four nights, a huge outlay for would-be Irish visitors who had to add the considerable travel expenses. By 1882 as *Hibernia* noted,[16] prices had come down to 28 shillings for the first performance of *Parsifal*, but this still only enabled the upper echelons of society to see Wagner in Bayreuth. Certainly with his *Parsifal* Wagner had endeared himself to Irish Catholics, and Catholics as well as Protestants were drawn to Bayreuth. This becomes clear in one of the first Irish accounts of a visit to Bayreuth which appeared in the Jesuit journal *Irish Monthly* in 1888. In that year Thomas F. Woodlock made what he called 'a pilgrimage to the shrine of Wagner'. The author is 'sworn to detest the sparkling champagne of Donizetti or the cloying juices of the Verdian and Bellinian grapes' and declares himself a Wagnerian for whom 'is reserved the delicious sherbet of irregular intervals and crashing combinations of unprepared discords, that appeal only to the educated palate.'[17] He thus displays the elitism which was to remain a strong feature in Irish Wagnerism: Wagner was particularly for the initiated and intellectual music lovers. Bayreuth was a meeting place of many nationalities and Woodlock was not the only one who indulged in ethnographic speculation, a very popular intellectual past-time and a vulgarized version of what Gobineau, Chamberlain and other racial theorists produced clothed in philosophical jargon around the same time. Massive stereotyping abounded, 'Golden-haired Gretchen and her soft blue eyes' took Woodlock's special fancy. His jocular linguistic advice highlights wide-spread anti-French sentiments in Germany: 'English is a safer resource than French, especially if one inverts the order of the sentence, putting the verb last, and using the longest words that suggest themselves'.[18] He was, like most travellers, largely ignorant of the German language. This made it easier to maintain the preconceived notion that, as George Moore put it: 'music is the art of Germany just as poetry is the art of England'.[19] Music was the only thing these visitors clearly understood. Woodlock's article ends with a longish description of *Parsifal*: 'one of the most remarkable works that mortal man has ever created [...]. It is more than opera and more than drama, and only less than a religious service', its music 'is beyond the expressive power of words.'[20]

Such Catholic appropriations of Wagner jarred somewhat with Ireland's most avid Wagnerian, the *enfant terrible* of the Celtic Renaissance, the novelist George Moore, Protestant landlord and *fin-de-siècle* aesthete. Rather than *Parsifal*, *The*

15 Gerald Molloy, *The Passion Play at Oberammergau* (London: Burns & Oates, 1872). **16** *Hibernia*, July 1882, 112. **17** T.F. W[oodlock], 'A pilgrimage to the shrine of Wagner', *Irish Monthly*, 16 (1888), 581. **18** Ibid., 582. **19** George Moore, *Hail and Farewell: Ave, Salve, Vale*, ed. Richard Allen Cave (Gerrards Cross: Smythe, 1985), p. 174. **20** Woodlock, 'A Pilgrimage', 591.

Ring he judged to be the composer's greatest musical work. Moore had perhaps the most sustained and intense relationship with Wagner's works, and he also produced perhaps the best known Irish account of a journey to Bayreuth. Moore had become acquainted with Wagner's music in July 1892 when his cousin Edward Martyn convinced him he should accompany Martyn to London's Drury Lane Theatre to hear *Rheingold* and *Tristan und Isolde*. Moore went to Bayreuth numerous times, mostly together with Martyn, for the first time in August 1894. In August 1897 he met Cosima Wagner. The account in Moore's autobiography *Hail and Farewell*, first published in three volumes between 1911 and 1914, is a collation and distillation of all these journeys.

What remained unreflected in Woodlock's article, Moore drags to the surface, mainly to pique Martyn, his devout Catholic cousin and travel companion: 'Bavaria comprises two spectacles: the Asiatic Gods in the South on the Tyrolean frontier, while the original Rhine Gods display themselves in the North at Bayreuth'.[21] There was indeed something curious in Catholics admiring the Pagan Germanic myths which Wagner brought onto the stage. This kind of questioning and critical reflection was, however, untypical for Irish Wagner reception. Moore is often taken as the prime example of Irish Wagnerism. This is correct in terms of the influence which Wagner had on his works, but his reception of Wagner is utterly untypical. Martyn probably reflected Irish attitudes much better. If it is true what Moore wrote in his account, Martyn did not like the discussion on Asiatic and Pagan gods, and did not speak to Moore for days. Also, admiration for Wagner tended to go hand in hand with an appreciation of Germany and what it stood for, often with a strong nationalist slant. In this regard again Moore was highly unrepresentative, as he disliked most of what he saw in Germany. In his typical cynical style Moore, after identifying the spot where Alberich robbed the Rhine Maiden's gold, says about the Rhineland:

> We are in the country of Günther and Hagen. It must have looked better in those days than it does now; otherwise Siegfried would not have left Brünnhilde. [...] mile after mile of ugly hills, disfigured by ruins of castles in which one would fain believe that robber-barons once lived, but one knows in one's heart that they were only built to attract tourists [...]

The Germans do not fare much better: he has hardly crossed the frontier at Aachen when 'large-bellied' Germans enter his compartment, 'their *Frauen* – swaying, perspiring German females, hugely breasted, sweating in their muslin dresses, and tediously good-humoured.'[22] 'Heavy' is one of his most frequently used adjectives, German thought is 'clumsy, quaint, heavy',[23] all of which upsets Moore's aesthetic sensibilities. His lack of interest in the real Germany may very well be the explanation for the curious fact that there is almost nothing about Germany and the Germans in his two Wagnerian novels, *Evelyn Innes* (1898) and

21 Moore, *Hail and Farewell*, p. 172.   22 Ibid., p. 151.   23 Ibid., p. 170.

Sister Theresa (1901) in which the heroine experiences one Wagnerian situation after another. In *Evelyn Innes* the only German, Mr Goetze, is a London stage manager and his most remarkable characteristic is his toothache. In his autobiography, the daily working lives of ordinary people are presented as particularly ugly. Bayreuth was for Moore simply an object of artistic desire. Moore's account appeared when the author was living in London, and it is an interesting question to what extent Moore's criticism of Germany can be linked to the political climate in Britain, and the rising Anglo-German antagonism in those years expertly described by Paul M. Kennedy.[24] When Mainz is described as a 'pompous town – imitation French'[25] we begin to sense that Moore's sympathies are more with Germany's neighbour and rival across the Rhine, where the author actually spent many years of the earlier part of his life. The admiration for Wagner in the works of Yeats and other Anglo-Irish Wagnerians similarly hardly ever translates into interest in the country and its people. Much as the Protestant authors of the Celtic Renaissance were influenced by Wagner and imbibed certain philosophical tenets of Nietzsche they kept their distance from the politics as well as the social and economic actualities of Germany. Literary images of Germany from the pens of Celtic Revivalists which we have from this period are, unlike Wagner's operas, unpolitical escapes into the distant past, often centred on the Rhine: 'The foamy beard of old Father Rhine' envelopes a Romantic tale inspired by Wagnerian themes in John Todhunter's libretto for Dublin composer James Cooksey Culwick's opera *The Legend of Stauffenberg*.[26]

There are indications that for Catholic writers Wagner was embedded in broader appreciation of Germany. The country's mythical past also casts its spell over Edward Martyn. In his drama *The Heather Field* published in 1899 the two brothers Carden and Myles reminisce about their travels to Germany down the Rhine with Boppart and Cologne as highlights and recall the German myths of the Lorelei and the Rhinegold. But Martyn was also an ardent supporter of the Cecilian movement and as his article 'Wagner's Parsifal, or the Cult of Liturgical Aestheticism' of 1913 shows he saw Wagner's works as a guiding star for building a new Catholic Irish music culture.[27] Martyn admired the German people and the role that state-supported theatre played in Germany as an educational institution. Contrasting this situation with England he wrote: 'popular drama has turned the English theatres into the dreariest wilderness. Coming back from the continent England appears to be a comparatively half-civilised country'.[28]

We find another Catholic response to Wagner and German mythology in the works of the most popular Catholic author of the time, Canon Patrick Sheehan. Sheehan was an even more enthusiastic admirer of German culture than Martyn. His novels abound in references about German literature, philosophy and music

---

24 Paul M. Kennedy, *The rise of the Anglo-German antagonism, 1860–1914* (London, Atlantic Highlands, NJ: Ashfield Press, 1980). **25** Moore, *Hail and Farewell*, p. 151. **26** John Todhunter, *The Legend of Stauffenberg*. Music by James Cooksey Culwick (Dublin: Gibbs, 1890), p. 6. **27** *Irish Review*, 3 (1913), 535–40. **28** Edward Martyn, 'The modern drama in Germany', *DE*, 11 February 1899.

in glowing terms. No doubt he had a more significant impact on the Irish perception of Germany than his contemporary Protestant literary colleagues who wrote largely for the Anglo-Irish elite and/or an English readership. Sheehan's article on 'The German and the Gallic Muses' which appeared in the *Irish Ecclesiastical Record* of 1887 is illuminating. Going right back to medieval German literature, with the *Nibelungenlied* as an example of 'purely Gothic' art, he argues that German poetry is utterly superior to French poetry. German literature is the product of its landscape, of

> broad majestic rivers, castlecrowned, and jewelled with green islets, its giant forests, dark and gloomy, as if still haunted by the spirit of Druidical worship, its mountains with their brockens and witches, its historic cities that were swept by the storm of political strife, and rent with the rage of battles ...[29]

whereas the French landscape 'of broad, tame, fertile plains [...] smooth, bare levels, dotted with poplars, arranged with the mathematical precision which nature detests, and shallow rivers flowing by dull towns' could only produce a literature full of 'the silly nonsense that forever attaches to purely erotic poetry.'[30] The French language 'of the drawing-room or cabinet, of pastoral loves and sweet simplicities' is like the country associated with the feminine. German on the other hand with its 'rough gutturals of war' is a masculine language. Sheehan's fascination with the Germanic goddesses, the Valkyries, 'who, forgetting their sex, went out on the battle field by night and slew the wounded'[31] is material for a closer psychoanalytic study. Do we have here some deeper psychological roots for Irish Catholic Wagnerism where the cold, male dominated, unerotic, hierarchically structured world of Germanic myths corresponds to certain aspects of the life experience of devout Catholics in general and Catholic clerics in particular? In any case, these passages show that the themes of Wagner's *Ring*, inconsistent as it seemed to Moore, could appeal to Catholics just as much as the Christian tale of *Parsifal*, even if they were priests.

Sheehan's war rhetoric was however mere sublimation. His outlook was conservative, and anti-modernist as well as nationalist; but he was never politically active and attacked the ideologies of the separatists who wanted more than just to admire and dream about national ideals but make them reality. What fascinated him about Germany was that 'everything favours the poetic and philosophic spirit', which is always 'in alliance with the lofty ideas and emotions'.[32] He contrasted this with the low materialist and political thinking he found in Ireland. In his second novel, *The Triumph of Failure*, published soon after the above article in 1899, one of Sheehan's German heroes uses Wagner's higher abstract and metaphysical notions of national being as a weapon against nationalist politics: Professor Messing, a family man with lofty morals and ideals,

---

29 *Irish Ecclesiastical Record*, 3rd series (1887), 48.   **30** Ibid., 49   **31** Ibid.   **32** Ibid.

exclaims '*Yees*, Wagner, *dot* teach you something better *dan de* 'Wearing of the Green,' played upon union pipes *und* a wheezy *goncertina*. Go away, *ye are zhildren!*'[33] Through his German mouthpiece Sheehan uses Wagner to support authority, and categorize all those who intend to upset the status quo as immature and naïve.

There were, however, hardly surprisingly, admirers in these radical separatist circles as well. Even before Woodlock, Maud Gonne had been whisked away to Bayreuth by her father in 1886 when she was 19 years of age. She was to go back there on a regular basis. In her letters to Yeats she relates her excitement during later visits in 1896 and 1901. *Parsifal* she says 'is worth travelling round the whole world to hear.'[34] When the Dublin Transvaal committee visited Paris in 1900 during the Boer War, its members were invited to a performance of *Die Walküre*. They were unable to go but Maud Gonne expresses her conviction in her autobiography that the opera would have pleased Arthur Griffith.[35] She was not the only one who saw a link and a high level of compatibility between Wagner's operas and separatist ideology. On 26 September 1902 *Tristan and Isolde* was performed in the Gaiety Theatre by the Carl Rosa Opera Co. The daily papers focus on the music exclusively but a critic calling himself 'Black Knight' in the ultra-nationalist *The Leader* with a long history of condemning everything foreign was very surprised at the audience's positive reaction to such a serious, 'heavy' piece. He gives the following explanation:

> The audience was Irish, and the legend, though in the hands of a German was Irish. It was the deep yearning, incomprehensible to ourselves, for things Irish which was making itself known. Why had we, whose love of music was proverbial, no master to sing for us in our own tongue the glories of our heroic age. Why had we no minstrel who should keep the spirit of nationality alive, as Germany was kept alive after the disgrace of Jena? The age of English music is passed. Italy is on the wane. Is our star set too, or are we to look forward to the time when Ireland will have its Gounod, its Wagner, and its Mozart?[36]

This sounds almost like Yeats' justification for setting up the Irish Literary Theatre Society and it was very strange that the views of the *Leader* writers, most of whom detested the Anglo-Irish intellectuals even more than the foreigners, should converge to such a degree. Wagner was an extraordinary integrative force: he expressed nationalist yearnings felt by many, his use of legends not only impressed the Protestant Anglo-Irish cultural and literary establishment and devout Catholic intellectuals alike, but also the extreme fringes of Irish nationalism. They all found their Wagner. In the vague and hazy mists of the

---

[33] Patrick Sheehan, *The triumph of failure* (London: Burns & Oates, 1899), p. 179.   [34] *The Gonne–Yeats letters, 1893–1938: always your friend*, ed. Anna MacBride White and A. Norman Jeffares (London: Hutchinson, 1992), p. 142.   [35] Maud Gonne MacBride, *A servant of the queen: reminiscences* (London: Gollancz, 1938), p. 287.   [36] *The Leader*, 4 October 1902, 94.

heroic past in which Germanic and Celtic myths merged all those who had or professed to have Ireland's national future at heart were able to meet.

When the *Ring* sung in English was first performed in Dublin by the Thomas Quinlan Co. from 12 to 16 May 1913 the *Irish Times* gave a detailed account of the history of the tetralogy and a detailed description of each opera. All other Dublin papers followed the event as well in daily instalments. C.H. Cox had doubted the success of the cycle in the *Sunday Independent* of 11 May 1913: 'The Ring – as often happens in domestic life – will be less a matter of joy than of duty. Wagner will long continue to be more admired than loved.' It turned out, however, that the audience loved it. And so did most of the critics, despite some musical inadequacies, in particular the curious exchange of one singer against another for the title role of Siegfried in *Götterdämmerung*. The performance was taken as proof that Wagner could very well be staged in Ireland. In the *Freeman's Journal* W. O'Leary Curtis quoted G.B. Shaw: 'Wagnerism, like charity, begins at home.'[37]

When in 1914 war broke out it was a time for taking sides. In a book published by Maunsell in Dublin in 1914 Joseph Hone pointed out the role which Wagner had played in the theory of Pan-Germanism and German racist ideology. The book was entitled *The German Doctrine of Conquest: A French View* and contained a collection of articles by the French political scientist Ernest Seillière to which Hone added a long introduction. It included Seillière's 'Wagnerian Germanism'. The role which Count Gobineau and Wagner's son-in-law Houston Chamberlain played in the development of German racial mysticism are outlined. Those who were willing to read, found out to what extent Wagner was part of this intellectual movement that underpinned the German war mentality.

But war is hardly ever a time for elaborate philosophical considerations. Naked propaganda was the rhetoric of the day. During the First World War Wagner was largely kept out of the pro- and anti-German propagandist battles, though the images he helped to create as we saw in the beginning moved centre stage.[38] Apart from the Kaiser, Bismarck, Nietzsche and Treitschke were defined as the arch-enemies in the pages of Redmond's *National Volunteer*, the mouth piece of those nationalists who supported the British war efforts. No doubt the clusters of hard voiceless plosives and fricatives made these names particularly suitable for the propagandist task at hand; the gentle sound of Wagner's name would not have fitted in as well. Up to the war, Nietzsche's popularity had reinforced interest in Wagner, both together were regarded as the essence of contemporary German intellect and art. Now they were separated. The Catholic writer Shane Leslie, in his book *The Celt and the World* of 1917 which aimed to condemn the Teutonic view of the world, still had good things to say about Wagner, and once again, *Parsifal* in particular:

---

[37] *FJ*, 13 May 1913.   [38] For further discussion of pro- and anti-German propaganda see Fischer, *Das Deutschlandbild der Iren 1890–1939*, chapter iv.

To Wagner's Parsival [*sic*] Celt and Teuton must bow. It is the supreme idealisation of the Legend of the Grail. [...] Wagner let the old Celtic and Catholic legend flower in the melody of his soul. No wonder that Nietzsche, the singer of the monstrous superman, cursed him from his sick-bed, but the holy music of Wagner will outlive the Caliphate of Krupp.[39]

Wagner's break with Nietzsche had clearly helped to safeguard the image of the composer.

As we have seen in Sheehan, German mythology had also created an image of the German woman, strong and at times cruel. The pagan mythic figure of Brünnhilde marked one pole of the Irish image of the German woman, Gretchen the other. It is highly likely that operas contributed to both images, the latter being more a creation of Gounod's *Faust*, popular around the same time as Wagner's works, rather than Goethe's play. The Brünnhilde figure, hardly surprisingly, was exploited in World War I anti-German propaganda. In an anti-German satire written by Mary Carbery in 1916 *The Germans in Cork* all German women are of this type, one, interestingly enough, a piano teacher by the name of Louisa Vogel who gives another German woman, Baronin von Kartoffel, the advice to protect her husband by violent means from Irish women: 'I long to see you annihilate these shameless ones who buss around Government House like vultures round the innocent turtle dove',[40] referring to Frau Baronin's bumbling husband.

Little remained of literary Wagnerism after World War I, with Thomas MacGreevy's 'Crón Tráth na nDéithe' (Irish for 'Götterdämmerung') containing one of the few literary allusions.[41] Wagnerism like European symbolism, which it was considered a part of, had run its course. It was to take almost 90 years and a politically much less explosive and divisive post-modern Celtic Tiger Ireland before Wagner's key work, *The Ring*, was performed again in Ireland. This time (2002) the venue was University Concert Hall in Limerick, and as in 1913, it played to a packed and hugely appreciative audience. Whether, and of what, this might indicate the beginnings of a revival remains to be seen.

---

39 Shane Leslie, *The Celt and the world: a study of the relation of Celt and Teuton in history* (New York: Scribner, 1917), pp 75ff.   **40** Baron von Kartoffel [pseudonym for Mary Carbery], *The Germans in Cork* (Dublin: Talbot, 1917), p. 100.   **41** Thomas MacGreevy, 'Crón Tráth na nDéithe', *Collected poems of Thomas MacGreevy: an annotated edition*, ed. Susan Schreibman (Dublin: Anna Livia Press; Washington D.C.: Catholic University of America Press, 1991), pp 14–24. It was written on Easter Sunday, 1923 and first published in 1929.

Chronology

SIGNIFICANT EVENTS AND PEOPLE ASSOCIATED WITH MUSICAL LIFE IN NINETEENTH-CENTURY IRELAND

AXEL KLEIN

1792
Belfast Harp Festival organised by Belfast Library and Society for Promoting Knowledge.

1794
William Michael Rooke [O'Rourke, Rourke], composer, b. Dublin (d. London, 1847).
William Henry Kearns, composer, b. Dublin (d. London, 1846).

1795
William Forde, folksong collector, composer, b. Cork (d. London, 1850).

1797
Samuel Lover, writer, composer, painter, b. Dublin (d. St Helier, Jersey, 1868).
John Smith, composer, professor of music, b. Cambridge (d. Dublin, 1861).
Edward Bunting (b. Armagh, 1773; d. Dublin, 1843) publishes *A General Collection of Ancient Irish Music* (London); two further volumes appeared in 1809 (London) and 1840 (Dublin).

1799
Francis James Robinson, tenor, organist, composer, b. Dublin (d. Dublin, 1872).

1801
Thomas Augustine Geary, composer, d. Dublin (b. Dublin, 1775).
Joseph Augustine Wade, composer, b. Dublin (d. London, 1845).

1806
George Alexander Osborne, pianist, teacher, composer, b. Limerick (d. London, 1893).
Tommaso Giordani, composer (b. *c.*1733, Naples) d. Dublin.

1808
Michael William Balfe, composer, b. Dublin (d. Rowney Abbey, England, 1870.)
Edward Bunting establishes the Belfast Harp Society (active until 1813: see also *1819*).

Thomas Moore's first volume of *Irish Melodies*, with accompaniments by John Stevenson, continued serially to 1834 (London).

1810
Joseph Cooper Walker, antiquarian, d. Dublin (b. Dublin, 1761).
Francis Robinson founds The Sons of Handel (choral society).

1811
Richard Michael Levey [O'Shaughnessy], violinist, writer, arranger, b. Co. Meath (d. Dublin, 1899).

1812
William Vincent Wallace, composer, violinist, b. Waterford (d. Chateau de Haget, France, 1865).

1814
First Dublin Grand Musical Festival organised by Lord Mayor and Corporation.
Belfast, Anacreontic Society founded (orchestral).

1815
John William Glover, composer, professor of vocal music b. Dublin (d. Dublin, 1899).
Joseph Robinson, baritone, conductor, composer, b. Dublin (d. Dublin, 1898).

1817
Joseph Francis Duggan, composer, b. Dublin (d. London, 1900).

1819
Bunting establishes the Irish Harp Society (active until 1839).

1821
Theatre Royal in Hawkins Street opens (replaces Crow Street Theatre) until 1880.
Moore, *Irish Melodies, with an Appendix, containing the original Advertisements and the Prefatory Letter on Music* (London: J. Power & Longman Hurst, Rees, Orme and Brown).

1825
Catherine Hayes, soprano, b. Limerick (d. Sydenham, Kent, 1861).
Robert Prescott Stewart, composer, professor of music, critic, b. Dublin (d. Dublin, 1894).

1826
Dublin Philharmonic Society founded, succeeded Anacreontic Society.

1827
William Vipond Barry, pianist, composer, conductor b. Bandon, Co. Cork (d. Port of Spain, Trinidad, 1872).

1830
The Festival Choral founded (to 1836 succeeded by Dublin Choral to 1841).

1831
Second Dublin Grand Musical Festival, organised by the Philharmonic and Anacreontic Societies.
Fanny Robinson [née Arthur], pianist, composer, professor of music, b. England (d. Dublin, 1879).
James Hardiman, *Irish Minstrelsy, or Bardic Remains of Ireland with English Poetical Translations, collected and edited with notes and illustrations*, 2 vols (London: Joseph Robins).

1833
Moore, *Irish Melodies with Miscellaneous Poems, with a Melologue upon National Music* (Dublin: John Cumming).
John Andrew Stevenson, composer (b. Dublin, 1761) d. Kells, Co. Meath.
Philip Cogan, composer (b. Cork, 1748) d. Dublin.

1834
Dublin, The Society of Antient Concerts founded.

1835
Allan James Foley ['Signor Foli'], bass, b. Cahir, Co. Tipperary (d. England, 1899).
George William Torrance, organist, composer, b. Dublin (d. Dublin, 1907).
Paul Bonaventure Alday, composer (b. Perpignan? or Paris? *c.*1763) d. Dublin.

1837
William Charles Levey, composer, conductor, and Richard Michael ['Paganini Redivivus'] Levey, violinist, b. Dublin (d. London, 1894; Portsmouth, 1911 respectively).
Victoire Balfe, soprano, b. Paris (d. Madrid, 1871).
Dublin, University Choral Society founded.

1840
Belfast Anacreontic Society builds its Music Hall in May Street (renamed Victoria Memorial Hall).

1842
Dublin, Metropolitan Choral Society founded (to 1847).

Revd John McHale translates into Irish A Selection of Moore's Melodies (Dublin: James Duffy, *c.*1842, [and 1871]).

1843

Dublin, Antient Concert Rooms are opened.

William McNamara, Downes, *Temperance Melodies for the Teetotallers of Ireland*, 3rd edn. (Cork).

1845

James Cooksey Culwick, composer, conductor, b. West Bromwich (d. Dublin, 1907).

Thomas Davis et al., *The Spirit of the Nation: Ballads and Songs by the writers of "The Nation" with Original and Ancient Music arranged for the voice and piano forte* (Dublin: William Duffy & Sons).

1846

Cork, Antient Concerts Society founded.

Johann Bernhard Logier, pianist, inventor, teacher (b. Kassell, 1777) d. Dublin.

1847

William Ludwig [Ledwidge], baritone, b. Dublin (d. London, 1923).

Augusta Holmès, composer, b. Paris of Irish parentage (d. Paris, 1903).

1848

Dublin, Irish Academy of Music founded (see *1872*)

1851

The Society for the Preservation and Publication of the Melodies of Ireland founded.

Royal Choral Institute founded (to 1855).

1852

Charles Villiers Stanford, composer, professor of music, writer, b. Dublin (d. London, 1924).

Thomas Moore, biographer, poet, and musician, (b. Dublin, 1779) d. Sloperton Cottage, near Devize.

Cork, National Exhibition.

1853

Great Industrial Exhibition organised by the Royal Dublin Society.

Cork, Theatre Royal, George's Street re-opens.

Limerick, Athenaeum opened.

1854
Percy French, entertainer, b. Dublin (d. Liverpool, 1920).

1855
Michele Esposito, composer, pianist, professor of music, b. Castellamare di Stabia (d. Florence, 1929).
Cork, Athenaeum opened.
George Petrie, *The Petrie Collection of the Ancient Music of Ireland* (Dublin: The University Press).

1858
Richard Michael Levey, *The Dance Music of Ireland*, 1st part (London).

1859
Victor Herbert, conductor and composer, b. Dublin (d. New York, 1924).
William Henry Grattan Flood, musicologist, b. Lismore (d. Enniscorthy, 1928).
Michael William Balfe publishes two collections of Moore's *Irish Melodies*.

1861
Thomas O'Brien Butler, composer, b. Caherciveen, Co. Kerry (d. 1915 Co. Cork).

1862
Heinrich Bewerunge, church music scholar, b. Leitmathe, Westphalia (d. 1923, Maynooth).
Frederick St. John Lacy, professor of music in Cork, b. Cork (d. 1935).
Robert O'Dwyer, conductor, critic, composer, professor of Irish music at UCD, b. Bristol of Irish parentage (d. Dublin, 1949).
Belfast, Ulster Hall founded.

1863
Alicia Adelaide Needham, composer, b. Downpatrick (d. London, 1945).

1864
Antient Concerts Society ceases to function.
Joseph O'Mara, tenor, opera manager, b. Limerick (d. 1927, Dublin).
Dublin, Harmonic Society of St Cecilia founded to promote Catholic Church music.
Charlotte Milligan Fox, composer, author, b. Omagh, Co. Tyrone (d. London, 1916).

1865
Great Dublin International Exhibition of Fine Arts and Manufactures, at Exhibition Palace, Earlsfort Terrace.

Harry Plunket Greene, baritone, writer, b. Old Connaught House, Co. Wicklow (d. London, 1936).

1866
Charles Wood, composer, teacher, b. Armagh (d. Cambridge, 1926).

1868
Annie Wilson Patterson, composer, conductor, lecturer, journalist, organist, b. Lurgan (d. 1934, Cork).

1869
Carl Gilbert Hardebeck, organist, composer, professor of music, b. London (d. Dublin, 1945).

1871
Vincent O'Brien, conductor, singing teacher, b. Dublin (d. Dublin, 1948).
Dublin, Gaiety Theatre opens.

1872
Belfast Musical Society founded.
Irish Academy of Music receives royal charter.

1873
Patrick Weston Joyce, *Ancient Irish Music* (Dublin: Mcglashan & Gill).
Richard Michael Levey, *The Dance Music of Ireland*, 2nd part (London).

1874
Belfast Musical Society and Classical Harmonists amalgamated to form the Belfast Philharmonic Society

1875
Dublin Musical Society founded by Joseph Robinson (to 1903).

1879
Hamilton Harty, composer, b. Hillsborough, Co. Down (d. Hove, 1941).
Dublin Orchestral Union starts under W.H. Telford.
Lyria Ecclesiastica founded, journal of the Irish Society of St Cecilia (to 1893).

1882
Herbert Hughes, composer, b. Belfast (d. London, 1937).
Geoffrey Molyneux Palmer, composer, b. Staines, Middlesex (d. Dublin, 1957).
C.V. Stanford, *Songs of Old Ireland: A Collection of Fifty Irish Melodies Unknown in England; The words by Alfred Perceval Graves* (London: Boosey & Co.).

1883
Arnold Bax, composer, b. Streatham (d. Cork, 1953).

1884
John McCormack, tenor, b. Athlone (d. Dublin, 1945).
John Francis Larchet, composer, professor of music, conductor, b. Dublin (d. Dublin, 1967).

1886
Royal Dublin Society established a series of chamber music recitals.

1889
Ina Boyle, composer, b. Enniskerry, Co. Wicklow (d. Co. Wicklow, 1967).
Margaret Burke-Sheridan, soprano, b. Castlebar (d. 1958, Dublin).

1897
May, first Feis Ceoil and Oireachtas festivals.
Dublin, (new) Theatre Royal opened.

1898
Orpheus Choral Society (later the Culwick Choral Society) founded.

1902
Palestrina Choir founded.

Select bibliography

ARTICLES AND BOOKS ON MUSIC IN IRELAND OR WITH IRISH
INTEREST FROM THE LONG NINETEENTH CENTURY

ARTICLES

Best, R.I., 'The Feis Ceoil', *Irish Yearbook* (1908), 154–6.
Bumpus, John Skelton, 'Irish church composers and the Irish cathedrals', 2 parts, *Proceedings of the Musical Association* (Session 26, 1899), 79–113, 115–59.
Bewerunge, Heinrich, 'The teaching of music in Irish schools', *Irish Ecclesiastical Record*, 4th series, 2 (December 1897), 481–7.
——'The special *charm* of Irish melodies sung "traditionally"', *Irish Ecclesiastical Record*, 4th series, 8 (August 1900), 140–54.
——'Cecilian Music', *New Ireland Review*, 13:2 (1900).
——'Irish traditional singing', *New Ireland Review*, 19 (1903), 20–32.
——'The neumatic notation', *Church Music*, 1 (1905) 33–44; 2 (1906), 303–14.
Citizen, 'The ancient music of Ireland', 2 (1840), 207–13.
Darley, Arthur, 'Irish music', *An Claidheamh Soluis* (13 November 1909).
Davis, T., 'Essay on Irish songs' in M.J. Barry, *Songs of Ireland*, 2nd edn (Dublin: 1869).
De Chlanndiolúin, Séamus, 'Irish traditional music', *An Claidheamh Soluis* (29 July 1911).
Dublin Journal of Temperance, Science, and Literature, 'Music for the people', 1:10 (2 July 1842), 145–6.
Dublin University Magazine, 'An apology for harmony', 17 (May 1841), 570–84.
——'Polyhymnia: or, Singing for the million', 21 (January–June 1843), 16–28.
——'Our portrait gallery, second series, No. 14, – Sir Robert Prescott Stewart', 85 (March 1875), 266–72.
Ferguson, Samuel, 'Review of James Hardiman, *Irish Minstrelsy; or, Bardic remains of Ireland with English poetical translations* [1831]', *Dublin University Magazine* (April, August, October and November 1834).
Flood, W.H. Grattan, 'Ancient Irish harmony', *Journal of the Irish Folk Song Society*, 3 (1905).
Gaynor, E., 'Irish music according to Dr. Henebry', *An Claidheamh Soluis* (12 December 1903).
Glynn, Joseph, 'Irish minstrelsy', *Dublin Journal*, 1:18 (1 December 1887).
Gmür, Theo, 'The choral singing in our schools: the intermediate system', *Journal of the Ivernian Society*, 5:17 (October–December 1912), 43–8.
Hardebeck, Carl, G., 'Traditional singing: its value and meaning', *Journal of Ivernian Society*, 3:10 (January–March 1911), 89–95.
——'Irish Music', *An Claidheamh Soluis* (numerous issues between September 1916 and June 1917).
Henebry, Richard, 'Irish music – a reply to some of my reviewers', *An Claidheamh Soluis* (28 November 1903).

Select bibliography

Hibernia, 'Review of music in Ireland ... late George Petrie', 1 (1 February 1882), 29 [and letter to the editor on above].
——'Music in Dublin 1' (2 January 1882).
——'Music in Dublin 2' (1 April 1882).
Irish Builder, 'Our "musical festivals" and "musical" critics' (15 January and 15 February 1873).
——'Irish music', 15:315 (1 February 1873), 36–39.
——'Musica Hibernica, lectures delivered by Sir Robert Stewart at Trinity College', 15:315 (1 February 1873).
——'Irish musical biography', 22:487 (1 April 1880), 96, 99.
Irish Musical Monthly, 'Lectures by Mr W.H. Grattan Flood' (April 1902), 24.
——'Lecture on Irish music', 1:11 (January 1903), 116–21.
——'To develop the school music of a whole nation', 1 (May 1902), 25–7.
——'Some remarks on the "theory of music": papers set at the Intermediate Education Examination, 1902', 1:5 (1 August 1902), 65–6.
Irish Teachers Journal, 'Vocal music', 2 (1 May 1868), 112.
Joyce, Patrick Weston, 'Music', *A social history of ancient Ireland* (Dublin: 1903; 2nd edn. Dublin: M.H. Gill and Son, 1913).
Lacy, F. St. John, 'Notes on Irish music', *Proceedings of the Musical Association* (Session 16, 1890), 171–98.
Martyn, Edward [signed 'M'], 'The musical season in Ireland 1899–1900', *New Ireland Review*, 13 (August–October 1900).
——'The RDS and the regeneration of the Irish musician', *New Ireland Review*, 14 (December 1900), 240–2.
——'The Gaelic League and Irish Music', *Irish Review*, 1 (1911).
Moore, Thomas, 'Letter on Music' (1810) cited in Seamus Deane (ed.), *The Field Day anthology of Irish writing*, i (Derry: Field Day, 1991), 1054–5.
——'Mr Moore's suppressed preface to the *Irish Melodies*', *Dublin Examiner* (June 1816), 107–9.
Musical Times, 'Music in Dublin', 32:575 (1 January 1891), 29–30.
Musical World, 'Music past and present in Ireland' (10 July 1875).
Nation, 'Modern music and musicians' (12 January 1850).
——'Music, the interpreter of nationality and literature' (2 February 1850).
——'The national music of Ireland' (1 December 1849).
——'Irish national music' (22 December 1849).
Ní Maeleagain, Éilís, 'Irish music and the traditions', *An Claidheamh Soluis* (30 July 1910).
——'Traditional music and other matters', *An Claidheamh Soluis* (20 August 1910).
Oldham, Edith, 'The Eisteddfod and the Feis Ceoil' [Abstract], *Belfast Natural History and Philosophical Society, Proceedings, Session 1897–8* (1899), 54–9.
Osborne, G.A., 'Musical coincidences and reminiscences', *Proceedings of the Musical Association*, 11 (1882–3), 95–113.
——'The emotional aspects and sympathetic effects of the sister arts: poetry, painting, and music', *Proceedings of the Musical Association* (Session 11, 1884–85), 81–98.
O'Brien, Grace, 'The national element in Irish music', *Irish Monthly*, 43 (November 1915), 704–14.
Ó Ceallaigh, Séamus, 'The Feis Ceoil agus Irish music', *An Claidheamh Soluis* (29 May 1909 and 12 June 1909).

Ó D. [P.], 'Grattan, W.H., *The history of Irish music*,' *An Claidheamh Soluis* (13 May 1905).
O'Dwyer, Robert, 'The modern aspect of Irish music', *Irish Yearbook* (1908), 251–4.
O' Sullivan, P.J., 'Irish music', *An Claidheamh Soluis* (24 March 1900).
——'Irish music', *An Claidheamh Soluis* (19 December 1903).
Patterson, Annie, 'Notes on music, art, etc.', *Journal of the Ivernian Society*, 1:3 (March 1909), 199–201.
Petrie, George, [Reviews of Moore, Bunting, Beethoven, Holden, Fitzsimons and Smith], *Dublin Examiner* (August 1816), 241–53.
——[signed 'P'], 'The ancient music of Ireland' [review of Bunting's volume], *Irish Penny Journal*, 1:1 (4 July 1840), 8.
——[signed 'P'], 'Paddy Coneely, the Galway piper', *Irish Penny Journal*, 1:14 (3 October 1840), 105–8.
——[signed 'P'], 'Our portrait gallery. No. 41 – Edward Bunting. With an etching', *Dublin University Magazine*, 29:99 (January 1847), 64–73.
Rogers, Brendan, 'An Irish school of music', *New Ireland Review*, 13 (1900), 149–59.
Russell, Edmund C., 'The national music of Ireland', *Dublin Journal*, 1:12 (1 August 1887).
Russell, T.O., 'Our Irish music: what is to be its future', *Evening Telegraph* (8 September 1894), 8.
School Music Review, 'School singing competition in Ireland', 1 (1 November 1892), 95.
Sheehan, Canon Patrick, 'The German and the Gallic muses', *Irish Ecclesiastical Record*, 3rd series (1887), 48.
Stanford, Charles Villiers, 'Some thoughts concerning folk song and nationality', *Musical Quarterly*, 1:2 (1915), 232–45.
Stewart, Robert P., 'Music (with illustrations): a lecture', *Lectures delivered before the Dublin Young Men's Christian Association* (Dublin: Hodges Smith, 1863), 107–71.
——'Irish church music', *Ulster Journal of Archaeology*, 2nd series, i (1895), 128–32.
——'Swift and Handel', *Irish Builder*, 16:344 (15 April 1874), 112, 115.
——'The Wagner Festival', *Daily Express* (1, 2 and 4 September 1876).
——'A New Work by Balfe', *Daily Express* (19 October 1881).
——'Organs', *Irish Builder*, 30:676 (15 February 1888), 55.
——'The Clarseach', *Daily Express* (23 December 1889).
——entries on Bach, Berlioz and Sterndale Bennett in *Cassell's biographical dictionary containing original memoirs of the most eminent men and women of all ages and countries* (London: Cassell, Petter & Galpin, 1867–69).
——'Irish music', *Grove's dictionary of music and musicians*, ed. J.A. Fuller Maitland (London: Macmillan, 1906), 2, 507–11.
——'Moore, Thomas', ibid., 3, 256–58.
——'O'Carolan', ibid., 3, 423–24.
'T', 'On the cultivation of music in Ireland', *Carlow College Magazine*, 1 (March 1870), 620–7.
T.H. M'C, 'Musical reform', *Irish Magazine and National Teachers Gazette*, 1:3 (1 July 1860), 47–8.
Vignoles, Olinthus J., 'Reminiscences of Sir Robert P. Stewart', *Musical Times*, 35 (1894), 318–319.
W[oodlock], T.F., 'A pilgrimage to the shrine of Wagner', *Irish Monthly*, 16 (1888).

Select bibliography 315

BOOKS

Barry, William Vipond, *Dissertation on the emotional nature of musical art and its media of operation* (London: 1863).
Barrett, William Alexander, *Balfe: his life and works* (London: Remington, 1882).
Bernard, William Bayle, *The life of Samuel Lover, R.H.A., Artistic, Literary and Musical* (London: H.S. King & Co., 1874).
Bumpus, John Skelton, *Sir John Stevenson*: *a biographical sketch* (London: Thomas B. Bumpus, 1893).
Collins, Charles MacCarthy, *Celtic Irish songs and song-writers, with an introduction and memoirs* (London: J. Cornish & Sons, 1885).
Collison, W.A. Houston, *Dr Collison in and on Ireland: a diary of a tour, with personal anecdotes, notes, autobiographical and impressions* (London: Robert Sutton, 1908).
Conran, Michael, *The national music of Ireland, containing the history of the Irish bards, the national melodies, the harp and other musical instruments of Erin* (Dublin: Duffy, 1846; 2nd edn, London: 1850).
Culwick, James Cooksey, *The rudiments of music* (2nd edn., Dublin: Ponsonby, 1887).
——*Handel's Messiah; discovery of the original word-book used at the first performance in Dublin, April 13, 1742, with some notes* (Dublin: Ponsonby & Weldrick, 1891).
——*The distinctive characteristics of ancient Irish melody: the scales: a plea for restoration and preservation* (Dublin: E. Ponsonby, 1897).
——*Sir Robert Stewart: with reminiscences of his life and works* (Dublin: Chadfield, 1900).
——*The works of Sir Robert Prescott Stewart: catalogue of his musical compositions* (Dublin: University Press, 1902).
——*Fifty years in the life of a great Irish musician* (Derby: Chadfield & Son, 1903).
Dublin Musical Festival programme books of the words of six concerts ... ms notes by Sir G. Smart (Dublin: W. Underwood, 1831).
Feis Ceoil, Irish Musical Festival, Dublin, May 18th, 19th, 20th, and 21st, 1897 [Programme] (Dublin: Dollard Press, 1897).
Feis Ceoil, Irish Musical Festival Dublin, May 15th, 16th, 17th, 18th, 19th, and 20th 1899 [Programme] (Dublin: Waller & Co., 1899).
Flood, William Henry Grattan, *The story of the harp* (London: Scott; New York: Scribner, 1905).
——*A history of Irish music* (Dublin: Browne & Nolan, 1905; 3rd edn. 1913).
——*William Vincent Wallace, a memoir* (Waterford: Waterford News, 1912).
Fox, Charlotte Milligan, *Annals of the Irish harpers* (London: Smith, Elder & Co., 1911).
Graves, Alfred Percival, *Irish literary and musical studies* (London: Elkin Mathews, 1913).
Greene, Harry Plunket, *Interpretation in song* (London: Macmillan, 1912).
Henebry, Richard, *Irish music*, (Dublin: c.1903) [see Henebry in *Articles* above].
Kelly, Michael, *Reminiscences of Michael Kelly*, 2 vols. (London: H. Colburn, 1826; [ed. Roger Fiske, Oxford University Press, 1975]).
Kenny, C.K., *A life of Michael William Balfe* (London: 1875).
Levey, R.M. and O'Rorke, J., *Annals of the Theatre Royal, Dublin, from its opening in 1821 to its destruction by fire, February, 1880; with occasional notes and observations* (Dublin: Dollard, 1880).

Logier, J.B., *A refutation of the fallacies and misrepresentations etc.* (London: 1818): this was a response to *An exposition of the musical system of Mr Logier with strictures on his chiroplast etc. etc. by a committee of professors in London* (London, 1818). [see also *Strictures on Mr Logier's pamphlets ... by a professor of Dublin* (Dublin: 1817)].

MacDonnell, Hercules, *A book of dates, operatic, dramatic and musical, compiled for The Strollers* (Dublin: Browne & Nolan [for private circulation], 1878).

O'Keeffe, John, *Recollections of the life of John O'Keeffe written by himself*, 2 vols. (London: 1826).

Renehan, Laurence F., Very Revd DD, *History of music* (Dublin: C.M. Warren, 1858).

Stanford, C.V., *Studies and memories* (London: 1908).

—— *Pages from an unwritten diary* (London: 1914).

Stewart, Robert P., *Programme of the afternoon recitals of chamber music, Autumn Course, 1886, with analytical notes by Sir Robert Prescott Stewart* (Dublin: Ponsonby & Weldrick, 1886).

—— and Ebenezer Prout: *Royal Dublin Society recitals of classical chamber music, session 1898–99* (Dublin: Ponsonby & Weldrick, 1899).

Stokes, William, *The life of George Petrie* (London: 1868).

Symington, Andrew James, *Samuel Lover: a biographical sketch* (London: Blackie & Son, 1880).

Townsend, Horatio, *An account of the visit of Handel to Dublin; with incidental notices of his life and character* (Dublin: James McGlashan, 1852).

Vignoles, Olinthus J., *Memoir of Sir Robert P. Stewart* (Dublin: Hodges, Figgis, 1898).

Walker, Joseph Cooper, *Historical memoirs of the Irish Bards* (Dublin: for the author, 1786; London: T. Payne & Son, 1786; 2nd edn., 2 vols. Dublin, 1818; facs. reprint New York: 1971).

Young, William, *The Catholic choralist* (Dublin: Catholic Choralist Office, 1842).

Index

Aachen [Aix-la-Chapelle], 123 n. 51, 124 n. 55, 128 n. 75
Act of Union (1800), 11, 54, 59, 278, 280
Adam, Jean Louis, 90
Adare, Viscount, 213 n. 11
Akenson, Donald, 163
Alcock, John, 138
Alday, Paul, 256
Algair, W.H., 116 n. 9
Allegri, Gregorio, 132
Allen, George Benjamin, 137, 245, 246, 248, 251, 251 n. 57
 By the waters of Babylon, 137
 In the beginning was the word, 137
 It is a good thing, 137
 Let my complaint, 137
 The Lord is my shepherd, 137
Allgemeiner Deutscher Cäcilien-Verein, 116
 Musica Sacra, 116
Allott, Richard ['Fiddling Dick'], 131, 136, 142, 145, 146
Amnesty Association, 50
Andrassy, Count, 265 n. 63
Anster, John, 17,
Antrim (town), 235, 236
Aran Islands, Co. Galway, 52 n. 1, 66
Arcadelt, Jacques, 122
 Ave Maria, 122
 Jesu Dulcis Memoria, 122
Ardee, Co. Louth, 124
Ardfinnan, Co. Tipperary, 124
Argyle and Sutherland Highlanders (1st battalion), 51
Armagh, 12, 130–5 passim, 137, 138, 142, 142 n. 58, 144, 145
 Armagh Amateur Harmonic Society, 131
 Armagh Guardian, 133 n. 13, 136
 Armagh Musical Society, 131, 140–4 passim
 Armagh Orchestral Society, 131
 Armagh Philharmonic Society, 131, 141, 141 n. 58, 142, 142 n. 58, 143, 144
 Armagh Philharmonic Society: representative programmes (various composers and performers), 147–8
 Armagh railway disaster, 135
 Ballyshannon Church, 141
 Music Hall, Vicar's Hill, 131, 131 n. 4, 139, 141, 142, 142 n. 58, 144
 St Patrick's Church of Ireland Cathedral, 130, 131, 131 n. 4, 133–45 passim, 245, 251 n. 57
 St Patrick's Church of Ireland Cathedral Collection (Robinson Public Library), 130–45 passim
 St Patrick's Church of Ireland Cathedral Orchestral Society, 140, 141, 142, 144
 Tontine Room, 143, 144
 Very Revd Dean of Armagh, 144
Arnold, Carl, 123, 123 n. 51
Ashe, Andrew, 236, 236 n. 5
Ashton-in-Makerfield, 124
 St Oswald's church, 124
Athenaeum, The, 204, 266
Attwood, Thomas, 132, 136
 Evening Service in F, 136
Auber, Daniel-François-Esprit, 282
 La muette de Portici, 282
Augsburg, 126 n. 67
Austen, Jane, 74, 93
 Emma, 74, 93
Avison, Charles, 131 n. 6
 Eight Concertos, 131 n. 6
Aylward, Theodore, 135

Bach, Johann Sebastian, 120, 132, 132 n. 10, 178, 187, 187 n. 2, 188, 193, 194, 264
 B minor Mass, 132 n. 10, 222 n. 47, 293
 Christmas Oratorio, 132 n. 10
Bailieborough, Co. Cavan, 155
Balfe, Victoire, 228 n. 67
Balfe, William, 17, 18, 19, 20, 20 n. 12, 23, 24, 25, 26, 29, 40, 42, 140, 190, 202, 252, 268, 271, 274, 280
 The Bohemian Girl, 17, 23, 280, 280 n. 11
 The Siege of Rochelle, 140
Balfour, Mary, 83
 Ballet Lute Book, 95

317

318

Ballymena, Co. Antrim, 163
Baltimore (USA), 117 n. 14
Bandon, Co. Cork, 244
Bantry, Co. Cork, 159
Barker, Granville, 27 n. 31
Barnum, T.P., 273
Barry, William Vipond, 244, 245
Bath, 234, 236 n. 5
Battle of the White Mountain, 278 n. 2, 283, 285
Bayreuth, 27, 192, 194, 253, 293, 297, 298, 299, 300, 302
Bayreuth Festival, 253, 265, 297, 298
Beale, William, 243
Beauford, William, 75
Beausang, Ita, 12, 257 n. 17
Becker, 144
Beethoven, Ludwig van, 26 n. 27, 88, 90 n. 56, 104, 140, 150, 178, 187 n. 2, 191, 193, 199, 201, 203, 210, 222, 222 n. 48, 225, 226, 227, 29 n. 71, 244, 258, 260–4 passim, 268, 274, 274 n. 9, 293
  Die Ruinen von Athen, 199, 201
  Fidelio, 229 n. 70
  'Kreutzer' Sonata, 227, 229 n. 70, 263
  Mass in C, 229 n. 70
  Mass in D 'Missa Solemnis', 203
  Mount of Olives, The [Christus am Oelberge], 104, 258 n. 20, 260, 274 n. 9
  Razumovsky Quartets, 199
  Symphony no. 9 'Choral', 150, 261, 261 n. 37, 262
Belfast, 12, 26, 41, 55, 75, 77, 78, 80, 82, 96, 114, 117 n. 14, 121, 155, 156, 163, 176, 177, 204, 234–51 passim, 275
  Arthur Street (now Arthur Square) Theatre, 237, 238, 240, 241, 245
  Belfast Anacreontic Society, 239, 240, 241, 241 n. 37, 242–6 passim, 248, 250, 251 n. 57
  Belfast Amateur Band, 241
  Belfast Band, 41
  Belfast Choral Society, 244
  Belfast Harp Festival (1792), 11, 55, 75, 78, 80, 96, 236, 289, 290
  Belfast Musical Society, 234–5, 236, 239, 248
  Belfast Philharmonic Society, 248, 251
  Belfast Saving Bank Concert Room (King Street), 240–5 passim, 250

Index

  Belfast Society for Promoting Knowledge, 75, 84, 236
  City Hall, 249
  Classical Harmonists, The, 244–51 passim
  Clonard Monastery, 117 n. 14, 121, 121 n. 39, 122
  Clonard Domestic Archive, 121
  Clonard Domestic Chronicle, 121
  Commercial Buildings, Waring Street, 238, 239, 241, 242, 245, 250
  Corn Exchange, 245
  Exchange Rooms, 235–42 passim, 250
  Fever Hospital (later Belfast General Hospital and Royal Victoria Hospital), 243
  First Presbyterian Church, 243
  Fisherwick Place Presbyterian Church, 244
  Grosvenor Hall, Grosvenor Street, 249
  High Street, 234, 235
  Linen Hall Library, 77, 241 n. 37
  Music Hall, May Street, 242, 243–8 passim, 250
  Queen's University, 249, 249 n. 56
  Queen's University Library, 78, 81 n. 30
  St Anne's Cathedral, 77
  St Anne's Church, 77, 236, 244
  St George's Church, 248
  St Mary's Hall, Bank Street, 249
  Second Presbyterian Church, Rosemary Lane (now Street), 236–8, 237
  Ulster Hall, Bedford Street, 246, 246 n. 50, 247, 248, 250, 251, 251 n. 57
  Ulster Hall Company, 246, 248, 250, 251
  Victoria Hall, Victoria Street, 245, 247, 250
  Vocal Union, 251 n. 57
  Waterfront Hall, 249
  Wellington Hall, Wellington Place, 249
Bell, David Richard, 37
Bell, George, 190
Bellens, Jozef, 119, 119 n. 25
  Ave Maria, 119
  Missa prima, 119
  Salva nos, Domine, 119
Bellini, Vincenzo, 19, 26 n. 27, 252, 260, 284, 298
  La sonnambula, 252, 260
  I Capuletti e i Montecchi, 284
  Norma, 260, 284
Bendl, Karel, 286, 288
Benedict, Julius, 17, 19, 20 n. 12, 23–6 passim, 29, 30, 40, 265 n. 59

The Lily of Killarney, 23, 24, 24 n. 21, 26, 30, 276
Bennett, Joseph, 266
Berlioz, Hector, 187, 192, 274
Best, William Thomas, 246, 251 n. 57
Bermingham, Revd James, 169, 170
  A Memoir of the Very Rev. Theobald Matthew, with an Account of the Rise and Progress of Temperance in Ireland (1840), 169
Bewerunge, Heinrich, 120–7 passim, 277, 296
Birmingham, 31, 214, 225, 246
Bishop, Mrs, 241
Bishop, Sir Henry, 146, 230, 256
Bismarck, Otto von, 296, 297, 303
Bizet, Georges, 201
  Carmen, 201, 276
  Pearl Fishers, The, 201
Blackburne, Francis, 213 n. 11
Blake, Donal S., 158
Blewitt, Jonathan, 256
Blomfield, Bishop Charles James, 133
Bochsa, Nicholas Charles, 241
Boer War, 302
Bohemia, 278 n. 1, 279, 283, 289
Böll, Heinrich, 293
Bond, Oliver, 49
Boppart, 300
Boston Public Library, 104, 105 n. 34
Boucicault, Dion, 23, 24, 27, 29, 29 n. 34, 37 n. 9
  The Corsican Brothers, 37 n. 9
  The Shaughran, 24
Bourke, Marie, 63
Boyce, William, 132, 138
  Cathedral Music, 138
Boydell, Barra, 12, 98 n. 15
Boydell, Brian, 11, 205, 279
Boyland, Blazes, 51 n. 87
Bowdich, Thomas Edward, 196, 197
  A Mission from Cape Coast Castle to Ashantee, 197
Bradford, 246
Braham, John, 240
Brahms, Johannes, 32, 32 n. 41, 187 n. 2
Bray, Co. Wicklow, 50, 123
Bray Brass Band, 50 n. 82
Breathnach, Breandán, 94, 95, 113
Brendel, Franz, 192
Brewer, James N., 98 n. 17
'Brian Boru' (harp), Trinity College Dublin, 73 n. 52
Bristol, 70

Bristol Museums and Art Gallery, 69
Britten, Benjamin, 18
Brooke, Charlotte, 74, 74 n. 3
  Reliques of Irish poetry, 74, 74 n. 3
Brown, Clive, 80 n. 27, 89, 89 n. 54, 90
  Classical and Romantic Performing Practice 1750–1900, 89
Browne, Bishop Robert, 119, 119 n. 29, 124
Brunetti, Giovanni Gualberto, 130 n. 1
  Gloria in D, 130 n.1
Bryan, Albertus, 132
Bull, Ole, 241
Bumpus, John Skelton, 137, 138
Bunting, Edward, 38, 40, 52, 55, 58 n. 21, 60, 60 n. 29, 72, 74–97 passim, 101, 103, 104, 106, 107, 112, 113, 236, 236 n. 8, 237, 238, 238 n. 14, 239, 270, 288
  A General Collection of the Ancient Irish Music (1796), 38, 75, 77, 79, 80–4 passim, 87, 87 n. 50, 88, 93, 96
  A General Collection of the Ancient Music of Ireland (1809), 82–7 passim, 96
  Ancient Music of Ireland (1840), 85, 87, 88, 89, 270, 288
  Ancient Music of Ireland, The (pub. W. Power & Co., 1969), 78 n. 18
  Manuscripts various (QUB Library), 78, 79, 85 n. 43, 89
Burke, Br Dominic, 158, 160, 163
Burney, Sir Charles, 96, 103, 104, 191, 197, 206, 279, 288
Burns, Robert, 44
Burton, Frederick William, 62–4 passim, 71, 98, 99
  'The Aran Fisherman's Drowned Child', 63
  'Paddy Conneely, Galway Piper', 63, 64, 99
Bussell, Henry, 261
Byron, Lord George, 259

Caldwell, John, 16, 16 n. 4, 25
Cambrensis, Giraldus, 87, 87 n. 49
Cambridge, 188, 248
Cameron, John, 242
Campbell, Thomas, 60, 60 n. 29, 82
Cappoquin, Co. Waterford, 275 n. 14
Caradori-Allan, Maria, 240
Carbery, Mary, 304
  The Germans in Cork, 304
Carey, John
  'Irish Piper' (postcard), 73
Carleton, William, 269
Carracciolo, Luigi, 41

Carlow, 120 n. 32, 124, 127
   Cathedral of the Assumption, 120 n. 32, 127, 128
   St Patrick's College, 127
Carolan [O'Carolan], Turlough, 52, 54, 54 n. 11, 97, 104, 187, 271
   'Signor Carrollini', 52
Carrickfergus, Co. Antrim, 176
Carter, Frederick George, 131
Casement, Roger, 294
Cassell's Biographical Dictionary, 187, 192
Catalani, Angelica, 236, 238, 240, 269
Catholic Choralist, The, 178, 180
Causton, Thomas, 133
Ceoltóirí Chualann, 78 n. 17
Cecilian movement (society), 116, 116 n. 12, 117, 118, 124–8 passim, 251 n. 57, 253, 296, 300
Čelakovský, František Ladislav, 291
   Slavonic national songs, 291
Chamberlain, Houston, 298, 303
Chappell (music publishers), 101
Chappell, William, 197
Charlemont, earl of, 37
Charles IV (Holy Roman Empire), 278
Chateaubriand, François-René de, 57
Cheng, Vincent, 35
Cherubini, Luigi, 26 n. 27, 281, 284
   Les deux journées, 281, 284
Childers, Erskine, 30 n. 35
Chipp, Edmund Thomas, 248, 251, 251 n. 57
Chopin, Fryderyk, 264, 274
Chorley, Henry, 204
Christian Brothers, 155, 158, 160, 165, 176
Church Education Society, 155
Clare Almanack, 116
Clark, M., 133
Clarke-Whitfield [Clarke], John, 132, 135, 137, 139
   A Morning and Evening Service with Six Anthems, 137
   I will lift up my eyes, 139
   In Jewry is God known, 137
   Twelve Anthems, 137
Clementi, Muzio, 77, 84, 93
Clonmel, Co. Tipperary, 43, 156, 159
Close, Maxwell H., 43, 44
Cloyne, Co. Cork, 119
   Cloyne Diocesan Centre, 119 n. 29, 124
   St Colman's Cathedral, 119, 128
Cobh, Co. Cork, 119, 119 n. 29, 123, 128

Coleraine, Co. Derry, 163
Collins, Derek, 280 n. 13
Collins, Paul, 12
Collison, William Alexander Houston, 208
Cologne, 128 n. 75, 300
Comerford, Vincent, 289, 290
Committee of Council on Education, 153 n. 13
Coneely [Conneely, Conneally], Paddy, 62, 62 & 36 and 37, 97–99 passim, 105, 106, 107, 109, 110, 112, 113
Connaught, 78
Connemara, Co. Galway, 62, 63
Connor, Denis, 54 n. 11
Conradh na nGaeilge, 93
Conran, Michael, 51
Cooke, Bartholomew [Bartlett], 76,
   Cooke's Selection of Twenty One Favourite Original Irish Airs, 76
Cooke, R., 134, 135
Cooke, Thomas, 236, 256, 256 n. 8
   'Sonata Fugata', 256 n. 8
Cooper, David, 12
Corelli, Archangelo, 132, 139
Cork, 26, 43, 103, 115, 117, 123–7 passim, 158, 160, 163, 166–77 passim, 184, 202, 204, 261, 275, 276, 277, 296
   Antient Concert Society, 261
   Batty's Circus, 176
   Choral Union, 126
   Cork Amateur Opera Company, 275 n. 14
   Cork Amateur Orchestral Society, 275 n. 14
   Cork Examiner, 166, 173, 252, 261, 262, 272–7 passim, 297
   Cork Musical Club, 275 n. 14
   Cork School of Music, 275 n. 14
   Cork Total Abstinence Society (CTAS), 168, 173, 186
   Corn Exchange, Great Hall, 167
   Filedha Ladies Choir, 126
   Globe Lane Temperance Reading Room, 172
   Imperial Clarence Rooms, 176
   Independent Church, 184
   Mrs Sexton Baylee's College, 176
   North Monastery, 158, 160
   North Monastery School, 160
   St Mary and St Anne's Cathedral, 115, 125, 126 nn 63 & 65
   St Vincent's Church, 125, 126 n. 65
   St Vincent's Palestrina Choir, 125

Index

School of Music Choral Society, 126
South Monastery School, 174, 176
Theatre Royal, 252
Corri, Domenico, 81
   A Select Collection of the Most Admired Songs, Duets &c, 81
Cowen, Frederic, 25
Cox, C.H., 303
Cramer, Johann Baptist, 74, 76, 93
   Irish Melodies, 74
Crocker, Crofton, 60, 62
   Fairy Legends and Traditions in the South of Ireland, 60, 62
Croft, William, 136
   Funeral Service (Burial Service), 136
   I am the Resurrection, 136
Croke, Dr Thomas, Archbishop of Cashel, 43, 44, 45
Cromer, Lord, 198
   Modern Egypt, 198
Cromwell, Thomas K., 98 n. 17
Crooke, Elizabeth, 97
Crotch, William 200, 203
   Specimens of Various Style of Music, 200, 203
Cruise, Dr, 45
Cruvelli, Sophie, 269
Cú Cullainn, 295
Cullen, Fintan, 68, 69, 70
Culwick, James Cooksey, 47 n. 67, 48, 187, 205, 205 n. 16, 300
   Greenoge (overture) 47 n. 67
   The Legend of Stauffenberg, 300
Curran, John Philpot, 38
Curtis, W. O'Leary, 303
Cusack, Michael, 43, 44
Cuthbert, Mrs, 131 n. 6

Dachau, 125 n. 61
   Church of St Jakob, 125 n. 61
Dahlhaus, Carl, 16, 16 n. 4, 260, 267
Daily Express, The, 197, 204, 295, 297
Daily News, The, 265 n. 63, 272
Dallis Lute Book, 95
Dalton, Charles, 244
Darwin, Charles, 43, 191
   The Descent of Man, 191
David, Félicien, 199, 201, 201 n. 5
   Désert, Le, 199, 201, 201 n. 5
Davis, Thomas Osborne, 42, 43, 49, 51, 151, 162, 177, 177 n. 41, 186, 271, 273
Davison, J.W., 264, 264 n. 55, 266
Davitt, Mary (née Yore), 44, 45

Davitt, Michael, 41–6 passim
Deane, Seamus, 22, 23,
Debussy, Claude, 201
   La Mer, 201
Delaney, Mrs, 55 n. 11
Delibes, Léo, 201
   Lakmé, 201
Democrat and People's Journal, 120 n. 31
Demetz, Peter, 284
Dempsey, Anne, 12
De Prins, Francis Prosper, 115–19 passim
De Prins, Leopold, 115–19 passim, 125 n. 58
Derry (Londonderry), County, 78
Dibble, Jeremy, 25, 27, 28
Dibdin, Charles, 80, 81, 81 n. 30
Dillon, John, 46, 46 n. 54, 177, 177 n. 41
Distins (Distin Family), 241
Dobrovský, Josef, 285, 289
Donato, Juliano, 282
Donaueschingen, 280
Doncaster, 106
Donegal, County, 169
Donegall, earls and marquises of (various), 234, 235, 238, 239, 244, 250
Donizetti, Gaetano, 19, 26 n. 27, 146, 282, 298
   Lucrezia Borgia, 271, 282
Donnelly, Bishop James, 251 n. 57
Dow, Daniel, 75
   A Collection of Ancient Scots Music, 75
Down, County, 55 n. 11
Downes, William MacNamara, 180, 181, 182, 183
   Temperance Melodies for the Teetotallers of Ireland, 180–3 passim
Doyle, J.C., 51 n. 87
D'Oyly Carte, Richard, 25
Dragonetti, Domenico, 257, 260
Drennan, William, 83, 84
Drummond, William, 236, 238
Dublin, 12, 17, 20–7 passim, 32–43 passim, 47–50 passim, 54 n. 11, 69, 74, 76, 77, 82, 83, 95, 100–5 passim, 116, 116 n. 12, 117 n. 18, 123–5 passim, 136, 150, 154, 155, 156, 160, 162, 170, 176, 177, 184, 187, 193, 194, 195, 201–6 passim, 211–34 passim, 236, 236 n. 5, 238, 240–6 passim, 253, 256–65 passim, 270, 275, 278, 279, 280, 280 n. 13, 281, 284, 296, 297, 302, 303,
   Academy of Music, 150
   Amateur Harmonic, 212
   Amateur Melophonic, 212

Dublin *(contd)*
  Ambassador Cinema, 217 n. 31
  Anacreontic Society, 212, 222 n. 44
  Antient Concert Rooms, 37, 218, 231 n. 82, 233, 263 n. 50
  Antient Concerts Society, 150, 201, 201 n. 5, 211–34, 261
  Antient Concerts Society programmes (various composers), 216 Table 11.1, 220, Tables 11.2 and 3, 221 11.4, 223 Table 11.5, 224 Table 11.6,
  Arbour Hill military prison, 50
  Blackrock, 230 n. 76
  Brass Band of Trade, 41
  Christ Church Cathedral, 37, 42, 193, 203, 212–14 passim, 219, 230 n. 76
  Christchurch Place, 50
  Citizen or Dublin Monthly Magazine, The, 104, 105, 109, 111, 113, 274 n. 9
  City Hall, 49
  City Hospital, 44
  Clarendon Street Church, 47 n. 61
  Concert Hall, 41
  Concert Rooms, Great Brunswick Street, 217 n. 32, 218 n. 33, 225, 261 n. 37
  Dominick Street Church, 47 n. 61
  Dublin Almanac, 215
  Dublin Castle, 50, 51
  Dublin Choral Society, 212, 233
  Dublin Corporation, 258 n. 17
  Dublin Daily Express, 213, 266
  Dublin Evening Mail, 226–9 passim, 257–63 passim
  Dublin Evening Packet, 272
  Dublin Festival Choral, 212, 258
  'Dublin First Grand Musical Festival' (1831), 104, 253, 257, 261 n. 37, 270
  Dublin Journal, The, 77
  Dublin Liberties, 40
  Dublin Lying In Hospital, 217 n. 31
  Dublin Magazine, 256
  Dublin Mechanics Institution, 274
  Dublin Morning Mail, 264
  Dublin Oil Gas Light Company (Great Brunswick Street), 217
  Dublin Orchestral Society, 284
  Dublin Philharmonic Society, 212, 218, 218 n. 33, 222 n. 44, 227, 228, 229 n. 69, 261, 263 n. 50
  Dublin Transvaal Committee, 302

Dublin University Calendar, 206
Dublin University Choral Society, 150, 195, 212, 212 n. 5, 220 n. 40, 224 n. 50
Dublin University Magazine, 81, 97, 260, 270
Dublin Weekly Herald – A Temperance, Agricultural, Commercial and Mechanics Journal, 170, 171
Dublin YMCA, 189
Exhibition of Irish Arts and Manufactures, Rotunda (1882), 42
Exhibition Palace, 41, 42
Feis Ceoil, 33, 46, 47, 47 n. 62, 48, 114, 253, 276, 277, 292
Gas Company Employees' Brass Band, 50 n. 82
Gaiety Theatre, 264, 302
Glasnevin Cemetery, 50
Grand Dock, 217 n. 32
Great Exhibition, 196
Great Industrial Exhibition, Leinster Lawn, 1853, 39, 42
Great Musick Hall, Fishamble Street, 279
Harold's Cross, 105
Hibernian Catch Club, 212, 212 n. 5, 214
Incorporated Brick and Stonelayers, 41
International Exhibition (1853), 150
Irish Temperance and Literary Gazette, 170 n. 17
Irish Traditional Music Archive, 100, 102
Kilmainham Jail, 42, 43
Ladies Land League (St James' Branch), 42
Leinster Hall, 41, 45, 46. 48
Madrigal Society, 212
Mansion House, 41
Marlborough St, 154, 156
Marlborough St Model Schools, 156, 162
Mendicant [Mendicity] Society, 216, 217 n. 30
Metropolitan Choral Society, 212, 219
Moore Statue (College Green), 39, 40
Mount Argus church, 40
Music Hall, 37 n. 11
National Library of Ireland, 101, 105 n. 34, 211, 253 n. 3, 258 n. 17
National Theatre, 21,
Normal Training College, 150
O'Connell Monument, 42

Index 323

O'Connell Street, 217 n. 31
Orpheus Choral Society, 47 n. 67
Palestrina Choir, St Mary's Pro-Cathedral, 47 n. 61
Parnell Square, 217 n. 31
Pearse Street, 217 n. 32
Pearse Street Station, 217 n. 32
Philanthropist and National Temperance Advertiser, 170
Phoenix Park, 297
Political Prisoners' Aid Society, 42
Portland Jail, 42
Presbyterian Scots' Church, Ushers' Quay, 212
Queen's Theatre, 37 n. 11
Rathfarnam, 49
Rathmines Church, 47 n. 61
Rathmines Ladies' Association, 268
Recollections of Dublin Castle (Anon.), 232 n. 87
Released Political Prisoners' Fund, 41
Richmond St Schools, 160
Rotunda Rutland Square, 37 n. 11, 40–51 passim, 215, 217, 217 n. 30, 218, 236, 236 n. 5, 262
Royal Choral Institute, 150
Royal Dublin Society, 39, 187, 203
Royal Irish Academy (1785), 94, 100, 102
Transactions of the Royal Irish Academy, 75
Royal Irish Academy of Music, 25 n. 22, 36, 37 n. 9, 41, 47 nn 60 and 67, 124, 194, 150, 211, 211 n. 3, 214, 264, 277
Royal Irish Institution, 38
Sacred Harmonic, 212
St Andrew's Church, Westland Row, 116 n. 12, 124, 125, 177
St Ann's Choral Union, 47 n. 67
St Catherine's Church, 50
St Kevin's Fife and Drum Band, 50 n. 82
St Laurence O'Toole Church, 40
St Mary's Pro-Cathedral, 36, 116 n. 12
St Michan's, 50
St Michael's and St John's Church, 177
St Patrick's Cathedral, 37, 136, 212–14 passim, 219
St Peter's Church, Phibsborough, 41, 120 n. 32
St Saviour's Church, 40
St Stephen's Green, 50
Smock Alley Theatre, 236 n. 5

Sons of Handel (Antient Concerts Society), 150, 213
Theatre Royal, 18, 37 n. 11, 236, 263 n. 50, 265 n. 59
Trinity College Dublin, 28, 36, 43, 102, 187–9 passim, 195, 196, 201, 202, 205, 206, 211, 212, 214, 230 n. 76, 270
1798 Rebellion, 28
University Choral Society, 201, 201 n. 5
Westmoreland Street, 213 n. 9
Duffy, Charles Gavan, 42, 177, 177 n. 41
Duggan, Br, 160
Dundalk, 50, 117 n. 14, 119, 120, 120 n. 31, 123, 161, 185
Dundalk Infant School, 161
Emmet Bras Band, 50 n. 82
St Joseph's Church and Monastery, 117 n. 14, 120
St Patrick's Church, 120
Dundee, 251 n. 57
Kincaird Hall, 251 n. 57
Dunmanway, Co. Cork, 156
Dunraven, earl of, 213 n.11
Durham Cathedral, 132
Durych, Václav, 290
Dušek, Václav, 284
Düsseldorf, 128, 203, 251 n. 57
Dvořák, Antonín, 280–92 passim
Alfred, 287
Cypresses, 286, 287
Dimitrij, 283
Incidental music to the play J.K. Tyl, 291
String Quartet in D major, 291
Symphony no. 9 'From the New World', 292, 292 n. 63
The Devil and Kate, 288
The Jacobin, 287, 288
The King and the Charcoal-Burner, 287
Vanda, 283, 290
Dwight's Journal of Music, 179
East, Michael, 132
Edgeworth, Maria, 19, 55 n.11
Edgeworth, Richard, 54–5 n. 11
Edinburgh, 188, 234, 251 n. 57
St Paul's Church, 251 n. 57
Edward, Lord, 50 n. 82
Eglinton, Countess of, 263
Elgar, Edward, 19, 31, 32
Elsner, Wilhelm, 41, 227
Elvey, George Job, 133
Ely Cathedral, 248, 251 n. 57

Emmet, Robert, 50
Engel, Carl, 203
Ennis, Co. Clare, 115, 116, 129
  Amateur Band, 116
  St Flannan's College, 116
  Sts Peter and Paul's Pro-Cathedral, 115
  Town Hall, 116
  Tulla courthouse, 116
Eogan, George, 96
Ehrlich, Cyril, 249 n. 56
Erben, Karel Jaromír, 291
  Czech Folksongs and nursery rhymes, 291
Eschrich, G., 218
Esposito, Michele, 47, 47 nn 60 and 67, 48, 284, 292
  Deirdre (cantata), 47 n. 67

Fagan, Robert, 59, 70
  'Portrait of a Lady as Hibernia', 59
Fanning, James, 40
Farmer, Edward, 104, 105
Farrenferris, Cork, 127
Farset ('Belfast River'), 235
Fellowes, Devd. Edmund, 136
Fenians, 41
Ferguson, Samuel, 19, 37 n. 9, 86, 97
Ferris, Catherine, 211 n. 3
Festa, Constanzo, 217
Fétis, François-Joseph, 197, 199
Fibich, Zdeněk, 283
  Šárka, 283
  The Bride of Messina, 283
Field, John, 84, 277
  Figaro, Le, 257 n. 13, 266
Fischer, Joachim, 12, 194 n. 51
Fleischmann, Aloys (senior), 123–6 passim, 296
Fleischmann, Aloys, 11, 74, 75, 76, 88, 101, 102, 120 n. 32
  Music in Ireland, 120 n. 32
  Sources of Irish Traditional Music c.1600–1855, 74, 88
Fleischmann, Matilda ('Tilly'), 127
Flood, William Henry Grattan, 38, 205
Flotow, Friedrich von, 26 n. 27, 263 n. 50
  Martha, 263 n. 50
Forde, William, 95–8 passim, 101–6 passim, 109, 111, 112, 166
  A general Collection of the Music of Ireland, 102
Forty-Third Light Infantry, 40
Foster, Roy, 27

The Irish Story: Telling Tales and Making It Up, 27
Fourth Battalion of the King's Royal Rifles, 276
Fowler, Trevor Thomas
  'Children Dancing', 68, 69
Fox, Charlotte Milligan, 81 n. 30
Franco-Prussian war, 40
Franz Joseph I (Austria), 284
Freeman's Journal, The, 221, 225, 229, 231, 232, 253, 253 n. 3, 255, 257–72 passim, 276, 297, 303
Friel, Brian, 35 n. 47
Fripp, Alfred D., 69–72 passim
  'A Pilgrim at Clonmacnoise', 70
  'Interior of a Galway Cabin', 70
  'The Bog Cabin', 70
  'The Holy Well', 70
  'The Irish Piper', 70, 71
  'The Rosary', 70
Fuller Maitland, John Alexander, 25, 25 n. 24, 187 n. 3

Gaelic Athletic Association (GAA), 21, 43, 44
Gaelic League, 21, 43, 43 n. 40, 46, 51, 69, 275, 276
  Central Branch of the Gaelic League, 51
  Gaelic Union, 43, 43 n. 40, 44
Galway, County, 62, 64, 71, 95, 97, 105, 112, 120, 121 n. 34, 155
  Pro Cathedral, 120
Gandsey, 97
Garbett, John, 137
  Responses in A and F, 137
Garcia, Viardot, 263 n. 50, 269
Garrett, George 135
Garvin, Tom, 283
Gater, William Henry, 208
Gauntlett, Henry J., 226, 226 n. 59, 251 n. 57
Gaynor, Edward, 125, 126 n. 65
Gazette Musicale, 264
Geary, Gustavus, 37, 38, 39
Geldern, Rhine-Prussia, 125
Gibbons, Orlando, 132
Gilbert, William Schwenk, 24, 26, 29
Gillies, Alexander, 290
Glenosheen, Co. Limerick, 95
Glover, Emilie, 41, 93
Glover, John William, 20 n. 12, 36, 37, 38, 40, 41, 42, 47, 92, 162
  One hundred years ago (choral fantasia), 42

Index

St Patrick at Tara (cantata), 41
School Songs, 161
The Deserted Village, 20 n.12,
Glover, Madeline, 41
Gluck, Christoph Willibald, 268
  Orfeo, 268
Glynn, John, 40, 42
Gmür, Theo, 296
Gobineau, Joseph-Arthur de, 298, 303
Goddard, Arabella, 212
'God save Ireland', 40, 44, 45, 276
'God save the Queen', 50, 144, 148, 162, 276
Goethe, Wolfgang von, 293, 304
Goldsmith, Oliver, 231 n. 82
  She Stoops to Conquer, 264
  The Captivity, 231 n. 82
Goller, Vinzenz, 126
Gonne, Maud, 302
Goodman, James, 105
Goodwyn, Elizabeth, 131 n. 6
Goodwyn, Henry, 131 n. 6
Goethe, Johann Wolfgang von, 57
Gonne, Maud, 44
Goodman, James, 94, 101, 112
Goodman, Peter, 41
Goodwin, Mr, 155
Gorges, Mrs M., 201
Goss, John, 132, 135
Göteborg, 280
Göttingen, 244
Gounod, Charles, 26 n. 27, 41 n. 33, 45, 126, 265 n. 59, 268, 302, 304
  Ave Maria, 45
  Faust, 265 n. 63, 269, 304
Gormley, Mr, 177
Graff, Alphonsus, 119, 124
Graham, Farquahar, 101
Granard, 236 n. 8
Grass, Günther, 293
'Grattan's Parliament', Henry, 74
Grand Irish National Concerts, 38
Graves, Alfred Perceval, 28
Graves, Charles, 37 n. 9
Green Mountain Manuscript, 289
Greene, Maurice, 132, 136, 222 n. 48
  Lord, let me know mine end, 136
Griffin, Gerald, 23,
  The Collegians, 23
Griffith, Arthur, 295, 302
Grimm, Jacob, Wilhelm ('the brothers Grimm'), 60
Grindle, W.H., 142

Grisi, Giulia, 263 n. 50, 269
Grove, Sir George, 253 n. 5
Grove's Dictionary of Music and Musicians (1906, 1907, ed. J.A. Fuller-Maitland), 187
Gruber, Franz Xaver 127
  Mass in honour of St Ignatius, 127
Grunieson, Charles Lewis, 266
Guerini, Vincenzo, 239

Haan, Alphonse, 124, 127
Haan, Gustav, 124, 127, 128
Haberl, Franz Xaver, 116
Habsburg, 278, 281, 284, 285
Halek, Vítězslav, 290
  The Heirs of the White Mountain, 290
Halévy, Fromental, 282
  La Juive, 282
Hall, Wayne E., 97
Hallé, Charles, 204, 212, 228, 229 n. 70, 264
Hallé Orchestra, 276
Haller, 118, 128
  Confirma hoc Deus, 128
  Missa Assumpta est, 118
  Missa Quarta, 118
Ham, Albert, 208
Hamilton, William Rowan, 37 n. 9
Handel, George Frideric, 18, 42, 131–6 passim, 138, 146, 188, 190–4 passim, 202, 203, 215, 220–3 passim, 229, 229 n. 71, 230, 238, 258, 293
  Acis and Galatea, 143, 203, 215
  Alexander's Feast, 36 n. 4
  Crystal Palace Commemoration 1859, 138
  'Hallelujah' chorus, 42 n. 38, 136
  Handel Commemoration (1834), 214 n. 14
  Israel in Egypt, 191, 192, 223, 230
  Jephtha, 215, 221, 223, 258 n. 20
  Judas Maccabeus, 36–7 n. 4, 215, 230
  L'Allegro, il Penseroso ed il Moderato, 222
  Messiah, 36, 36 n. 4, 131, 135, 136, 143, 190–3 passim, 217, 218, 222, 225, 229 nn 69 and 71, 238, 238 n. 14, 244, 245, 247, 258 n. 20, 279
  Messiah: items from (various, not including the 'Hallelujah' chorus), 131 n. 5, 135, 136, 218, 227

Handel, George Frideric *(contd)*
   Samson, 36 n. 4, 229, 229 n. 71
   Saul: 'Dead March', 136
   Solomon, 215
   The Ways of Sion Do Mourn, 136
   Zadok the Priest, 215, 223
Hanka, Václav, 289
Hanrahan, C.J., 124
Hanslick, Eduard, 192
Hardiman, James, 95, 97
   'Irish Minstrelsy', 97
Harrach, Count Jan, 281, 281 n. 19, 282, 283
Harrison, Frank Llewelyn, 103 n. 27
Harty, Sir Hamilton, 284, 291, 292
   An Irish Symphony, 291, 292
Harvey, Richard Frederic, 274 n. 7
Haughton, Samuel, 43
Haverty, Joseph, 65, 66
   'The Blind Piper' 65, 66
   'The Blind Piper' ('Limerick Piper'), 67
Hawkins, Sir John, 96
Haydn, Joseph, 42, 79, 83, 83 n. 37, 84, 85, 88, 90, 90 n. 55, 93, 126, 132, 132 n. 8, 139, 146, 178, 187 n. 2, 193, 203, 217, 217 n. 30, 222, 222 n. 46, 227, 229, 229 n. 71, 258–62 passim
   Insanae et vanae curae, 217, 217 n. 30, 222 n. 46
   Mass in D minor 'Nelson', 229 n. 71, 230
   Symphony no. 97, 227
   The Creation, 36 n. 4, 42 n. 38, 132 n. 8, 143, 193, 229 nn 69 and 71, 245, 258 n. 20, 259, 260
   The Seasons, 222, 261
Hayes, Catherine, 228 n. 67, 229 n. 72, 252, 253, 271–6 passim, 282
Head, Sir Francis, 162
Hempson [O'Hampsey], Denis, 58, 91, 92, 97
Henry VIII (England), 81
Henry, Bishop Henry (Down and Connor), 122
Herder, Johann Gottfried von, 55, 60, 74, 289, 290, 291, 295
   Abhandlung ueber den Ursprung der Sprache, 289
   Ideen zur Philosophie der Geschichte der Menschheit, 290
   Stimmen der Volker in Liedern, 74
Herity, Michael, 96
Her Majesty's Commissioners on Endowed Schools in Ireland (1857–8), 160

Hermann, the Brothers (string quartet) 241, 241n. 25
Hess, Albert, 76, 76 Figure 4.1
Heurmann, Alphonse, 123
Hibernia, 268, 298
Hill, Jane, 53
Hoffman, Francis, 92
   Ancient Music of Ireland from the Petrie Collection (1877), 92
Hogan, John, 39 n. 20
Hogan, Thomas, 171
Hohnerlein, 128
Holden, Francis, 107
Holroyd, Michael, 32 n. 41
Holts, Herr, 116 n. 9
Holy Faith Sisters, 155 n. 21
Holy Roman Empire, 278
Hone, Jospeh, 303
   The German Doctrine of Conquest, 303
Hoogstraten, 119
Hopkins, 135
Horncastle, Frederick William, 38, 138
   Kyrie in D major, 137
   Te Deum and Jubilate in E flat major, 138
Horsley, William, 232
Hostinský, Otakar, 287
Houdin, Robert, 37 n. 11
Howells, Herbert, 132
Hudební listy, 286
Hudson, Henry Philerin, 37 n. 9, 95, 97 n. 13, 98, 103, 104, 105 n. 34, 106, 107, 109–13 passim, 274, 274 n. 9
Hudson, William Elliot, 37 n. 9, 95, 97, 98, 103, 104, 105 n. 34, 107, 109
Hugo, Victor, 195
Hullah, John, 153–6 passim, 161, 162
   Wilhelm's method of teaching singing, 153, 154, 161, 162
Hume, David, 286
Hummel, Johann Nepomuk, 222 n. 45, 264
   Quodquod in orbe revinctum est, 222 n. 45
Hunt, Henry George Bonavia, 208
Hunt, Leigh, 263
Hyde, Douglas, 21–2, 34, 43 n. 40, 47, 51

Incorporated Brick and Stonelayers' Brass Band, 50 n. 82
Incorporated Society of Musicians, 276
Indian Civil Service, 195
Ingram, John Kells, 42

Index

Ireland's Eye, 253, 255
Ireland, John, 132
Irish Artisans Exhibition, 1885, 45
Irish Builder, 254, 256, 257, 264, 269, 275
Irish Ecclesiastical Record, 301
Irish Ecclesiastical Society, 133 n. 13
Irish Folk Song Society, 28 n. 33
Irish Free State, 11
Irish Fusiliers, 141
Irish Harp Revival Festival, 41
Irish League, 285
Irish Literary Revival, 20, 21, 22,
Irish Literary Society, 28, 233
Irish Literary Theatre, 48
Irish Monthly, The, 298
Irish Musical Fund Society, 281
Irish National Foresters, 44
Irish National League, 45
Irish National League of America, 46 n. 54
Irish National School System, 149, 152, 153, 155, 159, 161, 162
Irish Parliamentary Party, 43
'Irish Piper' (postcard), 72
'Irish Ring', 19, 23, 23 n. 19
Irish Sisters of Charity, 155 n. 21
Irish Society of St Cecilia, 114, 116–18 passim, 124 n. 58, 296
Irish Teachers Journal, The, 159
Irish Times, The, 189, 202, 263–9 passim, 276, 297, 303
Irish Traditional Music Archive, 52

Jackson, N., 219
Jackson, Walker, 97, 104
James, Revd, 131 n. 6
Janáček, Leoš, 283, 283 n. 26, 291
    Šárka, 283
    The Beginning of a Romance, 283 n. 26
Jessop, George, 29
Joachim, Joseph, 212, 222 n. 47, 227, 229 n. 70, 230, 264
Johnston, Roy, 12
Jomelli, Niccolo, 130 n. 1
    Requiem in E flat major, 130 n.1
Josquin des Prez, 193
Josef II, 285
Joyce, James, 12, 15, 18, 20–4 passim, 26, 34, 40 n. 23, 51, 51 n. 87, 233
    A Portrait of the Artist as a Young Man, 24 n. 21
    Dubliners, 24 n. 21, 34
    Finnegans Wake, 24 n. 21
    The Dead, 35
    Ulysses, 18, 19 n. 10, 21 n. 13, 24 n. 21, 34, 51 n. 87, 233
Joyce, Patrick Weston, 47, 60, 72, 92–6 passim, 100, 112
    Ancient Irish Music (1872 or 3), 92, 93, 95 n. 2
    Irish music and song (1888), 95 n. 2
    Old Irish folk music and songs (1909), 95 n. 2
Joyce, Stanislaus, 35
Jozé, Dr Thomas Richard Gonsalvez, 125, 209
Jullien, Louis, 262, 263
    Quadrille: The Fall of Sebastopol, 262
Jungmann, Josef, 286, 289, 290

Kabbani, Rana, 196
    Imperial Fiction: Europe's Myths of Orient, 196
Kaim, 127
Kalivoda, Jan Václav, 280
Kalkbrenner, Frederich, 240
Keane, Andrew, 40
Keenan, Patrick, 153, 161
Keleher, William, 176 n. 38
Kelly, Michael, 77
Kennedy, Brian, 70
Kennedy, Paul M. 300
Kennedy (Piper), 112
Kerbusch, Leo, 246, 248, 251, 251 n. 57
    Mass for St Cecilia, 251 n. 57
Kiberd, Declan, 19, 272
Kilkenny, 123, 124 n. 52, 230 n. 76, 231 n. 83
    St Mary's Cathedral, 124 n. 52
Kilronan (village), Co. Galway, 66
King, Alexander, 184, 185
Kingstown, (Dun Laoghaire) Co. Dublin, 41 n. 27, 50
Kinsella, Thomas, 19,
Kirjule, 144
Klebelsberk, Count, 281
Klein, Axel, 15–17 passim, 20, 20 n. 12, 22, 31, 34
Knight, 41 n. 33
Koczwara, František, 280
    The Battle of Prague, 280
Kohl, Johann Georg, 161
Kollár, 289, 290
Kolovrat, Count, 281
Komzák, Karel, 284
Koss, Joseph A., 124, 124 n. 55
Kozeluch, Leopold, 83, 93

Krásnohorská, Eliška, 286, 287
Kremens, 120 n. 32

Lablache [La Blache], Luigi, 258, 269
La Borde, Jean-Benjamin de, 197, 200
   Essai sur la musique ancienne et moderne, 197, 200
Lacedaemonia, 191
Lagan River, 235, 243
La Marseillaise, 40
Lamentations of Jeremiah, 226, 226 n. 57
Land League, 43
Lane, Edward William, 197
   An account of the manners and customs of the modern Egyptians, 197
Langdon, 135
Larchet, John 205
Lasso, Orlando di, 128 n. 75
Lauder, E. W., 141
Lauer, Carl, 41
Laurence, Dan H., 27 n. 31
Lawless, George R., 131 n. 6, 144
Leader, The, 275, 276, 277
Lebrecht, Norman, 34 n. 46
Lee, John, 54 n. 11, 76
   John Lee's Collection of Country Dances for the Present Year 1791, 76
Lee, Vandaleur, 32 n. 41
Leersen, Joep, 55, 57, 61
Le Fanu, Sheridan, 27–30 passim
   Phaudrig Crohoore, 30 n. 37
Leighton, Lord, 31
Leipzig, 230 n. 76
Lemmens, Jack Nikolaus, 114, 118, 123 n. 50, 124
   Messe en re, 118
Leslie, B., 44
Leslie, Shane, 303
   The Celt and the World, 303
Lessing, Gotthold Ephraim, 293
Levey [O'Shaughnessy], Richard Michael, 38, 41, 41 n. 33, 45
Limerick, 26, 65, 104, 115–19 passim, 123–4 passim, 155, 168, 176, 204, 275, 304
   Limerick Chronicle, The, 181, 272, 297
   Mount St Alphonsus (church), 115–19 passim
   St John's Cathedral, 123 n. 51
   University of Limerick, 67, 304
Lind, Jenny, 263 n. 50, 272, 273
Lindpaintner, Peter Josef von, 232, 261
   The Widow of Nain, 261

Lismore, Co. Waterford, 275 n. 14
Liszt, Franz, 192, 243, 244, 274
Liverpool, 124, 243, 246, 259 n. 23
   Liverpool Choral Society, 258
   St George's Hall, 246
Lloyd, David, 18, 21–2,
Logier, Johann Bernhard, 20 n.12
   Brian Boroimhe, 20 n. 12
London, 17, 18, 22, 25–7 passim, 32, 75, 138, 140, 150, 173 n. 28, 176, 184, 188, 196, 199, 204, 213–14 passim, 222, 229, 232, 234, 236 n. 5, 238, 244, 246, 248, 251 n. 57, 253, 261 n. 37, 264, 299
   Academy of Ancient Music, 75
   Academy of Vocal Music, 75
   Chapel Royal, 248, 251 n. 57
   Concerts of Antient Music (1776), 75, 214, 222 n. 49
   Covent Garden, 34 n. 46
   Crystal Palace, 138
   Drury Lane Theatre, 299
   Great Exhibition (1851), 199
   Hanover Square concerts, 236 n. 5
   Her Majesty's Theatre, 39 n. 21
   House of Commons, 152
   Illustrated London News, 71, 199
   Inquirer, 176
   London Philharmonic Society, 232, 261
   London Pianoforte School, 78, 84
   National Gallery, 62
   Piccadilly, 199
   Royal Academy, 68
   Royal Italian Opera, 265 n. 59
   Royal Musical Festival (Westminster Abbey, 1834), 214, 214 n. 14, 222 n. 49
   Royal Panopticon, 248, 251 n. 57
   St Olave's Church, Southwark, 251 n. 57
   Savoy Opera, 24, 25, 26,
   Society of Painters in Watercolours, 70
   South Kensington Museum, 203, 203 n. 11
   Theatre Royal, Drury Lane, 140
   Westminster Abbey, 251 n. 57
Longford, 124, 127, 236 n. 8
   St Mel's Cathedral, 127, 127 n. 71
Loos, Karel, 285
   Chimney Sweep, 285
Loreto Sisters, 155 n. 21
Loughrea, Co. Galway, 124, 124 n. 55
Louvain, 117
   Dominican Church, 116

Lover, Samuel, 20 n.12, 40, 44, 62, 63, 64
   'An Irish Piper', 62, 63
   Il Paddy Whack in Italia, 20 n. 12
Lucretius, Diodorus, 192
Ludwig, William, 45, 46, 46 n. 53, 49, 51
Lynch, Patrick, 84
Lyndsay, Charles Dalrymple (dean of Christ Church Cathedral, Dublin, and bishop of Kildare), 213 n. 11
Lyra Ecclesiastica, 114, 117–18, 124–8 passim, 296

MacDonnell, Hercules, 201, 214, 214 nn 17 & 18, 253, 266, 267
Macfarren, Sir George, 199, 201
   The Sleeper Awakened, 199, 201
MacGreevy, Thomas, 304
Mackenzie, Alexander, 25
MacKenzie, John, 200
Maclise, Denis, 73 n. 52
   'Marriage of Aoife and Strongbow', 73 n. 52
Macmillan's Magazine, 253–4 n. 5
MacNeil, Eoin, 47
Macpherson, James, 74, 82, 82 n. 34, 83, 289
   Ossian, 82, 289
Madden, Frederick, 37 n. 9
Magilligan, Co. Derry, 58
Mahon, Derek, 15
Mahon, John, 236, 236 n. 5
Mail, The, 186
Mainz, 123 n. 50, 300
Mainzer, Joseph, 166, 167, 172–5 passim, 178, 184
   Mainzer's Musical Times and Singing Circular, 166, 173, 175, 177
   Singing for the Million, 167, 174, 177
Malcolm, Andrew, 243
Malibran, Maria, 258
Malines [Mechelen], 114, 118, 119, 121, 123 n. 50, 124
   Cardinal Archbishop, 115, 118
   Lemmens Institute (Academy of Sacred Music), 114, 115, 119, 120, 120 n. 32, 121, 122
Mallow, Co. Cork, 275 n. 14
Manchester, 204, 214 n. 14, 246
   Gentlemen's Concerts, 214 n. 14
Manchester Martyrs, 40, 50
Mangan, James Clarence, 19,
Manning, Henry Edward, Cardinal, 123 n. 51
Marchand, Mr, 125

Marchant, Charles G., 209, 277
Mario, Giovanni Matteo, 263 n. 50
Marks, Thomas Osbourne, 134, 137, 143, 144
   Magnificat and *Nunc Dimittis* in G, 137
Martin, Timothy, 21 n. 13
Martyn, Edward, 277, 295, 299, 300
   The Heather Field, 300
Masaryk, Tomáš G., 289
Mathew, Theobald, 38, 167–86 passim
Maunsell (publisher), 303
May, Frederick, 11
Maynooth, Co. Kildare, 120–4 passim, 127, 296
   St Patrick's College, 122, 124
Mayr, Jan, 282
McCarthy, Denis Florence, 42, 44
McCarthy, Canon Richard, 126 n. 66
McCarthy, Jane, 157
McCarthy, Marie, 12
McDermott, 'Miss', 218
McGuire, James K., 293, 294
   What Could Germany Do for Ireland?, 293, 294
McHale, John, Cardinal Archbishop, 41, 158
McHale, Maria, 12
McIntosh, John, 50
McKee, Joseph, 132–8 passim, 142, 142n. 61
Meagher, William, 43
Meath, County, 127
   Oldcastle, 127
Mendelssohn, Felix, 42, 132, 132 n. 9, 140, 141, 146, 187 n. 2, 190, 193, 194, 214, 222–32 passim, 261, 262, 264, 274
   A Midsummer Night's Dream Incidental Music: Wedding March, 132 n. 9
   Athalie, 229
   Die erste Walpurgisnacht, 222
   Elijah, 36 n. 4, 41, 143, 221, 223, 225, 227, 228
   Festgesang an die Künstler, 222, 229 n. 71
   Hear my Prayer, 230
   Lauda Sion, 229 n. 71
   Piano Concerto in G minor, 227
   Piano Trio in C minor, 227
   Piano Trio in D minor, 229 n. 70
   Psalm 42, 225, 229 n. 71, 231
   Psalm 55, 229 n. 71
   Psalm 114, 132 n. 9, 141
   St Paul, 132 n. 9, 140, 223
   Symphony no. 2, Hymn of Praise, 42 n. 38, 132 n. 9, 143

Meix [Marx], Hans, 123, 124, 124 n. 33, 128, 128 nn 75 and 76
Messing, Professor, 301
Meulemeester, Arthur de, 114, 121–3 passim, 126 n. 63, 129
   Hymn to St Cecilia, 122
   The Reform of Church Music, 114
Meyerbeer, Giacomo, 26 n. 27, 33, 222 n. 45, 229 n. 70, 274
   Dinorah, 222 n. 45, 229 n. 70
Midleton, Co. Cork, 275 n. 14
Milner and Co. (Fleet Street), 218
Milton, John, 37
   The Death of Lycidas, 37
Mitchell, John, 46
Mitterer, 128
Moeran, Mr, 171
Molique, Bernhard, 228
Moloney, Colette, 78, 78 n. 20, 79, 89
Monck, Viscount, 213 n. 11
Monthly Museum, The, 256
Moody-Manners Opera, 276
Moomaier [Moosmair], Herr, 123, 123 n. 52
Moore, Christopher, 39 n. 20
Moore, George, 298–301 passim
   Evelyn Innes, 299, 300
   Hail and Farewell, 299
   Sister Theresa, 300
Moore, Thomas, 11, 17, 18, 19, 22, 28, 30, 36–44 passim, 48, 49, 51, 54, 55, 61, 74, n. 1, 81–6 passim, 107, 151, 154, 158, 163–5 passim, 180–3 passim, 187, 290, 291
   Centenary celebrations (1879), 41, 44
   'Grand National Commemoration of our Gifted Countryman, Thomas Moore Esq', 36–7
   Moore's Irish Melodies (1808–1834), 22, 37–43 passim, 54, 55, 61, 74 n. 1, 83, 84, 86, 151, 154, 158, 163, 164, 165, 180–2 passim, 290
   Lalla Rookh, 28
   'Melologue on National Music', 37
   Moore Statue (College Green), 39. 40
   Songs various, 42 n. 38, 43
   'The harp that once', 41–3 passim, 55
   'The Veiled Prophet of Khorassan' (Lalla Rookh), 28
Moran, D.P., 276
Morash, Christopher, 15, 17
Moravia, 278, 283
Moscheles, Ignaz, 228 n. 65, 261
   Hommage à Handel, 228 n. 65

Mozart, Wolgang Amadé, 26 n. 27, 37 n. 4, 41 n. 33, 84, 93, 126, 140, 146, 163, 178, 187 n. 2, 188, 193, 210, 215, 222–3, 228 n. 65, 229, 258–61 passim, 274 n. 9, 279, 281, 282, 302
   'Coronation' Mass, 223
   Don Giovanni, 34, 265 n. 59, 279, 282
   La Clemenza di Tito, 279
   Le nozze di Figaro, 228 n. 65, 279
   Orchestration of Handel's Messiah, 258 n. 20
   Requiem, 36–7 n. 4, 215, 215 n. 23
   Sonata for Piano in C minor K457, 193
   Symphony no. 41 'Jupiter', 229 n. 70
   Thamos, Konig in Aegypten, 222 n. 46
Mulholland, Andrew, 246, 250
Mulholland organ, 248, 250
Müller, C.F.W., 196
Mullingar, Co. Westmeath, 129
   St Finian's College, 129
Munich, 126
   Königliche Akademie der Tonkünste, 126
Munster Feis, 276
Munster News, 117
Murphy, John 'the Boss', 112 n. 46
Murphy, Canon Martin, 126 n. 67
Murphy, Michael, 12, 194 n. 51, 282 n. 21, 297 n. 11
Murphy, Tom, 35 n. 47
Murphy, William, 112 n. 46, 274
   'National Music of Ireland', 274
Murray, John, 116 n. 12
Musical Times, The, 138, 176 n. 38, 264 n. 55
Musical World, The, 215, 219, 264 n. 55

Naas, Co. Kildare, 172
Napier, William, 83
Naples, 240
Napoleon, 198
Nares, James, 135
Nation, The, 40, 41 n. 2, 167, 169, 170, 171, 177–86 passim, 269, 271–6 passim
National Anthem (British): 'God save the Queen' 50, 144, 148, 162, 276
National Anthem (Irish): 'God save Ireland' 40, 44, 45, 276, 'St Patrick's Day' 50
National Board of Education, 36, 152, 154, 155, 162–5 passim
National Music of Ireland, 51
National Literary Society, 46, 47, 48, 51, 285
National Volunteer, The, 303

Index

Neal, John and William, 52, 54, 95
  A collection of the most celebrated Irish tunes (1724), 52, 54, 95
Nejedlý, Zdeněk, 285, 285 n. 40
Nenagh, Co. Tipperary, 43
New Ireland Review, 122
Newell (School Inspector), 157
Newry, Co. Down, 80, 163
Newton, Rev. John, 259
New York, 293
Nibelungenlied, 301
Nicolai, Phillipp, 222 n. 47
Niebuhr, Carsten, 197, 199, 200
  Voyage en Arabie, 200
Niermann, Rudolf, 123, 124
Nietzsche, Friedrich, 300, 303, 304
Ní Houlihan, Cathleen, 294
'98 Centenary Committee, 49
Nono, Charles Louis, 115 Illustration 6.1, 115, 116, 116 n. 7, 116 n. 9 and 10
Nono, Donatus [Donat, Dominic], 116, 116 n. 11
Normal Training College, 36
Norwich, 214
Nostitz-Rhinek, Count Franz Anton von, 279
Novello, Clara, 229 n. 69
Novello Octavo Editions, 138
Novello, Vincent, 104

O'Beirne, Hugh, 109
Oberammergau, 298
Oberhoffer, George, 124
Oberthür, Charles, 41 n. 33
O'Boyle, Seán, 151
O'Brien, Patrick, 65
O'Brien, Vincent, 47, 47 n. 61, 49
O'Brien, William, 45,
O'Brien Moran, Jimmy, 12, 62 n. 36, 63 n. 37, 274 n. 9
O'Byrne, Ellen [Madame Nono], 116
O'Byrne, Robert, 217 n. 32
O'Casey, 23 n. 19, 35 n. 47
  The Shadow of a Gunman, 23 n. 19
  Juno and the Paycock, 23 n. 19
  The Plough and the Stars, 23 n. 19
Ó Catháin, 97
Ó Comhraigh, Eoghan [Eugene Curry], 100
O'Connell, Daniel, 38, 41, 46 n. 53, 184, 185, 186, 259, 270, 297
O'Curry, Eugene, 66, 66 n. 42, 109
O'Dea, Bishop Thomas, 120, 124 n. 55

O'Donnell, Frank Hugh, 295
  'For the free Republics', 295
O'Donnell, John, 43, 44, 45
O'Donovan, Ite, 18 n. 7, 253 n. 3, 256 n. 9
Offenbach, Jacques, 280
O'Hagan, Thomas, Lord, 42, 42 n. 34
Oireachtas, 46, 47, 277
O'Keefe, John, 20 n. 12,
  The Wicklow Mountains, 20. n. 12
O'Leary, John, 49
O'Meara, James, 124
O'Mullane, Br, 158
O'Neill, Francis, 94, 95
O'Neill, John, 235, 236, 250
Oram, Hugh, 264
Ordnance Survey, 66 n. 42, 98, 100
Ó Riada, Seán, 77–8 n. 17
O'Reilly, Edward, 104, 105
O'Shea, Katharine, 45
Osborne, George Alexander, 190, 266, 274
Ostrčil, Otakar, 283
  The Death of Vlasta, 283
Ouseley, Sir Frederick Gore, 199
Owenson, Sydney (Lady Morgan), 37, 53–60 passim, 72, 260
  Original Hibernian Melodies, 53, 54
  The Lay of the Irish Harp, 55
  The Wild Irish Girl, 53, 57, 59, 60, 72
Oxford, 188, 189, 203, 235 n. 5
  Holywell Music Room, 236 n. 5
  Magdalen College, 189
Oxford Movement, 134

Packenham, Henry (dean of St Patrick's and Christ Church cathedrals), 213 n. 11
Paganini, Nicolò, 241, 258, 259, 260
Palacký, Frantizšek, 286, 289, 290
Palestrina, Giovanni Pierluigi da, 118, 123, 127, 128 n. 75, 188, 222 n. 48
Paris, 214, 283, 302
Parker, Lisa, 12
Parks, Thomas Vincent, 120
Parnell, Charles Stewart, 42–46 passim
Parry, Hubert, 25, 31
Parry, John, 75
  Antient British Music, 75
Parry, William Edward, 195 n. 53
Pasta, Giuditta, 258
Patterson, Annie, 47, 47 n. 59, 48, 205
Pearse, Patrick H., 47
Pepusch, Johann Christoph, 217
  'Charming sounds that sweetly languish', 217

Percy, Bishop Thomas, 95
  Reliques of Ancient English Poetry (1765), 95
Pergolesi, Giovanni Battista, 191, 222 n. 48
  Stabat Mater, 191
Petrie, George, 18 n. 7, 28 n. 33, 37 n. 9, 52, 52 n. 1, 60–7 passim, 72, 86, 86 n. 47, 92, 94–101 passim, 105–12 passim, 150, 236 n. 8
  Irish Penny Journal, 63, 63 n. 37, 64, 97–9, 102, 103, 110, 112
  'St Brigid's Well' 66 n. 41
  'The last circuit of the pilgrims at Clonmacnoise', 66 n. 41
  The Petrie Collection of the Ancient Music of Ireland (1855), 92, 94, 97, 100, 102, 110, 151
Petrie, Marianne, 102
Philadelphia, 126 n. 63
  Visitation Church, 126 n. 63
Phillips, Thomas, 234, 235
Phipps, Constantine Henry (Earl Mulgrave), 215 n. 27
Piccolomini, Marietta, 39, 39 n. 21
Pigot, David, 213 n. 11
Pigot, John Edward, 95, 111, 274, 274 n. 9
Pigott, Mr, 217
Pinsuti, Ciro, 144
Pius X, 121, 126, nn 63 & 65
  Moto Proprio, 121, 126
Pleyel, Ignace, 79, 79 n. 23, 83, 93, 178
Plzeň, 283 n. 29
Powis Commission Report (1868–70), 155, 160, 161
Prague, 278–85 passim
  Národní listy, 282
  National Theatre, 280, 281 n. 17
  Prague Organ School, 281, 284, 288 n. 47
  Provisional Theatre, 280–4 passim
  Society for Artists, 284
Presentation Sisters, 155 n. 21
Preston and Son, engraver (Bunting 1796), 77
Prout, Ebenezer, 47 n. 67, 135, 205
Puccini, Giacomo, 201
  Madama Butterfly, 201
  Turandot, 201
Purcell, Henry, 19, 136, 194, 215, 222 n. 48
  Burial Service, 136
  The Tempest (incidental music), 215
Pyne, Louisa, 228 n. 67, 229 n. 72

Queen's Court Manuscript, 289
Queenstown, (Cobh) Co. Cork, 276
Quin, Mr, 155

Randeggar, Alberto,144
'Ranz des vaches', 191
Ratisbon, 116, 125, 127
  Kirchenmusikschule, 116, 125
Rauzzini, Venanzio, 236 n. 5
Redemptorists, The [Congregation of the Most Holy Redeemer], 114–21 passim
Regge, Ernest de, 129
Regondi, Giulio, 241
Reilly, Seamus, 23
Rembrandt van Rijn, 66, 67
Rennison Very Revd. Henry, 132–8 passim, 141, 145
Report from the Select Committees on Foundation Schools and Education in Ireland (1835–7), 152, 164
Rheinberger, Joseph Gabriel, 126
Rhine, 295, 297, 299, 300
Richter, Hans, 251 n. 57
Ries, Ferdinand, 258–61 passim
  Triumph of Faith, The, 258–60 passim
Rimsky-Korsakov, Nicolai, 201
  Scheherazade, 201
Roberts of Kandahar, Lord, 51
Robinson (family), 36, 213, 213 nn 9 and 12, 226
Robinson, Fanny, 227
Robinson, Francis, 213–18 passim, 227
Robinson, John, 213
Robinson, Joseph, 40–3, 47, 211–15 passim, 218, 222 nn 44 & 48, 225–31 passim
  March, 42 n. 38, 233
Robinson, William, 213–18 passim
Roch, Sampson Togwood, 61, 62
  'Piper and Dancers Co. Waterford', 62
Roche, Francis, 95
Rodmell, Paul, 12, 25
Roe, Henry, 203
Roeselare, 116
  Academie van Schone Kunsten, 116
Rogers, Brendan, 43, 43 n. 41, 116 n. 12
Rogers, Edward, 131
Rolston, R.W., 131 n. 6, 144
Rome, 278
Rooke, Bartholomew Warburton, 17, 209, 271
Rosa [Rose], Carl (Carl Rosa Opera Company), 46 n. 53, 49, 253, 266–8 passim, 296, 297, 302

Index 333

Rossini, Gioacchino, 26 n. 27, 36–7 n. 4, 42, 106, 140, 214, 222 n. 45, 228 n. 65, 231, 252, 267, 268, 270, 271, 282, 284
  Il barbiere di Siviglia, 282
  La gazza ladra, 222 n. 45, 228 n. 65
  Otello, 106, 284
  Semiramide, 222 n. 45
  Stabat Mater, 36–7 n. 4, 231
  The Maid of Judah, 270
  William Tell 'overture', 42, 42 n. 38
Rossmore (Henry Robert Westenra, 3rd Baron Rossmore), 98, 98 n. 16
Roulers, 123 n. 51
Rouse, I., 133
Rousseau, Jean-Jacques, 57, 191, 206, 286
  Dictionnaire de musique, 191
Rothe, Carl William, 124
Royal Choral Institute, 36, 36 n. 4, 37
Royal Hibernian Academy, 63, 64, 65
Royal University, 47
Rubinstein, Anton, 187 n. 2
Rudersdorff, Hermione, 229
Rudolf II, 278
Rushdie, Salman, 19 n. 10
Russell, George, 294
Russell, Thomas, 84
Ryan, Joseph, 15, 150

Šafařík, 289, 290
Sainton, Prosper, 229 n. 72
Sainton-Dolby, Charlotte, 229 n. 72
Saint-Saëns, Camille, 187 n. 2
Salomon, Johann Peter, 236 n. 5
Šamberk, František, 291
  J.K. Tyl, 291
Sampson, Revd, 58
Santley, Charles, 46 n. 53
  St Cecilia, 117
St James' Brass Band, 50 n. 82
'St Patrick's Day', 50
St Petersburg, 280
Saunders' Newsletter, 225, 229 n. 72, 261, 262
Scahill, Adrian, 52
Schallehn, 241
Scherrer, Maximilian, 124
Schiller, Friedrich, 293
Schindler, Anton, 261
Schubert, Franz, 187 n. 2
Schumann, Robert, 36–7 n. 4
  Paradise and the Peri, 36–7 n. 4
Schweitzer, Anton, 127

Scilière, Ernest, 303
Scoales, John, 214
Scott, Mr, 125,
Scott, Mrs, 59 n. 28
Scott, Walter, 25, 26, 45
Searle, 'Misses', 217
Sexton, Thomas, 43
Seymour, Joseph, 116 n. 12, 124, 125 n. 58, 209
Seymour, Mr, 240
Shakespeare, William, 263
Shane's Castle, 235, 236
Shannon, Co. Clare, 295
Shaw, George Bernard, 12, 19–20, 13, 25–7 passim, 31–5 passim, 205, 253, 265, 303
  John Bull's Other Island, 33
  Man and Superman, 21 n. 13, 34
  Widowers' Houses, 33
Shaw, Lucy, 32 n. 41
Sheehan, Canon Patrick, 300–4 passim
  'The German and Gallic Muses', 301
  The Triumph of Failure, 301
Sheil, John Barclay, 169, 170, 170 n. 16, 184
  History of the Temperance Movement in Ireland, 169, 184
Shiel, Mr, 155
Shields, Philip, 25 n. 22, 211 n. 3
Shore, William, 222 n. 47
Shrewsbury, 231
Sigerson, George, 47, 47 n. 62, 48, 49
Simpson, William Woolsey, 170 n. 16
Singenberger, 122, 127, 128
  Mass in honour of the Holy Spirit, 128
Sinn Féin, 93, 295
Sireaux [Siraux], Joseph, 119, 120, 120 n. 31
Sisters of Mercy, 155 n. 21, 157
Sjoden, Adolf, 41, 41 n. 33
Skibereen, Co. Cork, 185
Skinners' Band, 40
Škoda, Emil, 283 n. 29
Škroup, František, 282
  'Where is my home?', 282
Škroup, Jan Nepomuk, 290
  The Swedes in Prague, 290
Sligo, County, 43
Smaczny, Jan, 12
Smart, George, 135, 214 n. 14
Smetana, Bedřich, 280–91 passim
  Dalibor, 283, 287
  Libuše, 283, 289, 290
  My Country, 289
  The Bartered Bride, 288

Smetana, Bedřich (contd)
 The Brandenburgers in Bohemia, 283, 290
 The Devil's Wall, 287
 The Kiss, 287
 The Secret, 287
Smith, John, 36, 188
Smith, Richard, 37, 227
Smith, Stafford, 132
Society for the Preservation of the Irish Language, 43 n. 40, 47
Society for the Preservation and the Publication of the Melodies of Ireland (SPPMI), 94, 100, 111, 150
 Ancient Music of Ireland (1856), 94
Sotheby (Auction House), 52
Southern Reporter, The, 103 n. 28
Spencer, Herbert, 192
 'The Origin and Function of Music', 192
Spirit of the Nation, The, 186, 274 n. 9
Spohr, Louis, 136, 146, 178, 190, 214, 227, 251 n. 57, 261
 Blessed are the departed, 136
 The Last Judgement, 136
 Was treibt den Waidmann, 227
Sporck, Franz Anton, 279
Stafford, Fiona, 82
Stafford, William, 191, 192, 193, 206
 A History of Music, 191, 192
Stainer, Sir John, 133, 135, 136
 The Crucifixion, 135, 136
Standard, The, 297
Standish, James O'Grady, 295
Stanford, Charles Villiers, 20 n. 12, 25–34 passim, 46, 205, 228 n. 68, 253, 266, 275, 276
 Irish Songs and Ballads, 28
 Requiem, 30, 31, 32
 Shamus O'Brien, 20 n. 12, 25–34 passim, 275, 276
 Songs of Old Ireland, 27
 Symphony no. 3 Irish, 33, 34
 The Irish Melodies of Thomas Moore: the Original Airs Restored, 30
 The Veiled Prophet, 25 n. 22, 28
Stanford [Stamford], John, 28 n. 32, 225
Steggall, Charles, 135
Stein, Herr, 123
Steinhaur, Professor, 128 n. 75
Stephens, James, 49
Sternberk, Count, 281
Sterndale Bennett, William, 187

Stevenson, John, 20 n. 12, 81–6 passim, 202, 256
Stevenson, Patrick J., 214 n. 18
Stewart, Robert Prescott, 25, 32 n. 41, 36, 41, 41 n. 33, 46, 47, 125, 187–206 passim, 226 n. 58, 253, 263, 266
 Eve of St John, The, 192
 'Musical Education', 202
 'Natural Music and its Relation to Modern Musical Art' (lecture series), 187, 195
 Ode for the Installation of the Earl of Rosse as the Chancellor of the University of Dublin, 189
 Tercentenary Ode, 189
Stoker, Bram, 264
Stokes, William, 37 n. 9, 66, 67, 107
Straight, Thomas (engraver; Bunting 1796), 77
Strangways, Revd James Henry Michael, 131 n. 6, 139, 144
Strauss, Johann (band), 241
Stuyck, Jan Juliaan, 120, 120 n. 30
 Ave Maria, 120 n. 30
 Toccata for organ, op. 21, 120 n. 30
Sunday Times, The, 280
Sullivan, Arthur, 17, 25, 25, 29, 29 n. 34, 135, 136
 Blessed are the dead, 136
 Brother thou art gone before us, 136
 Haddon Hall, 26
 Ivanhoe, 25, 26 n. 25, 29
 Patience, 24, 25
Sullivan, Frank, 253, 255
Sullivan, Timothy Daniel, 40, 41 n. 27, 44
Sunday Independent, The, 303
Sušil, František, 291
 Moravian folksongs, 291
Sweetman, Walter, 37 n. 9
Swertz, Hans Conrad, 123–6 passim
Swift, Jonathan, 37, 83
Synge, John Millington, 35

Tarleton, Vicar Choral Armagh, 144
Tartini, Giuseppe, 227, 228
 'Devil's Trill' Sonata, 227, 228
Taruskin, Richard, 16
Teahan, John, 77
Teeling, Batholomew, 50
Telegraph, The, 266
Telford, Henry, 218
Telford, William H., 209
Temperley, Nicholas, 16 n. 4, 18 n. 8, 77
Terpander, 191
Terry, R.R., 121

Index 335

Thackeray (vicar choral, Armagh), 137
   Open me the gates, 137
   Thou O God, 137
Thackeray, William Makepeace, 161
Thalberg, Sigismond, 212, 243
Thinnes, Herr, 123, 125
Thomas, John, 25
Thomas, Ambroise, 26 n. 27
Thomas Quinlan Co., 303
Thomson, George, 79 n. 23, 83, 84, 84 n. 40, 88
   A Select Collection of Original Scotish [sic] *Airs* (1793), 83
   A Select Collection of Original Scottish Airs (1803), 88
Thomson, Samuel Smith, 243, 246
Three Choirs Festival, 236 n. 8, 238
Thurles, Co. Tipperary, 116 n. 12, 124
   Cathedral of the Assumption, 116 n. 12
Tils, Heinrich, 277
Times, The, 25 n. 24, 272
Tinel, Edgar, 119, 121
Tingadee, 199
Tipperary, County, 53, 171
Tisdall, Charles Edward, 42–5 passim
Titiens [Tietjens], Therese, 263 n. 50, 269
Tohill, Bishop John, 121
Tone, Matthew, 50
Tone, Wolfe, 50
Torrance, George William, 209, 230–1 passim
   Abraham, 230 n. 76
   The Captivity, 231 n. 82
   William of Normandy, 230 n. 76
Tours, Berthold, 135
Townend, Paul, 167
Treitschke, Heinrich von, 303
Trim, Mr, 155
Trollope, Anthony, 30
   The Landleaguers, 30
Tuam, Co. Galway, 124, 128
   Cathedral Church of the Assumption, 128
   St Jarlath's College, 128
Tuam Herald, 128
Turle, James, 133, 134, 137, 138, 139, 142, 146
   Almighty and Everlasting God, 137
   Morning chants in E and A, 137
Tyl, Josef Kajetan, 282
Tyrolese Vocalists, 37 n. 11
Tyrone, County, 78
Tyrrell, John, 285, 288

Ulster, 58, 78
Ulster Folk and Transport Museum, 62
   Illustration 3.2
Ulster Gazette, 133 n. 13, 140, 141, 143
United Irishmen, 49, 55
United Irishman, The, 277, 295
Urbánek, Mojmír, 289

Vaccai, Nicola, 282
   Giulietta e Romeo, 282
Valentine, 275 n. 14
Van Craen, Jan Baptist, 120, 120 n. 32, 127
Van de Velde, Firming, 120, 121 n. 34
Velasquez, Diego, 26
Verdi, Giuseppe, 26, 26 n. 27, 194, 201, 252, 263, 263 n. 50, 268, 298
   La traviata, 39, 39 n. 21
   Macbeth, 263, 263 nn 50 & 51
   Otello, 268
   Rigoletto, 265 n. 63
Victoria (Queen), 39, 49, 135, 162, 196, 224, 275
   Jubilee, 135
   Queen's Private Band, 248, 251 n. 57
Vienna, 281, 283, 291
   Gesellschaft der Musikfreunde, 291
Vignoles, Olinthus, 187
Villoteau, Guillaume-André, 197, 198, 199
Volkmer, Alois, 123, 124, 124 n. 58, 125, 125 n. 60, 125 n. 58

Wagner, Cosima, 299
Wagner, Richard, 12, 20, 21 n. 13, 26 n. 27, 27, 33, 188, 194, 194 n. 51, 203, 210, 264–9 passim, 285, 293, 295–304 passim
   Die Walküre, 302
   Flying Dutchman, The, 266, 267, 268, 297
   Gesamtkunstwerk, 21 n. 13, 295
   Götterdämmerung, 303
   Lohengrin, 265, 297
   Parsifal, 298–304 passim
   Rheingold, 299
   Ring, The, 265 n. 63, 297, 301, 303, 304
   Siegfried, 265 n. 63
   Tannhäuser, 268, 269 nn 83–7, 276
   Tristan und Isolde, 299, 302
Wagnerian singing roles, 46 n. 53
Wales, Prince of, 196
Walker, Joseph Cooper, 58, 74
   Historical Memoirs of the Irish Bards, 58, 74
Wallenstein, Count, 283

Waller, John Francis, 37 n. 9
Wallace, Vincent, 17, 20, 23, 24, 40, 42, 44, 190, 252, 280
　Maritana, 23, 276, 280
Walmisley, Thomas, 226, 226 n. 58
　'Remember thou, O Lord', 226
Walsh, Edward, Archbishop of Dublin, 45
Walsh, Henry, 77
Wandsworth (London), 60 n. 28
Ware, William, 236
Washington, George (Belfast), 155
Washington, James, 155
Waterford, County, 26, 43, 61, 168, 275
Webb, Daniel, 178
Weber, Carl Maria von, 17, 24, 26 n. 27, 40, 140, 199, 200, 201, 201 n. 5, 210, 222 n. 45, 228 n. 65, 261, 267
　Concert-stück op. 79, 228 n. 65
　Der Freischütz, 146, 199, 200, 201 n. 5, 229 n. 70, 247
　Oberon, 199, 200, 201 n. 5, 222, 222 n. 45
　Preciosa, 199, 200, 201 n. 5
　Turandot, 199, 200
Weekly Irish Times, The, 205
Weichsell, Carl, 236
Weichsell, Charles, 236
Weickert, Herr, 123
Weir [Ware], Mr, 77
Weinberger, Jaromir, 282, 288
　Švanda the Bagpiper, 282
Weldon, John, 215 n. 22
Wenzig, Josef, 289
Weseke, Münsterland, 124 n. 55
Wexford, Co. Wexford, 116, 161, 172
　Wexford Independent, The, 272
　Wexford Temperance Union, 171
Whateley, George (Anglican archbishop of Dublin), 213 n. 11

White, Harry, 12, 84, 180 n. 51, 205, 271 n. 96, 278, 285, 296
White, Mr (organ builder), 116, 128
Wilde, Oscar, 24, 25
Wilde, William, 37 n. 9, 100
Wilhelm I (Germany), 297, 303
Wilkie, David, 68, 70
Wilkinson, James, 222 n. 48
Williams, Evan, 75
　Antient British Music, 75
Willis, John, 244
Wilson, Revd S.E., 145
Windsor, 136
　St George's Chapel, 136
Wiseman, Cardinal, archbishop of Westminster, 160
Witt, Franz Xaver, 116, 127, 128
Wolfe Tone Co., 293
Wood, Charles, 138
　I will arise, 138
　Magnificat and Nunc Dimittis in E flat major, 138
Wood, Mrs (singer), 270
Woodlock, Revd Dr Lord, 127
Woodlock, Thomas F., 298, 299, 302
Wordsworth, William, 68
Wötzel, Caspar Anton, 123, 123 n. 50, 155
Wright (Travel Guides), 98 n. 17
Wyse, Sir Thomas, 152
　Education Reform (1836), 152

Yeats, William Butler, 28, 48, 295, 300, 302
Youghal, Co. Cork, 128
Young Ireland (Irelanders), 17, 41, 42, 60, 151, 177, 295
Young, William, 178, 179, 179 n. 47, 180

Zangl [Zange], Narcissus, 118, 127